Corner Offices
&
Corner Kicks

How Big Business Created
America's Two Greatest Soccer Dynasties,
Bethlehem Steel and the New York Cosmos

Roger Allaway

s⊥p

St. Johann Press
Haworth, New Jersey

ST. JOHANN PRESS

Published in the United States of America
by St. Johann Press
P.O. Box 241
Haworth, NJ 07641

Copyright © 2009 by Roger Allaway

Library of Congress Cataloguing in Publication Data pending

The paper used in this publication meets the minimum requirements of the
American National Standard for Information Sciences—Permanence of Paper
for Printed Library Materials, ANSI/NISO Z39/48-1992

Manufactured in the United States of America

Contents

Preface   v
Acknowledgments   ix

ONE   **A Matched Pair**   1
TWO   **Lehigh Valley Boys**   35
THREE   **Gothamites**   63
FOUR   **Men of Steel**   87
FIVE   **The Greatest Show on Earth**   119
SIX   **Second Fiddle**   149
SEVEN   **. . . The Harder They Fall**   183
EIGHT   **The End . . . Or Not?**   213

Appendix A Some Bethlehem Steel
             and Cosmos Team Records   221
Appendix B Record Goalscoring Seasons
             by Chinaglia and Stark   228
Notes   231
Bibliography   249
Index   255

Preface

The idea for this book, like the one for my previous book, *Rangers, Rovers and Spindles*, had been rattling around in my head for a few years before I decided to write it. That previous book, which was about the early soccer history of several textile-manufacturing centers in the northeastern United States, was published in the summer of 2005. In August 2005, during the six-hour drive home from the annual induction ceremonies at the National Soccer Hall of Fame, I made up my mind to write this one.

At the time, I was not yet the historian of the Hall of Fame. I also was not yet a former newspaperman. I was still an active newspaperman, a copy editor at the *Philadelphia Inquirer*. I retired just a few months later, however, and much of my time since has been taken up with researching and writing this book.

I'm not sure how many years ago it first occurred to me that Bethlehem Steel and the New York Cosmos would make a good combination for a book. I know that I wished for many years that the literature on the history of soccer in the United States included a book about the history of the Cosmos (since 2006, it has included one, as that was the year that Gavin Newsham's *Once in a Lifetime* was published). During those years, any time the thought occurred to me that I might write such a book myself, that thought included the corollary that pairing the Cosmos with Bethlehem Steel seemed a good idea. I never covered the Cosmos myself, but I had more than enough knowledge of the Bethlehem Steel team to bring an interesting perspective to the subject of the Cosmos, viewing them in the light of their earlier twin (and vice versa).

In 1997, when I wrote the foreword to Colin Jose's book about the original American Soccer League of the 1920s, I said that many people knew all about the North American Soccer League but few knew that something very similar to that league's ups and downs had happened before, a half-century earlier, with the original ASL. It's very much the same with the Cosmos and Bethlehem Steel. The Cosmos' ups and downs didn't exactly mirror those of Bethlehem Steel, but because of the Steelworkers, the Cosmos were not an entirely new phenomenon.

My most important research technique on this book's dual subject has been the same one that I have used many times before in researching various other subjects, poring over old newspapers on microfilm in libraries. I have no idea how many hours I have logged in front of microfilm reading machines over the last 45 years. I know that the last few have been especially heavy. Others who have written books about events of a few decades before have relied primarily on interviews with many of the participants in the events they describe. I have taken the tack that there is more to be learned from newspaper accounts written at the time than from first-person memories of distant events. Equally important have been the many books on subjects related to the Bethlehem Steel and Cosmos sagas, books that I have referred to constantly and quoted from often. The small bookshelf closest to the computer on which I have written this book contains copies of more than a dozen such books. On the floor next to the computer are three plastic bins filled with research files. I have managed to keep those files in reasonably organized and logical shape, so that I have only a few times had to say to myself: "I remember a quote that might work perfectly here. I wonder where I put it." That computer itself is adorned with two good-luck charms that have accompanied me throughout the writing of this book. Almost a year before I started writing, about the time that I started compiling the outline that served as a guide to me, I taped those good-luck charms, photos of the Cosmos in 1979 and the Bethlehem Steel team in 1919, to the front of the computer. More than three years later, they're still there.

That outline, in the same sort of Roman numeral, capital letter, Arabic numeral, lower-case letter format that's taught to grade-school students, was very important to the writing of this book. The first two books that I wrote (co-authored, actually), involved a series of items that made them relatively easy to write. You just kept writing the items, one by one, and eventually you were done. The third book, *Rangers, Rovers and Spindles*, was different, a continuous narrative, much longer than any narrative I had ever written before. I couldn't have written it if I hadn't plotted it all out in outline form before I started writing, and then followed that outline religiously. Deciding to follow the same technique with this book, which is nearly twice as long as that one, was a no-brainer. It took nearly a year to compile that 16-page outline, first sketching the general form and then filling in the details and fine-tuning it all. I spent nearly as much time on that as I did on writing the book itself, but it was worth it. Once again I couldn't have written the book without my detailed "road map."

Roger Allaway
Abington, Pa.
March 2009

Acknowledgments

I could never have written this book without the assistance of Colin Jose. That's true of a few other people, too, but particularly Colin, who was the historian of the National Soccer Hall of Fame from 1997 to 2007 and probably is the ranking expert on the history of both the original American Soccer League and the North American Soccer League. His files, his books, his answers to the many questions I have bounced off him and his suggestions after reading chapters in manuscript form have been invaluable.

By far the most important source of information for the Bethlehem Steel portions of this book was the newspaper articles on the website concerning the Bethlehem Steel team that is maintained by Dan Morrison, the grand-nephew of Bethlehem Steel player Bobby Morrison. This is an amazing website, with more than 3,500 articles, mostly from the *Bethlehem Globe-Times* (which was the *South Bethlehem Globe* until 1917 and then the *Bethlehem Globe* until 1925). Because my use of these articles has been so heavy, I have included citations for quotations from them, but not for most places where my own words have been based on facts learned from these articles. Those places have been numerous. There are paragraphs in this book, without any direct quotations, where I could have cited a different *Globe* article at the end of each sentence. It is not an exaggeration to say that these articles, and Dan Morrison's work in compiling them, have been the foundation for the Bethlehem Steel part of this book.

Dan Morrison also is one of two people to whom I am particularly indebted for giving me the green light to write this book. They are the people whom I considered to have first call on writing books about the two teams that this book is about, Morrison, the ultimate Bethlehem Steel expert, and Alex Yannis, who covered the Cosmos for the *New York Times* throughout their 15 years. I talked with both of them before starting out on this venture, to make sure that I had their approval. I have relied on their help and suggestions throughout the writing of this book. I am additionally indebted to Dan Morrison for his assistance with photographs; he has allowed me to use a number of pictures from his personal collection. I also found a number of useful photographs in the archives at the National Soccer Hall of Fame.

I am extremely grateful to the six people who read this book in manuscipt form as I was writing it: Wendell Plumlee and Don McKee, former colleagues of mine at the *Philadelphia Inquirer*; George Brown, the former president of the National Soccer Hall of Fame; Colin Jose, who was my co-author on two previous books, and Paul Moyer, the athletic director at Moravian College in Bethlehem. Those five people suggested a huge number of valuable editing changes and saved me repeatedly from making factual errors.

As with my previous books, I have depended heavily on libraries in the preparation of this book, particularly ones with good microfilm machines and open stacks of old newspapers on microfilm. Those that I have used as I researched this book have included the Abington (Pa.) Free Library, the New Jersey State Library in Trenton, the Free Library of Philadelphia, the Bethlehem Area Public Library, the Elkins Park (Pa.) Free Library, the Fairchild-Martindale Library at Lehigh University in Bethlehem and the Philadelphia Newspapers Inc. Newsresearch Library.

I was certainly aided in writing this book by the fact that a number of books dealing with subjects related to the New York Cosmos have been published in the last few years, particularly books by David Wangerin, Clive Toye, Gavin Newsham and David Tossell.

The section on the formation of the U.S. Football Association in Chapter Two was adapted from part of an article that I wrote for the Third Quarter 1996 edition of *Fussball Weltzeitschrift* (World Football Journal), a magazine published in Weisbaden, Germany. That article also appears on the American Soccer History Archives website.

I must give great thanks to Dave Biesel, the owner of St. Johann Press, the publisher of this book. This is the third book of mine that Dave has published (and the fourth that he has been involved with as either publisher or editor). The study of the history of soccer in the United States owes a huge debt to Dave Biesel, without whose interest in the subject a number of books by several different authors might never have seen the light of day.

A number of people have helped me in various ways in the preparation of this book. They have included Ann Bartholomew, Dave Biesel, George Brown, Connie Bruck, Paul Bunting, Ted Howard, Jack

Acknowledgments

Huckel, Colin Jose, Frank Litsky, Brian Meagher, Kristal Meagher, Thomas Misa, Lloyd Monsen, Dan Morrison, Don McKee, Lance Metz, Paul Moyer, Walt Murphy, Michael Panzer, Peppe Pinton, Wendell Plumlee, John Kenley Smith, Melvin Smith, Hank Steinbrecher, David Sullivan, Clive Toye, Jim Trecker, David Wangerin, David Wasser and Alex Yannis. I am grateful to all of them.

ONE

A Matched Pair

On April 2, 1978, Giorgio Chinaglia scored three goals as the
New York Cosmos opened their North American Soccer
League season with a 7-0 pasting of the Fort Lauderdale Strikers. Chinaglia's hat trick raised his career total of goals in NASL
games to 46, a count that would eventually reach 242 and make him
the No. 2 scorer of first-division goals in American soccer history.

Among the more than 44,000 spectators watching Chinaglia that
day at Giants Stadium was one, an 80-year-old former player from
nearby Kearny, N.J., who had a special interest in the Cosmos star's
exploits. For when Chinaglia retired five years later with his second-
of-all-time ranking, the one goalscorer still ahead of him was that man
in the stands from Kearny, Archie Stark, first by virtue of the 260 goals
he scored for Bethlehem Steel and two other teams in the original
American Soccer League of the 1920s.

The fact that Bethlehem's legendary goalscoring machine was
among the fans watching the Cosmos' legendary goalscoring machine
put the ball in the net a half-century later is only one of the connec-
tions—and maybe not all that substantial a one—between the two
most dominant teams that American soccer has ever produced. Some
of the other parallels between the two teams are striking. Both the
Steelworkers and the Cosmos were owned by huge corporations, a
change from the far more common situation in American pro sports
of ownership by a wealthy individual or group of individuals, and
both were greatly affected by the financial ups and downs of those
companies. Both the Steelworkers and the Cosmos relied heavily on
players imported from overseas, while some teams in their eras
spurned that method. And both the Steelworkers and the Cosmos

1

came and went very quickly, rising rapidly to the top rung of American soccer and folding with equal suddenness after a relatively short time at the top. These parallels are why the story of Bethlehem Steel and the story of the New York Cosmos are a matched pair.

Bethlehem Steel and the New York Cosmos are unquestionably the two greatest teams in the history of American soccer, their dominance of their eras unmatched by any other teams. They are not without rivals, such as the Fall River Rovers and Fall River Marksmen in Bethlehem's era, the Chicago Sting and Tampa Bay Rowdies in the Cosmos' era and teams like D.C. United, Ukrainian Nationals of Philadelphia and Stix, Baer & Fuller of St. Louis at other times. All of those contenders are competing for third place, however. First and second are spoken for, although in which order is unclear.

Giving this sort of designation to Bethlehem Steel and the New York Cosmos does involve a good deal of making comparisons between teams from far different eras, teams that never came close to meeting (the Cosmos played their first game 41 years after Bethlehem played its last). Such comparisons can involve problems, the chief one being that athletic performance has improved over the years in all sports, a result of such factors as better nutrition and training methods and improvements in the basic human material from which athletes are made. There is little question that if an outstanding soccer team from 1920 and a mediocre team from 1980 were put on the field, the 1980 team would win easily, despite its poor results against other 1980 teams. A demonstration of the fact that this is the way it goes in sports can be seen in sports in which performance is measured against unchanging standards such as minutes and seconds, sports like track, swimming and speed skating. When Bethlehem Steel was at its peak around 1920, the world record holder in the one-mile run was an American named Norman Taber, who had run the classic distance in 4 minutes, 12.6 seconds in 1915. When the Cosmos were at their peak 60 years later, the world record in the mile was being tossed back and forth between Britons Sebastian Coe and Steve Ovett, whose best times were in the 3:47-3:49 range. Had the Norman Taber of 1915 been around, he would have been left 200 yards behind by Coe and Ovett. But that doesn't really matter in comparing them, because had Taber been born 60 years later than he was and benefited from the same nutritional and training advantages that Coe and Ovett did, he might have been quite competitive with them. What it adds up to is the fact that in comparing athletes and teams from different eras, you have to disregard the way that athletic performance in general has improved over the years and simply judge a team or athlete by how they fared against their contemporaries. And by that standard, Bethlehem Steel and the New York Cosmos look far ahead of any other American teams and almost even with each other.

The Cosmos' greatness, to a good degree, was built on their record in league play, in the North American Soccer League. Once they hit their stride, after the signing of Pelé in 1975 and several other key players shortly afterward, they consistently outclassed the rest of the NASL. In the six seasons between 1977 and 1982, they won the NASL championship four times and came close in the other two. They finished atop the NASL's regular-season standings for six years in a row, from 1978 through 1983.

Bethlehem's domination was built more on its success in cup competitions, an area in which the Cosmos don't have a comparable record because the NASL didn't allow its teams to enter the U.S. Open Cup. Between 1915 and 1919, Bethlehem Steel reached the final of the U.S. Open Cup (which was then called the National Challenge Cup) five times in a row, winning four of those. After a few lean years, they won that title again in 1926. They also won the American Football Association Cup, a slightly lesser competition, six times over the years. While Bethlehem's league record was not the main jewel in its crown, it still was impressive. Playing in a succession of different leagues as their horizons widened, the Steelworkers won their league title 10 times in 15 seasons between 1912 and 1927. In their last seasons, they faded a bit in league standings, just as the Cosmos did toward their end, but for more than a decade they finished either first or second in their league every season except one.

A good bit of the Cosmos' lasting reputation is based on their play against foreign teams, particularly preseason and postseason tours in Europe and Latin America. They began making foreign tours in 1975 after Pelé's first season with them. From then until the end of the North American Soccer League after the 1984 NASL season, nearly a third of the Cosmos' more than 500 games were against non-NASL opponents. They tried not to look like a barnstorming sideshow, the Harlem Globetrotters of soccer, but rather like ambassadors of American soccer to the world. They were semisuccessful, both in that effort and in their results. At times, particularly on wearying postseason tours of Europe against in-season European opponents, their results were not impressive. But they did produce a few outstanding performances, and they unquestionably accomplished another significant objective, that of publicizing the name of their owner, entertainment giant Warner Communications, before foreign audiences that Warner was eager to cultivate.

Bethlehem also played overseas, although on a much more limited basis. In the summer of 1919, the Steelworkers became the first American club team to undertake a foreign tour, playing 14 games in Sweden and Denmark, and losing only two of those. Numerous other foreign tours, including one that was cancelled just minutes before the ship carrying the players to Brazil was to sail from New York, were talked about but never took place.

Both teams, particularly the Cosmos because communications were so much faster and more pervasive in their era, left lasting legacies on the sport in the United States. Jim Trecker, who was the Cosmos' public relations man in the 1976 season before going on to similar posts with the NASL and the 1994 World Cup organizing committee, says: "Without the Cosmos there would not have been a 1994 World Cup [he concedes that this is arguable]. Without the Cosmos there wouldn't have been any so-called 'youth boom' and the concomitant increase in interest across the country. The Cosmos were the first of the world mega clubs, the precursor of Manchester United, Chelsea, Marseilles of the early '90s, Bayern, etc. Yes, Real Madrid was a legendary club in the '60s, but the concept of buying up the world's greatest names and players was born with the Cosmos."[1] Clive Toye, the Cosmos general manager who signed Pelé, had similar thoughts on the 30th anniversary of that event in 2005: "Without it, Tim Howard wouldn't be playing for Manchester United, if he was playing soccer at all. Brad Freidel wouldn't be playing for Blackburn. Kasey Keller wouldn't have had a long career in England, Germany and Spain. Claudio Reyna wouldn't be playing for Manchester City. The United States wouldn't have reached the quarterfinals of the last World Cup."[2]

Three of the leading histories of American soccer comment glowingly on Bethlehem's legacy. In *Offside*, Andrei Markovits and Steven Hellerman note that the early years of the U.S. Open Cup were dominated by the "legendary" Bethlehem Steel team, which they call "the only American soccer team with any pedigree and general name recognition."[3] In *Soccer in a Football World*, David Wangerin notes how surprising it is that the top American team of the early part of the 20th century came not from one of the primary soccer hotbeds like St. Louis or Fall River but "from the steel mills of eastern Pennsylvania...[where] the town of Bethlehem and the mammoth Bethlehem

Steel Corporation created what many still consider to be the most successful of American soccer clubs."[4] And Sam Foulds and Paul Harris in *America's Soccer Heritage* say that Bethlehem Steel "epitomized the ultimate in American professional soccer. In an era when professional baseball and collegiate football represented the acme of team sports, the charisma that surrounded this soccer power was amazing."[5]

The mark that these two teams left on the sport in the United States can be seen starkly in the number of people associated with them who have been inducted into the National Soccer Hall of Fame in Oneonta, New York, 14 from Bethlehem Steel and 15 from the Cosmos, numbers unchallenged by any other team. Eleven of the 14 from Bethlehem are players, as are 10 of the 15 from the Cosmos (and each group also includes one man who was a player in the team's earliest years but gained his greatest fame in later roles). The fact that about 10 percent of the Hall of Fame's current membership comes from either Bethlehem or the Cosmos says volumes about the exalted place that these two teams occupy in American soccer history.

But what sets the Steelworkers and the Cosmos apart from their contemporaries and all other American soccer teams involves more than just their achievements on the field. The two are the prime examples of the difference that ownership by a huge, deep-pocketed business corporation can make for an athletic team.

Bethlehem Steel was owned, obviously, by the Bethlehem Steel Corporation, which in its heyday was one of the largest manufacturing companies in the world. It was easily the largest of the "independent" American steelmakers, companies that had been left out of the mix when the interests of Andrew Carnegie and J.P. Morgan were merged in 1901 to form the gigantic U.S. Steel Corporation, and it managed to compete successfully against U.S. Steel in certain areas of the steel business for decades. Not surprisingly, the success of the Bethlehem Steel soccer team coincided with some of the years of greatest profitability of the Bethlehem Steel Corporation.

The Cosmos were owned by Warner Communications Inc., a conglomerate involved in many facets of the entertainment industry and built around the hallowed Warner Brothers movie studio. Here, too, the success of the soccer team mirrored the rise and fall of the company's fortunes, particularly the Atari video-games division that supplied much of Warner's profits during the early 1980s.

If ownership of athletic teams by big corporations were a common thing, perhaps the similarities in the ownership of Bethlehem Steel and the ownership of the Cosmos would not be so striking. But both in

American professional sports and in professional soccer elsewhere in the world, the more usual models have been quite different, and Bethlehem Steel and the Cosmos stood out, off the field as well as on it.

Bethlehem and the Cosmos also were alike in their heavy dependence on importing large numbers of foreign professional players, the former most strongly from Britain and the latter from a number of countries in Europe and South America.

Edgar Lewis, who played for Bethlehem Steel in the team's early years, briefly managed it and then oversaw it from the executive suite in its last years, had been born in Wales and came to America as a teenager. Many of the other players he recruited were from Britain, but not Wales. The majority of them were from Scotland, including two of the earliest of Bethlehem's great stars, forward Whitey Fleming and defender Jock Ferguson. In later years, the man who dominated the Steelworkers was one who had been born in Scotland but moved to New Jersey when he was 12 years old, Archie Stark.

The Cosmos had a few foreign stars in their first years, players like Randy Horton from Bermuda, Mordechai Speigler from Israel, Juan Masnik from Uruguay and Josef Jelinek from Czechoslovakia. Those were nothing, however, compared to the polyglot flood that followed the signing of Pelé in 1975. Taped to the computer monitor in front of me is a team photo of the 1979 Cosmos. Among the 21 players in the picture, I can count 11 different nationalities. The 10 Cosmos players in the National Soccer Hall of Fame represent six different countries. In the five Cosmos teams that won the NASL championship, each lineup contained players from at least seven countries. The Cosmos were the first soccer team anywhere in the world to field a squad that included the captains of the winning teams at the previous two World Cups.

Even so, the Cosmos' claim to have been the first club to field an international all-star team may be a little shaky. The New Yorkers didn't necessarily go around signing the players who were the best in the world at the time they signed them. The four biggest international stars who played for the Cosmos—Pelé, Franz Beckenbauer, Carlos Alberto and Johan Neeskens—each were past their prime by their NASL years. Of the four, only Beckenbauer was still the star of his national team when the Cosmos signed him, and even he had been in three World Cups by that time. By comparison, the international stars at Real Madrid in the late 1950s, while fewer in number, were still closer to their peak. Hungarian Ferenc Puskas, Argentinian Alberto DiStefano, Frenchman Raymond Kopa and Brazilian Didi all were still major international stars during their time at Real. So the answer to that debate may be a tossup. Either way, the two certainly paved the way for games like the 2008 European Champions League final between Manchester United and Chelsea, in which the two teams were represented by players from 12 different countries.

The last major similarity between the Steelworkers and the Cosmos has to do with their lack of longevity. Look at some of the most famous dynasties in other American sports. Baseball's New York Yankees were founded in 1901, football's Green Bay Packers in 1922 and basketball's Boston Celtics in 1946. The leading European soccer dynasties have been around even longer, Manchester United since 1885, Real Madrid since 1898 and AC Milan since 1899.[6] As of 2008, those six teams had lasted an average of 99 years each. In contrast, the Bethlehem Steel soccer team lasted only 23 years and the New York Cosmos only 15. Both came and went quite quickly.

The two teams had somewhat similar ends, both driven by economic forces that buffeted the corporations that owned them.

The Bethlehem Steel team's demise came about six months after the Stock Market Crash of October 1929 that set off the Depression. It has never been completely clear just how much the disbanding had to do with the Crash and the Depression, which didn't begin to have serious effects on the Bethlehem Steel Corporation until 1931. It has long been throught that the team's end was brought about by Edgar Lewis' disillusionment with professional soccer after the "Soccer War," a jurisdictional battle between the American Soccer League and the United States Football Association that paralyzed American soccer during most of 1928 and 1929. Both matters, plus Lewis' departure from the Bethlehem Steel Corporation, may have been factors.

The reasons for the Cosmos' end are clearer. They ran out of money. A business' balance sheet is a matter of income and outgo, and there was plenty of outgo with the Cosmos and with Warner Communications. They spent wildly, particularly on the purchase of star players from European clubs. For a long while, there was plenty of income as well, but when that dried up in 1982 and 1983, the Cosmos' days became numbered. They always were a frill at Warner Communications, Steve Ross' plaything, and when Warner ran into rocky financial times, frills became expendable.

The leagues that the two teams played in, the original American Soccer League for Bethlehem and the NASL for the Cosmos, ran into trouble at the same time as the teams. The American Soccer League collapsed in stages, and it is difficult to pinpoint exactly when its end occurred, although the accepted date is 1931. The league re-formed it-self, on a more cautious financial basis, in 1933, and its second incar-nation lasted until 1983. In any case, the league was already in trouble when Bethlehem pulled out in April 1930. Even if the Steelworkers had stayed in, the league might not have lasted much longer than it did. The Cosmos outlasted their league, but only by a few months. By the time the NASL closed its doors in March 1985, the handwriting had been on the wall for a few years. Ever since, the causes of the NASL's demise have been a subject for endless debate. The chief sus-pects seem to have been runaway spending on foreign players as teams without the Cosmos' deep pockets spent themselves dry in an attempt to keep pace, the extremely rapid expansion of the league after attendance increased in 1977 and 1978, and the loss of the league's na-tional television contract with ABC in 1980. The Cosmos, who played a large role in the NASL's final death scenes, tried to continue without the league in 1985, but lasted for only a few games more.

The ends of the two teams and the leagues that they had played in did not mean the ends of the corporations that had owned them. Bethlehem is defunct now, but it lasted for 73 years after the end of its soccer team, and had some very prosperous times along the way. It recovered from the Depression with the help of the big-city build-ing boom of the 1930s, when steel structural beams made by Bethle-hem were used to build San Francisco's Golden Gate Bridge, New York's George Washington Bridge, New York's Chrysler Building and dozens of other landmarks across the country. The company fur-ther thrived during World War II, when its shipyards on both coasts turned out naval vessels at an incredible rate. Warner, which sold its majority interest in the Cosmos in July 1984, recovered within a few years from the troubles brought about by the video-game collapse and downturns in other divisions. By 1990, it had reinvented itself via a merger with Time Inc. to form the gigantic TimeWarner com-bination, which survives to this day. However, neither TimeWarner nor Arcelor-Mittal, the European-based current owner of the last re-mains of Bethlehem Steel, has any major interest in American soccer today.

Evidence of the way that Bethlehem Steel and the New York Cos-mos dominated their rivals on the soccer field during their relatively short lives can be easily seen in the records of the National Soccer Hall of Fame, underscoring their status as unquestionably the two great-est American soccer dynasties. Of the more than 270 players, coaches, referees and administrators who have been inducted into the Hall of

A Matched Pair

Fame since its beginning in 1950, 29 were connected in one way or another with Bethlehem Steel or the Cosmos. They make quite a dazzling roll call:

- Harold Brittan, a recent arrival from England who had played for Chelsea, took over as Bethlehem's top scorer in 1920 after the departure of Harry Ratican and led the Steelworkers to several league championships, including the first season of the American Soccer League.

- Davey Brown is most famous for his goalscoring exploits with other ASL teams, but he did play for Bethlehem as a guest player on its Scandinavian tour in the summer of 1919, appearing in 12 of the 14 games on that tour and scoring two goals.

- Thomas W. Cahill was a prominent American soccer official from about 1905 to 1930, perhaps the most important administrator the sport has seen in this country. Although he often occupied influential positions in competitions in which Bethlehem Steel played, his only direct involvement with the team was as its manager on the 1919 Scandinavian tour.

- Ned Donaghy was a star forward for Bethlehem Steel in the team's earlier years. He later gained fame as one of the country's leading soccer referees, and became the first American ever to referee a game between two other countries when he handled a World Cup qualifier between Mexico and Cuba in 1937.

- Jock Ferguson was a rock in the center of the Bethlehem defense for years, probably the greatest defensive player Bethlehem ever fielded. He played in all four of Bethlehem's National Challenge Cup victories between 1915 and 1919, and then was a reserve with the Steelworkers through most of their years in the American Soccer League.

- Whitey Fleming, a star winger, was one of the first outstanding foreign players Bethlehem ever signed. He was a mainstay of the Bethlehem attack throughout its years of cup domination, playing in every one of its 10 cup finals between 1914 and 1919.

- John Jaap became a star of the Bethlehem forward line during its years in the American Soccer League. He played for Bethlehem in its ASL championship season in 1921-22, then left the team, but returned for five more Bethlehem seasons later in the decade.

- Edgar Lewis was the driving force behind the Bethlehem team for years, probably the most significant figure in the team's history. He was a player in Bethlehem's early seasons, before his tremendous rise through the executive ranks of the corporation. By the time he left in 1930, he was executive vice-president of Bethlehem Steel and had been able to be of great benefit to the soccer team from his management position.

- Bob Millar played only one full season for Bethlehem, plus part of another, but in the 1914-15 campaign he set a team goalscoring record that wasn't surpassed until Archie Stark came along more than 10 years later.

- Bobby Morrison was one of Bethlehem's early stars, joining the team in 1913 and playing in cup final victories in 1914, 1915 and 1916 before his career was ended early by an injury.

- Harry Ratican was an unusual figure for his day in American soccer, a native St. Louis player who came east to gain his greatest fame. The goalscoring star played in the National Challenge Cup finals of 1918 and 1919 for Bethlehem before moving to teams in Brooklyn and Fall River.

- Archie Stark was Bethlehem Steel's greatest star, even though he didn't join the team until the 1924-25 season, nearly 10 years after he won his first major championship at the age of 17. Stark scored 67 American Soccer League goals in his first Bethlehem season, and remains today as the greatest scorer of goals in first-division play that American soccer has ever seen.

- George Tintle, perhaps the leading American goalkeeper before 1920, was a guest player with Bethlehem Steel on its Scandinavian tour in the summer of 1919.

- Jimmy Walder is most famous as one of the greatest of referees in American soccer history, particularly in the 1920s and '30s. His connection with Bethlehem came in the 1921-22 season, when the Steelworkers played as the Philadelphia Field Club and Walder was their manager.

- Franz Beckenbauer was the player, perhaps more than any

other, whose arrival transformed the Cosmos from a good team into a great one. Beckenbauer, who was still captain of the West German national team when he joined the Cosmos, played five seasons with them and won three NASL titles.

- Vladislav Bogicevic was probably the best midfielder in the history of the NASL, a man who didn't score many goals himself but whose pinpoint passes set up plenty for others. The Yugoslavian national team star was the NASL's all-time career leader in assists.

- Gordon Bradley was the longest-serving coach of the Cosmos, managing that team in its first five seasons and again in portions of the sixth and seventh seasons. After departing from the Cosmos in 1977, he had a successful run as coach of the NASL's Washington Diplomats.

- Carlos Alberto joined the Cosmos late in the 1977 season and was a significant factor in pulling them out of mid-season doldrums toward the NASL title. The former Brazilian national team captain had a number of memorable moments, both good and bad, during his five Cosmos seasons.

- Giorgio Chinaglia was the greatest goalscorer in Cosmos history and one of the team's most controversial players. In between goalscoring sprees, the former Italian national team star was said to have exerted considerable behind-the-scenes influence in the running of the team. After retiring as a player following eight Cosmos seasons, he became an official of the team and ended up presiding over its demise a year later.

- Rick Davis was one of the leading American players in the history of the NASL, and one of the few Americans who were able to fit in well with the Cosmos' international galaxy of stars. Davis was captain of the United States national team through most of the 1980s.

- Ahmet Ertegun was the younger of the two Turkish brothers who conceived the idea that became the Cosmos and were significant executives for most of the team's existence. He took over as president of the Cosmos in 1977 and later was a member of the board of directors of the 1994 World Cup organizing committee.

- Nesuhi Ertegun was the older of the two brothers and served as president and later chairman of the board of the Cosmos. He was responsible for much of the early contact between Kinney National, the forerunner of Warner Communications, and the NASL that resulted in the creation of the Cosmos franchise.

- Pelé was certainly the most influential player in Cosmos history, although he was nearing the end of his skills when he joined them. He had been been a top-level professional player for nearly 20 years, during which played for Brazil in four World Cups and gained recognition as the greatest player in the history of the game. His arrival in the United States in 1975 is considered the most significant event in sparking the American soccer boom of subsequent decades.

- Tab Ramos never did play for the Cosmos after signing with them straight from high school in 1984. Although the NASL folded before he could get onto its fields, Ramos later became one of the most honored players in American soccer history, playing in three World Cups and starring in pro leagues in Spain, Mexico and the United States.

- Steve Ross was the chairman of Warner Communications Inc. during the 13 years that it owned the Cosmos and was a major figure in building the team into a great dynasty. Ross was not a soccer man, but his enthusiasm certainly inspired those in his employ who were.

- Werner Roth stands alongside Rick Davis and Bobby Smith as the Cosmos' leading American stars. Roth was the only member of the original 1971 Cosmos squad who was still with the team when it won NASL titles in 1977 and 1978, and was captain of the Cosmos in both of those championship seasons.

- Bobby Smith played four of his nine NASL seasons with the Cosmos, and was one of the team's best American players between 1976 and 1979. He played a total of 23 games for the Cosmos teams that won the 1977 and 1978 NASL championships.

- Clive Toye, more than anybody else, was the man who built the Cosmos. First general manager and later president of the Cosmos, Toye pursued Pelé, pen in hand, for more than four years before signing him in an event that turned the soccer world on its ear. Toye, who also signed Franz Beckenbauer,

A Matched Pair

Giorgio Chinaglia and others, left the Cosmos in 1977 and later was president of the Chicago Sting and the Toronto Blizzard.

- Bruce Wilson was one of the best soccer players Canada has ever produced, and was a key figure in the Cosmos' 1980 NASL champion team, although most of his long NASL career was spent elsewhere, particularly Vancouver and Toronto.

Another 49 players from either Bethlehem Steel or the Cosmos are on the Hall of Fame's eligibility list, the roster of former players who have met the Hall of Fame's eligibility requirements and are on the ballot for the Hall of Fame's annual elections.

When it's all added up, the cups, the league titles, the international victories, the Hall of Famers, it is clear that Bethlehem Steel and the New York Cosmos stand head and shoulders above every other team as the two most dominant that American soccer has ever seen.

Sponsorship—which sometimes has meant ownership—of successful teams in American soccer has usually fallen into one of two categories: teams backed by ethnic organizations like the Kearny (N.J.) Scots, Chicago Slovak and Ponta Delgada of Fall River, Mass., and those backed by commercial businesses like Brookhattan of New York (sponsored by a trucking company); Morgan Strasser of Morgan, Pa. (sponsored by a jeweler), and the colorfully named National Slug Rejectors of St. Louis.

Of the two, the ethnic organizations have very regularly been the longer lasting in their involvement in soccer, which helps to explain the relatively short life of the business-backed Bethlehem Steel and New York Cosmos soccer teams. For commercial investors, soccer is a business opportunity, one that may come and go depending on factors like changes in the leadership of a company, in the company's financial situation and in how the company perceives the tastes of the consuming public. But people who run ethnic organizations, who by definition tend to be people who have resisted rapid Americanization, often are people for whom soccer is a large part of the heritage that they grew up with. They don't bail out of involvement with the sport casually and suddenly the way that corporate sponsors and owners sometimes have. For instance, while Kearny Scots may be nothing like they were in their heyday, when they won five consecutive American Soccer League championships in the 1930s and '40s, they do still exist, both as a social club and as one of New Jersey's leading amateur teams, more than 75 years after their founding. Meanwhile, Brookhattan, which was founded around the same time and played against Kearny Scots in the ASL, has been gone for half a century.

Some of the greatest ethnically-based American soccer teams of decades ago, teams like Schwaben of Chicago, Ukrainian Nationals of Philadelphia and Maccabi of Los Angeles still exist, albeit usually in amateur leagues today. The same cannot be said for most of the commercially sponsored soccer teams of decades ago. Brookhattan, Strasser, Bethlehem Steel and Warner Communications are long gone from the soccer scene, and so are many more trucking companies, steelmakers, shipyards, brewers, textile mills and others.

Corporate involvements in soccer teams are often a fleeting thing, and at the top levels of sports—the levels at which Bethlehem Steel and the Cosmos played—they are relatively rare to begin with. The trend is sometimes even formalized, as in the National Football League's prohibition on corporate ownership of teams. That's part of the NFL's efforts to maintain competitive balance, which deep corporate pockets like those that sustained the Cosmos theoretically could upset, but it's not the only reason, as former Cleveland Browns owner Art Modell pointed out in a 2004 interview: "We never allowed corporate ownership and we shouldn't allow it now. It's about individual accountability for [the] franchise. You can't lay it off on a board of directors. There has to be accountability."[7] Another NFL owner, Arthur Blank of the Atlanta Falcons, said somewhat the same thing in 2006: "At the end of the day, it [ownership by individuals] creates that personal sense of accountability. And in a [private] ownership, you have flexibility to do things that in a public company it is harder to do....You don't have to think about what shareholders are going to say."[8]

Other leagues, both in the United States and elsewhere, don't take as harsh a line on corporate ownership as the NFL does, but it still is often considered a poor idea from a corporate viewpoint, and particularly the viewpoint of stockholders. Joe Leccese, a New York lawyer specializing in sports matters, told the *Seattle Post-Intelligencer* in 2006 that professional sports franchises don't work well for corporations "because their financial patterns don't match what Wall Street wants to see—predictable, steadily increasing earnings." Instead, the *Post-Intelligencer* said, the picture in the pro sports industry tends to include such things as "fits and starts in earnings" and "increased debt loads to buy teams," with the result of often scaring off potential investors.[9]

A Matched Pair

Owning a professional sports team is not necessarily a money-losing proposition, but the potential profit is in eventually selling the team for more than it was bought for, not something that produces substantial dividends in the short term.

The negative effects of team ownership for a corporation can be seen at work in the actions of Warner Communications concerning the Cosmos. When Warner finally sold a majority interest in the team in 1984, it did so as a result of pressure from a dissident stockholder who saw getting rid of losing assets such as the Cosmos as a necessity in a time of financial crisis for the company[10] (although "increased debt loads" were not among those problems, as Warner had bought the Cosmos in 1971 for one dollar).

Instead of corporations, the most common model for ownership of professional sports teams, both in the United States and in Western Europe, is a wealthy individual who has made his money elsewhere and now is looking for someplace to spend it. Sometimes that can be a group of individuals, often staying in the background as a front man becomes the public face of the ownership, or a family after the death of the person who once was the sole owner.

By far the best known example of a wealthy individual team owner in American sports in recent years has been George Steinbrenner of the New York Yankees. To a good degree, Steinbrenner's fame is a result of his being a classic "meddling owner," one who tends to interfere frequently in the on-the-field running of the team he owns, and of the legal troubles that dogged him during the first two decades of his ownership of the Yankees.

Although Steinbrenner is of relatively recent vintage to be called the most famous team owner in baseball history, he seems to fill that bill. Steinbrenner bought the Yankees in 1973, when huge amounts of the team's storied history were already past. Not only were Babe Ruth, Lou Gehrig and Joe DiMaggio long gone, so were more recent heroes like Mickey Mantle, Whitey Ford and Yogi Berra. Despite his late start, Steinbrenner still has managed to make plenty of headlines.

Although Steinbrenner has become a national figure via sports, he didn't make his original money that way. Like the typical pro sports team owner, he earned it elsewhere, specifically in the ship-building business. Steinbrenner came into wealth as the owner of the American Shipbuilding Company, operator of a string of shipyards on the Great Lakes (since becoming a celebrity, Steinbrenner has moved his base of operations from Cleveland to more-glamourous Tampa). Of course, Steinbrenner could make a lot more money if he ever sold

15

the Yankees, who in 2006 were valued by *Forbes* magazine at more than 100 times the $10 million that Steinbrenner paid for them in 1973.[11] Nevertheless, Steinbrenner is the current archetype of the most common type of team owner, a wealthy individual who gained his original wealth in something other than sports and bought his team as an avocation rather than as a way to make money.

Sometimes, a team has become so closely identified with the company where the owner made his money that it tends to cloud the issue of just who does own it. There are a lot of longtime pro basketball fans who will tell you that the NBA's Detroit Pistons, previously the Fort Wayne Pistons and originally named the Zollner Pistons, were once owned by the Zollner Corporation of Fort Wayne, Ind. In reality, the team was owned by Fred Zollner, who also owned the Zollner Corporation. Similarly, baseball's Chicago Cubs were long tied in the public mind with the William Wrigley Jr. Company, but the company, one of the nation's leading makers of chewing gum, never did own the team. The team owner was Philip K. Wrigley, the owner of the company. Zollner and Wrigley, despite the frequent public confusion about the ownership of their teams, were really just the same as Steinbrenner, wealthy men looking for a place to spend their money.

Some team owners, particularly in the first half of the 20th century, were not especially wealthy before they got involved with professional sports, however. These were mostly men who were pioneers in their sports, getting involved before doing so became monstrously expensive. One such was Art Rooney, who was a semipro athlete in Western Pennsylvania in the 1920s, a regular at Pittsburgh-area racetracks and for the last 55 years of his life the owner of the Pittsburgh Steelers of the National Football League. Rooney bought the Steelers in 1933 for $2,500, and spent the rest of his life hearing talk (interesting but untrue) that the stake that got him into the NFL had resulted from a good day at the track.[12]

Rooney was one of several longtime NFL team owners who got into pro football in the NFL's rough-and-tumble early days, when making money was still more of a motive than the glamour of owning a pro sports franchise, because there was not yet any glamour to be had in pro football. Besides Rooney, the group included George Halas of the Chicago Bears, Tim Mara of the New York Giants, George Preston Marshall of the Boston Redskins, Charlie Bidwill of the Chicago Cardinals and Bert Bell of the Philadelphia Eagles. Some of them had made their money in ways quite different from chewing gum. Several were gamblers, Mara was a bookmaker and Bidwill was a bootlegger.[13] Other sports had their pioneer owners too, like Zollner, Connie Mack of the Philadelphia Athletics in baseball and Eddie Gottleib of the Philadelphia Warriors in basketball.

There have been several American soccer pioneers who have owned teams. Erno Schwarcz, like George Halas and Connie Mack, got into the sport as a player and for many years was coach of the team he owned, the New York Americans of the American Soccer League. Nat Agar, one of the founders of what later became the U.S. Soccer Federation, owned the Brooklyn Wanderers of the original ASL. The trend has continued in more recent years, although as the price of a franchise has risen, those pioneers have more often been men who were already well heeled and first got involved in the sport at a relatively high level. Lamar Hunt, one of the sons of legendary Texas oilman H.L. Hunt, owned pro soccer teams beginning in 1967, when he founded the Dallas Tornado of the North American Soccer League. Hunt was involved in various other sports ventures, including owning a team in the NFL. Several other NASL team owners could be classified as pioneers in the sport, especially Robert Hermann of the St. Louis Stars. Hunt has been matched in his soccer investment in recent years by the equally wealthy Philip Anschutz, the owner of several Major League Soccer teams.

Although George Steinbrenner has gained huge amounts of publicity in recent decades, he is only one among many in the category of wealthy individuals owning teams. Besides Steinbrenner, Fred Zollner and Phil Wrigley, other particularly famous ones have included Tom Yawkey of the Boston Red Sox, Jerry Buss of the Los Angeles Lakers, John Galbraith of the Pittsburgh Pirates, Walter O'Malley of the Brooklyn Dodgers, Charles Comisky of the Chicago White Sox, Walter Brown of the Boston Celtics and Ed Snider of the Philadelphia Flyers. One such baseball team owner, Charles Stoneham of the New York Giants, also had a brief and unhappy involvement with pro soccer.

This model of the wealthy individual team owner has not been confined to the United States. It has become the rule in much of European soccer as well, particularly in capitalist Western Europe. The man most prominently filling that role in recent years has been Russian billionaire Roman Abramovich, who owns the Chelsea team of the English Premier League and has spent truckloads of money assembling a squad of stars from various parts of Europe and Africa. The classic, however, was Gianni Agnelli, the Italian automaker whose family controlled the Fiat Group of Turin. Agnelli owned the dominant Turin soccer team, Juventus, which for decades has been among the greatest in Europe. Ironically, Agnelli also was a major stockholder of Warner Communications at the time that Warner owned the Cosmos.[14]

The most widespread exception in European and South American soccer to team ownership by wealthy individuals is not corporate ownership. Rather it is control of a team by a nonprofit multisports club whose members are the team's "owners" and also its main ticket-buyers. This sort of club was particularly common in Eastern Europe before the fall of the Iron Curtain, although in those countries, the clubs that fielded major soccer teams were likely to be under the thumb of organizations with political ties. For a long time, the four big teams in Moscow were Dynamo (sponsored by the Interior Ministry, which to a degree meant the secret police), Spartak (trade unions), Lokomotiv (railroads) and CSKA (the army). There were army-connected teams in many different Soviet-bloc countries, such as Legia Warsaw in Poland, Dukla Prague in Czechoslovakia, Honved in Hungary, Steaua Bucharest in Romania and CSKA Sofia in Bulgaria.

Clubs owned by their members, which are found in many parts of the world, are usually run by officials elected by the membership, with campaigns for those offices often revolving around the candidates' promises concerning the star players they will sign if they are elected. In Spain, where this type of club organization is standard, the biggest soccer event of July 2006 was not the World Cup final (which didn't include Spain anyway), but the election of a new president at Real Madrid, which has 66,000 members.[15] Even so, the winner, Ramon Calderon, is far from the most famous, or infamous, club president in the Spanish capital's soccer history. The most famous is the legendary Santiago Bernabeu, who was president of Real Madrid from 1943 to 1978, including the team's greatest years of the late 1950s, and for whom the team's gigantic stadium is named. The most infamous is Jesus Gil, who was president of Atletico Madrid, Real's crosstown rival, from 1987 to 2003. Gil was often in hot water in matters having to do with his business and political dealings, and perhaps the hallmark of his time in charge of Atletico Madrid was the fact that in 16 years he hired and fired 23 different managers, a revolving door that puts George Steinbrenner's to shame by comparison.[16]

The South American counterpart of Gil is Eurico Miranda, the controversial president of the Vasco da Gama club in Brazil. In his

A Matched Pair

2002 book *Futebol: Soccer, the Brazilian Way,* author Alex Bello described Miranda and his operating methods in some detail:

> For Eurico, the end justifies the means. And the end is always Vasco. In a 1999 match, Vasco were tying 1-1 when the referee sent off three Vasco players. Eurico came down from his presidential perch, invaded the pitch and forced the match to be suspended. Among the other tricks in his ample repertoire is an occasional refusal to let visiting teams warm up. Eurico is loathed by most football fans, but idolized at Vasco because he puts his love for the club above the rules. Vasco fans, called 'Vascainos,' do not care that he is rude, confrontational and authoritarian . . . .
>
> Like almost all of Brazil's clubs, Vasco is a non-profitmaking organization governed by its members, who choose a ruling council. In practice, this amateuristic structure is hijacked by authoritarian leaders, like Eurico, who climb their way to the top based on personal relationships, patronage and exchanging favors . . . .
>
> Under Vasco's constitution, the election [Bello was describing an election held in 2000] is between slates. The winning slate receives 120 members on the ruling council, and the second slate receives thirty. It is a way of ensuring that the opposition always has a say in club affairs. Vasco, Rio's first champions to field black players, is proud of its democratic heritage. At this election, however, United Nations monitors would be horrified. Halfway through the afternoon Eurico realizes that his slate will win, so he starts a second one. When voting is over, a row of old men—the electoral committee— sit at a long wooden table to count the ballot papers. Gradually the results come through. Eurico's slates have come in first and second. This means he has all 150 councillors.[17]

From George Steinbrenner and Art Rooney to Gianni Agnelli and Eurico Miranda, there are plenty of men who stand as examples of the usual manner of sports ownership, one that puts corporate ownership of the sort enjoyed by Bethlehem Steel and the New York Cosmos very much in the minority. This is not to say that those two have been the only exceptions, however.

Perhaps the first and certainly one of the most famous corporate owners in major-league baseball was the Anheuser-Busch brewery of St. Louis, which owned the St. Louis Cardinals of the National League from 1953 to 1995. That partnership did not grow out of any sort of financial consideration, however, but out of civic pride. In 1953, Cardinals owner Fred Saigh was convicted of income tax evasion and forced to sell the team. Saigh had offers of about $4.5 million from buyers who wanted to move the team out of St. Louis, to Milwaukee or Houston. Anheuser-Busch was only able to bid $3.75 million for the team, but that was enough to satisfy Saigh, who accepted the lower offer, making less money on the deal but keeping the team in St. Louis and making something of a local hero of himself.[18]

Anheuser-Busch's purchase of the Cardinals was not the first connection between a brewery and a big-league baseball team, but with the earlier ones, the team was owned by the owner of the brewery, not by the brewery itself, as in the case of Jacob Ruppert's famous ownership of the New York Yankees from 1914 until his death in 1939. Anheuser-Busch president Gussie Busch took great pleasure in running the Cardinals, much more so than did his heirs after his death in 1989. They eventually sold the Cardinals in 1995, but Anheuser-Busch has maintained strong ties to the team, particularly in buying the naming rights to the new Cardinals stadium that opened in 2006.[19]

Anheuser-Busch managed to make considerable use of its ownership of the Cardinals in marketing its products. The next big corporation to buy into major-league baseball didn't do as well. The Columbia Broadcasting System (CBS) bought the New York Yankees in 1964 from Del Webb and Dan Topping, the men who had bought the team from Jacob Ruppert's family 20 years earlier, but CBS owned the Yankees for less than 10 years.

CBS has been followed by several other broadcasting companies in owning major pro sports teams, but most of the more recent ones have been able to make some indirect profit from their investment, via gaining inexpensive programming for the television stations they own. But CBS' ownership of the Yankees came before the era of cable television, when team ownership has become particularly lucrative for media companies. CBS wasn't even able to make money from selling the Yankees. The $10 million for which it sold the team to George Steinbrenner in 1973 was $3.2 million less than what it had paid for it in 1964.

More recent instances of media corporations that have owned teams have included the Tribune Corporation, which has owned baseball's Chicago Cubs since 1981; the Walt Disney Co., which owned the NHL's Anaheim Mighty Ducks from 1993 to 2005 and baseball's Anaheim Angels from 1996 to 2003; Cablevision Systems, which has owned the NBA's New York Knicks and the NHL's New York Rangers since 1994; Comcast Corporation, which has owned the NBA's Philadelphia 76ers and the NHL's Philadelphia Flyers since

A Matched Pair

1996; News Corporation, which owned baseball's Los Angeles Dodgers from 1997 to 2004 and Rogers Communications of Canada, which has owned baseball's Toronto Blue Jays since 2000.

Then there is Warner, the same Warner that owned the Cosmos. As Warner Communications, it bought a minority share in baseball's Pittsburgh Pirates in 1983, but sold it just two years later as part of the same effort to divest itself of losing properties that resulted in the sale of the Cosmos. As TimeWarner, its name since the 1990 merger with Time Inc., it inherited baseball's Atlanta Braves, the NBA's Atlanta Hawks and the NHL's Atlanta Thrashers in 1996 when it bought Turner Broadcasting System, the owner of the three teams. It sold the Hawks and Thrashers in 2004 and the Braves in 2007.

The beer and sports connection, which has been strong for decades in many places, gained another direct link when the Molson brewery of Canada bought the NHL's Montreal Canadiens in 1978. Molson sold the Canadiens in 2001, but like Anheuser-Busch in St. Louis, it maintains substantial ties to the team it once controlled, and still owns a minority share. (Molson also owned the Montreal Manic of the NASL from 1981 to 1983. Other corporate owners in the NASL, besides Warner and Molson, were Lipton Tea, which owned the New England Tea Men from 1978 to 1981; Madison Square Garden Corp., which owned the Washington Diplomats from 1974 to 1980, and Louisiana-Pacific lumber, which owned the Portland Timbers from 1975 to 1982.) Not every recent corporate owner in North American pro sports is connected to brewing or broadcasting. One that isn't is electronic game manufacturer Nintendo of America. The company has long held a minority interest in baseball's Seattle Mariners, and in 2004 it pushed its ownership of the team over the 50-percent mark by buying retired Nintendo president Hiroshi Yamauchi's 32-percent interest.

Another involvement of corporations in sports teams, now long gone, came in the middle of the 20th century, when company-owned semipro basketball teams played at a level almost on a par with the then-fledgling NBA. The ranks of AAU basketball were dominated by teams like the Phillips 66 Oilers of Bartlesville, Okla., the Akron Goodyears of Ohio, the Peoria Caterpillers of Illinois and the Denver-Chicago Truckers of Colorado. Today, medium-sized companies like the ones that owned those teams have other ways to use sports to put their names in front of the public. The primary one is to buy stadium naming rights. Now, the names on stadiums and arenas are less likely to be those of team owners like Charles Comisky or civic leaders like

William Shea than airlines (United Center, Delta Center, Continental Airlines Arena) and banks (Lincoln Financial Field, Bank One Ballpark, Citizens Bank Park). The oddest sounding one may have been the basketball and hockey arena in Miami, for which the naming rights once were owned by the National Car Rental Co. Visitors from out of town could be forgiven for thinking that the National Car Rental Center was a garage, not a sports arena.

Corporations are not as common in the top ranks of European soccer as they are in the top ranks of American sports, but they're not unheard of, either. Perhaps the most famous—and most successful— is PSV Eindhoven of Holland. PSV is owned by the Philips Electronics Co. and its initials stand for Philips Sport Vereniging, which means Philips Sports Union. The team, one of the big three of Dutch pro soccer along with Ajax of Amsterdam and Feyenoord of Rotterdam, is located in Eindhoven, a small city in the southwestern part of Holland that formerly was the headquarters of Philips' multinational business empire. PSV's origins are somewhat similar those of the Bethlehem Steel team. It was started by Philips in 1913 as a sports club for the company's employees. While the next few years after 1913 were quite different in Holland than in Pennsylvania, Philips righted itself after the end of World War I and PSV eventually rose to the top ranks of Dutch soccer, which didn't become officially professional until 1956. PSV won the Dutch championship for the first time in 1929 and has won it many times since.

Just on the German side of the Rhine River, only about 70 miles from Eindhoven, is another big-time soccer team with a corporate owner. That is Bayer Leverkusen, owned by Bayer AG, the pharmaceutical giant that makes Bayer Aspirin and many other products. Leverkusen is a relatively small town a few miles from the far bigger and more famous Cologne. Like PSV Eindhoven, Bayer Leverkusen was started as a sports club for employees. The official name of the multisports organization of which the soccer team is a part, TSV Bayer 04 Leverkusen, reflects the date that it was founded, 1904. Bayer Leverkusen did not reach the top division of the German national Bundesliga until 1979, but has been one of the best German teams in recent years.

Two French first-division teams, Paris Saint-Germain and Sochaux, have corporate owners. Paris Saint-Germain was owned from 2001 to 2006 by French television company Canal Plus, but then was sold to a group of investment banking houses led by the American firm Morgan Stanley. Sochaux is connected with the Peugeot auto works, where it was founded in 1928. Parma, an Italian first-division team in the city of the same name, was partially owned by Parmalat, a huge international dairy business, from 1990 until the company's collapse in 2003. Since 2005, Gazprom, one of the world's largest oil corporations, has owned a controlling interest in Zenit, the main St. Petersburg team, which followed its first-ever Russian championship in 2007 by beating some of Europe's best teams to win the UEFA Cup in 2008.

The largest corporate owner of pro soccer teams in Latin America, maybe anywhere, is Televisa, the Mexican national television network. Televisa, turning an eye toward its programming needs the same way American firms like Comcast and Cablevision have, owns three Mexican first-division teams, Club America, Necaxa and San Luis. Club America, one of Mexico's best-supported teams, plays at Mexico City's 110,000-seat Estadio Azteca, which also is owned by Televisa.

In Japan, where the current J-League has been in operation only since 1993, most first-division soccer teams are owned by corporations, a model copied from baseball, which has been a Japanese staple for nearly a century. Robert Whiting discussed the ownership of Japanese baseball teams in his 1989 book on Japanese baseball, *You Gotta Have Wa*:

> Most teams are owned by corporations for public relations purposes. For example, the Hanshin Tigers and the Kintetsu Buffaloes are owned by private railway companies. The Yomiuri Giants, Japan's most popular team, and the Chunichi Dragons belong to newspapers, while the Yakult Swallows and the Taiyo Whales are the property of a health food firm and a fish company, respectively. The Hiroshima Carp are jointly owned by the citizens of Hiroshima and Toyo Kogyo, a leading car manufacturer. The Nippon Ham Fighters are owned by a pork producer and the Seibu Lions by a leading land developer. In the fall of 1988, two long-standing Osaka-based franchises owned by railroad companies were sold. The Orient Leasing Company, a financial firm that leases computer office equipment, bought the Hankyu Braves while the Dalei Corporation, a supermarket chain operator, purchased the Nankai Hawks.[20]

Thus, it's only natural that the J-League should be heavily populated by corporate-owned teams like the Kashima Antlers (Sumimoto Metal Industries) and Urawa Red Diamonds (Mitsubishi Motors). Similarly, in South Korea, many top teams, such as the Pohang Steelers, Daewoo Royals and Lucky Goldstar Bulls, are owned by the *chaebol* conglomerates that dominate Korean business.

In America, by far the most common form of corporate involvement with soccer has been sponsorship rather than full ownership, sponsorship of the sort that produced teams like the aforementioned Brookhattan, Morgan Strasser and National Slug Rejectors. The greatest extent of that has taken place in St. Louis, where the ethnic organizations that flourished in soccer elsewhere were relatively rare. During St. Louis' time as a leading hotbed of American soccer, from the 1920s to the 1960s, corporate sponsors whose teams were particularly successful included a hatmaker (Ben Millers), a steelmaker (Scullin Steel), a department store (Stix, Baer & Fuller), an auto dealership (Joe Simpkins Ford) and a funeral home (Kutis). It seems only appropriate that the first big corporate venture into big-league baseball ownership took place in St. Louis in 1953, considering the long tradition of corporate involvement with soccer in that city.

Corporate sponsorship has caused some confusing team names in American soccer. Historians at the National Soccer Hall of Fame have had to explain many times over the years that the Indiana Flooring team, one of the members of the original American Soccer League in the 1920s, was from New York, and the Manhattan Beer team, a finalist in the U.S. Open Cup in 1939, was from Chicago. And Brookhattan was based in neither Brooklyn nor Manhattan, but at Starlight Park in the Bronx.

In both Europe and elsewhere (including America), companies have paid a lot of money in recent decades to buy advertising space on the uniforms of teams they do not own. Thus, nearly all of the world's biggest clubs have taken the field with names emblazoned across their chests—Vodafone, Siemens, Carlsberg, Pirelli, Samsung and hundreds of others—that are not the names of the teams, nor of the cities they play in nor of their owners. In one comical instance, Italian first-division club Napoli, having sold shirt advertising space to an American candy manufacturer, wore uniforms that said Mars across the front. And while shirt advertising has been expanding from European soccer into American soccer, the selling of stadium naming rights has expanded from American sports into European soccer, as witness the names of two of the most spectacular new soccer stadiums in Europe, the Emirates Stadium in London and the Allianz Arena in Munich, Germany.

In all, it is safe to say that while corporate ownership of teams has been the exception to the rule in both American pro sports and in worldwide soccer, corporate money has been everywhere.

The effects of corporate ownership were both good and bad for the Steelworkers and the Cosmos. Obviously, the teams benefited greatly from their owners' financial successes. Bethlehem Steel's growth from a struggling company to one of the world's industrial giants began with the first production in 1908 of the "Grey beam" and took off with the upsurge in orders that accompanied the start of World War I. The corporation's revenues soared from $16.8 million in 1908 to $452.2 million in 1918.[21] It was in the midst of that fabulous growth, in 1915 and 1916, that Bethlehem Steel made its initial grant to the company's athletic program and built Steel Field for the soccer and baseball teams. The Cosmos' equivalent of World War I was Atari. Warner Communications hit a gold mine with its purchase in 1976 of the small maker of video-game equipment, a few years before the market for Atari's products took off.[22] Atari fueled Warner's profits during some of the Cosmos' greatest years. As had been the case at Bethlehem Steel 60 years earlier, when the corporation was flush, the soccer team reaped the benefit.

Similarly, corporate downturns hurt the two teams, as they have other pro sports teams with corporate owners. The Cosmos' slide from their wild success of the late 1970s to their demise in the mid-1980s paralleled fairly closely a series of financial troubles for Warner Communications, particularly the collapse of the video-game business in 1982 and '83 that turned Atari from Warner's prime asset into a major liability. The blame for the end of the Bethlehem Steel soccer team can be laid partly at the feet of the 1929 Stock Market Crash, which preceded the disbanding of the soccer team by six months and started the slide that put Bethlehem Steel into the red in 1932 after three straight decades of profits.

Today, there is a new corporate owner beginning to make noises in American pro soccer. In the spring of 2006, Red Bull GmbH, the Austrian maker of the Red Bull energy drink, became the "owner" of the Major League Soccer team playing at the Meadowlands, in the same stadium where the Cosmos did from 1977 to 1985. MLS teams do not have real owners because of the league's single-entity structure, in which both teams and individual players are owned by the league. The title that MLS uses for its team "owners" is investor / operators. They invest in the league, which then grants them rights to operate particular franchises. The team that Red Bull operates, and may someday own if MLS changes that single-entity structure, is one that was originally operated by John Kluge of the Metromedia conglomerate and was named the New York/New Jersey MetroStars when MLS began play in 1996. That mouthful was later shortened to MetroStars (a step reminiscent of the New York Cosmos' change to Cosmos when they moved to New Jersey in 1977). When Red Bull became involved in 2006, the name was changed to New York Red Bulls, briefly upsetting some MetroStars fans who had become attached to that name despite 10 disappointing seasons and some New Jersey politicians who objected to the New York label on a team that played exclusively in New Jersey.

The Cosmos were a part of the reason why the MetroStars existed in the first place. Although one of the things that MLS tried hardest to do in its early years was to avoid repeating mistakes made by the NASL, it did imitate the NASL by putting several of its original teams in places that had been among the NASL's biggest success stories, such as Northern New Jersey, Tampa, Fla., and San Jose, Calif. Putting a team in the stadium where the Cosmos had played was a natural once there were local investors like Kluge.

MLS' demand for local investors for its sites obviously has changed some since 1996. Red Bull GmbH, which began producing the Red Bull energy drink in 1987, is headquartered in Fuschl am See, Austria. The drink is a slightly changed version of one that had been sold in Thailand since 1962 and was discovered there in 1982 by Dietrich Mateschitz, the Austrian businessman who founded Red Bull GmbH. Over the years between 1987 and 2006, the company had gotten heavily involved in sports sponsorship, particularly in various forms of auto racing. In 2005, it bought a first-division soccer team in Salzburg, Austria, previously called SV Austria Salzburg. It changed the team name to Red Bull Salzburg, sparking far more local unhappiness than did the later name change in New Jersey. A year after that, it expanded its soccer horizons to America. Its MLS investment and the name change to New York Red Bulls were announced on March 9, 2006.

Red Bull quickly made it clear that it was eager to spend money to improve the often-bedraggled MetroStars, who reached the MLS semifinals only once in 10 seasons. Their first international signing was fairly mundane, however, an Austrian journeyman who did little to put fans in the stands in New Jersey. The new coach they hired in the middle of the 2006 season, former U.S. national team coach Bruce Arena, lasted only until the end of the 2007 season. MLS's passage in 2006 of the "Beckham rule," designed to give teams more freedom in signing international stars despite restrictions imposed by the league's salary cap, gave promise of a more interesting future for the Red Bulls, although one of the players they signed under that rule in 2007 proved a marked disappointment. It was encouraging, however, that after a short hesitation, Red Bull backed the plan the MetroStars had been working on for several years to build a new stadium in Harrison, N.J. In its first season as the Red Bulls, the team lost a lot of money, but Red Bull had bought it to advertise its energy drink, not to make money.

Over the years, American soccer has had to base much of its growth potential on the strength of the game in other countries. Bethlehem Steel and the New York Cosmos both show very clearly one of the effects this has had, something that is second only to their corporate backgrounds as a similarity between the two teams. This is the way that both built their success very heavily on the play of stars they imported from elsewhere in the world. By far the most famous of those is Pelé, who played for the Cosmos from 1975 to 1977 and whose arrival in New York was a huge factor in advancing the soccer boom that overtook the United States in subsequent decades. There were many others, however.

No one knew the Cosmos and the NASL better than Clive Toye, the driving force behind the team during their first seven seasons and the general manager who pursued and eventually signed Pelé, but even Toye's crystal ball was sometimes out of focus. "The signing of Pelé is not the start of a massive influx of foreigners," Toye said a few weeks after that landmark event. "It is the start of developing many better Americans. Pelé's presence means that there will be a decreasing number of foreigners, only those of a higher standard."[23] But the tide was moving inexorably in the direction of more foreign players, and not even Toye, someone who understood how important the development of American players was, could stop it. Toye later signed Giorgio Chinaglia and Franz Beckenbauer for the Cosmos, and saw them add the likes of Carlos Alberto, Johan Neeskens, Vladislav Bogicevic and many other expensive foreign stars after he was gone. As part of the keeping-up-with-the-Joneses trend that infected the rest of the NASL, other teams signed international superstars who included Johan Cruyff of Holland, Gerd Muller of West Germany, George Best of Northern Ireland, Bobby Moore and Gordon Banks of England, Teofilo Cubillas of Peru and Kazimierz Deyna of Poland. In the NASL's last nine seasons, 1976 through 1984, the league's 99 first-team all-star selections included 71 from Europe, 11 from South America, five from Africa, four from Asia, six from elsewhere in the CON-CACAF region and only two from the United States. And it wasn't just big stars. In 1975, the year Pelé joined the Cosmos, 202 of 337 NASL players, 59.9 percent, were foreign (meaning neither American nor Canadian). Three years later, in the 1978 season, 385 of 577 (66.7 percent) were.[24] Expansion had opened up a lot more roster spots, but about three-quarters of those openings had been filled by foreign players. The lack of playing time for Americans in the NASL drew the ire of a number of American players, including Cosmos like Bobby Smith and Shep Messing. When Major League Soccer began in 1996, it received a lot of criticism from former NASL players for its lesser quality of play. The standard was lower, but for a reason: MLS was more concerned with developing American talent than with being the sort of showcase for foreign players that the NASL had been.

Perhaps MLS shows that Toye was right in saying that the arrival of Pelé was the start of developing many better Americans. It just didn't happen within the NASL's lifetime.

The NASL had something of a reputation as a haven for over-the-hill European players. Toye characterizes this as an over-generalization: "Were some NASL players past their best? Yes. Were some as good as they ever were? Yes. Were some still at the dawn of successful careers at the highest levels in the world? Yes."[25] Indeed, along with the Pelés, Bests, Moores and Mullers, there were plenty of young players in the NASL who would go on to great stardom with big clubs in Europe in later years, players like Peter Beardsley, Bruce Grobelaar, Trevor Francis, Graeme Souness and Hugo Sanchez. Still, there were a fair number who had been journeyman players in Europe, particularly England, and who became stars when they crossed the Atlantic. Typical of them was Derek Smethurst, a South African forward who had had an inconsistent career in England. In his last stop there before crossing the Atlantic, he scored only nine goals in 70 games at Millwall in the second division. Playing in the NASL gave him a new life, however, and in 126 games for Tampa Bay, San Diego and Seattle he scored 75 goals.[26]

Bethlehem Steel likewise benefited from a lot of foreign players, although these were not the polyglot group that populated the Cosmos and the rest of the NASL. Bethlehem didn't look far beyond Britain to fill its roster. In the biographical section of his 1998 book *American Soccer League, 1921-31*, soccer historian Colin Jose included biographical sketches of 17 men who had played for Bethlehem Steel at one time or another. Every one of the 17 had been born in England,

Scotland, Wales or Northern Ireland.[27] They did include several who had moved to America as children rather than after their soccer careers had begun, but there is no doubt that Bethlehem Steel was dominated by British players.

The rest of the ASL was similarly dominated, to a degree that caused some alarm on the other side of the ocean. Jose tells about that situation:

> In Scotland it was known as the "American menace"—the drain of players from top-class Scottish clubs to the new American clubs springing up across the Atlantic. In fact, the leaders of the Scottish Football Association were so concerned about the problem that a special meeting was held in Glasgow on August 19, 1925, to discuss what to do about it....Economics, as is so often the case, was a factor in many players leaving their homelands to play in the American Soccer League. One of the players signed by Boston for the 1924-25 season was Scottish international winger Alec McNab. One year later, on his return to Scotland for a vacation, he was asked by a reporter for the Evening News of Glasgow if he would be returning to the United States. "Going back!" McNab is quoted as saying. "It will need to be a very tempting offer indeed to keep me in Scotland. From what I have heard on the other side and since I came home, terms here for next season are nothing to boast about."[28]

They certainly weren't. Wages paid to soccer players in Britain in those days were dismal. Before he left for America in 1924, McNab had been offered four pounds a week to continue playing for Greenock Morton in the 1924-25 Scottish season. From the "other side," the Boston Wonder Workers offered him the equivalent in dollars of about 12 pounds a week.[29] It wasn't a difficult decision.

Where the American Soccer League sometimes crossed the line was in signing foreign players who were under contract overseas. This started in the summer of 1924 with Johnny Ballantyne, a Scottish forward who moved to the Boston Wonder Workers at the same time as McNab. According to Jose, Ballantyne "had accepted close-season, or summer, wages from his club, Partick Thistle, something considered akin to accepting a contract for the coming season, before signing for Boston."[30] Something equivalent to baseball's reserve clause of later years didn't exist in British soccer of the 1920s, but those close-season wages were about as close a thing as there was. Dealings between clubs and players were relatively unstructured in those days, and the fact that this movement was not just from one club to another or even from one country to another, but from one continent to another made it much more difficult to control. There was the option of protest to FIFA, which at this point was only 20 years old and not as powerful as it later became, but this was not yet used at this point.

One reason why the FIFA option wasn't used was that the trans-Atlantic traffic was not all in one direction. Many players took the route of Alex Jackson, who after his one-season American sojourn became a star at several clubs in Scotland and England and was one of the stars of the famous "Wembley Wizards" team, scoring three goals in Scotland's legendary 5-1 victory over England in London in 1928. Jackson and his brother Walter played for Bethlehem Steel in the 1923-24 ASL season, with Alex scoring 22 goals in 36 games and Walter, who was a bit older, scoring 26 goals in 31 games. The two brothers went home for a visit to Scotland in the summer of 1924, amidst promises that they would be back within a few weeks.[31] Walter came back three years later. Alex never did.

While Scotland never protested to FIFA over the signing of players by ASL teams, some other countries eventually did, as a result of an American tour in the spring of 1926 by an Austrian club, Hakoah, some of whose players decided to stay in America and join ASL teams. The matter was decided, Colin Jose says, at the FIFA Congress in Helsinki, Finland in 1927, when the national associations of Austria and Hungary sought the suspension of the United States Football Association from FIFA. An appeal by Andrew M. Brown, one of the greatest early leaders of American soccer and then the president of the USFA, saved the USFA's skin and the matter was settled peacefully.[32]

Interestingly, Jose notes that "Among the first to violate the new agreement were the Scottish clubs Hearts and Aberdeen; each signed players still under contract to ASL clubs."[33]

Some in Europe saw the spectre of a second "American Menace" in the Cosmos and the NASL. This fear surfaced particularly after Franz Beckenbauer, who had captained West Germany to victory in the 1974 World Cup, decided to pass up the 1978 World Cup in order to stay with the Cosmos, whose spring-to-fall season didn't allow for a break in June and July the way the European fall-to-spring season did.

Brian Glanville, one of the leading English soccer writers, expressed this fear in the spring of 1978:

> The American threat to future World Cups is now alarmingly plain. Already the NASL and the Cosmos have prevented Franz

Beckenbauer from taking part in the Buenos Aires tournament [that year's World Cup in Argentina]. But if, as Giorgio Chinaglia promises (or threatens) a host of famous players up stakes and leave for America after the World Cup tournament, then what will the position be by the time the 1982 tournament is played in Spain?...If, as seems probable, many players of renown are playing in the NASL by 1982, and if, as seems quite ineluctable, the NASL continues to be, Heaven help us, a summer league, the conflict of interests is both manifest and inevitable.[34]

Glanville went on to refer to the NASL as a "parasite" and showing "every prospect of becoming a damned nuisance to the game." The events that he feared never happened, of course. The only NASL player who was still a current member of one of the 24 teams in the 1982 World Cup, Teofilo Cubillas of Peru and the Fort Lauderdale Strikers, was released to his national team and became the only NASL player ever to play in the World Cup.

Both the Bethlehem Steel team and the New York Cosmos were supernovas on the American soccer scene. They were dazzling at their brightest, but that light didn't shine for very long. The Cosmos' peak, from the signing of Pelé to their last NASL championship, occupied only seven years. Bethlehem's peak, from its first National Challenge Cup title to its last, occupied only 11 years. The combined total of the two teams' existence adds up to only 38 years.

Such short-livedness is not particularly surprising. Corporate involvement in sports is a fickle thing, and these were not established teams in established leagues who could survive a loss of corporate interest. The New York Yankees, legendary long before CBS bought them, easily survived being sold by CBS. The same is true for the St. Louis Cardinals after Anheuser-Busch sold them and the Montreal Canadiens after Molson sold them. But the corporate owners of the Steelworkers and the Cosmos had been the only owners of those teams, and the teams did not survive being dropped (officially, the Cosmos did exist for another 11 months after being sold by Warner, but there are many who believe that Warner never really did sell the team[35]).

Corporate ownership of a team can bring a large, sudden influx of cash, but that spigot can be quickly shut off. Teams are at the mercy of nonsports economic forces, such as the Stock Market Crash of 1929 that played a role in the doom of the Bethlehem Steel team and the collapse of the video-game market in 1982 that played a role in the doom of the Cosmos. Changes in corporate leadership also can have an effect. Herb Siegel, the stockholder who saved Warner from a takeover bid in 1984 and then became the Warner board's cost-cutting maven,[36] was not the Cosmos fanatic that Steve Ross was. Eugene Grace, who took over from Charles M. Schwab as president of Bethlehem Steel in 1916 and occupied that post until the 1950s, had been an outstanding college baseball player in his day,[37] and Bethlehem Steel sponsored an active amateur baseball league as well as its pro soccer team. Corporations' interests come and go. They can move on to other novelties. In the cases of the Steelworkers and the Cosmos, they did.

Rapid come and rapid go is a well-established trend in American soccer. A major component of it is early success, of the sort enjoyed by the Philadelphia Atoms. In 1973, the Atoms were a first-year expansion team in the NASL. In a magical season, one in which they found the perfect player combinations on the field and everything seemed to go right, they won the NASL championship. Just three years later, attendance had evaporated and the local investors who founded them had sold them to a combination of four pro teams from Guadalajara, Mexico. According to reporter Don McKee, who covered the Atoms throughout their four-season life for newspapers in Philadelphia and Camden, the new owners then sealed their doom by moving the team (which had become known locally as the "Mexican Atoms") from new Veterans Stadium to crumbling Franklin Field and populating it with obscure Mexican players.[38] Just a year after that, the Atoms had folded.

The Atoms are not the only case of such rapid success in American pro soccer. 1973 was only the first of three years in a row that the NASL title was won by a first-year expansion team, the Los Angeles Aztecs repeating the Atoms' feat in 1974 and the Tampa Bay Rowdies doing it in 1975. In MLS, the expansion Chicago Fire were champions in 1998. In the original American Soccer League, the Fall River Marksmen finished only third in their inaugural season, 1922-23, but they then won the title the next three seasons in a row, and the Boston Wonder Workers won the league cup and then the U.S. professional championship in their first season. Such early success has usually been hailed as a remarkable achievement by the backers of the clubs that have done it, but it may really be much more an indication of the weakness of the existing teams than the strength of the new ones.

As with the Atoms, burnout can happen quickly. The Aztecs

lasted only eight seasons, and never won another NASL title. The Marksmen moved away from Fall River eight years after they were founded. The Rowdies did last through the NASL's last season, 1984, but without another NASL title, and Tampa's reputation as a soccer hotbed didn't continue very long into the MLS era. The Tampa Bay Mutiny folded after six MLS seasons without ever coming close to a title. The standards in this area are held by a pair of American Soccer League teams, the Philadelphia Nationals and the New Bedford Whalers. The Nationals were the defending ASL champions when they folded in 1953 and the Whalers were the U.S. Open Cup champions when they folded in 1932.

Bethlehem Steel lasted a bit longer than the Cosmos. The Steelworkers played their first game in November 1907 and their last in April 1930, a span of more than 22 years. For the first few years of that time, they were an amateur club, and while they were built around Bethlehem Steel employees from the start, they didn't change their name from Bethlehem FC to Bethlehem Steel FC until 1915, after a grant from the corporation. Although they won a few championships in their later years, their greatest achievements were in the middle part of those 22 years. From 1914 to 1922 they didn't go a single year without winning either the National Challenge Cup, the American Football Association Cup or the championship of their league.

The demise of the Bethlehem Steel soccer team seems to have revolved around two factors, first the weakening of the American Soccer League by the "Soccer War" jurisdictional battle of 1928 and '29 and the Stock Market Crash of October 1929 and second Edgar Lewis' departure from Bethlehem Steel early in 1930. When the Steelworkers did disappear, they did so quite suddenly. On March 23, 1930, they were still in the thick of the battle for the National Challenge Cup. A week before, they had played a 1-1 tie in New York in the semifinals of that competition against their traditional rival, the Fall River Marksmen. Then, on that day, the Marksmen eliminated them, scoring a 3-2 victory in the replay in New Bedford, Mass. Three weeks later, on April 14, 1930, the disbanding of the team was officially announced. By the end of April, the team was history.

The Cosmos lasted from December 1970 to June 1985. Their decline was a gradual one, but the final steps were brutally sudden. They suffered through the general decline of the NASL, in which the handwriting was on the wall for several years, a lingering sort of death. They also suffered through changes at Warner Communications that included the collapse of the video-game market that had provided much of the profits that had kept them flying. In the spring of 1985, they continued to play without the NASL, announcing a schedule of 11 exhibition games. Attendances were disappointing, but they seemed to be making a good attempt at survival. After the second of those games, a 2-0 victory over a touring Portuguese team, a New York soccer newspaper announced in a banner headline that "Cosmos Are For Real."[39] Things went downhill very suddenly after the third of those games, however, and the end came just a few days later, only a week after that exultant headline.

The two greatest teams that American soccer has seen both died unhappily and both died young.

TWO

Lehigh Valley Boys

The Bethlehem Steel soccer team started small. Today, that's not the way it works with professional soccer teams in the United States. Today, they don't grow gradually in the manner of a Bethlehem Steel or a Philadelphia Nationals. They're born big, in the manner of a Los Angeles Galaxy or a Chicago Fire.

In Bethlehem Steel's day, the model was different. By the time of the 1913-14 season, during which it started competing successfully outside its immediate area, the team had been around for a half-dozen years as an amateur eleven in the Lehigh Valley, one that had grown out of some barely organized kickabouts among a few Bethlehem Steel employees. Perhaps that was appropriate, mirroring the way the company itself had grown. The Bethlehem Steel Corporation had been around for a while, under one name or another. It, too, had started small and gradually gained in size and strength as it grew into the industrial giant that supported the Bethlehem Steel soccer team.

One of the greatest chapters in American soccer history had its roots with the formation in 1857 of a firm that was originally called the Saucona Iron Company. The valley of Saucon Creek, a few miles east of South Bethlehem, Pa., contained substantial deposits of iron ore, and the company's objective was to mine the ore and use it to make iron rails for railroads, which were becoming a growing factor in America.

Although it retains a place in history as the earliest ancestor of Bethlehem Steel, the Saucona Iron Company never was more than a paper company. Before it ever rolled a single rail, some major changes were made through the actions of the Lehigh Valley Railroad, whose principal stockholder was one of Saucona's initial investors. The railroad needed a better supply of iron rails than the inferior ones it was buying from one of the few American makers,[1] and in 1858, it used its financial resources to take control of the Saucona Iron Company. Among its first acts were to reorganize the company under the name Bethlehem Rolling Mill and Iron Company, choose a plant site in South Bethlehem (Bethlehem, on the north side of the Lehigh River, and South Bethlehem, on the south side, were separate municipalities until 1917) and hire an engineer named John Fritz away from the Cambria Iron Works in Johnstown, Pa.[2]

In 1857 at Cambria, Fritz had developed a system that greatly eased the problem of inferior rails, which often cracked or warped and could be a cause of serious railroad accidents. He didn't actually invent the system, but rather improved on one that had been invented in Wales, particularly by adapting it to American technology. A large reason for the problems with the rails had to do with the fact that two passes through the rollers were required to shape the square bars of iron correctly. By the time the bars had finished the first pass and been hauled back to the front of the rollers to begin the second pass, they often had cooled sufficiently that the second pass couldn't do its job properly, resulting in rails that were susceptible to cracks and other problems. Fritz' solution was what was called a "three-high" system of rollers, which basically was one set of rollers stacked on top of another. The bar was passed through the lower set of rollers, and then, while it was still warm and malleable, passed through the upper set in the opposite direction.[3]

As with a number of developments in the iron and steel industries over the years, the end product wasn't the real invention. Rather, the invention was the mill required to make that end product. Fritz moved to Bethlehem in 1860 as general manager and superintendent. His "three-high" rolling mill began producing Bethlehem's first rails in 1863 (by which time the name of the company had been shortened to Bethlehem Iron Company). Historian Gerald Eggert says that "Fritz' invention became standard for the industry and remained such until the appearance of steel rails at the close of the Civil War."[4] Bethlehem's timing in getting into the business of making rails couldn't have been more perfect. Between 1863 and 1865, the law of supply-and-demand caused the price of iron rails to more than double in the United States, because the builders of the transcontinental railroad then under construction had begun buying rails, and federal law required that they buy only American-made ones.[5]

The steel rails to which Eggert refers were made in England. They were much more expensive than iron rails, and got many American ironmaking companies interested in switching to steelmaking, thus heralding the next major advance for what was to become Bethlehem Steel. The difference between iron and steel is small but meaningful. "Steel is iron united during production with a small but critical percentage of carbon," notes Eggert. "In use it can withstand extremely heavy wear and flexing."[6] In the 1850s, English inventor Henry Bessemer had developed what was to become a widely used method for producing steel in large quantities. Methods for making steel had existed for centuries, but were so expensive as to be impractical for producing steel in large quantities. Nevertheless, they continued to be used for some time for producing small quantities of very high quality steel for use in things like eating utensils, cutting tools and razor blades.

What Bessemer invented was a type of cauldron, called the Bessemer converter, that could be tipped on its side on an axis and in which large amounts of steel could be produced without the huge expense of earlier methods. Eggert tells how it worked:

> In the mid-1850s, Henry Bessemer in England and William Kelly in Kentucky independently discovered that steel could be made directly from pig iron by melting it in a large pear-shaped 'converter.' As the iron melted, a strong blast of cold air, blown through holes in the bottom of the converter, passed through the molten iron. This created such intense heat that the carbon and silicon in the iron were burned off. As the process began, the flame at the mouth of the converter burned red. Then, with rising temperatures and consumption of the carbon and silicon, the flame turned a white so brilliant that it could scarcely be viewed by the naked eye. The loss of the flame after nine or ten minutes into the 'blow,' signaled that only molten, pure wrought iron remained. The converter was then turned on its side, the blast shut off, and enough carbon and manganese added to change the iron into steel. When completed, the Bessemer steel was poured into ingot molds and the ingots, in turn, rolled into slabs, blooms and billets preparatory to further refining.[7]

Bessemer and Kelly were not alone in their discoveries. Methods of producing steel by blowing air through molten iron were developed by several other English and American inventors, but Bessemer's converter won out as the preferred method.[8] Bringing that method to America wasn't easy, however. A group from Troy, N.Y., held the American rights to Bessemer's English patents. A midwestern group held the rights to Kelly's American patents for a related method. Neither group could put its method into use without infringing on the other's patents. Eventually, the legal gridlock was cleared through a series of out-of-court settlements in the late 1860s, and the way was cleared for the patentholders to begin selling licenses to American companies (who much preferred the Bessemer method).[9]

By 1873, Bethlehem Iron had joined the growing crowd of American companies making steel rails using the Bessemer process. The Bethlehem board of directors voted in 1868 to make the change from ironmaking to steelmaking. John Fritz did not go along eagerly. In particular, Bethlehem's plant superintendent worried that the Bessemer process required iron ore lower in phosphorus content than the ore Bethlehem normally used.[10] Because of its location, Bethlehem didn't have access to the low-phosphorus ore from the Upper Peninsula of Michigan that was used by companies in western Pennsylvania and the shores of the Great Lakes. But after Bethlehem's Bessemer mill was completed in 1873, it managed to make a go of steelmaking, using ore from one mine in north-central New Jersey that was lower in phosphorus than other New Jersey mines and from several other mines overseas.[11]

Bethlehem Iron's steel railmaking operation survived the ore problem that threatened to prevent it from getting off the ground, and it also survived a national financial panic in the 1870s. But it met its match in a fuel problem caused by its eastern Pennsylvania location. Western Pennsylvania and West Virginia are underlain by one of the world's largest deposits of bituminous coal, or "soft coal." Western Pennsylvania steel mills used coke, which was derived from bituminous coal, to fuel the blast furnaces that produced pig iron, which then was turned into steel in the Bessemer converters. Bethlehem couldn't use coke because the coal under eastern Pennsylvania was a different type, anthracite, but it had stayed competitive with western Pennsylvania steelmakers by using high-pressure blasts of air in its anthracite-fueled blast furnaces. When western Pennsylvania mills tried that technique in coke-fueled blast furnaces, they produced pig iron of significantly better quality than the eastern anthracite-fueled furnaces had.[12]

By 1881, Metz says, "coke-fueled furnaces in the Pittsburgh region were beginning to dominate the iron industry and the rail market."[13] Bethlehem Iron was forced into a new direction. Where it ended up going was the munitions business, particularly steel armor plate for large warships and steel guns for those ships, a change that would prove to be of tremendous profit to the company in the future, particularly during the World War I years when the Bethlehem Steel soccer team was at its peak.

This time, John Fritz led the movement for change, rather than opposing it as he had with the change from iron to steel. Bethlehem Iron's directors, led by railroad man Asa Packer, wanted to stay with their policy of making rails and nothing else. "The directors' conservatism irritated John Fritz," says Misa. "By the early 1880s Fritz became convinced that Bethlehem needed to cut its dependency on the rail market. The declining profits on rails—the result of a flood of cheap rails from Carnegie's Edgar Thompson mill [near Pittsburgh] and its counterparts—made a decision on diversification critical. He formulated plans for making structural shapes, plates for ships and heavy forgings, but company directors rejected every one of them."[14]

Fritz managed to carry the day anyway, thanks to the support of board member Joseph Wharton, who gained effective control of the company after the deaths of Packer and several of his conservative allies on the board. Wharton took Bethlehem out of rails altogether and then began the steps that had Bethlehem already moving in the right direction when the United States Navy sought bids on huge contracts for armor plate and guns in the mid-1880s.[15]

The timing of Bethlehem's move into munitions was fortuitous. For years, the U.S. Navy had been largely a coastal force, designed mostly for blockading ports the way it had during the Civil War. In the 1880s, the decision was made to greatly expand the navy, turning it into an ocean-going force that needed new ships, with heavy armor and big guns. Besides the good timing, Bethlehem benefited from several other advantages in its move into munitions, particularly the fact that the president of the biggest Pittsburgh steelmaker, Andrew Carnegie, was a pacifist who was willing to make armor plate, but not guns.

When the bids on the new navy contract were opened in March 1887, Bethlehem Iron was the only bidder on both armor plate and guns, meaning that it got the contracts for both. Bethlehem and the navy finished negotiating the prices and amounts of steel a few months later. The contracts were worth nearly $4.5 million, a huge figure in 1887.[16]

Bethlehem didn't yet have the technology or equipment it needed to begin producing the steel called for in the contracts, but it had negotiated agreements with British and French firms for the use of their processes. Over the next few years, Bethlehem began receiving equipment needed for those processes from its European partners. In addition, it began building a new mill on its property that included four open-hearth furnaces. These furnaces were not a new development, having been invented by German engineer Charles Siemens a quarter-century before, but they were the type of furnace required for making armor plate.[17] At one time, they had been thought to require low-phosphorus iron ore just as the Bessemer process did, but then an English chemist, Sidney Gilchrist-Thomas, developed a way by which, in an open-hearth furnace, the phosphorus could be drawn out of the molten iron as slag.[18]

Bethlehem's contract with the navy called for it to begin making deliveries of armor plate in December 1889, but a number of problems, particularly a delay in the arrival of equipment from Europe, prevented it from meeting this deadline. This allowed Carnegie Steel to get a foot in the door.[19] Carnegie had built several open-hearth furnaces at its Homestead mill in Pittsburgh in 1889 and, by the time Bethlehem did begin producing armor plate, an 1890 contract with the navy had given Carnegie a share of the business.

For several years in the early 1890s, there was a furious debate over which of several different types of armor plate (meaning different chemical compositions of the steel being used) was better able to withstand direct hits from shells.[20] The debate, which included questions of whether Bethlehem's or Carnegie's armor was better, was rendered moot by the mid-1890s when two new processes for hardening armor plate, one developed by American engineer Hayward A. Harvey and the other by the legendary firm Friedrich Krupp AG of Essen, Germany, proved vastly superior to all others—and somewhat similar to each other.

Rights to the Harvey process were controlled by British armsmaker Vickers' Sons & Maxim. "Under the Harvey United Steel Company, which existed only on paper and whose chairman was Albert Vickers, the patents were exchanged," wrote historian William Manchester. "All member organizations—Krupp, Vickers, Armstrong, Schneider, Carnegie and Bethlehem Steel—agreed to pool information about refinements of hardening techniques, and Krupp received a royalty of $45 on each ton of hull armor produced."[21] The armor plate "wars" seemed to have concluded, with the companies, including Bethlehem, that held rights to make armor plate by the Harvey-Krupp methods the clear winners.

Bethlehem Iron's situation seemed to have stabilized a bit, too, but that didn't last. The turn of the century, including the years just before and after it, brought some huge upheavals in the ownership of the company, which in the course of those upheavals became the Bethlehem Steel Corporation.

The first step in that revolution was a relatively gentle one, although it was something of a landmark in that it involved the first use of the word "steel" in the company's name. In 1899, the directors of Bethlehem Iron created a holding company, called the Bethlehem Steel Company, which would lease the facilities of the Bethlehem Iron Company, sell stock and use the proceeds to expand those facilities.[22]

Two years later, the steel industry was turned upside down by one of the most gigantic mergers that has ever occurred in American business. The vast Carnegie Steel company was sold to financier J. Pierpont Morgan and merged with Morgan's similarly vast steel-making holdings to create the U.S. Steel Corporation, which also included some smaller steel companies that the new combination felt could be advantageous to it. Bethlehem Steel was not one of those included. The leaders of U.S. Steel didn't want to include units that they felt duplicated ones they already had, and Bethlehem Steel, whose only business at this point was munitions making, was felt to be too similar to parts of Carnegie Steel that did the same thing.[23] So Bethlehem Steel was left out, and started on the route to becoming the number-one thorn in U.S. Steel's side.

The man who put together the merger and became president of the new corporation was Charles M. Schwab, who had been president of Carnegie Steel since 1897. Because of the merger, he became a fabulously wealthy man. In his years as a high-ranking executive at Carnegie Steel, he had repeatedly been given bonuses in the form of Carnegie Steel stock. By the time of the merger, he owned six percent of Carnegie Steel, and as a result was showered with $25 million worth of U.S. Steel bonds.[24] This new-found wealth enabled him, a few months later, to outbid Vickers and buy Bethlehem Steel for $7.2 million. Shortly after buying Bethlehem Steel, he turned around and sold his new purchase to Morgan for the same price he had paid for it.[25] But a year later, he bought it back from Morgan so that it could be included in a combination of shipyards on both coasts that was being put together as the U.S. Shipbuilding Company.[26]

Things didn't go well for Schwab at U.S. Steel. Although he was president of the company, he was outranked by its chairman, Elbert Gary, who had come from the Morgan side of the merger, and the two men clashed repeatedly, particularly over company policies and

41

Schwab's *bon vivant* lifestyle.[27] That lifestyle also got Schwab into trouble with his straight-laced mentor, Andrew Carnegie, who hit the roof after Schwab was seen playing roulette in the casino at Monte Carlo during a European vacation in 1901 (it wasn't Schwab's first visit to those tables, only the first one Carnegie found out about). Although Schwab later got back into Carnegie's good graces, he and Gary remained foes for years, long after Schwab finally threw in the towel and resigned as president of U.S. Steel in August 1903. His position at U.S. Steel hadn't been helped by the fact that the U.S. Shipbuilding Company had become a money-losing disaster, with some, including the head of a government investigation of the matter, accusing Schwab of having planned the disaster for his own personal gain.[28]

Schwab certainly did benefit in one way from the U.S. Shipbuilding collapse. The deal under which Bethlehem Steel was included as part of U.S. Shipbuilding was structured in such a way as to enable Schwab to retain control of Bethlehem should U.S. Shipbuilding fail.[29] Coming out of the shipbuilding collapse with Bethlehem Steel still in his hands (plus some shipyards), he kept it there this time and made it the project that occupied him for much of the rest of his life. Schwab turned to running Bethlehem Steel—as opposed to just buying and selling it—in 1904.

Schwab was 42 years old when he took command of Bethlehem Steel, whose name became the Bethlehem Steel *Corporation* in December 1904. He was a small-town kid from Loretto in central Pennsylvania who had gone to seek his fortune in the big city, Pittsburgh, and found it at Carnegie Steel's Edgar Thompson Works in Braddock, Pa., just south of Pittsburgh on the Monongahela River. He started there in 1879, when he was 17, in a menial job, carrying a leveling rod on a surveying crew.[30] His intelligence and his zeal for hard work enabled him to rise rapidly, and he became a draftsman, then an aide to the superintendent of the mill and by age 24 superintendent of Carnegie's nearby Homestead mill. At 35 he was the president of Carnegie Steel, at 39 the president of U.S. Steel and at 42 picking up the pieces of his career at Bethlehem Steel.[31]

Bethlehem Steel in 1904 was not the giant it was to become. When Bethlehem had gotten out of the rail business in the 1880s, it hadn't really diversified. It had switched from nearly total concentration on making a single product, rails, to nearly total concentration on making a different product, munitions. In 1904, it was a specialty steelmaker, in a specialty that made it very heavily dependent on government contracts for its revenue.[32]

Lance Metz describes the start of Schwab's efforts to bring Bethlehem Steel out of that situation:

> Schwab possessed an intimate knowledge of U.S. Steel's strengths and weaknesses. During the first decade of his ownership of Bethlehem Steel, he counterprogrammed its expansion to exploit chinks in his larger competitor's armor [the figurative armor, not the literal stuff]. He installed a crucible steel plant since U.S. Steel did not own such a facility, built an open hearth rail mill that produced products superior to the Bessemer steel rails produced by U.S. Steel, and added a drop forging plant since U.S. Steel was not willing to enter this market.[33]

Schwab's biggest move involved what was called the "Grey beam," a product that eventually became so closely identified with Bethlehem Steel that it was adopted as part of the corporation's logo. He could have bankrupted Bethlehem Steel with this move, but decided that it was worth the risk.

The Grey beam, or rather the mill needed to make it, had been invented in 1897 by Henry Grey, an English engineer working at the Ironton Structural Steel Company in Duluth, Minn. The beam was similar to the familiar I-beam, but had much wider lips, or flanges, giving it more the shape of a sideways H and making it much stronger than the I-beam for supporting weight and building to great heights. Actually, similar strength could be obtained with more conventional beams, but not without a lot of expensive and difficult riveting together of separate pieces of steel. The beauty of the Grey beam (which eventually became known as the "Bethlehem beam") was that it could be rolled in a single piece.[34]

By the early 1900s, Grey and Ironton had patented their 1897 invention and hoped that the big steel companies would pay them richly for the right to make the revolutionary beam, but they had miscalculated its appeal. The big steel companies resisted the change. The only major steel executive who showed any interest in the Grey beam was Charles M. Schwab of U.S. Steel, but he was overruled by U.S. Steel's finance committee. He didn't forget the Grey beam, however. In 1905, by which time he was running the show at Bethlehem Steel, he twice inspected the one steel mill where Grey beams were being produced, a German-owned mill in Luxembourg. After deciding that Bethlehem Steel should begin making Grey beams, he informed U.S. Steel of his plans, a diplomatic necessity, since he had first learned about the beam while employed there. U.S. Steel still wasn't interested in the Grey beam, so Schwab and Bethlehem took the plunge.[35]

There was a lot more to making the Grey beam than just deciding to do so and paying Henry Grey for the right to, and this may have been one reason why other steelmakers were reluctant to get involved. In particular, an entire new mill had to be built, at a cost of $12 million.[36] This was done, on 250 acres that Bethlehem Steel purchased just east of its main plant,[37] but outside economic forces almost doomed the project. The Panic of 1907, a nationwide financial crisis in which the credit markets temporarily dried up, caused Schwab great difficulty in finding financing for the construction of what became known as the Saucon plant. That construction eventually went ahead, however, and Bethlehem began producing Grey beams in July 1908. Eight years later, the Saucon plant had been operating at full capacity since the day it opened without a single break.[38] U.S. Steel was forced to play catch-up, and it spent the next 20 years looking for ways either to create a beam that was the equal of Bethlehem's or skirt the Grey beam patents. It never succeeded at either.

By 1913, as the Bethlehem Steel soccer team began to emerge from local competition and start winning games against top teams from New England, New Jersey and elsewhere, the Bethlehem Steel Corporation had positioned itself very successfully as a truly diversified steelmaker. It was involved in each of the major areas that were available to a steelmaker in that day. In structural steel, its Grey beam had made it a leader in the heavy construction business east of the Appalachians (U.S. Steel built Chicago, but New York was Bethlehem's turf). In munitions, it was dividing the armor-plate market with U.S. Steel and Philadelphia's Midvale Steel, and dominating the gun-forgings market. In steel rails, its open-hearth rail mill had it as firmly back in the market as it had been in the days when the "three-high" mill revolutionized the making of iron rails. And in shipbuilding, an area that it had gotten involved in as a result of the U.S. Shipbuilding complications, it owned two of the largest shipyards in the country, Harlan & Hollingsworth of Wilmington, Del., and the Union Iron Works of San Francisco, and was about to buy a third, the Fore River Shipyard of Quincy, Mass.

Bethlehem Steel's workers, meanwhile, had already begun to take an interest in leisure-time activities—like soccer.

American soccer was just coming out of a doldrums around the time that both Charles M. Schwab and the first soccer ball arrived in

Bethlehem. Soccer had made its first appearance in the United States in the 1860s. Perhaps the debut was the games played by a group of schoolboys, called the Oneida Football Club, on the Boston Common early in the decade, although the game they were playing may have been more like rugby than soccer. If it wasn't the Oneidas, then it probably was a game between Carroll College students and local residents in Waukesha, Wisc., on Oct. 11, 1866. The colleges turned toward rugby instead in the 1870s, but soccer really took hold in the working classes, particularly immigrant working classes, in a number of places in the 1880s. Those places principally included Fall River, Mass.; Kearny, N.J.; St. Louis, Chicago, New York and Philadelphia. But the Panic of 1893, which triggered one of the most severe depressions in American history, put soccer on the shelf for a while. Both the American Football Association Cup, which was the closest thing there was to a national championship, and the National Association Foot Ball League, a New York-New Jersey circuit that was probably the strongest league in the country, shut down after their 1898 editions.

Soccer's American comeback seems to have been inspired by the 1905 tour of the Pilgrims, a team of English amateur players. The Pilgrims' 1905 American tour, the first of two that they made, lasted from Sept. 5 to Oct. 26 and included stops in Detroit, St. Louis, Chicago, Philadelphia, Fall River, Boston and New York. They played 12 games in the United States and five in Canada. Of the games in the United States, the Pilgrims lost one, to a Chicago all-star team, and won the other 11 by a total of 72-7. Besides promoting the game of soccer, the tour also was intended to assist President Theodore Roosevelt's campaign against the growing violence in American college football, and at the end of the tour two Pilgrims players visited Roosevelt at the White House.[39]

After that Pilgrims tour, it was less than a year before the AFA Cup and the National Association Foot Ball League got back on their feet again. The AFA Cup was reorganized in February 1906 and the league in August 1906.[40] In each, the first competition since 1898 was won by a new club on the scene, West Hudson AA of Harrison, N.J. The area that West Hudson was from, the western part of Hudson County, was one of the leading hotbeds of soccer in the country at the time, a result of the immigrant population drawn there by companies that included the Clark Thread Mill and the Nairn Linoleum Company, both the American branches of large Scottish firms. Kearny, next door to Harrison, had a reputation that has lasted into the 21st century as a "Little Scotland." The first winner of the AFA Cup in 1885, and thus the first champion of American soccer, was ONT of Kearny (the club was sponsored by the Clark Thread Mill and the initials stood for one of its products, Our New Thread). Other teams from northern New Jersey that were among the best in American soccer before World War I included Kearny Scots, Paterson True Blues, Newark Caledonian and Kearny Clark. Teams like those are the reason why the National Association Foot Ball League, most of whose clubs were from northern New Jersey, is considered to have been the best in the country at the time, slightly better than excellent leagues in New England, St. Louis, Chicago, Philadelphia and elsewhere.

That the steelworkers in Bethlehem, Pa., should begin playing soccer and eventually organize a team was quite in keeping with the trend of the day. In the first quarter of the 20th century, factory teams flourished in American soccer. Perhaps chief among these were shipyards, particularly in the years during and just after World War I, when American shipbuilding was booming and many shipyard workers were exempt from the draft. Among the shipyard-based teams that became prominent in American soccer in these years were Fore River Shipyard of Quincy, Mass.; Robins Dry Dock and Morse Dry Dock of Brooklyn; Federal Shipyard of Kearny, N.J.; New York Shipbuilding of Camden, N.J., and Merchant Shipbuilding of Bristol, Pa. There were teams connected with textile mills, like J&P Coats of Pawtucket, R.I.; Clark AA of Kearny and Farr Alpaca of Holyoke, Mass. There were steel mill teams: Homestead of Pittsburgh; Scullin of St. Louis; Joliet of Illinois and, of course, Bethlehem. There were other heavy industries represented as well, with teams like Disston AA of Philadelphia (sawmaking), Howard & Bullough of Pawtucket (mill machinery) and Babcock & Wilcox of Bayonne, N.J. (boilers). Bethlehem Steel fit right in.

When Bethlehem Steel played its first real soccer game in 1907, the sport had been played in Bethlehem on a sandlot basis for several years. According to the *Bethlehem Globe* in 1925: "In 1904 a soccer ball was brought from Scotland and kicked around on a vacant lot on Buttonwood street facing the plant of the Bethlehem Steel Co. and later used on a more adapted lot at the rear of the O'Reilly grocery and dry goods store on East Third street. The introduction of the ball in this city created quite a lot of excitement among the athletically inclined."[41] Soccer in Bethlehem then entered a sort of intramural phase, which Edgar Lewis referred to in a speech in 1915, by which time he was retired as a player and managing the team. The *South Bethlehem Globe* (which became the *Bethlehem Globe* when the two cities were merged in 1917) said that Lewis spoke of the time eight years before "when there were but two teams in the county, Bethlehem and Allentown, and on alternative Saturdays one would play the other on the home grounds."[42]

In the fall of 1907, Bethlehem decided to step out into some real competition and play its first official game. At this time, the team was still called the Bethlehem Football Club. Although the team was composed almost entirely of steelworkers, the word "steel" wasn't added to the team's name until 1915. But if they didn't yet have Bethlehem Steel's name, they had its hubris. For that first game, they bit off far more than they could chew, West Hudson, which may have been the best team in the country at the time. Perhaps they were inspired by the origins two years before of the West Hudson team itself. A fan from Harrison, watching a champion team from New York City, declared that he could organize a team of Harrison players that would beat the New Yorkers—which he then did.[43] If the Bethlehem people were hoping to repeat that feat, they came up considerably short when they played their first game on Nov. 17, 1907, at the West Hudson team's home ground in Harrison, just across the Passaic River from the city of Newark. The predictable result was described by the next day's *Newark Evening News*: "The West Hudson Association Football Club had an easy time yesterday afternoon at Harrison Oval, Harrison, defeating the Bethlehem Football Club, the reputed champions of the Lehigh Valley, to the tune of 11 goals to 2. The visitors were outclassed and put up a poor exhibition. The management of the [Bethlehem] team stated that some of the regular players of the club were unable to be present and another contest has been arranged between the clubs to be decided in Bethlehem next month."[44] One of the Bethlehem goals was an own goal, the other was scored by center forward Jack Cassidy, making him the Steelworkers' inaugural goalscorer.

(The spot in Harrison where Bethlehem and West Hudson played, between Middlesex and Burlington streets, is now a parking lot operated by Kinney Parking, which was involved in the founding of the New York Cosmos in 1970.)

Those absences from the Nov. 17 game probably reflected the fact that soccer was still something the players did in their time off from full-time jobs at Bethlehem Steel. Among the players who weren't there that day was Edgar Lewis, later the man more responsible than any other for the success of Bethlehem Steel soccer. The team is referred to as the "reputed" champion of the Lehigh Valley. There was no official champion, but this may indicate that the series of informal

Bethlehem vs. Allentown games had gone mostly in Bethlehem's favor and that most of the Lehigh Valley's best players were on the Bethlehem team. However, any hope that the return to the lineup of those missing players would turn the score around was misplaced. When Bethlehem and West Hudson met again in December, West Hudson won by 9-0.

At this point, Bethlehem decided that while it might have outgrown its back-and-forth series against Allentown, it still would be a good idea to seek some lesser opposition than mighty West Hudson. It started playing teams from elsewhere in eastern Pennsylvania, particularly from Reading, from Lansford in the anthracite coaling-mining region of Carbon County and from Bangor in the "Slate Belt" region north of the Lehigh Valley. In 1910, the team's progress was slowed by the first major strike at Bethlehem Steel, over the issue of forced overtime. The strike involved only a minority of Bethlehem's workers, but nevertheless lasted 108 days, from February to May. The striking workers won little, only a concession by the company to make overtime and Sunday work optional. That was a moot point for many, however. The settlement included no increase in pay rates, so few could afford to give up overtime and Sunday work. The whole affair was another feather in Charles M. Schwab's union-busting cap.

Still, the team continued to advance, with Edgar Lewis playing a larger and larger part. The fact that Lewis later served as captain of the team was an indication that his standing with his teammates had not been hurt by the strike, despite the fact that he was an executive, not an ordinary steelworker. Of course, Lewis was not quite an ordinary executive, either. A 1936 article in *Time Magazine,* after he had been named chairman of Jones & Laughlin in Pittsburgh, referred to him as an "up-from-the-mill steelman."[45]

Lewis was born in 1882 in Pontardulais, Wales, in the valley of the River Loughor, about five miles north of the city of Swansea. His father was a roller in one of the tin mills that had proliferated in that valley in the mid-1800s. In 1896, the family moved to America, settling first in Harrisburg, Pa., then in Martin's Ferry, Ohio, just across the Ohio River from Wheeling, W.Va. Lewis entered the working world in 1899, at the Carnegie Steel Co.'s Duquesne Works in Pittsburgh. He didn't start all the way at the bottom like Schwab had at Carnegie 20 years before. Lewis' first job at the Duquesne Works was as a tool-dresser,[46] a skilled job that involved sharpening the cutting tools, usually made of very high quality hardened steel, that were used for machining the steel that came out of the furnaces into finished products. Ironically, 1899 was the same year that Eugene Grace, later Lewis' colleague and rival at Bethlehem Steel, started work at Bethlehem, as an electric crane operator. But Grace, like Lewis one of Schwab's "boys," as he called his protégés at Bethlehem Steel, was a few years older than Lewis and had just graduated at the top of his class from Lehigh University in South Bethlehem with a degree in electrical engineering. Lewis finished his formal education with high school in Martin's Ferry. Both men were excellent athletes. Grace had been a baseball star at Lehigh and had turned down an offer from the Boston Braves that would have paid him four times as much as Bethlehem was offering, while Lewis had been an outstanding American football quarterback with his high school team, and continued in that position with the Dravosburg semipro team near Pittsburgh while working for Carnegie Steel.

[Edgar Lewis' name has been rendered several different ways over the years. His full name was Horace Edgar Lewis, and that is what he is called by the National Soccer Hall of Fame, where he was a member of the 16-man first induction class in 1950. In published references to corporate affairs and soccer, he was often called H. Edgar Lewis or H.E. Lewis, and the latter is what he is called by Dan Morrison's voluminous and detailed website on the Bethlehem Steel soccer team. The people who knew him, both in soccer and in steel, seem to have most often referred to him as Edgar Lewis, and that is what this book will call him.]

Lewis was still with Carnegie Steel when it became a part of U.S. Steel in 1901, but he left a few years later for a brief time with the Passaic Steel Company in New Jersey. In 1906, he arrived at Bethlehem Steel, no longer in the mill but now in the office as chief of the accounting department,[47] crunching some big numbers for a company that had revenues of $17.5 million that year.[48]

Lewis' arrival in Bethlehem resulted in the native of Wales being introduced to soccer. "I had never seen a soccer game before I came to Bethlehem," Lewis remarked in a speech in 1919. "I was an American rugby [American football] player and only became interested in soccer when I journeyed to the athletic field with one of the shop foremen, more to participate in outdoor exercise than to really participate in the game. It was then that I became aware of the intricate features of the game."[49]

Lewis was a real player, not a figurehead. He starred at inside right for Bethlehem for quite few years. As he got older, the injuries and his corporate responsibilities both mounted, and Bethlehem began attracting more professional players, particularly from Scotland. Lewis' playing time waned until he finally retired from playing after the 1914-15 season. But as late as the 1913-14 season, he played more than half of Bethlehem's league games. The last important cup win that he played was the landmark victory over Braddock of Pittsburgh in December 1913, which was probably the biggest win the Bethlehem team had ever scored to that date.

After he stopped playing, Lewis managed the team for a few years, and then continued to oversee it from the executive suite. Having a former player in an executive position, with access to the corporate purse strings, was invaluable to the Bethlehem Steel team.

Lewis left Bethlehem Steel in 1930, the same year that the soccer team was disbanded, and there seems little question that there was some connection between the two events. After six years in charge of Jeffrey Manufacturing Co., a maker of heavy equipment for the coal-mining industry, in Columbus, Ohio, he returned to the steel industry in 1936 as chairman and later president of Jones & Laughlin in Pittsburgh, leading the nation's fourth largest steelmaker through World War II, a busy time for a steel company.

With Lewis' influence growing, both on the soccer field and in the corporate offices, the Bethlehem team took another step up the ladder at the start of the 1911-12 season, joining the Eastern Pennsylvania League.

The Eastern Pennsylvania League was not a high-level circuit. It covered a band of territory across the southeastern part of the state, from the Lehigh Valley at one end to Lancaster at the other, but it did not include any of the excellent Philadelphia teams, who had their own leagues. Bethlehem swept easily to the Eastern Pennsylvania League championship, going undefeated through a league schedule that was completed before Christmas, leaving the winter and spring months open for another competition to which Bethlehem was new, the Allied Amateur Cup. That event ended up giving Bethlehem its first taste of something that was going to become quite familiar to it in the coming years, a cup final.

When it was inaugurated in 1911, the Allied Amateur Cup had been restricted to teams from the three amateur leagues in Philadelphia, but this time it was opened to amateur clubs from nearby cities that included Wilmington, Del.; Camden, N.J.; Chester, Reading and Bethlehem.[50] The Steelworkers' cup run began on March 2, 1912, with a 2-0 victory over the Camden Rovers in Camden, and they had to go on the road again three weeks later for the quarterfinals, when two first-half goals by Edgar Lewis led them to a 4-2 victory over Kensington AA of Philadelphia. On April 22, they got past Centennial AA of Philadelphia, 1-0, in a semifinal that was played on the ground of one of Philadelphia's strongest professional teams, Hibernian. The final against Cardington of Upper Darby, Pa., was scheduled for that same field, but a one-week postponement and the start of the baseball season made the field unavailable, so the final was played at another Philadelphia field, Washington Park. Cardington, from just outside the Philadelphia city limits, had won its last three games by a total of 16-1. Bethlehem slowed it down only a bit in the final as the Steelworkers' cup run ended with a 3-1 defeat, their only loss of the 1911-12 season. That record indicated that they were destined for good things.

Those good things started happening, or rather continued happening, in the 1912-13 season, which ended with Bethlehem winning the Allied Amateur Cup this time and also taking its division of the Allied American League. In that league, a step up from the Eastern Pennsylvania League, the Steelworkers regularly faced Philadelphia teams like Centennial, Smith and Kensington, although not yet the top Philadelphia pros like Hibernian and Tacony. Their most satisfying victory, however, may have been not one of those "competitive" games but the friendly with which they opened the season on Sept. 23, 1912, against Cardington, the team that had beaten them in the Allied Amateur Cup final the previous May. By 1912, Bethlehem was playing most of its home games at East End field in northeast Bethlehem. Sometimes, however, big games were played at Lehigh University's football stadium in South Bethlehem, and this was one of those occasions. This also was the first game ever played in Bethlehem's colors by Thomas "Whitey" Fleming, later one of the leading lights of Bethlehem's greatest teams. The Scottish winger, who was then 22 years old, scored two of Bethlehem's goals in a 3-0 victory over Cardington (Edgar Lewis had the other). The *South Bethlehem Globe* said that Fleming "was easily the star of the game, time and again getting the crowd going with his acrobatic movements."[51] Bethlehem not only had a measure of revenge over Cardington, it also had a new star.

The 1913-14 season was a breakout one for Bethlehem. The Steelworkers took on, and beat, competition of a sort that they hadn't faced since those two ill-fated games against West Hudson in 1907. Their emergence as a force in American soccer was very much tied to the emergence of a new organization governing the sport in America, the United States Football Association.

At the beginning of 1913, the administrative situation in American soccer was in confusion, with the established organization, the American Football Association (AFA), being challenged by a new one, the American Amateur Football Association (AAFA).

The AFA had been formed in 1884 in Newark, N.J., ceased to exist in 1899, then was restarted in 1906. In its first incarnation, it had organized the American teams for two international games, against Canada in 1885 and 1886 (Those games are not recognized by the U.S. Soccer Federation as having been full internationals). It also had organized a cup competition, the AFA Cup. Both the teams that played Canada in 1885 and 1886 and the early years of the AFA Cup were dominated by players and teams from northern New Jersey, particularly ONT of Kearny. Five of the 11 members of the team that played Canada in 1885 and six of the 11 in 1886 had been from ONT, which won the first three AFA Cups, in 1885, 1886 and 1887.

The AFA had detractors, however. By the second decade of the 20th century, there were many factions within the sport in the United States that did not feel that their interests were really being represented by the AFA. Sam T.N. Foulds and Paul Harris described the problem in 1979:

> Over the years, the American Football Association developed an informal alliance with the British associations of England and Scotland rather than with the recently organized international FIFA confederation. The deference of the association to the British soccer powers hit a sour note with many American soccer people, who felt that the United States national body should be entirely devoid of ties with any other particular country except where the mutual interests of both were concerned.
>
> The American Football Association, despite its concern with soccer in the East, displayed very little interest in national expansion [through 1912, every winner of the AFA Cup had come from northern New Jersey, southeastern New England or Philadelphia]. This conservative attitude led to a growing feeling among rival soccer groups that there was room for a more aggressive and imaginative administration to govern soccer on a nationwide basis.[52]

In addition, there was the problem of the division between the amateurs and the professionals. Before 1899, the AFA had had an amateur inclination, but after its revival in 1906, it became concerned foremost with the affairs of the professional side of the game, which was beginning to flourish in a few places such as New Jersey and New England.

The situation began to come to a head in October 1911 with the formation of the American Amateur Football Association. The AAFA was an outgrowth of the Southern New York State Association, which had not become as involved with the AFA as had associations in neighboring states. One of the first acts of the new organization was to seek recognition from FIFA. Accordingly, Thomas W. Cahill, the secretary of the AAFA and a man who probably was more important to the early history of soccer in the United States than any other, was sent to the FIFA Congress that met in the summer of 1912 in Stockholm, Sweden. The AFA's interests also were represented at the FIFA Congress, by Sir Frederick J. Wall, the secretary of the Football Association in England.

Wall's position was not to seek FIFA membership for the AFA, however. Rather, it was to counsel FIFA against granting membership too hastily to the AAFA. He pointed out that the AAFA had no voice in the professional portion of the sport in the United States. He urged that FIFA instruct Cahill to return to the United States and seek an accommodation between the AAFA and the AFA that might yield a truly comprehensive United States federation, one that FIFA could then accept. FIFA agreed with the suggestion, and Cahill was so instructed.

The 1979 *Encyclopedia of World Soccer* told what happened next:

> After Cahill returned to New York, the two associations appointed committees to find a solution to their difficulties. . .A series of conferences between the two committees began on October 12, 1912 at the Astor House in New York City, but on December 8, when an agreement appeared imminent, the AFA voted to discontinue negotiations and dismiss the committee. This unpopular action gained the AAFA much support among local and regional associations. In March 1913, the Allied American F.A. of Philadelphia [one of whose members was Bethlehem] and the F.A. of Philadelphia switched their allegiance to the AAFA, and it was this newly found strength from two important Philadelphia associations that gave the AAFA the necessary stimulus to prevail.[53]

On April 5, 1913, the organizations now on the side of the AAFA, representing a wide spectrum of American soccer, met at the Astor House, which was a large hotel on Broadway in lower Manhattan, to found the United States Football Association (USFA). The organization that was established that day is the same one that governs American soccer today. The United States Football Association changed its name in 1945 to United States Soccer Football Association and in 1974 to the present name, United States Soccer Federation. This April 5, 1913 meeting holds a place in American soccer history not unlike the place occupied in English soccer by the famous meetings at the Freemasons Tavern in London in 1863.

America now was able to approach FIFA with a more united front than in 1912, and on Aug. 15, 1913 the USFA received notification from FIFA that it had been granted provisional membership in FIFA. The AFA had voted several days before not to accept membership in the USFA, but now that this word from FIFA had arrived, it gave up its struggle and joined the USFA. The following year that provisional membership was changed by the FIFA Congress into full membership in FIFA for the USFA as the representative of the United States.

By the fall of 1913, the USFA had started its first cup competition, the National Challenge Cup, using a trophy that had been donated to it two years before by Scottish distiller Sir Thomas Dewar and which had since been used in a local amateur competition involving New York teams. The National Challenge Cup started right away into territory where the AFA Cup had never been, with teams from Great Lakes points like Buffalo, Detroit and Chicago entering in the first year. One Pittsburgh team entered in 1913, to be joined by others later. Cleveland teams joined the following year, followed by St. Louis teams in 1919 and California teams in the 1950s. Bethlehem played its first game in the competition in which it was to earn its greatest laurels on Nov. 1, 1913. However, the AFA Cup didn't go away, despite having been reduced to secondary status. It lasted well into the 1920s, and Bethlehem also played its first game in that competition in the fall of 1913 (it had entered the previous year, but had forfeited its first-round game).

Bethlehem Football Club began the 1913-14 season secure in its status as one of Pennsylvania's best teams and looking around for new fields to conquer. It finished it riding even higher than that. It easily won the Allied Amateur Cup again, the beneficiary of forfeits in both the semifinals and final. It played in the top division of the Allied American League and won that in impressive fashion. It entered the AFA Cup for the first time and won that, beating teams from Massachusetts, New Jersey and Pennsylvania along the way. It reached the third round of the new National Challenge Cup before losing on a penalty to the eventual winner. And it started an amazing undefeated streak that lasted into 1915. The season certainly was the most successful Bethlehem had had yet, perhaps one of the most successful any American soccer team has ever had.

That 1913-14 season also provides a good demonstration of the way that soccer teams, both then and now, have had to juggle a variety of competitions at the same time. This is something many American sports fans aren't used to. They see the top teams in pro baseball, pro basketball and pro football concentrating on a single objective, straight from opening day to the final game of the World Series, the final game of the NBA playoffs or the Super Bowl. Soccer is different, both in the United States and elsewhere. Bethlehem played in four different competitions in the 1913-14 season, plus several friendlies. Suppose that the letter "a" represents a National Challenge Cup game, "b" is an AFA Cup game, "c" is an Allied American League game, "d" is an Allied Amateur Cup game and "e" is a friendly. Bethlehem's 1913-14 season followed a pattern that looked like this: e-b-e-b-a-c-c-b-c-c-a-c-b-c-b-b-c-a-b-c-e-d-c-b-b-c-d-c-c-b-d-c-b-e-d-e. The Steelworkers were constantly switching back and forth between competitions. Nowhere in a 36-game season did they play more than two games in a row in any one competition. Seven times, they played games in three different competitions in the same month. And there was nothing particularly remarkable about this. That's the way it was, and is, in big-time soccer.

It does seem as though league officials have always been upset by the disruptions that cup games have caused in their schedules, and Bethlehem's 1913-14 season certainly shows why, particularly since the disruption was even more serious in the days when cup games that ended in ties were replayed rather than settled by penalties. An Allied American League official, Oliver Hemingway, commented on this in a review of the season in the 1914 *Spalding Guide*, saying: "The season was an eventful one. First and foremost was the fact that one of the Allied members, Bethlehem, won the American Foot Ball Association Cup, the first time any Allied club played in that competition. Its tie games caused replays, which completely upset the Allied schedule, and it was necessary to close the season with two first division games unplayed."[54] Bethlehem seems to have been both the local boy who made good and the prodigal son at the same time.

Of Bethlehem's achievements in the 1913-14 season, winning the Allied Amateur Cup certainly was the easiest, and not just because of the two forfeits. Bethlehem only played two games, against teams from lower divisions of the Allied League. Third-division Centenary was beaten by 9-0, on Feb. 28, 1914, and second-division Putnam fell, 3-0, on April 11. Then came the two forfeits that handed the Steelworkers the cup. Philadelphia Electric pulled out of the semifinals at the last minute, and West Philadelphia refused to play the final after the schedule had been changed to make room for a replay of Bethlehem's AFA Cup final.

The Allied American League championship was only a little more difficult. Bethlehem won every one of its 13 games, by a total score of 68 goals to eight. West Philadelphia was second, five points behind Bethlehem's 26. The Steelworkers took the lead early in that competition, with victories in the first month of the schedule over the only other teams in the division that finished over .500, West Philadelphia and Schuylkill Falls. They clinched the title in their next-to-last game, a 6-0 victory over Smith AA in Philadelphia on April 25, 1914. Whitey Fleming scored three of the Bethlehem goals that day. By this time he and Edgar Lewis had been joined in the Steelworkers' lineup by two more future Hall of Famers, Ned Donaghy and Bobby Morrison.

The National Challenge Cup was an adventure for the Bethlehem team. The Steelworkers may have been the first team ever to win a game in this event, which survives nearly 100 years later, now known as the Lamar Hunt U.S. Open Cup. The first round was played on the weekend of Nov. 1 and 2, 1913. Because Pennsylvania and Massachusetts laws did not allow Sunday sports events, three of that weekend's eight games (22 teams had byes) were scheduled for the Saturday, in Bethlehem, Philadelphia and New Bedford, Mass. The game in Philadelphia produced a forfeit, so either Bethlehem or New Bedford FC has to have been the first winner.

Bethlehem met one of its Allied League rivals, Disston, in that opening-day game and breezed past the Philadelphia team, 8-0. That put it into a second-round matchup against Braddock FC, the champion of western Pennsylvania. The Dec. 6, 1913 game in Pittsburgh was billed in some quarters as a meeting that would decide the state championship, but Bethlehem really had no official claim to the eastern Pennsylvania title. The setting did have a championship feel about it, however. The game was played at Forbes Field, and it was a special occasion in 1913 for soccer teams to get a chance to play at a major-league baseball stadium.

Braddock, Pa., near Pittsburgh, was where Charles M. Schwab had started his steel career in 1879 at Carnegie's Edgar Thompson Works, but it is not clear if any of the Braddock FC players were steelworkers. The Edgar Thompson Works, which now was owned by U.S. Steel, had its own team, in the same league that Braddock FC played. The Pittsburgh area did not yet have the reputation for strong soccer teams that it developed a few decades later, but it has always had a hard-nosed aura in sports generally. As a result, both teams seem to have been quite impressed with their opponents, and newspaper accounts following Bethlehem's 3-2 overtime victory indicate that supporters of both were satisfied with their performance.

From the *South Bethlehem Globe*: "East proved beyond a doubt its superiority over the West. . . . The fighting spirit and training of the Bethlehems team was never better demonstrated than on Saturday in Pittsburgh and too much credit cannot be given the Bethlehems team for its great victory away from home."[55]

From the *Pittsburgh Post*: "The winners are a great eleven, admittedly, but they found their match in the opponents of yesterday . . . . Braddock was unlucky to lose a [game] that they seemed to have won in the second half. By its display against such renowned opponents, Braddock has put Pittsburgh on the soccer map for all time. Manager Trend of the Bethlehem team acknowledged that Braddock had given his eleven the hardest fight in any game in two years. . . . The game was cleanly contested throughout and Braddock was defeated but not disgraced."[56]

Braddock did have a very good run at winning the game. The Pittsburghers took a 2-1 lead midway through the second half, after a penalty by Fleming had given Bethlehem the halftime edge. But just a minute after the second Braddock goal, Fleming equalized with a startling 30-yard free kick. Two minutes from the end of overtime, it was Fleming again, gathering the ball 40 yards out, dribbling past the defense and sharply putting his third goal of the game into the net. The *Pittsburgh Post* stated the obvious when it said that "The star of the contest was Fleming, without whom the visitors would have been a beaten lot."[57]

Bethlehem's National Challenge Cup run came to an end seven weeks later in the first game it had ever played in New York City, where it would play more than 100 times in coming years. On Jan. 25, 1914 at Marquette Oval in the Gowanus section of Brooklyn, the deciding play came 25 minutes into the second half, after the ball hit Edgar Lewis in the arm in Bethlehem's goalmouth. Brooklyn Field Club scored on the rebound after Bob Millar's penalty was saved and that was that. The defeat was Bethlehem's first of the season, after 13 victories and three ties. It also was the last game Bethlehem would lose for nearly 14 months.

Those three ties all had come within a few weeks of each other, and were typical of the horrendous struggle the Steelworkers had en route to their first championship outside Pennsylvania, in the American Football Association Cup. Bethlehem's participation in the AFA Cup began placidly enough. In the first three rounds, it beat Wissinoming of Philadelphia by 5-0, gained a forfeit over Trenton Caledonians of New Jersey and traveled to Massachusetts for a 3-1 win over Farr Alpaca of Holyoke, the first New England team it had ever faced. Then the difficulty began.

On Dec. 27, 1913, Bethlehem was beating West Hudson, 1-0, in their AFA Cup quarterfinal at East End field when the Harrison team's Jimmy McHolland scored an equalizing goal with five minutes left. Five weeks later, his teammates probably were wishing that his shot had gone wide, for in the meanwhile they had been dragged through the mud, both figuratively and literally, only to end up right where they would have if McHolland had missed—out of the competition.

The tie on Dec. 27 in Bethlehem meant that there would be a replay eight days later in Harrison, on the same field—sort of—where Bethlehem had made its debut six years and six weeks before. The West Hudson team on Jan. 4, 1914 included three players from the 1907 game, Duncan Lawson, Frank Carter and George Knowles. Bethlehem had no such veterans. It did have four future Hall of Famers in its lineup, but this was not the day they were honored for. It was a day when rain, snow and sleet caused sports events to be cancelled or postponed throughout the New York area, but in Harrison, the AFA insisted that the show must go on. The result of that insistence was summed up in a headline in the next day's *Newark Evening News*: "Soccer Cup Teams Wallow in Slush." The story contained the gruesome details:

> In the opinion of the management of the West Hudsons the contest should never have been started. The field was covered with mud, while numerous puddles of water dotted the field. In addition, a steady downpour of rain, accompanied by hail and flurries of snow drenched the players to the skin. . . .
>
> Good football was out of the question under the circumstances of field and weather. The ball was soon covered with mud, and the soft earth and water would stop the oval while the players went skimming through the water full length at times like a boat. . . . Before the game had been in progress many minutes the uniforms of both teams were almost entirely covered with mud. . . .
>
> During the intermission the West Hudsons hurried to their headquarters, where dry suits were procured, while the Pennsylvanians

were compelled to keep on their water-soaked garments, which were covered with a layer of hail and snow and practically frozen on their bodies.[58]

It all sounds a bit like the famously rain-drenched 1996 Major League Soccer final between D.C. and Los Angeles in Foxboro, Mass., but with the temperature about 30 degrees lower. The referee halted the game 20 minutes into the second half, on the grounds that the lines were so obliterated that further play was impossible. The score was 1-1. They would have to do it again.

So do it again they did. On Jan. 11 in Harrison, the two teams played yet another 1-1 tie, including 30 minutes of overtime that failed to break the deadlock. A delay in the start of the game resulted in its finishing by the light of a full moon. At this point, the two teams had played 275 minutes of soccer without settling the issue and Oliver Hemingway of the Allied League was probably tearing his hair out. The third replay, on Jan. 31, was played on neutral ground, Tacony's field in Philadelphia. There was more rain and a long delay before the game was started, but finally there was a decision. At halftime, the score was the dreaded 1-1, but Bethlehem goals by Jack Lance and Whitey Fleming in the first 10 minutes of the second half opened it up and Fleming added another goal before the end.

After that struggle, the semifinals and final were anticlimactic, but they involved replays as well. On March 29, Bethlehem and the Jersey City AC played a 2-2 tie in their semifinal in Jersey City, but the Steelworkers won the replay, 2-1, on their home ground a week later. The final against Tacony in Paterson, N.J., on April 19 produced a scoreless tie, but two weeks later in Newark, Ned Donaghy's goal in the 15th minute of that replay gave Bethlehem the cup.

The Jan. 31 victory over West Hudson was more than just an end to the four-game battle between the two teams. Coming six days after Bethlehem's defeat in Brooklyn, it was the start of a new undefeated streak, one that had reached 16 games (not including the two forfeits) by the end of the season.

In the fall of 1914, Bethlehem picked up right where it had left off the previous spring. In their 16 games between the beginning of the season and the end of the year, the Steelworkers scored 87 goals to their opponents' 13. Of course, they didn't lose any of those 16, although a string of three straight ties in October did produce some momentary concern. In all, the 1914-15 season didn't contain quite the drama that the 1913-14 season had, but it did contain the victories.

Bethlehem had acquired a number of strong players over the summer. Three, Neil Clarke, Bob Millar and James Ford, were from the Brooklyn Field Club team that had just won the first National Challenge Cup. James Campbell was from the Philadelphia Tacony team, whose franchise had been taken over by Disston. Bethlehem still wasn't classified as a professional team (Clarke, Millar, Ford and Campbell had to apply to the USFA that summer for reinstatement of their amateur status[59]), but it didn't compete in the Allied Amateur Cup any more. It also had graduated once more to a new league, playing in Philadelphia's American League, against some old rivals like West Philadelphia, Disston and Schuylkill Falls and some new ones like Hibernian and Victor. (Actually, there were two Victor teams in the league, one in Philadelphia and one across the river in Camden, N.J. The Philadelphia team was called Victor, while the Camden team, operated by the company that made Victrola phonographs, was called Victor Talking Machine.)

Once again Bethlehem raced through its league schedule undefeated, with 11 victories and those three ties among 14 American League games. That only gained it a one-point margin, however, as Philadelphia Victor finished with 11 victories, one defeat and two ties. Victor's one defeat, which made all the difference, came on Jan. 16, 1915, when Bethlehem's visit to Victor's field in Philadelphia resulted in a 5-2 win for the Steelworkers.

Bethlehem's great undefeated streak finally came to an end on March 14, 1915 in the semifinals of the AFA Cup. As it had the year before, Bethlehem had it fairly easy in the early rounds of the AFA Cup, with a 6-0 victory over West Philadelphia, a 2-0 victory over Clan McDonald in Brooklyn and a 6-1 victory over Farr Alpaca of Massachusetts. The bid to repeat as AFA Cup champions ended in the semifinals, when Brooklyn Celtic handed Bethlehem a 3-1 defeat on the same field where its last loss had occurred, Marquette Oval in Brooklyn.

Once again Bob Millar was playing, this time in a blue-and-white Bethlehem uniform, although this proved to be his only full Bethlehem season (Millar, who changed clubs quite often, also played part of the 1918-19 season for Bethlehem). The former Brooklyn Field Club star at this point was well on his way to a total of 59 goals for the season (including all games in various competitions), which stood as the most ever by a Bethlehem player in one season until Archie Stark's 75-goal outburst in the 1924-25 season.

Brooklyn Celtic ended the suspense early that day, with Bethlehem never able to overcome the New York team's two first-half goals. So, the streak ended at 41 games (43 if you count the two forfeits). In those games, Bethlehem outscored its opponents by 191-31. It suffered five ties to mar the perfection a bit.

This season had a happy ending however, and one that included a good measure of revenge. The Steelworkers finished the season as champions of the National Challenge Cup, and the team that they beat in the final was none other than Brooklyn Celtic.

Their route to that final had begun with victories over three Philadelphia teams, Putnam, Peabody and Victor. In the quarterfinals on March 20, 1915, they played Kearny Scots in Bethlehem. This was a fairly ordinary game. Bethlehem scored a routine victory, 3-0, without overtime or much drama. The Bethlehem goals were scored by Whitey Fleming, Fred Pepper and Bob Millar. What is interesting, at least in retrospect, is that the Kearny team's inside right that day was Kearny resident named Archie Stark, then 17 years old and playing his first game ever in Bethlehem. Stark would be back as a visiting player with a few other teams before joining Bethlehem Steel in 1924.

Next was Homestead, and history. When Bethlehem had played Braddock 17 months before, it had played a team that was from a Pittsburgh-area steel town but did not represent the mill itself. This time, it did. The Homestead team was from U.S. Steel's Homestead Works, where Bethlehem Steel owner Charles M. Schwab had been the superintendent 20 years before, when he was working for Carnegie Steel. Although the Bethlehem team was not yet officially named Bethlehem Steel, Schwab was aware that it was facing a team from his old stomping ground in an important game just a few miles from his South Bethlehem office. He may also have been aware that in the past decade company-sponsored athletic teams had become a cornerstone of the Homestead Works' efforts to keep unions at bay and avoid a repetition of the bitter and bloody strike there in 1892.[60] Interestingly, Homestead had reached this game via a quarterfinal victory over the team from Chicago's Pullman railway car works, the scene of a similarly infamous strike in 1894.

In the end, Bethlehem won handily, 4-1, after a two-day delay caused by an early-spring snowstorm. Despite an early goal by Homestead, Bethlehem had taken a 2-1 lead by halftime. Fleming evened the score on a penalty kick and James Ford put the Steelworkers in front just before the intermission. The second half belonged to Bethlehem. Ford scored two more goals and, according to the *Philadelphia Inquirer*, "Homestead did not, with the exception of one corner, have a try for goal in the second half. . . . Homestead grew noticeably weak as the game progressed."[61]

The final was played almost a month after the Bethlehem-Homestead semifinal, and Bethlehem had completed its league season. To keep in trim, the Steelworkers undertook their first trip to another place that, like New York, they were to visit many times in the future. In mid-April they played two games in Fall River, Mass., the first a 4-1 victory over the Fall River Rovers and the second a 1-0 win over a local all-star team. They then turned their attention to the National Challenge Cup final, which, like the Homestead game, was held at Lehigh University's Taylor Stadium.

Two months before in Brooklyn, two first-half goals by Brooklyn Celtic had spelled Bethlehem's doom, its elimination from the AFA Cup and the end of its long streak. This time, things were reversed and Bethlehem was in command most of the way. Ford, who had scored the winning goal in the previous year's final for Brooklyn Field Club, was involved in all three Bethlehem goals. First, Fleming's cross set up a goal for Ford. Just before halftime, Ford did the same for Bob Millar. In the second half, a Brooklyn player handled a shot by Ford in the area and Fleming scored from the penalty spot. A Brooklyn goal reduced the final margin to 3-1.

Bethlehem was the national champion and Schwab had taken notice. He had recently donated $25,000 to the team, and by the time the Steelworkers began their 1915-16 season, they had changed their name from the Bethlehem Football Club to the Bethlehem Steel Football Club. Perhaps the donation can be attributed to the fact that Bethlehem Steel was flush with money at this point, with orders coming in at a great rate because of World War I. Perhaps it was because developments at Homestead had helped Schwab to realize the value of company-sponsored athletic teams. Perhaps it was out of the goodness of his heart. Whatever it was, it put an exclamation point on the fact that in less than eight years, the Steelworkers had left their days of losing games by scores like 11-2 and 9-0 far behind.

THREE

Gothamites

The North American Soccer League didn't have a team in New York during the 1969 and 1970 seasons but, despite the collapse of the New York Generals after the 1968 season, it was inevitable that the NASL would want to return sooner or later to the United States' largest city. A few other cities such as St. Louis and Fall River might have had brighter soccer histories, but New York was always the key to the hopes of making a success of professional soccer in America.

The first signs of soccer had appeared in New York about the same time they did in a few other American cities, around 1870. Even so, New York was soon behind a smaller neighbor across the Hudson River in that respect. The real soccer hotbed of the New York area was the New Jersey cities of Newark and Kearny, facing each other across the Passaic River about 10 miles west of New York City. The American Football Association, formed in Newark in 1884, was only the second "national" football association founded outside the British Isles. New York was not completely uninvolved, however. While the first three AFA Cup titles were won by ONT, from Kearny, ONT's opponent in the first of those was a team called the New York Club.

The people playing soccer in New York City in those days were a bit different from those in Newark and Kearny. They were British expatriates also, but upper-crust ones, not the textile mill workers who were playing the game in New Jersey. Their teams had names like

Nonpareils and Longfellows and they occasionally played their American counterparts in games like Old Etonians vs. Yale.[1] Foreshadowing future events, there also was a team in New York in the 1890s called the Cosmopolitans.

The domination of New York teams by New Jersey teams continued into the first dozen or so years of the 20th century, with the New Jersey case being argued particularly well by West Hudson and Paterson True Blues. When things began to turn around, the first New York teams to really assert themselves were from Brooklyn. In the first final of the new National Challenge Cup, the Brooklyn Field Club defeated a local rival, Brooklyn Celtic. Brooklyn Celtic was the runnerup again a year later, to Bethlehem. The same trend started to show itself in the National Association Foot Ball League, whose first 12 winners all had been from New Jersey. The Brooklyn Field Club broke that string in 1914 and, as the start of the original American Soccer League in 1921 approached, other New York teams like Robins Dry Dock, Morse Dry Dock and the New York Football Club started winning some games.

That first ASL was founded in the spring of 1921, and basically was a combination of the National Association Foot Ball League and the Southern New England Soccer League, which had been flourishing in the area of Fall River, Pawtucket and New Bedford. There were two New York teams in that first ASL season, New York FC, which played its games in upper Manhattan, and Todd Shipyards, which was a renamed version of Robins Dry Dock (Robins was a subsidiary of Todd) and played in Brooklyn. The league began to play that September with eight Eastern seaboard teams, two in New York, two in New Jersey, three in New England and one in Pennsylvania.[2] The strength of New Jersey's representation was a bit down from what the sport had been there 10 or 12 years before, because three of the best New Jersey teams, Paterson True Blues, West Hudson and Kearny Scots, had folded before 1920, doomed partially by the lack of players caused by the military draft in World War I.[3]

New York teams did not set the world on fire in that original ASL. None of them won an ASL title until the New York Giants did it in 1931. That same team, under the name New York Nationals, had won the National Challenge Cup in 1928.

Todd Shipyards lasted only that first ASL season before being replaced by another Brooklyn team, Brooklyn Wanderers, who were owned and managed by Nat Agar, one of the founders of the USFA. They played in the original ASL until it folded but never won the title. There was a team by the same name in the second ASL, and while those Brooklyn Wanderers lasted until 1948, they never won an ASL championship either.

New York FC played a lot of good games, and usually was a difficult opponent for Bethlehem Steel, but the name only lasted the first three ASL seasons. Before the 1924-25 season, New York FC was taken over by the Indiana Flooring Company and also lost Archie Stark, who had been its goalscoring star in its first three years, to Bethlehem. The team played three seasons under the name Indiana Flooring, but it was bought out before the 1927-28 season by Charles Stoneham, owner of the New York Giants baseball team. Stoneham would have liked to call his soccer team the Giants, too, but that name was already taken. New York fur dealer Maurice Vandeweghe had bought the Paterson Silk Sox franchise in 1923, moved the team to New York and named it the Giants, so Stoneham had to call his team the New York Nationals. The situation reversed itself in 1930 when Vandeweghe sold his Giants to a company that changed the name yet again, leaving Stoneham free to grab the name Giants for his team.[4]

But amidst all the name changing and franchise selling, victories by New York teams were somewhat lacking, and the situation improved only slightly in the second American Soccer League, which began play in the fall of 1933. In the first 23 seasons of the second ASL, the championship was won 18 times by teams from either Philadelphia or Kearny (including the revived Kearny Scots), leaving little room for New York. However, only three teams in those 23 years won the "double," taking both the ASL title and the National Challenge Cup (which by this time was sometimes called the U.S. Open Cup) in the same year, and all three were from New York. Brooklyn Hispano won the double in 1943, with a team that included future Hall of Famers Billy Gonsalves, Gene Olaff and Fabri Salcedo. New York Americans did it in 1954. In between, Brookhattan captured a rare triple in 1945, taking the ASL, the U.S. Open Cup and the Lewis Cup, which was a sort of league cup, with ASL teams competing for a trophy that had been donated in the 1920s by Bethlehem Steel's Edgar Lewis.

New York Americans and Brookhattan shared Starlight Park in the Bronx, so that one or the other was playing a home game there nearly every week. New York City is dotted with the sites of long-gone fields once used by former soccer teams. Most have met relatively mundane fates, being turned into warehouses or supermarkets and their parking lots (former urban soccer fields seem to make excellent parking lots). But Starlight Park's headstone is a little more showy. That field now lies underneath the Cross-Bronx Expressway, a seven-mile, six-lane slash that was completed in 1960. Only one of those old-time fields has continued to thrive. Metropolitan Oval, on the border between Brooklyn and Queens, has been turned into a shrine of New York soccer, making it a sort of memorial to the many departed fields.

New York's teams might not have won as many games from the 1920s to the 1950s as their rivals from Philadelphia and New Jersey, but New York still managed to remain a center of the American soccer world in another way. A major feature of American soccer in those decades was the visits of touring foreign teams, particularly European ones. This really started with two English amateur teams, the Pilgrims and Corinthians, who had five American tours between 1905 and 1911. The most noteworthy tours of later decades were usually arranged by the American Soccer League or the German-American Soccer League. Outranking all the others were the 1926 and 1927 tours of Hakoah, an all-Jewish team from Vienna that had won the Austrian championship in 1925. A game between Hakoah and a combined squad of two New York ASL teams drew a crowd of 46,000 to the Polo Grounds on May 1, 1926, setting a record for a soccer crowd in the United States that lasted until 1976 (the next-best crowd for a touring-team game was 43,177 at Yankee Stadium in 1947 for a game between Hapoel from Palestine and a New York all-star team).

Besides Hakoah, the best of the touring teams included the Uruguayan national team in 1927, Glasgow Rangers in 1928 and 1930, Glasgow Celtic in 1931, Scottish FA selections in 1935 and 1939, Liverpool in 1946 and 1948 and Santos of Brazil nine times in the 1960s and '70s (helping to establish Pelé's name as a magical one in the United States). The American tours were beneficial to the touring teams as well as the hosts. Liverpool used its 1946 tour to build up its strength on American food en route to winning its first English Football League title in more than 20 years, beating teams that had stayed home and spent their preseason training coping with British post-war rationing. In 1949, the directors of Belfast Celtic from Northern Ireland voted before an American tour to disband the team, but didn't tell the players and made the lucrative tour anyway.

The tours led in the direction of the NASL, as David Wangerin explained in *Soccer in a Football World*, his 2006 history of American soccer:

> The success of these tours was not lost on promoters from outside the incestuous American soccer world. In the early 1960s, New York-born Bill Cox became the most conspicuous of them. A one-time art

dealer and lumber company executive, Cox had dabbled in sport for decades. . . . by the late 1950s Cox had turned his attention to soccer, having ventured to big matches in London, Madrid and Rio de Janiero and marvelled at the size of the gates. . . .

Cox was convinced the reason for the Americans' indifference was that they had never seen the game played as foreigners did: in a big-time, high-calibre competition. He also suspected that the New York sporting public would welcome a new summer diversion after two of its three major league baseball teams, the Giants and the Dodgers, moved to California in 1957. . . . By inviting foreign clubs to participate in a summer competition, Cox hoped to offer fans an attractive standard of play through something more than a series of meaningless exhibitions [although the players may not have regarded these games as being especially meaningful].

His International Soccer League, as it was christened, lasted from 1960 to 1965. From time to time, it proved capable of attracting sizeable crowds: the first final, between Kilmarnock [of Scotland] and Bangu of Brazil, drew more than 25,000 to the Polo Grounds. It also brought across the odd talented team, none better than the young Dukla Prague side that won the competition in 1961. . .

While the ISL didn't make Cox any money, it didn't lose him much, either, and its ambitions toward becoming a proper domestic league grew more transparent.[6]

In 1966, Cox started to put those ambitions into action. The group of investors that he put together was one of three petitioning the U.S. Soccer Football Association for a chance to start what would become the North American Soccer League. The American broadcast of the World Cup final between England and West Germany on July 30, 1966 is sometimes said to have been the spark that set off American interest in a pro soccer league, but the three-way race to attract the USSFA's approval really had begun months before that game.

By 1968, when the first real NASL season took place, the situation had sorted itself out into a single league. A year earlier, there had still been two leagues, one of which had been given (for a fee), official recognition by the USSFA as the United States' new first-division league. Clive Toye, an English newspaperman who was starting out on what would be a long involvement with the NASL, the New York Cosmos and American soccer generally, was connected to the other group, Bill Cox's group. It had not gotten the official nod and apparently wasn't particularly bothered by that fact, especially since it did have a national television contract. Says Toye: "We, the National Professional Soccer League, were the outlaws, frowned upon from on high by FIFA and banned from the game. It was a ban which had the salutary effect of a wet lettuce thrown from fifty paces, i.e. none. Coaches coached, players played, referees refereed and by the time they had done that for a season or less, reality was setting in."[7]

That reality was financial reality, in the form of the realization that the United States was not ready to support two professional soccer leagues. One thing the two leagues did have in common was red ink, which was the key factor in persuading the rivals to accept a merger in December 1967. That didn't stem the losses, however, and there was a mass exodus of teams and investors from the NASL after the 1968 season. Between 1967 and 1969, the number of leagues shrank from two to one, which was good, but the number of teams shrank from 22 to five, which was not.

That the NASL survived its crisis year of 1969 is due largely to the efforts of three men, Toye, Phil Woosnam and Lamar Hunt. Toye and Woosnam both were British expatriates and both had come to America for supporting roles in this new soccer venture that was beginning there. Woosnam, a veteran star with several Football League teams and a rarity among British soccer players, a college graduate, had come to be coach of the Atlanta Chiefs (in 1968, he ended up coaching the U.S. national team in World Cup qualifying as well) and by this point was executive director of the NASL. Toye, who had been the chief soccer writer for the *Daily Express*, a huge London newspaper, had crossed the Atlantic in 1967 to become general manager of the Baltimore Bays and by 1969 was Woosnam's assistant. Hunt, the son of legendary Texas oilman H.L. Hunt, was a money man, of whom there were a number (at least at the start), but he was not like the others. Hunt was committed to this venture and didn't join the scramble for the exit at the end of the 1968 season.

Woosnam and Toye were squeezed into a tiny office in the bowels of Fulton County Stadium in Atlanta, but contrary to what is sometimes believed, they were not painting on a completely blank canvas in trying to advance the cause of soccer in the United States. There were 277 American colleges that fielded soccer teams in 1966, the year before the NASL started to gear up.[8] There are no corresponding numbers available for high school teams, but interpolating between the numbers for 1963 (1,650) and 1971 (2,217) indicates that there may have been nearly 2,000.[9] Those college and high school teams were playing in a style, based on hard running and frequent substitutions, that may not have been very pleasing to European eyes, but they were playing.

The German-American Soccer League of New York had been around for 43 years in 1966, the American Soccer League for 45 years, the National Soccer League of Chicago for 46 years, the U.S. Open Cup for 53 years and the Greater Los Angeles Soccer League for 64 years. The names of the leading teams in those leagues — Ukrainian Nationals, Roma, Schwaben, Scots, Slovak, Hellenic, etc. — imply a heavy ethnic orientation, but hyphenated Americans are Americans.

There has been a tendency for some people who came to the United States for the NASL to discount the degree to which the sport was present in the United States before the NASL. Likewise, there is a tendency for some people who participated in American soccer before the NASL to belittle the contribution of the NASL to the American soccer boom of recent decades. Both viewpoints are mistaken, but it is true, as a *Soccer America* columnist said in 2008, that "what pushed soccer into the mainstream was the NASL, particularly the New York Cosmos."[10]

The efforts of Phil Woosnam and Clive Toye to advance American soccer may have gotten more notice at the time, but the contribution of Lamar Hunt was crucial to the NASL's survival. Hunt was an unassuming millionaire, and the fact that he was willing to stick to his commitment to soccer in 1969 and invest his time as well as his money in efforts to keep the league afloat may be the number-one factor in why American soccer has the respectability that it does today.

Alex Yannis talked about the effect of Hunt's work in his 1980 book, *Inside Soccer*:

> The total collapse of the NASL was narrowly avoided through the singlehanded efforts of Lamar Hunt. There were rumors that Hunt subsidized four of the franchises. . . .
>
> "The main reason we stayed alive," [Phil] Woosnam says, "was the presence of Lamar Hunt. He gave the league credibility. People knew who Lamar Hunt was and that he would not stay with a league he didn't believe had a future in the United States.". . .
>
> "Phil and everybody else in the league give me too much credit," Lamar Hunt said [in 1976]. . . . "Phil Woosnam is the guy who really kept it alive. He went out and knocked on doors. I just gave the league a little stability because of my involvement in other sports."[11]

There was a New York team in the NPSL in 1967 and the NASL in 1968, but it did not produce very memorable results. Over those two seasons, the New York Generals won 23 games, tied 20 and lost 21. They didn't make the playoffs either year, and television commentator Paul Gardner years later referred to that 1967 Generals season as "a depressing summer."[12] But in their next-to-last game, against the Detroit Cougars, on Sept. 1, 1968, the attendance at Yankee Stadium suddenly jumped to 36,904, whereas the Generals had never before drawn more than 8,000 for a league game. The reason had little to do with them, however. The Generals and Cougars were the first game of a doubleheader. The big crowd came for the second game, Santos vs. Benfica. There were four future Cosmos on the field at Yankee Stadium that day. In addition to Pelé and Carlos Alberto for Santos, the Generals had Gordon Bradley and the Cougars had John Kerr.

The Generals are more noteworthy for who than for what. The players included Cesar Menotti, who gained fame when he coached Argentina to the World Cup title in 1978, future Cosmos Bradley and Barry Mahy, and future NASL marksmen Warren Archibald and Leroy DeLeon, who between them scored 105 NASL goals. The coach in both seasons was Freddie Goodwin, an Englishman who later was one of the NASL's leading coaches with Minnesota.

The NASL started to rise again early in 1970 when two American Soccer League teams, the Washington Darts and the Rochester Lancers, agreed to jump leagues. It was a narrow thing according to Toye. Washington agreed to switch to the NASL, but only if Rochester would also. So the negotiations with Rochester owners Charlie Schaino and Pat DiNolfo really were for two teams, not one. Maybe more than two in a sense, considering that the NASL would have folded without them. After considerable back and forth, Schaino and DiNolfo agreed to make the move and the NASL stayed in business.[13]

After having completed two seasons since the mass departure of teams that followed the 1968 season, the NASL was ready to look elsewhere. Specifically, it was ready to move back into New York. Gavin Newsham sets the scene in his history of the Cosmos, *Once in a Lifetime*:

> Crucial to the NASL's progress, though, was the re-establishment of a franchise in New York. Without a team since the New York Generals folded in 1968, America's economic capital was a key background in the drive to develop soccer on a national level. If the league was ever going to get that vital coverage in the press and on television—the major TV networks were all based in New York—they needed that "major league" appeal that other sports enjoyed, and that meant bringing soccer back to the Big Apple. "In our youth-

ful enthusiasm/arrogance, Phil [Woosnam] and I decided early on that one of us would run the league and one of us New York," explains Toye, who opted to handle the New York drive.[14]

It was all figured out.

Actually, Clive Toye had to share the job of "running" New York. A large slice of that role would go to a man who knew precious little about soccer, but tons and tons about making money. Steve Ross originally was just one out of 10 Cosmos owners, the Kinney National executives who pooled some money to buy an NASL franchise in 1970. Then, they decided to sell the team to Kinney, which in late 1971 was renamed Warner Communications.

Nominally, Steve Ross was co-CEO of Warner Communications with William Frankel, but even before Frankel's death in June 1972, Ross really was in sole charge of the company,[15] and thus the boss of the Cosmos. Ross was yet another person who had started small, not that he ever intended to remain small. In 1956, when he was 28, he was running his father-in-law's business, a string of funeral homes on the Upper West Side of Manhattan. Over the next few years, the man the *New York Times* later referred to as "an instinctive financial conglomerator"[16] managed to expand the funeral business into car rental and parking lot operations and take the company public as Kinney National Services. In those early business dealings, Ross began to display the personality traits that would serve him well in his later Warner, Cosmos and TimeWarner years. Said Joe Albritton, a newspaper magnate in later years who attempted to sell Ross his own funeral business in 1958, of Ross' negotiating style: "He would never put a foot wrong. He may appear to be charming, which he is, and he may appear to be relaxed, which he is—but if you think the brain is not working, you're wrong. He has what I would call a relaxed intensity."[17]

Kinney National continued to grow through various acquisitions until, in 1969, it bit off its biggest chunk, the famous Warner Brothers movie studio, for $400 million. Ross had climbed through the mortuary, car rental, parking lot and office-cleaning businesses, but as the *New York Times* noted in 1972, he "never seemed to have mustered much enthusiasm"[18] for those services. The entertainment business was far better, and the outgoing Ross was in his element rubbing shoulders with Hollywood celebrities. The Warner Brothers purchase also included a factor that was much more important to the future of the New York Cosmos than movie stars. In 1967, Warner Brothers had acquired—and Kinney now owned—a division called Atlantic Records, run by two Turkish-born brothers named Ahmet Ertegun and Nesuhi Ertegun, who were the people who got Ross into soccer.

The Erteguns were considerably more famous than Ross, despite his growing stature as a New York wheeler-dealer. Eventually, their activities over the years earned each of them election to both the National Soccer Hall of Fame in Oneonta, N.Y., and the Rock 'n' Roll Hall of Fame in Cleveland, a most unorthodox parlay.

The two brothers came to the United States in the 1930s, when their father was Turkey's Ambassador to the United States, and remained in the United States after his death in 1944. "My father was a diplomat who was ambassador to Switzerland, France and England before he became ambassador to the United States, and we lived in all those countries and we always had music in the house," Ahmet Ertegun once told a reporter. "By the time we came to Washington, we were collecting records and we amassed a collection of some 25,000 blues and jazz records."[19] In 1947, Ahmet Ertegun, whom the Rock 'n' Rock Hall of Fame calls "one of the most significant figures in the modern recording industry"[20] co-founded Atlantic Records, which grew into an extremely influential jazz label, with artists who included Ray Charles, John Coltrane, Charlie Mingus and Ornette Coleman. That influence continued to grow after Nesuhi Ertegun, who had moved to California in 1944, joined the company in 1955.

"[Ahmet Ertegun] was an astute judge of both musical talent and business potential, surrounding himself with skillful producers and remaking rhythm and blues for the pop mainstream," the *New York Times* said after Ertegun's death in 2006. "As Atlantic Records grew from a small independent label into a major national music company, it became a stronghold both of soul, with Aretha Franklin and Otis Redding, and rock, with the [Rolling] Stones, Led Zeppelin and Yes."[21] Ahmet Ertegun even wrote a few blues songs himself under a pseudonym and sang backup on a few recordings.

The first informal contact between Kinney and the NASL took place in Mexico City, during the World Cup held there in the summer of 1970. Phil Woosnam and Nesuhi Ertegun talked at a party and agreed to continue their discussions in New York. Woosnam remembers his early impressions of the Erteguns positively: "Ahmet and Nesuhi came from a football background. As such, they had a passion for the game that many investors didn't."[22]

Nesuhi Ertegun knew of Steve Ross' sports interests. A part of the Ross legend, which started as a joke but which Ross chose not to deny, was that his American football career had been ended by a broken arm suffered while playing for the professional Cleveland Browns in the late 1940s. Actually, Ross had suffered the break while playing for a junior college in upstate New York, the highest level at which he ever played.[23] He was a very real sports fanatic, however, and when the idea of investing in an NASL team was broached to him he liked it, although he would soon realize the downside. Says Gavin Newsham:

> Convinced that the plan had legs, Steve Ross rounded up a group of like-minded colleagues and suggested that between them they privately meet the NASL's expansion fee of $350,000, which was levied on new clubs entering the league. In total ten men, including Ross, the Ertegun brothers, Jay Emmett and the chairman and CEO of Warner Bros., Ted Ashley, would all put up $35,000 apiece to launch Gotham Soccer Club Inc.
>
> Within months, however, the team of investors would come to realize that financing a soccer club, even one as seemingly irrelevant as theirs, was a money pit . . . . [Emmett] went to the chairman [Ross]. "I said that this is something Warner [actually then still Kinney] should take, not us, because this is going to lose quite a bit of money."[24]

The 10 men sold their investment to Kinney for one dollar. "It was an entertainment vehicle; [Kinney was] an entertainment company," Emmett says.[25] The move not only removed Ross, Emmett and their eight colleagues from the financial line of fire in case the Cosmos' expenses should get out of hand, it also gave the Cosmos some deep pockets. After all, these were the pockets that had paid $400 million for Warner Brothers just a few years before.

So Ross was in charge of a soccer team. Most of the rest of the people at Kinney didn't know soccer any better than Ross did, but his novice status was noticeable to some outsiders. Paul Gardner, perhaps the dean of American soccer writers, says of the Cosmos' ruling triumvirate: "In that group, the only one you could have a real soccer conversation with was Nesuhi. Ahmet, to a lesser degree. Steve Ross, not at all."[26]

It took a while for Ross to become as fixated on the Cosmos as he later did. As late as August 1972, a 2,500-word profile of him in the *New York Times* contained no mention of the Cosmos, and it indicated that American football was still Ross' first love, saying: "And who can tell what other Warner acquisitions might be thrown into the mix? Mr. Ross has indicated he'd like to soft-pedal his football past, though he and friends once tried and failed to buy the New York Jets in a personal deal. 'If Warner ever did acquire a ball club, I can see what would happen to the stock,' he said, smiling and feigning dread. 'They'd all say Ross has to have his football team.' "[27]

If his British colleagues like Clive Toye and Gordon Bradley read that article, it probably occurred to them that he already had one.

Clive Toye may have had to answer to some higher-ups in running the Cosmos, but he still ranks as the man who made the Cosmos what they were. He started doing that right from the beginning of the Cosmos, whose addition to the league was announced on Dec. 10, 1970. Phil Woosnam spoke with foresight and understatement that day when he said, "We look upon this as a breakthrough for the league."[28]

Toye had come to America four years earlier, making a career move whose boldness might terrify most people. He gave up a job as the chief soccer writer at one of the world's largest newspapers to cross the Atlantic Ocean for a job doing public relations for a tiny soccer team in a league that hadn't even kicked its first ball yet. Toye had grown up in Devonshire in the West of England, fought in the Korean War with the British Army and had been climbing the ladder through the English newspaper business, working for papers in Exeter, Birmingham and London. On that last stop, he wrote for the *Daily Express*, whose circulation of 4.5 million made it the largest anywhere in the English-speaking world, but he felt after the excitement of the 1966 World Cup in England that the job had become boringly routine. [29]

When his PR job with the NPSL team in Hartford, Conn., evaporated before it started, as a result of the team itself evaporating, Toye took another route and ended up as general manager of the NPSL team in Baltimore, the Bays. After two seasons, Toye's contract in Baltimore had expired and he landed in that basement office in Atlanta, assistant to Phil Woosnam as they tried to save the dying embers of the NASL. Thanks to the success of that effort, when the still nameless New York team began operation in December 1970, it had its general manager all ready and waiting for it. After all, Toye and Woosnam had figured it out.

Three of Toye's first actions as general manager of the Cosmos, long before the team played its first game, had a particularly great effect on the future of the team. The first, in January 1971, was the hiring of Gordon Bradley, who would be coach of the Cosmos for more than five seasons. The second, in February, was to choose the team's

name. The third, also in February, was a trip to Jamaica for a visit with
Pelé, the first step in the long siege that would result in Pelé signing
with the Cosmos more than four years later.

The 32-year-old Bradley was an excellent choice for this sort of
venture, someone with a good grounding in soccer on both sides of
the Atlantic. Bradley, a native of Durham in England's northeast,
played parts of five injury-filled seasons with various English pro
clubs in the 1950s and '60s, followed by several seasons in Canada. He
came to the United States in 1964, and played for the NASL's New
York Generals in 1968 and the NASL's Baltimore Bays in 1969. By this
time, his playing career was seemingly winding down (although he
actually ended up playing more games for the Cosmos than he had
for the Generals and Bays combined) and he was gravitating toward
coaching. In 1971, he was both playing for and coaching Hota of New
York's German-American League and had Hota headed toward that
year's U.S. Open Cup championship when he was named as coach of
the Cosmos.[30]

The choice of Bradley as coach was Toye's pick and so was the
choice of the name, even before the contest that supposedly selected
it. On Feb. 5, 1971, the newspapers announced that the name Cosmos
had been chosen from among 3,000 contest entries. Toye tells the real
story: "Mets is short for Metropolitan and I wanted something bigger
and better than mere Metropolitan and, running through all the
words I could come up with, came up with Cosmopolitan. . . . So what
about shortening it to Cosmos, then? Perfect. At least I thought so. . .
. With Pelé in mind, I chose the colors of Brazil and ran a competition
(two free tickets to Zurich, courtesy of Swissair) and waited for the entries to come in, discarding them all (well, amounting to fewer than
40 all told) until I came to one from two schoolteachers in Queens.
'Cosmos,' they said, so with a genuine winner in hand, I could man-
ufacture several other Cosmos entries and declare it the people's
choice. Well mine anyway."[31]

The meeting with Pelé at a hotel poolside in Jamaica, where Santos was playing a friendly, was polite, cordial and noncommittal. Toye
didn't expect a commitment from Pelé that day. He just wanted to
give him the pitch that was to become a mantra in the next few years,
about how he could only win championships elsewhere but could
win a country in New York, and to make Pelé aware that if ever he became available, the Cosmos were interested (boy, were they interested).[32]

In March, the Cosmos began signing players, beginning with

Jorge Siega, a Brazilian-born forward playing in the German-American League. Siega set the tone. Every one of the 18 players the Cosmos signed before the start of the season in April had been born overseas and was playing for a semipro team in the New York area or Philadelphia.

A few days before the Cosmos' opener, with the roster not yet quite full, Bradley signed himself as a player. (Several years later, when Bradley was coaching the U.S. national team in a game against Israel, he put himself on the field as a defender. That made him the only player-manager in the history of the U.S. national team and the American goalkeeper behind him, 22-year-old Bruce Arena, none too comfortable, or so Arena laughingly has claimed.[33])

After a meeting with Pelé, could the season itself be anything other than an anti-climax? Maybe, maybe not, but it wasn't one to remember. The Cosmos played that year at Yankee Stadium, as the Generals had in their only two seasons. They finished second behind Rochester in the NASL's four-team Northern Division, with a record of nine victories, 10 defeats and five ties. That second-place finish put them into the playoffs, but the Atlanta Chiefs polished them off in the semifinals. If there was a highlight to the Cosmos' play that year, it was Randy Horton, the Bermudian striker whose Afro made him even more imposing than his 6-foot-4 height. Horton, who was a full-time college student while playing for the Cosmos, scored 16 goals in 22 games, and he and midfielder Siggy Strizl became the first two of 39 Cosmos named first-team NASL all-stars over the years.

But spectacular success right off the bat wasn't what the Cosmos were looking for anyway. Toye had set a cautious keynote just before the start of the season, when he said: "We are going into this conservatively and with enough money to last for a while. We want to be around when those half a million kids who play the game now are college students."[34]

Adding emphasis to the already-known fact that Pelé was the number-one soccer drawing card in New York, the Cosmos played in front of by far their largest crowd that season when their NASL game was the first game of a doubleheader in which Santos played in the second. They did get to play the second game of a doubleheader a few weeks later, but the game wasn't the cause of any celebration. After a women's game in the opener, the Cosmos were routed, 6-1, by Bangu of Brazil in what Alex Yannis of the *New York Times* referred to as "the main attraction, if one could call it that."[35] Said Gordon Bradley after the game: "It was so bad I don't even want to talk about it."[36]

Gothamites

There was a small connection between the Cosmos and Bethlehem Steel that year. In their third game of the season, the Cosmos played the Toronto Metros at Varsity Stadium in Toronto. That was one of only two stadiums the Cosmos ever played at where Bethlehem Steel also had played, the other being Franklin Field in Philadelphia.

A few months after the season, the Cosmos announced that they would be moving to Hofstra Stadium on Long Island for the 1972 season. Apparently, being the tenant in a stadium where the baseball-playing landlord was very, very concerned about keeping the playing field in pristine shape had gotten to be too much.

At Yankee Stadium, the Cosmos had had to worry about damaging the field. At Hofstra, a commuter college in Hempstead, Long Island, they had to worry about the field damaging them. The drawbacks of artificial turf for soccer players (and some other athletes) include the fact that its hardness can deaden legs over time, especially if the surface underneath it is very hard, and the fact that it doesn't yield under a player's feet when he turns sharply the way grass does and can make knee injuries more likely. Hofstra, according to Cosmos midfielder Stan Starzell, had "the worst AstroTurf in the country. It was like putting carpet down on the expressway and playing on that."[37] (Admittedly, the Cosmos didn't seem as upset by the downside of artificial turf when they were dominating the NASL on it a few years later at the Meadowlands, although some of the players disliked it.)

The Cosmos did win a somewhat unexpected NASL championship at Hofstra. Their first season there also included some ventures into the international politics of soccer.

The championship came at the end of a 1972 season in which the Cosmos had compiled a regular-season record of seven victories, three losses and four ties. That wasn't overwhelming, but it was good enough to win the Northern Division title, which was followed by a 1-0 victory over Dallas in the playoff semifinals. They won their first NASL title a week later by beating the St. Louis Stars in front of 6,102 people at Hofstra Stadium. They took a first-half lead on a goal by Randy Horton, who was the league's MVP that season. After St. Louis tied the score early in the second half, Josef Jelinek scored the winner on a penalty kick with four minutes left.

Jelinek was the first European international the Cosmos had signed, in a sense the forerunner of Franz Beckenbauer, Giorgio Chinaglia, etc., although he was quite a bit past his prime years. The Cosmos press release announcing his signing in March 1972 said he was 27 years old, but he actually was 31 and had last played for Czechoslovakia in 1962, when he played five of Czechoslovakia's six games in the World Cup in Chile, including the final against Brazil. This wasn't the first time he had played in New York. He had been one of the stars of the Dukla Prague teams that dominated the International Soccer League in the early 1960s. Like the several Hungarian stars who had escaped to the west when their teams were on tour in Spain at the time of the Hungarian Revolution in 1956, Jelinek had escaped the Iron Curtain via an Italian tour by his Czech team.

Jelinek scored only three goals for the Cosmos in 1972, including the gamewinner in the final, but goals weren't really his thing. He was a winger, and led the Cosmos in assists that year. Two other internationals also joined the team in 1972, Israeli Roby Young, who captained the Cosmos, and Canadian John Kerr, who became the first Cosmo to make the step to another country when he signed with Club America of Mexico after the 1972 season.

Kerr was the engine of the Cosmos in 1972. Said teammate Barry Mahy: "Johnny is not only what you could call the hardest working midfield player in the league. He is more than that. He is the general out there. He plans things before the game and then puts them into effect on the field."[38] He did just that in the final, in which the winning goal came after Kerr had been fouled in the penalty area. Wrote Alex Yannis in the next day's *New York Times*: "It was not until the last four minutes that the Cosmos found the solution, and Kerr, as he has done all season, took matters into his own hands and made the move that resulted in Jelinek's penalty shot."[39]

Toye wasn't keen on seeing Kerr depart for Mexico, saying that "We will have to listen and see what they [Club America] have to say, but we are interested in building the Cosmos for the future more than breaking the team up."[40] But Kerr did depart, at least for a while, and Toye negotiated a compensation agreement that included Club America hosting a friendly against the Cosmos in 1973. That compensation game, played before the start of the 1973 NASL season, drew a crowd of 35,000 at the Estadio Azteca in Mexico City, the largest that had ever seen the Cosmos but still only enough to fill about a third of that huge stadium.

Four days after the 1972 NASL final, the Cosmos drew a sellout crowd at Hofstra, 13,205, for a friendly against Moscow Dynamo, one of the world's most famous teams. The game had originally been scheduled to be played in early June. A frantic trip to Europe by Toye had saved the day after the Soviet team attempted to back out of the game, citing an unexpected schedule conflict.[41] In the end, everybody involved with the Cosmos was happy after the game, despite Dynamo's 2-1 victory. The glow of the newly-won NASL title helped, as did the fact that the Cosmos had finally drawn a big crowd without Santos' help and the fact that the Cosmos had played an excellent game against Dynamo despite the narrow defeat.

"I think the game was most enjoyable, and the Cosmos played the best 45 minutes I've ever seen,"[42] said Bradley, in a marked contrast to his attitude after the Bangu debacle almost exactly a year earlier. "I'm very pleased," said Toye. "To lose 2-1 to Moscow Dynamo, I'll take that any day."[43]

In contrast to 1972, the 1973 season, again at Hofstra, was a letdown. After the Dynamo game, *Newsday* had written of "the belief that professional soccer has been permanently established on Long Island."[44] Toye had expressed bright hopes for the Cosmos' future at Hofstra. But in 1973, there were no championship, no sellouts and no MVP (not even any all-stars). What there was at the end of the season was a decision to move back into New York City, but not to Yankee Stadium. The destination was Downing Stadium, a 40-year-old, city-owned, ill-maintained, 22,000-capacity horseshoe on Randall's Island in the East River.

Virtually everybody connected with the Cosmos disliked Downing Stadium. Clive Toye remarks that after being built as a WPA project during the Depression, it had been "left by the City of New York to rot."[45] He recounts a few of the stadium's problems:

> There was often no water in the locker rooms, except that which overflowed from the toilets on the floor above; very little grass. . . . No regular security so that the Press Box was broken into regularly, no matter how many locks or reinforced doors and barricades we put in place; a City-employed, union work force which, in the main, considered manual labor (i.e. moving about) not in their maintenance and cleaning job descriptions.
>
> This led to the sight of the coach, Gordon Bradley, John O'Reilly, our PR man, and others grabbing brooms and sweeping the stands before games . . . so that our fans wouldn't be stepping through garbage to get to their seats and sitting on trash when they got there.[46]

Gavin Newsham comments that "there was more grass on the

road into Manhattan than there was on the field."[47] He also describes certain special preparations the morning of the day in 1975 that Pelé played his first game with the Cosmos: "Stan Cunningham, the stadium manager, gathered his team together and presented them each with a watering can into which he mixed green paint and water. His men were then dispatched onto the field of play to sprinkle over any suggestion that the playing surface was anything other than of a standard a three-time World Cup winner had come to expect."[48] TV viewers may have been fooled, but Pelé himself was not the ideal target for such a ruse. The first game he had ever played in the United States, in August 1966, had been at Randall's Island.

And where was Randall's Island? Under the Triborough Bridge, which connects Manhattan, Queens and the Bronx, accessible only via the bridge spans that link it with those three boroughs, a fact that was eventually to create massive traffic headaches for the Cosmos. Frank Litsky, who covered track meets there for the *New York Times* for decades, comments that "most people didn't know where Randall's Island was, and those who did often didn't know how to get there."[49]

Toye indicates that the reason why the Cosmos moved to Randall's Island was that he already had his eye on an eventual move to the new Giants Stadium, which was still under construction in 1974: "Hofstra is way out on Long Island. Giants Stadium is way over in New Jersey. I did not want to stay at Hofstra and then, one day, make the gigantic hike away from a market in which we would have played five years and set up shop almost another world away. Downing Stadium, bad though it was, put us in the center of things."[50]

Not everybody had quite such a dismal viewpoint of Randall's Island as did the Cosmos. Many New Yorkers, those involved with track and field, considered it a shrine rather than an eyesore. The stadium had hosted Olympic Trials in 1936 and 1964 and the U.S. national championships in 1942, 1945, 1961 and 1966 (and did again in 1991). Jesse Owens, Glenn Cunningham, Jim Ryun, Harrison Dillard and Billy Mills had run there. Owens and Bob Beamon had jumped there. Parry O'Brien and Al Oerter had thrown there. The list of men's track stars who competed at Randall's Island between the 1930s and the 1960s includes more than 50 Olympic gold medalists (the 1991 meet added several more, including Carl Lewis and Michael Johnson). And it also had been, if not quite a soccer shrine, at least a better-than-average soccer venue in the 1940s, '50s and '60s. New York's semipro teams played their weekly league games at hardscrabble fields like Starlight Park and Zerega Oval, but for big occasions like all-star games and the visits of touring foreign teams, Randall's Island often was the place.

Walt Murphy, the editor of *Eastern Track* and one of the leading track experts in New York for decades, is one of those who remember Randall's Island, where Downing Stadium was torn down in 2002 and replaced with a smaller stadium, more fondly than do the Cosmos. Says Murphy: "I have nothing but positive memories about Randall's Island . . . . I was there on the first day of the [1961] AAU Championships when Frank Budd set the world record in the 100-yard dash and I was forever hooked on the place. And I loved the way the stadium looked from the outside. . . . I always felt I was entering a special place. And I never noticed, or least didn't pay attention to, the perceived deficiencies of the stadium."[51]

Litsky, who did notice those deficiencies but wasn't terribly upset by them, comments: "I remember the press facilities as primitive, the bathrooms elementary and the locker rooms no better, but those shortcomings were common 30 or 40 years ago."[52] And the track people did sometimes share Toye's viewpoint about the level of maintenance. In some years, there were complaints, especially in the early part of the track season, that the cinder track was in bad condition and the city parks department, which was charged with maintaining it, was not doing its job.

Perhaps it all depends on your perspective. If your point of reference in assessing Randall's Island is Wembley, it looks very bad. If your point of reference is Zerega Oval, it looks a lot better. Of course, if you're hoping to get the world's greatest player to play for your soccer team, one piece of trash or one patch of bare dirt is one too many.

If the Cosmos had fared disappointingly in 1973 at Hofstra, they were even worse in 1974 at Randall's Island, which Alex Yannis called "a place almost as bleak as their record."[53] They finished last in their four-team division, winning only four NASL games while losing 14 and tying two. In 1975, they seemed started toward more of the same, with four defeats in their first six games, but by this time the attention of most Cosmos fans and all Cosmos officials was riveted on certain off-the-field events.

The Cosmos' pursuit of Pelé had proceeded through various isolated encounters between Clive Toye and Pelé since the 1971 meeting in Jamaica. In the spring of 1974, it picked up speed.

Three factors seem to have been the crucial ones in the eventual success of the Cosmos' pursuit of Pelé. One is that he was still quite young for someone who had played in four World Cups (and could have played in a fifth in 1974 if he had chosen to). Pelé had been only 15 years old when he made his first-team debut with Santos in 1956 and was only 34 when he signed with the Cosmos in 1975. Second was the relentlessness of Clive Toye's efforts. Toye was rebuffed repeatedly and never gave up. Third was the fact that after retiring from Santos in October 1974, Pelé began to realize that his financial picture was not as rosy as he had been thinking it was.

By the time the Cosmos pushed the throttle forward on their pursuit in 1974, Pelé was quite familiar with New York. Since his first game there in 1966 (which ended in a melee in the stands that had given soccer yet another black eye with many Americans) he had played in New York several times a year, thanks to Santos' seemingly endless barnstorming tours. Santos was a fairly small club to be the world's number-one gate attraction. Founded in 1913 in Santos, a port city for the huge Sao Paulo 30 miles inland, it won only one major title in its first 40 years, the 1935 Sao Paulo state league (because of Brazil's vast size, there was no national championship until the 1960s and the state leagues, particularly those in Sao Paulo and Rio de Janeiro, were the big attraction). Its prospects improved rapidly in the 1950s, as *The Encyclopedia of World Soccer* relates: "The rebirth of Santos began in 1952 with the signing of wing half—then multipurpose player—Zito, who led Santos to much-heralded *paulista* [Sao Paulo state league] championships in 1955 and 1956. In September 1956, Pelé, aged 16 [actually he was a month short of 16], gained a place on the first team in a friendly against AIK Stockholm, and with one stroke, the fortunes of Santos, and world soccer at large, changed dramatically."[54] By the mid-1960s, Santos had realized that it had a gold mine—the greatest player of all time in the world, up from its own junior team—that was not likely to happen twice and was not going to last forever.

As Pelé's career wound down, after his retirement from the Brazilian national team in 1971 and with his retirement from Santos looming, the barnstorming pace became frantic. Harry Harris, in his 2001 biography *Pelé: His Life and Times*, says:

> [Pelé] made his plans for retirement public to give Santos plenty of time to find a replacement for him. Instead they scheduled as many matches as possible to make as much money as they could while he was still wearing their colours . . . . [The lucrative touring

for which Manchester United was criticized in the 1990s] was nothing compared to what Santos were doing nearly thirty years earlier. . . . They were more like the Harlem Globetrotters. "We played around a hundred games [per year]," says Pelé. "Yes, it got to a hundred games. Santos were a club who had to pay a lot of money for its players, so they played many games on top of their Brazilian league commitments. January and February in Latin America. June and July in Europe. Every year we would go on tours. At this time there was no concept of selling TV rights for large amounts of money."[55]

Clive Toye may have picked up the pace in his pursuit of Pelé in 1974, but the Brazilian was no more eager to play for the Cosmos than he had been when Toye talked to him at poolside in Jamaica in 1971. In July 1974, they met in Frankfurt, West Germany, while Pelé was in Germany as an observer at the 1974 World Cup. The answer was a polite "no." In August, Toye buttonholed Pelé in the executive lounge of a terminal at JFK airport in New York, while Pelé was en route to Canada. The answer was a polite "no." In September, Toye flew to Brazil to meet Pelé and his main adviser, Julio Mazzei, at Pelé's house in Santos. The answer was a polite "no." In December, Toye wired Mazzei in Brazil about the matter. The answer was a polite "no."[56] Pelé, who retired from Santos in the fall of 1974, also was being courted by some big European clubs, but they were having no more success than the Cosmos.[57] Pele was firmly set against playing again, in particular because he feared the reaction of the Brazilian people if he took his talents to a foreign club.

Pelé's last game for Santos, after playing 1,114 games in 18 years with the club he had made world famous, had been against a league rival, Ponte Preta, at the Villa Belmiro stadium in Santos on Oct. 2, 1974. It was not long after that that he began to realize the holes in the financial network that he had built up during his playing years.

Pelé's financial arrangements were in disarray generally, but the most pressing problems centered around Fiolax, an auto-parts manufacturer in which Pelé owned a six-percent interest. The investment wasn't the problem. Pelé could easily have sustained the loss of that money. The problem was that Pelé had co-signed for a loan on which Fiolax had defaulted, and now he could either pay up or be blamed for allowing Fiolax to collapse, which he didn't want to do for public-relations reasons.[58]

Pelé discussed his plight in a 1977 autobiography:

When the loan fell due and the company could not pay, the bank came to me. In addition, at the same time there had been a rather serious breach of government regulations concerning the import of some raw material . . . and the government imposed a tremendous fine on the company. It was then I discovered that among the other papers I had signed were ones making me responsible for all liabilities of the company, so there was the fine as well as the bank loan . . . .

I had enough resources by that time to pay both the fine and the loan, but it would have meant selling off very valuable properties to raise the money, taking a large loss because of the forced sale, and that would have meant more than doubling the loss I would take for not having sought competent legal counsel. The final bill would be about $2 million.[59]

Pelé's advisors came up with a route around the problem, but it involved generating some new income by accepting the Cosmos' offer. Julio Mazzei presented him with a list of the pros and cons of signing with the Cosmos. There were many more pros than cons, and Pelé began to waver.[60]

The importance of Pelé's financial difficulties in leading him toward the Cosmos is indicated by Pelé himself in his autobiography when he mentions his admiration for the skill of a Brazilian lawyer hired by his advisors to help sort out his legal/financial entanglements. "After seeing Dr. [Sergio] de Brito at work," Pele said, "I wished I had had his services in the past on many occasions, and particularly when signing the papers relating to Fiolax! Still, if I had not signed those papers relating to Fiolax, it is very possible I would never have come to New York and Cosmos, and that was a decision I have never regretted."[61]

Meanwhile in New York, Clive Toye was smarting from the way that Northern Irish idol George Best, one of the two or three biggest stars in the world after Pelé, had suddenly decided to disappear just as he was on the verge of signing with the Cosmos in January 1975. That sting was eased when the Pelé prospects began to show some promise that they hadn't before.

A call from Mazzei to Toye restarted the process, and when talks between Toye and Pelé resumed in early spring, it no longer seemed a question of whether Pelé would be willing to play for the Cosmos. It had become a matter of money, of offers and counter-offers, of figures written on pieces of hotel stationery.

Toye believes a meeting on March 27, 1975 in Brussels, Belgium, was the crucial one. That was the one where Pelé first told him that, yes, he would play for the Cosmos, although he was not yet committing to the three seasons that Toye wanted. "We were almost there," Toye says. "As Sir Winston Churchill had said about something far more important after the Battle of El Alamein, it was not the end, it was not the beginning of the end, but it was the end of the beginning, albeit a beginning of four years and one month."[62]

Two weeks later in Rome, the two sides got even closer, but in on April 29 in Brazil, Pelé announced that he was rejecting the Cosmos' offer, saying: "I have to take care of my family and my business obligations."[63] Pressure from the Brazilian public seemed to have unhinged the Cosmos' plans. From the Cosmos' standpoint, it was George Best's January turnabout all over again.

Toye churned back into action, enlisting the help of American politicians and Warner executives who could fill Pelé in on the diplomatic advantages and marketing aspects of the deal he was being offered. Toye flew to Brazil once again to plead the Cosmos' case, with particular emphasis on the ways that the deal would be of benefit to the Brazilian people. Pelé agreed to a visit to New York in late May, and there he accepted the Cosmos' offer.[64] The actual signing of the contracts took place in early June in Bermuda.

Talking to reporters on May 28, at the beginning of that visit to New York and on a night when he said he was 60 to 70 percent certain he would sign with the Cosmos, Pelé had made reference to the way that the reaction of his Brazilian fans was worrying him, but also showed that the things Toye had been telling him had made an impression. "If this offer had come from West Germany, Spain, Italy or even Brazil, I would have to say No." Pele said. "But to return to playing in the United States would be a different principle. . . . I really feel if I came here I could give something to U.S. soccer. . . . If I come back, the Brazilian people would prefer that I come back to playing in Brazil. But I think the people would be proud of me if Brazil in some way can gain through me playing here. . . . If I sign it would be a great deal for Brazil."[65]

The actual size of Pelé's contract with the Cosmos has long been a cause of uncertainty. The three main figures that have been cited numerous times are $7 million, $4.5 million and $2.8 million. Then there is the question of whether that was before or after taxes. Toye was quoted in the *New York Times* a few days after the signing indicating that the middle figure was the closest one: "The club's general manager, Clive Toye, flatly denied yesterday that Pelé's contract was about $7 million, which was widely reported to include payment by the team of his income taxes. 'He will receive closer to $4.5 million for the three years,' said Toye. 'And it's ridiculous to think we'd pay his income tax. There are absolutely no income tax deals at all.' "[66] In a 2003 book, author David Tossell quoted Toye giving a lower figure: "We paid him a total of $2.8 million for three years as a player and 10 years of marketing rights. I found out later that Real Madrid had offered roughly the same."[67] Others have seconded that $2.8 million figure.

The star himself was noncommittal. The *New York Times* said: "Pelé and his business manager, Jose Roberto Ribeiro Xisto, try to avoid money specifics, pointing out that Pelé's promotional earnings are only estimates. Pelé said he would pay Brazilian income tax, but would take the matter up with the Finance Minister. 'After all, I'm exporting know-how and there exist incentives for firms exporting know-how,' he said, describing himself as 'raw material, very Brazilian raw material.' "[68]

Whatever it was, it was the most money an athlete had ever been paid, in the United States or elsewhere. The highest-paid athlete in American professional sports was New York Yankees baseball pitcher Catfish Hunter, who was making $740,000 a year. The soccer figure that Pelé's contract was most often compared against was the $2 million that Spanish power Barcelona had paid in 1973 to buy Dutch superstar Johan Cruyff from Ajax of Amsterdam, but that was a matter of apples and oranges. The $2 million did represent money that Barcelona had shelled out, just like the Cosmos had paid to get Pelé, but it was a transfer fee, not a salary, and went to Ajax, not to Cruyff. Cruyff's salary when he arrived at Barcelona was about $100,000 a year, less than what he made from endorsements.[69]

The Cosmos' signing of Pelé was officially announced at a press conference at the 21 Club in Manhattan on June 10, 1975, by which time the news had long since ceased to be a secret. There was a ceremonial signing at the press conference, although the real signing had happened the day before in Bermuda. The press conference, with about three times as many people jammed into the room as supposedly were allowed, was a madhouse. Pelé took it in stride. He had been one of the most famous people on earth for years and was accustomed to mob scenes. Still, the press conference at 21 was only the beginning of the hoopla greeting him in America.

FOUR

Men of Steel

It was no coincidence that the Bethlehem Steel soccer team rose to prominence around the same time that World War I was raging in Europe. Bethlehem Steel had gotten its start as a manufacturer of iron rails for the railroads of the mid-19th century. It gained perhaps its greatest fame for its heavy construction work in the 1930s. But over the years, the work that kept Bethlehem's mills busiest and its coffers fullest was the manufacturing of munitions. At the time of the soccer team's peak, the business generated by World War I had made Bethlehem Steel one of the leading arms makers in the world, a corporation with lots of money to spend.

The team's record in those war years is stunning. Between the 1913-14 season and the 1918-19 season, it won the National Challenge Cup four times, the American Football Association Cup five times and its league championship four times. During those six seasons, the Steelworkers won 171 games, tied 15 and lost only eight. They also won seven by forfeit.

That record owed a great deal to the fact that during those years, the Bethlehem Steel Corporation was taking in money at a fantastic rate. A picture of the boost that the war gave to Bethlehem Steel's prosperity jumps from the page in its revenue figures during the early years of the 20th century. From $14.7 million in 1905, the year after the company was incorporated, those revenues grew steadily during the decade before World War I. They were $22.3 million in 1909, the first full year of Grey beam production, and $47.7 million in 1914, the year the war started in August. They then skyrocketed, to $147.6 million in 1915, $217.9 million in 1916, $301.9 million in 1917 and $452.2 million in 1918.[1]

Bethlehem Steel's stock price was affected in a similar way by the war. According to John Steele Gordon in *An Empire of Wealth*, a history of American business published in 2004, Bethlehem "had never had a foreign contract larger than $10 million, but in November 1914 the British Admiralty offered it a contract for $135 million worth of ships, guns and submarines . . . . Bethlehem Steel's stock increased tenfold in 1915."[2]

Some of that newfound wealth found its way to the soccer team, beginning with the $25,000 grant that Charles M. Schwab gave to the soccer team and the rest of Bethlehem Steel's athletic program. The effect of that grant, only the start of the company's munificence, could be seen in the team's name. "In previous years the team was known as the Bethlehem soccer team, but this year it will be known as the Bethlehem Steel company soccer team and will be registered and known under that name in the future," the *South Bethlehem Globe* said shortly before the start of the 1915-16 season.[3] There had been many inaccurate references in previous years to the Bethlehem Football Club as the Bethlehem Steel Football Club. Now, any such references would be accurate.

Bethlehem Steel's prosperity in the war years got a tremendous boost right at the start via that $135 million British contract, a controversial one that became known as the "submarine deal." The controversy came from the fact that Schwab bent American neutrality laws about as far as he possibly could without breaking them (publicly, that is; secretly, he did break them). The name came from the fact that the heart of the contract called for 20 submarines to be built for the British Navy, although it also involved artillery, shrapnel and shells.[4] Within days after Schwab arrived back in New York on Nov. 20, 1914, carrying a check for the British downpayment of $15 million, President Woodrow Wilson and American Secretary of State William Jennings Bryan had informed him of their opinion that the deal violated American neutrality laws. In December, Schwab returned to London to face questions from First Lord of the Admiralty Winston Churchill as to why he had wasted British time by accepting a contract that the British felt he must have known he wouldn't legally be able to fulfill. Schwab had his answer ready. He asked permission to take over a British-owned shipyard in Canada and quietly transferred the heads of Bethlehem shipyards in Wilmington, Del., and San Francisco there, along with enough American shipyard workers to do the job.[5] All 20 submarines (some of which were secretly built at Bethlehem's Fore River Shipyard near Boston) were launched by September 1915.[6]

Men of Steel

Perhaps the most striking confirmation of how the submarine deal had propelled Bethlehem Steel into the forefront of armaments makers was the way that Germany sat up and took notice of its adversary—not the one across the English Channel, but the supposedly neutral one on the Lehigh River. Gordon explains: "The German government, unable to tap into American industrial capacity, tried to deny it to its enemies by buying it. In 1915, it offered Charles Schwab, president and principal stockholder of Bethlehem Steel, twice the market value of his stock for control of the company. Britain, able to read German diplomatic communications, learned of the bid and was prepared to make a counteroffer. But Schwab assured the British that he would fulfill his contracts and turned down the German offer out of hand."[7] Schwab must have enjoyed receiving the British bid, considering that it was conveyed to him by a banker who seven years before had turned down a loan application from Schwab for 1/100th of the sum the British now were prepared to offer him.[8]

The submarine deal was only the beginning. By the end of 1916, Bethlehem Steel was producing 25,000 artillery shells a day and had surpassed Krupp to become the world's largest manufacturer of munitions.[9] A government report after the war summarizing Bethlehem Steel's production included 11,000 gun barrels, 18 million artillery shells and 34,000 tons of armor plate.[10]

Besides the basic fact of support from a very prosperous company, one of the most important advantages that Bethlehem Steel could offer soccer players was dual employment. The company could pay players particularly well because it could offer them employment off the field as well as on. It was not alone in holding this edge. Some other industrial companies involved in American soccer in those days were able to do the same. In the case of Bethlehem Steel, this doesn't necessarily have meant work in front of a blast furnace or in a machine shop.

In its earliest years, the Bethlehem Football Club had been composed largely of real steelworkers. This trend seems to have been modified somewhat as the team improved over the years and advanced to better and better levels of competition. The work in a steel mill can be backbreakingly difficult and often very dangerous, and steelworkers in those days often worked six- or seven-day weeks with very little time off. By 1915, players on the Bethlehem Steel soccer team were making frequent weekend road trips, sometimes as far as New England and sometimes involving games on both Saturday and Sunday. Some of them were taking six-week summer vacations to visit their families in Scotland. They were occasionally attending banquets at Bethlehem hotels on weekday evenings and regularly going to practice on Bethlehem soccer fields on weekday afternoons. These are not things that it would have been possible to do while holding down a full-time job in a steel mill at the same time.

Nevertheless, there were a few real steelworkers, not insulated from the dangers inside the mill, who were still involved with the team in its peak years. One such, backup goalkeeper Robert Scaife, who had been the starter until just a few weeks before, saw his soccer fortunes wane after he lost a fingertip in an accident in the mill in March 1915.[11] But Bethlehem Steel was a huge company, which included lots of jobs that were safer and less arduous than working in the mill. One place that seems to have been a common destination for soccer players over the years was the company's drafting office.

Another advantage that Bethlehem Steel could offer players, starting in 1916, was a field that was considered the best in the country at the time. Late in the 1915-16 season, the soccer team moved out of East End Field, where it had been playing home games for years. By the start of the 1916-17 season, Steel Field, built on land that Bethlehem Steel had bought from Moravian College, was ready.

Then there was the question of the draft. The United States entered World War I in April 1917 and the draft went into effect two months later, after which employment by Bethlehem Steel carried a bonus of a sort. Workers involved in armaments making, of whom there were many at Bethlehem Steel, were exempted from the draft and safe from being sent to the trenches in France. The majority of players on the soccer team were British, and therefore unaffected by the American draft. Britain, which had been in the war since August 1914, had never used conscription in its centuries-long history. When a draft finally did become necessary during World War I, Britain entered into it cautiously. The first draft in British history went into effect in February 1916, and for some time applied only to single men and widowers with no children. Most of the British soccer players who played for Bethlehem during the war were already in America by that date, and various publications of the day show no indication that Bethlehem Steel ever fielded any soccer players who were fleeing the British draft.

The draft did have considerable effect elsewhere in Bethlehem Steel's athletic program, which included baseball as well as soccer. The Bethlehem Steel soccer team played at the top levels of its sport in America, but professional baseball was too far advanced compared to American pro soccer to allow for an equivalent baseball team. Instead, there was a semi-pro Bethlehem Steel baseball league, with teams at Bethlehem Steel plants in various locations. The team from the original mill in Bethlehem played against teams from more recently acquired facilities in Lebanon, Pa.; Quincy, Mass., and elsewhere. Beginning in 1916, its home games were at the new Steel Field, just like the soccer team's home games. By the summer of 1918, it and its league rivals were swamped with potential players, as steel mills and shipyards with baseball teams had become magnets for big-league players seeking protection against the draft.[12]

There may also have been a degree of protection against the draft conferred on workers by many textile mills. Particularly in Massachusetts, textile mills got a lot of government orders during World War I, mostly for woolen uniforms and cotton cloth used in airplanes, gas masks and bandages.[13] Many of those textile mills fielded soccer teams, but there is no record of soccer involvement by the other giant American arms maker, Dupont, whose prominent status in the armaments field was based heavily on its massive production of smokeless gunpowder.

Not too many other steelmakers attempted to challenge Bethlehem on the soccer field. U.S. Steel, which from 1901 onward was by far the largest of American steelmakers, fielded only isolated soccer teams, most notably at the Homestead Works near Pittsburgh, the Federal Shipyard in Kearny, N.J., and the Joliet Works near Chicago. At one time or another, Bethlehem Steel defeated all three of those U.S. Steel teams. However, it lost the only game it ever played against another Bethlehem Steel unit, a 3-2 defeat by Fore River Shipyard in 1920. Other steel mills fielding soccer teams were few and far between. A perusal of American soccer records before 1930 shows no mention at all of most of the biggest names in steelmaking, like Jones & Laughlin, Youngstown Sheet & Tube, Midvale, Cambria, Inland and Republic.

Perhaps the most successful steelmaker in soccer other than Bethlehem was Scullin Steel, a small specialty steelmaker located in St. Louis. Scullin reached the final of the National Challenge Cup three years in a row, 1921, 1922 and 1923. It won the title in 1922 by defeating Todd Shipyard of Brooklyn, the same team that had beaten it (under the name Robins Dry Dock) in the 1921 final. Scullin came close again in 1923, when it sent its team east for the final against Paterson FC of New Jersey. After playing a 2-2 tie in the final, Scullin decided to forfeit the title because, team leaders felt, injuries and departures had left the traveling squad too debilitated to put up a respectable performance in the replay. Scullin's time at the top in St. Louis play also was brief, as so often happened with company-backed teams. Scullin won the first of its three St. Louis Professional League titles in 1919 and the last in 1922.

By the start of the 1915-16 season, the Bethlehem Steel team's objectives had focused on three competitions, the USFA's National Challenge Cup, which it had won in the spring of 1915; the American Football Association Cup, which it had won in 1914, and the American League of Philadelphia, in which it was trying to add to its streak of having won titles for four consecutive seasons in various leagues.

Unquestionably Bethlehem Steel's primary target during the next few seasons was the National Challenge Cup. Bethlehem Steel had played a vital role, via the Allied American Association, in the founding of the USFA. By winning the National Challenge Cup in 1915, it had already begun the process of making its name synonymous with that competition. It saw that the new event was the truest national championship that existed in American soccer, and it wanted to make that event its main stage.

That Bethlehem Steel was so eager about the National Challenge Cup is ironic in view of the attitude of top-level pro clubs about that competition in later years. In the 1924-25 and 1928-29 seasons, most American Soccer League teams boycotted the National Challenge Cup, citing the disruption of their league schedules. North American Soccer League teams declined throughout that league's existence to enter what by then was known as the U.S. Open Cup. And when Major League Soccer began in 1996, it was only reluctantly that some MLS teams agreed to take part.[14] Severe schedule congestion in 1997 was often blamed on the U.S. Open Cup, with the result that two leading MLS teams, D.C. United and the Los Angeles Galaxy, declined to enter the cup in 1998.

There had been no such balking on Bethlehem Steel's part eight decades before. It saw the National Challenge Cup as an event in which it could make itself famous, and proceeded to do so. Only a one-goal defeat in the 1917 final separated Bethlehem Steel from the feat of winning the National Challenge Cup five times in a row. Nearly a century later, its two sets of back-to-back victories, 1915-1916 and 1918-1919, have only been bettered once, by the New York Greek-Americans team that won in 1967, 1968 and 1969.

The American Football Association Cup was reduced to a somewhat secondary status by the rise of the National Challenge Cup, but some teams didn't slacken their efforts in the old competition, and Bethlehem Steel was one of those.

The field for the AFA Cup was not as strong as the one for the National Challenge Cup. The main difference was that USFA's horizons were moving steadily westward, while the AFA's stayed where they were. The Pittsburgh, Buffalo, Cleveland, Detroit, Chicago and St. Louis teams that started appearing in the National Challenge Cup by 1920 had not played in the AFA Cup in earlier years and still didn't. Bethlehem and Philadelphia remained the westernmost outposts of the AFA Cup, which the *South Bethlehem Globe* characterized as "emblematic of the championship of the east."[15] Most of the eastern teams that had been major AFA contenders in the past were still there. Between the 1915-16 season and the 1918-19 season, Bethlehem's opponents in AFA Cup play included four past champions, West Hudson, Fall River Rovers, Kearny Scots and Philadelphia Disston (the former Tacony) and such newer powers as Robins Dry Dock of Brooklyn, Paterson FC and New York FC.

Whether those teams were giving it everything they had in the AFA Cup and not holding anything back for the National Challenge Cup is unknowable, but if newspaper reports are any indication, Bethlehem Steel seemed to be taking AFA Cup competition very seriously. There might have been a temptation to view the AFA Cup as a warmup for the "real thing," but Bethlehem Steel does not appear to have seen it that way.

The third of Bethlehem's three objectives was league play, which in the 1915-16 season meant the American League of Philadelphia. This would be Bethlehem's second season in the American League and also its last, after which it would continue an established pattern. It had jumped to higher leagues twice before, from the Eastern Pennsylvania League to the Allied American League in 1912 and from the Allied American League to the American League of Philadelphia in 1914. After leaving the American League at the end of the 1915-16 season, it would take a season off from league play in 1916-17 while it pondered its next move and then continue upward, joining the National Association Foot Ball League in 1917 and helping to form the American Soccer League in 1921.

The fact that Bethlehem kept changing leagues might imply that league play was not a major concern to it, but the opposite was true. There were no lateral moves in Bethlehem Steel's league-jumping.

Every move was an upward one, as the Steelworkers kept seeking tougher and tougher challenges.

With three objectives to shoot for, Bethlehem Steel seems to have done things the right way in the 1915-16 season. It won all three.

Actually, one of those, the American League, was a tie. Bethlehem finished even with Disston of Philadelphia in the standings at the end of the 10-game season. After a scoreless playoff game failed to settle the issue, the championship was allowed to remain a tie.

Bethlehem was developing quite a rivalry at this point with Disston, which was from the Tacony area of northeast Philadelphia and was sponsored by the Henry Disston sawmaking firm. They had first met in the 1913-14 season, when Bethlehem won three games by a total score of 20-1. That was an earlier version of Disston, however, before it took over the franchise and many of the players of the professional Tacony team, which had given Bethlehem a tremendous tussle in the AFA Cup final that season. In the 1914-15 season, Bethlehem played the improved Disston team three more times. The result was two Bethlehem wins and a tie.

In the 1915-16 season they played a total of five times, and the rivalry was now becoming a lot closer. The five games produced two wins for Bethlehem, one win for Disston and two ties. The first of those games was the Disston victory, and it really set Bethlehem Steel back on its heels. Since the defeat by Brooklyn Celtic in March 1915, Bethlehem had won 16 consecutive games, but on Nov. 20, 1915, Disston won, 2-1, on its own field in Philadelphia, and Bethlehem was forced to play catchup in the American League standings until very nearly the end of the season. Bethlehem went on a long winning streak in league play, but so did Disston, and remained a game ahead until May 11, 1916, when Bethlehem evened the standings with a 2-1 victory over the Sawmakers in its next-to-last game of the league season. The game was at Bethlehem, but not East End Field. The Steelworkers had been forced to vacate that field, but Steel Field was not yet ready, so they were temporarily playing their home games at Lehigh University.

Two days later, the American League season ended, with Bethlehem Steel and Disston each having nine victories and a loss on the other's turf. The playoff game on May 27 on Disston's field confirmed the evenness of the two teams and the season went into the books as a tie (in the spring, there was more of a tendency to let ties stand rather than replay them than at other times of the year, because the start of the baseball season made availability of both fields and players more difficult). Bethlehem's loss to Disston on Nov. 20, 1915 remained something of a bookend. A few days after that setback, the Steelworkers won a friendly against an all-star team from the Blue Mountain League, an amateur league in the Lehigh Valley, and began a new undefeated streak, which eventually would match the 41 games of its 14-month streak in 1914 and '15.

Bethlehem also met Disston in the second round of the National Challenge Cup that season and had a rather narrow escape, although the score of Bethlehem 3, Disston 0 on Dec. 25, 1915 would indicate otherwise. But that game was a replay. Two weeks earlier, Bethlehem had been three minutes away from elimination before tying the game at 1-1. The replay on Disston's field was a surprising cakewalk for Bethlehem, which took a 2-0 lead by the 30th minute and was never threatened. A few weeks later, in the third round of the National Challenge Cup, Bethlehem swamped Philadelphia Hibernian, 6-0, the same score by which it had eliminated Hibs from the AFA Cup in October.

In April, Bethlehem met West Hudson in Harrison in the National Challenge Cup quarterfinals. The Steelworkers went home 1-0 victors, on a penalty kick by Whitey Fleming 20 minutes into the game. The *Newark Evening News* indicated that a wider victory would not have been unjustified, saying: "The Bethlehems hold the United States championship cup and defended the trophy in great style. The visiting eleven played a far superior game to that put up by the Harrisonians."[16]

That victory set Bethlehem up for the longest road trip it had ever taken. Previously, the farthest from Bethlehem that it had travelled was Fall River, Mass., about 230 miles. Chicago, where it played Pullman in the semifinals of the National Challenge Cup on April 16, 1916, was more than 600 miles. The game, one of the biggest events in the history of soccer in Chicago to that point, wasn't played on the Pullman team's home field, but rather on the best that Chicago had to offer, the home ground of the Hyde Park Blues team. After all the buildup, the game produced a scoreless tie. The replay six days later at Taylor Stadium in South Bethlehem was better, particularly at the finish. Neil Clarke had given Bethlehem a 1-0 halftime lead, but Pullman tied it on a penalty early in the second half. With the game down to its last few minutes and overtime looming, Bethlehem gained four corner kicks in rapid succession. The first three produced nothing, but on the fourth, with less than a minute left, the ball got loose in a scramble in front of the net, and Bethlehem captain Bobby Morrison raced up from the back to score the winning goal.

The final was two weeks later in Pawtucket, R.I. Bethlehem Steel met the Fall River Rovers in a game that was memorable for several reasons. The two teams had played a friendly a year before, but this was the first competitive game in what was to become the first great intersectional rivalry in American soccer history. Another reason was that this game at the J&P Coats team's Lonsdale Avenue Ground produced the first significant American soccer riot—and a headline in the *New York Times* that ignored the outcome of the game and said: "Mob Referee at Big Soccer Game."[17] Both the riot and the goal by Whitey Fleming that gave Bethlehem its 1-0 victory came in the closing minutes. The *South Bethlehem Globe* told about them, although not necessarily from a completely impartial viewpoint:

> The play that helped decide the game came ten minutes from the end of the contest. Just as Clarke, the rangy center forward of the Bethlehem team jumped into the air to head the ball toward the Rover goal, Charlie Burns, the Rovers' left halfback, ducked into Clarke and threw him headlong into the turf. Instantly referee [David] Whyte's whistle sounded for a penalty kick and the Rovers swarmed around Whyte like a lot of wild men, gesticulating and even threatening the referee. "Sinker" Sullivan, the fiery inside right of the Rovers, persisted in protesting so violently that the hundreds of Fall River rooters in the stands, distinguishable by the yellow cards in their hats, took up the refrain and raised a fearful din of disapproval that continued through the remaining ten minutes of play. After cooler heads had prevailed the Rovers drew back and allowed Fleming, the blond outside left of the Bethlehems team to make the free kick . . . .
>
> The Rovers in the last ten minutes fought like demons for the equalizing score but they were so angry and excited that they had no semblance of teamwork. Their rough, plunging style of play, however, worked the fans into a frenzy. A few seconds before the time limit the ball glanced off one Bethlehems player and struck another on the wrist and the Rover fans and players yelled, "Penalty! Penalty!"
>
> Whyte, however, did not see the play and raised his whistle to his mouth to end the game. Even as he did he was struck in the back by a fan who had been in the lead in the wild rush at the referee. His failure to call what the Rovers thought was a penalty kick for their team seemed the last straw and in an instant Whyte disappeared in the seething mob. The Pawtucket police headed by Lieut.

D.A. Ballou drew their clubs and rushed to the assistance of the players who were doing their best to protect the referee, especially [William] Booth, who was beaten black and blue. Bottles began to fly and the tumult didn't cease until one of the officers drew his revolver. This cowed the rest into submission and Whyte and the Bethlehem players got off the field into safety.[18]

The Rovers had an opportunity for revenge two weeks later, when they played Bethlehem in a semifinal of the AFA Cup on their home ground in Fall River. They failed to take that opportunity, and this time there was no dispute about the result. Just before halftime, Bethlehem's George McKelvey scored to break a 1-1 tie. Early in the second half, he got an insurance goal, after Fred Pepper had eluded three defenders in bringing the ball down the wing and centered to McKelvey.

The finish of this game in Fall River was remarkably different from the one two weeks before and only about 25 miles away in Pawtucket, as least as described by the *Globe*. It said: "Pepper was given great applause from the crowd for his work in making the third point for Bethlehem and from then on the crowd cheered and clapped for every good play made by the Bethlehem team. When the game ended with Bethlehem winners three goals to one the crowd swarmed on the field and shook hands with the players and officials."[19] It sounds almost too polite to be true.

Before the game in Fall River, Bethlehem had played three relatively routine games in the AFA Cup, beating Philadelphia Hibernian by 6-0, Clan McDonald of Brooklyn by 2-0 and Jersey City FC by 5-0. The final against Kearny Scots was more of the same, a 3-0 Bethlehem victory. En route to winning the AFA Cup two years before, Bethlehem had played 11 games, five of which were ties. This time, they only needed five games, and no one came closer to them than a two-goal decision.

Actually, the final, in which Neil Clarke got all three Bethlehem goals, was a little closer than the score implied, particularly before halftime. Said the *New York Times*: "The Scots put up a wonderful struggle, especially in the first half, but were met at every angle by the clever work of the steelworkers. The first half was a grueling affair, and by far the best from a hair-raising standpoint. In the second half the Scots seemed to have shot their bolt, and the local eleven toyed with them at will."[20]

The *Newark Evening News* thought it was the crowd, rather than the game that was most interesting on this day, and made reference to one factor that may have had something to do with Bethlehem Steel's chronic attendance problems in later years. "All that section of Bethlehem which wasn't making shrapnel and cannon was on deck," the *Evening News* said. "Every nationality represented in this city of many nations gathered in the Lehigh University Stadium. It was a queer sight to see Poles and Czechs and Hungarians cheering the English national pastime."[21]

It had been a very eventful spring for Bethlehem Steel en route to its triple (or double-and-a-half as the case may be). The last three rounds of the National Challenge Cup, including the trip to Chicago and the controversial final in Pawtucket; the last three rounds of the AFA Cup and the last four games of the American League season, including two showdowns with Disston, had all come within a 10-week period. And that new undefeated streak, the one that had begun after the loss to Disston in November, was now at 22 games and counting.

The start of the 1915-16 season had seen the inauguration of a new name for the Bethlehem Steel soccer team. The start of the 1916-17 season saw the opening of a new field for it, on land that the company had bought from Moravian College about a mile north of the Lehigh River.

The team's new playground was initially referred to as the New Athletic Field and eventually came to be called Steel Field. The permanent grandstand, which is still there, is on just one side of the field, although temporary wooden bleachers sometimes were added. The brick-and-steel grandstand is a substantial thing, 17 rows high and more than 40 yards long, with the entire seating area raised enough that even the front-row spectators are more than 10 feet above the ground and have a good viewing angle. The grandstand has a large roof and is partially enclosed at both ends to protect spectators from the wind.

In a 1918 article about the history of the Bethlehem Steel team, the *Spalding Guide* put a price tag on the company's gift to the team, saying: "President E.G. Grace of the Bethlehem Steel Company set aside an appropriation of $100,000 to buy the athletic field as well as to put on it a magnificent clubhouse with gymnasium, grandstand and other necessary facilities."[22] Thomas W. Cahill, probably the leading official in American soccer in his day, corroborated that figure in a speech in Sweden during Bethlehem Steel's Scandinavian tour in the summer of 1919.[23]

Most American soccer fields of its day are long gone, but Steel

Field looks very much the same today as it did in 1916. The land is once again owned by Moravian College, which refurbished the grandstand in 2005 and uses Steel Field as its football, track and lacrosse stadium (with the artificial field itself named after a former coach). There is a plaque on the side of the grandstand commenting on its history, but perhaps a more poignant reminder of that history is the fact that the football field is surrounded by a blue-and-white all-weather track, the same colors as Bethlehem Steel's soccer uniforms.

The grandstand, which holds 1,000 spectators, isn't just an empty shell. Underneath the stands are locker rooms and a gymnasium, used in more recent years by Moravian students instead of the steelworkers they originally were intended for. Bethlehem Liberty High School's football stadium is just a few blocks away. The high school stadium is considerably larger, but Steel Field has history on its side.

According to Paul Moyer, the Moravian athletic director, the college was faced a few years ago with a choice of either refurbishing the grandstand or tearing it down and building something new. Engineering studies done by the college discovered that the grandstand had been built so solidly, including steel beams sunk far into the ground, that tearing it down would have been prohibitively expensive.[24] Bethlehem Steel's legacy may be a rust-covered brownfield elsewhere (or in the case of the Martin Tower on Bethlehem's northwest side, a white elephant), but thanks to Moravian, it's looking good at Steel Field.

Steel Field was dedicated on Sept. 23, 1916. The designated victim that day was West Hudson, which was involved in a program of rebuilding its team with young players after having finished an unaccustomed fourth in the National Association Foot Ball League the season before. The rebuilding program did help to get West Hudson to the AFA Cup final the following spring, where it had the misfortune to run into a Bethlehem Steel team looking to make up for the most stinging defeat in its history a week before. On Steel Field's opening day, Bethlehem Steel wasn't looking for any sort of retribution, but the score was the same as it was the following May: Bethlehem Steel 7, West Hudson 0. The *Newark Evening News* said: "Bob Lennox Saturday afternoon took his West Hudson soccer team to Bethlehem for the purpose of helping the National and American cup champions dedicate their new field. Bethlehem celebrated in great style and offered up the West Hudson aggregation as a sacrifice, 7 goals to 0 . . . . the West Hudsons were willing to admit that the new field of the Bethlehem club is the finest in the country."[25]

The newspaper stories made no mention of the attendance that day, but it probably was unimpressive. It certainly can't have compared with the throng the following weekend, when Steel Field was packed with Bethlehem Steel employees and their families there for a rather odd sports event, a competition among teams of steelworkers demonstrating their first-aid skills in the face of simulated calamities.

While Steel Field may have done some good things for the Bethlehem Steel soccer team, one thing it didn't do was solve its chronic attendance problem. The *Bethlehem Globe* commented on this problem repeatedly over the next 15 years, but American newspapers back then didn't go in for analyzing the events they reported as much as they do today, so the *Globe* never really explored the causes of the low attendance.

There were several reasons. The fact that Steel Field was located a long way from the South Bethlehem areas where many of Bethlehem Steel's workers lived probably didn't help the attendance, nor did the fact that the workforce in the mills was dominated by men from eastern and southern Europe[26] who can't have been very eager to watch a bunch of Scottish soccer players. Those may have been moot points however. Pennsylvania's laws banning Sunday sports forced the team to play its home games on Saturdays, when few steelworkers could attend them anyway. In the 1920s, one of Bethlehem Steel's leading ASL rivals, in Fall River, Mass., got around the Massachusetts blue laws, which were similar to Pennsylvania's, by putting its stadium barely across the state line in Rhode Island. Bethlehem didn't have that option, and references to Bethlehem's crowds as "a corporal's guard" became the standard.

Something else that can't have helped Bethlehem's attendance, but was no more a detriment in Bethlehem than in many other places, was the fact that in those days, top American soccer teams played fall-to-spring schedules. Snow-covered fields often caused games to be called off, but when there was no snow, the games went on, even if the cold meant that there were almost no spectators either. The fact that less-than-ideal fields were taken for granted is typified by a comment in the *South Bethlehem Globe* account of a January 1916 game at East End Field, which notes casually that "the field was frozen, but it otherwise was in good condition."[27]

The opening game at Steel Field was a friendly. The season opener on the road a week before had been a friendly against an amateur team. Friendlies were to be a regular theme in the 1916-17 season, in which Bethlehem Steel wasn't in a league, wanting one beyond the boundaries of Pennsylvania but not yet having found one.

In the end, Bethlehem Steel did find a league, joining the National Association Foot Ball League for the 1917-18 season. In the meanwhile, the lack of a league made for an interesting and different season in 1916-17. In the 1915-16 season, Bethlehem Steel had played 20 games against teams from Pennsylvania and 11 against teams from elsewhere. In 1916-17, the numbers were roughly reversed, with 14 against teams from Pennsylvania and 22 against teams from elsewhere.

Many of those games were played elsewhere. Of the many road trips, two in particular were demonstrations of one way in which soccer was viewed differently in 1916 than it is today. Today, professional soccer teams never play games on consecutive days. Even college teams rarely do, and the NCAA long ago gave up the practice of playing the semifinals and final of the national collegiate championship on consecutive days. But twice early in the 1916-17 season, once in mid-October and once in late December, Bethlehem Steel made trips that involved games on *three* consecutive days (plus more than a little traveling).

The first of those was a journey to New England that began with a game in New Bedford, Mass., on Thursday, Oct. 12 (Columbus Day was a major holiday in Massachusetts). Bethlehem Steel won impressively, beating New Bedford FC by 3-0. A day later in Fall River, Mass., about 25 miles from New Bedford, the Steelworkers got another shutout, 4-0 over Fall River Pan-American, a team that had taken its name after a soccer victory at the Pan-American Exposition in Buffalo, N.Y., in 1900.

The third game was against J&P Coats in Pawtucket, R.I. The *South Bethlehem Globe* called it "the hardest one of the trip, the Steelworkers having to play practically the pick of the New England states, the J&P Coats' management having gotten permission from the United States Football Association to use several professional players from the leading teams in that part of the country."[28] The Pawtucket team took a 1-0 lead 10 minutes into the second half, but Bethlehem rallied with two goals from Whitey Fleming and one from Harry Ratican to gain a 3-2 victory.

Ratican, Bethlehem's newest star, was particularly in the spotlight on Bethlehem's next long trip, which featured two games in Ratican's hometown, St. Louis. Ratican was among the first major stars in American soccer who had been born in the United States. He played for one of the best St. Louis teams, Ben Millers, from 1911 to 1915 before moving east, and the 1916-17 season was the first of three that he played for Bethlehem Steel.

By the time Bethlehem Steel left on its western trip, which began with a game in Chicago on Dec. 23, 1916, Bethlehem's undefeated streak had grown to 40 games and was threatening to overtake the 41 games of the 1914-15 streak. On Dec. 23 in Chicago, goals by Neil Clarke and George McKelvey enabled Bethlehem to beat a Chicago All-Star team, 2-1, and tie the streak record.

A tie was as far as it got. After an all-night train trip from Chicago to St. Louis, Bethlehem dominated the first half against a St. Louis all-star team, leading by 1-0 on a goal by Ratican, and seemed en route to certain victory. The *South Bethlehem Globe* described the turnabout in the second half, in which all five players in the St. Louis forward line switched positions: "One could have written his own ticket on the outcome at the end of the half, but when the All-Stars came on the field for the second half they presented a rearranged forward line and the fans' hope revived a trifle . . . . Thirty seconds after the kick-off it was evident that a marvelous change had been wrought in both the execution and spirit of the home team. The Stars played a whirlwind but systematic football and the visitors were swept off their feet by the fierce attack."[29]

St. Louis came out a 3-1 winner that day, and Bethlehem Steel's streak was ended. On Christmas Day, Bethlehem played a 2-2 tie with Ben Millers, on the same field where it had lost the day before. Ratican got one of the Bethlehem goals against his former teammates. The *South Bethlehem Globe* declined to blame the disappointing results on the strain of travel and was magnanimous in its assessment of St. Louis soccer, saying: "St. Louis now has a legitimate claim to premier ranking in soccer, having taken the series with the champion. You might even go so far as to credit six of the seven goals to St. Louis, for Harry Ratican, a local product, counted two of the Bethlehem markers. Take it any way you wish, you must award the crown to St. Louis."[30]

The trips to New England and the midwest accounted for only six of the 26 friendlies that Bethlehem played in that season without a league. Those friendlies included a number against teams from the NAFBL, the league they were to join the following season, and a 2-0 victory over Ben Millers when the St. Louisans came east in April. But the Steelworkers' main target still was the National Challenge Cup (which St. Louis teams were not yet entering). Their devotion to that competition brought about what may have been the most demoralizing defeat they suffered in their entire history.

On May 5, 1917 in Pawtucket, Bethlehem Steel seemed poised to claim its third consecutive National Challenge Cup. It had won its games in the first five rounds of that event by a total of 19-2. It was facing the Fall River Rovers, the same team it had beaten in the cup final the year before. It hadn't been defeated in 15 games since the loss in St. Louis more than four months before. It was undone by one of the most surprising goals in American soccer history.

Bethlehem certainly hadn't taken an easy route to the final. Of its five earlier victories, the last four had been against strong teams, 3-1 over Brooklyn Celtic, 3-0 over West Hudson, 2-1 over Homestead Steel and a resounding 6-0 over Joliet Steel in the semifinals.

The goal that ended that run in disappointment was scored by Thomas Swords, the captain of the Fall River team, less than a minute into the final, and gave the Rovers a startling 1-0 victory. The *Newark Evening News* carried a good account of the game:

> The early lead secured by the Rovers caused the Bethlehem aggregation to put up a hard battle throughout the contest. The Rovers started with a rush. The Rovers kicked off, Landy passing to Sullivan. The ball was then swung over to Swords, who eluded the backs and gave Duncan no chance to save.
>
> It was following this goal that the battle started in earnest. For the remainder of the game the spectators were treated to one of the great exhibitions of soccer football ever given in New England. There was not a dull moment. The Bethlehem players fought hard to even up the count and the Rovers tried just as hard to add another goal for the purpose of making victory more secure . . . .
>
> While it was the unanimous opinion that Bethlehem outplayed the Rovers fully eight-five minutes out of ninety, the goal at the start proved enough to win.[31]

There was some dispute over whether the Rovers, in the course of protecting a one-goal lead for more than 89 minutes, had simply played good defense or had overstepped that. It seems to have depended on one's viewpoint. The *Newark Evening News* and the *South Bethlehem Globe* printed very similar stories about the game, certainly by the same writer, perhaps the very same story before they were edited at each newspaper. Each story dealt with the question of the Rovers' tactics in the last sentence of the next-to-last paragraph. The Newark paper said: "Some of the Bethlehem players complained to Referee Taylor that the Rovers were playing roughly, but the complaint was not noticed."[32] The South Bethlehem paper said: "The Rovers tried all kinds of tactics which were not in the laws of the game and Referee Taylor was not too strict with them, Sullivan and Swords being the worst offenders."[33]

Perhaps the most important factor in Bethlehem's downfall, more than any tactics, legal or not, by the Rovers, was the fact that its shooting touch in front of the Fall River goal was badly inaccurate on this day.

The biggest prize was gone, but still there was the AFA Cup final to be played a week later. Bethlehem had been given some good battles in earlier rounds, particularly a quarterfinal on Jan. 28 at Harlem Field in New York. The New York FC, a relatively new club that had played before this season under the name New York Continentals, had taken the lead in the first half and held that lead 20 minutes into the second half before Bethlehem tied it at 1-1. George McKelvey then got the winning goal, taking advantage of a slip by a New York defender.

Bethlehem's semifinal was easier, 5-0 over Clan McDonald of Brooklyn on a neutral site in East Newark, N.J. The final was easier yet, 7-0 over West Hudson on a supposedly neutral site in Newark, only a few miles from Harrison. Bethlehem led by 3-0 at halftime and coasted to victory. Said the *Bethlehem Globe*: "It took Bethlehem 17 minutes to score its first goal, by McKelvey, but after that it was a procession."[34]

Despite the victory in the final game, it had not been the happiest of seasons for Bethlehem Steel. There was the lack of a league to play in. There was the defeat in St. Louis and the end of the unbeaten streak. There was the stunning upset in the National Challenge Cup final. And there had been the death on April 13 of Harry Trend, the manager of the company athletic program and one of the leaders of the soccer team. Trend, who died of pneumonia, was only 34.

Bethlehem Steel had a happier time in the 1917-18 season. The classic team photo of Bethlehem Steel was taken at the end of this season, with the players surrounding the two pieces of silverware they had just claimed, the National Challenge Cup and the AFA Cup. They nearly had a third, but an unfavorable ruling on a protest cost them the National Association Foot Ball League title.

The National Challenge Cup tournament was very similar to the previous year for the Steelworkers. Again they drew relatively easy assignments in the early rounds, faced Joliet Steel in the semifinals and faced Fall River Rovers in the final.

The first two rounds consisted of a first-round bye followed by a second-round meeting in early December with Veteran of Philadelphia, the same team that Bethlehem had eliminated from the AFA Cup five weeks before. The result was the same, although the 2-0 win was less impressive than the 7-0 score in the AFA Cup. The assignments got tougher in the third round, which brought on Disston. This game on Jan. 10, 1918 marked the fourth time that Bethlehem Steel had played Disston in just two months. The first of those was a stunning 3-1 defeat in an NAFBL game, one of the two defeats that doomed Bethlehem to second place in its first season in that league. There then followed a friendly at Franklin Field in Philadelphia, a war relief benefit that finally was abandoned in the midst of a blizzard with Bethlehem leading, 3-2, in the middle of the second half. Bethlehem got its revenge for the league defeat by beating Disston, 4-0, in a league game at Steel Field on Christmas Day.

The National Challenge Cup meeting was on Disston's field in Northeast Philadelphia, where the Sawmakers had scored their 3-1 victory in November. They almost got another win, forcing overtime by scoring a tying goal with less than a minute to play. But Harry Ratican's overtime goal gave Bethlehem the 2-1 victory. After that, the quarterfinals pitted Bethlehem against another Western Pennsylvania team, McKeesport, but this meeting proved relatively easy, a 5-0 victory on a muddy field in McKeesport, Pa.

As had been the case a year before, Joliet brought its press clippings east for the semifinal at Steel Field, but little else. Once again they arrived in Bethlehem with an undefeated record and once again they left without it. Whitey Fleming scored the first goal of the game in the eighth minute, got two more in the second half, and Bethlehem Steel walked off a 4-0 victor.

The final was again in Pawtucket, on the same field where Bethlehem Steel and Fall River Rovers had met in the last two finals. Once again, it was a titantic struggle, but this time it failed to produce a result. According to the *Bethlehem Globe*, "For more than three-fifths of the game, the Steel Workers did the attacking but over-anxiety prevented them from scoring on many occasions."[35] All four goals came in the first half. Whitey Fleming in the fourth minute and Harry Ratican in the 30th scored for Bethlehem, but both times Fall River tied the score. The last 75 minutes, of which 30 were in overtime, produced no more goals.

The Fall River team, which used every ounce of energy it had in beating Bethlehem in the 1917 final, seems to have done so again in gaining the tie a year later. It had nothing left for the replay, which took place two weeks later in Harrison, N.J., on the same plot of land where Bethlehem had played some memorable games in the past, including its 1907 debut. What stood there now was the Federal League baseball park, built for the Newark Peppers of the league that briefly challenged the existing structure in major-league baseball. The *Newark Evening News* left no doubt about Bethlehem Steel's superiority in the 3-0 replay: "The New Englanders were completely outclassed, and the 2-2 tie which the finalists played at Pawtucket, R.I., two weeks ago could only be accounted for by conceding the runner-up team a complete reversal of form since the Down East meeting . . . . Excepting only a few minutes, play was almost entirely in Fall River territory, and, when, in their widely separated spasms of offensive play, the Rovers carried the ball toward the steel men's goal there was always awaiting them that seemingly impenetrable defense which made their best efforts go for naught."[36] The caption under a cartoon accompanying the *Evening News'* story put it more succinctly when it said, referring to Bethlehem goalkeeper Bill Duncan, that "Kicking Duncan into the net was the nearest the Rovers came to scoring."[37]

Ratican scored two of the Bethlehem goals. In the 29th minute, he ran down a long free kick by Jock Ferguson and took advantage of some hesitation in the Fall River defense to shoot home. In the middle of the second half, he tapped the ball in after Fleming had done some brilliant work in breaking free and crossing the ball into the goalmouth. In between, Fleming scored after his penalty shot was saved but rebounded right to him.

The AFA Cup featured a semifinal clash with Disston, which was running a close second to Fall River Rovers as Bethlehem's biggest rival. The 7-0 victory over Philadelphia Veteran in the first round was followed by a forfeit win over Pan-American of Fall River in the second round and a 5-0 rout of New York IRT in the quarterfinals. By the time Bethlehem met Disston in the semifinals in late April, Disston was the one that was seeking revenge. The Sawmakers had lost to Bethlehem three times in a row in December and January, the third of those defeats knocking them out of the National Challenge Cup.

Even so, Disston should not have been such a difficult hurdle for Bethlehem. As the *Bethlehem Globe* noted, "Disstons were badly riddled by the draft and enlistment . . . . The Disstons have lost eight of its players since the season opened."[38] Despite those departures, Disston almost beat Bethlehem in that semifinal at Steel Field. An early Disston goal held up until a few minutes were left before Fred Pepper tied the game off a corner kick by Jimmy Murphy. After 30 minutes of overtime, the score was 2-2 and a replay was necessary. The Steelworkers left it late in that one, too, with Harry Ratican scoring the deciding goal of a 1-0 victory in the last minute of play

The final a month later in Pawtucket was more of the same. The final was against Babcock & Wilcox of Bayonne, N.J., a team Bethlehem had twice beaten by 4-0 earlier that season in NAFBL play. Again the game seemed headed for overtime before Bethlehem gained the winning goal with two minutes left. Whitey Fleming's corner kick was headed home by center half Jim Campbell, who was playing his fourth season in Bethlehem but had never before scored a goal for the Steelworkers.

In reporting on the final and reviewing the season, the *Bethlehem Globe* conceded a significant advantage that the war had given Bethlehem Steel when it said: "The Bethlehem team was also fortunate in keeping the squad intact all through the season. They have not lost a player, either through enlistment or the draft. Most all of the other teams were greatly handicapped in having to take the field toward the close of the season minus a good many of their regular players."[39]

Bethlehem had its double, taking both cups for the second time in three years, but a triple was not to be. Ever since the 3-1 loss to Disston on Nov. 10, Bethlehem had been battling neck-and-neck in the NAFBL standings with Paterson FC, which was starting to assert itself as the leading New Jersey team. It seemed that the Steelworkers might succeed in that struggle before a 4-2 loss to West Hudson on May 12 set them back again. That defeat came one day short of the first anniversary of Bethlehem's 7-0 win over West Hudson in the 1917 AFA Cup final, and the Bethlehem players may have been wishing they hadn't run the score up quite so high the year before.

Bethlehem's loss to West Hudson enabled Paterson to regain the lead. Bethlehem got it back with a 2-0 victory over Paterson on June 8, but the ruling that relegated Bethlehem to second place came six days later. A committee of the U.S. Football Association ruled that New York F.C. had used an ineligible player in a victory over Paterson earlier in the season, and the points that Paterson gained when that loss was turned into a forfeit victory gave it the NAFBL title.

Bethlehem Steel did get that triple in the 1918-19 season, when it enjoyed its best campaign yet. By this time, the war was having a big effect on American soccer, and Bethlehem Steel was reaping substantial benefit from the draft protection that it afforded its workers. At one point, according to the *Bethlehem Globe*, of 45,000 registered soccer players in the country, 18,000 were in uniform and more than 1,000 teams had been forced to disband for lack of players. The war ended about six weeks after Bethlehem Steel started its season, but the war's effects on soccer lasted well beyond the Nov. 11, 1918 armistice, particularly because of the time it took for soldiers to be mustered back into civilian life and the misnamed Spanish influenza epidemic.

Bethlehem Steel had to go to some lengths to maintain the protection against the draft that its war work enabled it to confer on soccer players. In 1918, teams were cropping up among shipyards, which afforded better protection than did Bethlehem Steel because nearly all the work going on in shipyards at that time was war related. Players from many clubs were flocking to the shipyard teams, and in the summer of 1918 Bethlehem team officials felt it necessary to deny that any Bethlehem players were among them. The *Bethlehem Globe* cited Billy Sheridan, Bethlehem's manager of athletics, as its source when it said that "the team will remain intact . . . . there is little likelihood of any of the players being induced to leave Bethlehem to take up work in any of the shipbuilding plants, especially as all the players were working on munitions and having been classified as such prevents them from being drafted."[40] The fact that every one of the soccer players was working on munitions was quite a coincidence—or maybe not.

The impact of the draft was considerably more pronounced in baseball than in soccer. Robert Creamer described it in *Babe*, a biography of Babe Ruth:

> There was no notable shortage of labor in essential industry, but Secretary of War Newton Baker, reflecting on the mood of the times, decided [in 1918] to issue a "work or fight" order. Draft-age men engaged in nonproductive work were liable to be drafted, even if they had been deferred previously. In theory, the order was designed to keep factories, steel mills, shipyards, munitions plants and the like well supplied with the workers they might need. In practice, it was to prevent able-bodied men of soldierly age from engaging in frivolous pursuits while their contemporaries were fighting and dying in France—or working behind a desk at the Brooklyn Navy Yard.
>
> The responsibility of executing the work-or-fight rule lay with the Provost Marshal of the army, General Enoch Crowder, who was

in charge of the draft. Anyone born after 1900 would be hard pressed to identify Crowder today, but the men who played baseball during World War I remembered him beyond Pershing, Foch, Joffre, Von Hindenburg or any of the other history-book generals. As the man in charge of the draft, he was the one the ballplayers [and soccer players] were aware of. A decade later when a fine righthanded pitcher named Alvin Crowder came into the American League he was instantly nicknamed General.

When the work-or-fight order was pronounced in the spring of 1918, local draft boards moved quickly to demonstrate their patriotism, and ballplayers who had thought themselves immune from service were advised that they were now subject to being called to military duty . . . . There were plenty of farm boys in the major leagues, and because farming was deemed productive they began to leave for home and the plow. Others looked for jobs in factories. Some went to work at steel mills and shipyards, particularly mills and shipyards that happened to have fast semipro baseball teams. Indeed, some mills and shipyards actively proselytized major league players.[41]

Three big-league baseball stars are known to have played for Bethlehem Steel units, Babe Ruth and Dutch Leonard of the Boston Red Sox and Shoeless Joe Jackson of the Chicago White Sox. Leonard left the Red Sox in June 1918, a few weeks after pitching three straight shutouts, one of which was a no-hitter. He spent the rest of the 1918 season working at, and playing baseball for, Bethlehem's Fore River Shipyard in Quincy, Mass., just south of Boston. Jackson, just a year away from infamy for his part in the Black Sox scandal, played briefly for Bethlehem's Harlan & Hollingsworth shipyard in Wilmington, Del.

Ruth, according to biographer Leigh Montville, "wound up in Lebanon, Pennsylvania, on the books as an employee of Bethlehem Steel . . . . He took the long route to his new job, playing a couple of exhibitions in New Haven and Hartford, then left Lebanon to play another one in Baltimore, where he wrenched his knee. Singeing his hand in a kitchen accident and catching the flu again limited him to one game for the steel plant against a barnstorming group of his Red Sox teammates."[42] Then came the armistice, the end of the draft and the end of Ruth's days as a Bethlehem Steel employee.

The armistice did not mean the end of the flu, which affected soccer teams, baseball teams and every other sort of activity, athletic or otherwise. The Spanish influenza pandemic of 1918-20 is considered the worst in human history and is believed to have killed between 50 million and 100 million people around the world. The flu did not come from Spain. It got its name because it was most widely reported in Spain, which was not a combatant in World War I and thus not affected by wartime censorship of news reports. It also wasn't caused by the war, although battlefield conditions and close quarters may have helped to spread it. The Bethlehem Steel soccer team did not suffer any casualties as a result of the flu, but the city of Bethlehem was not unaffected. The number of deaths is not known, but the city did impose a quarantine that resulted in all bars, movie theaters, soda fountains, ice cream parlors and schools being closed from Oct. 4, 1918 to Nov. 6, 1918.[43]

There wasn't any soccer in Bethlehem during that month of quarantine, either. Bethlehem Steel's only game during October was on the road, and it didn't play a home game between Sept. 28 and Nov. 9. When activity at Steel Field did resume, it was a National Challenge Cup game against the confusingly named New York Shipbuilding team of Camden, N.J. This was one of the shipyard teams that had sprung up as a result of the draft, and its lineup included none other than Thomas Swords, who had captained the Fall River Rovers in three National Challenge Cup finals against Bethlehem and scored the winning goal in one of those. Fall River Rovers had disbanded after the 1917-18 season. They were re-formed after the war, but folded again for good in 1921.

Two weeks after disposing of New York Ship, 3-0, in the first round of the National Challenge Cup, Bethlehem played its second-round game against another of the new shipyard teams, Merchant Ship of Bristol, Pa. That resulted in a 4-3 victory, after which Bethlehem Steel's sights turned westward. The Steelworkers gained a forfeit victory over Homestead Steel of Pittsburgh in the third round of the National Challenge Cup, a 5-0 victory over Akron Goodyear of Ohio in the quarterfinals and a 5-0 victory over Chicago Bricklayers in the semifinals. Along the way, they had another holiday trip to St. Louis, where they scored a 3-0 victory over the Innisfails club, were held to a 1-1 tie by a St. Louis All-Star team and were beaten by the All-Stars, 4-3, on New Year's Day.

The National Challenge Cup final on April 19, 1919 in Fall River was against Paterson FC, now Bethlehem's most serious rival for major honors. Paterson FC, founded only two years before after the True Blues folded, had become the dominant team in New Jersey soccer. The team had picked up some of its best players from clubs that

110

were foundering in those war years. The most noteworthy were Archie Stark and Davey Brown, who were to become the two most spectacular goalscorers in American soccer in the coming decade, with more than 440 American Soccer League goals between them. Stark, formerly of Kearny Scots, who had folded a few months before, and Brown, formerly of West Hudson, which had folded the year before, also played a few games for Bethlehem in 1919. Both Paterson stars were invited to accompany the Steelworkers on that summer's Scandinavian tour as guest players.

Paterson gave Bethlehem a close game in the National Challenge Cup final, although poor play by Bethlehem in the first half may have been the main cause of that. "In the first half of the game Paterson was the aggressor," the *Bethlehem Globe* said, "and Bethlehem seemed unable to settle down to their accustomed stride and only cool work on the part of Duncan, Wilson, Ferguson and Campbell prevented the champions from being scored upon. In the second half Bethlehem seemed to be an entirely different team and every man settled down to playing his part, with the result that Paterson was seldom in evidence."[44]

Bethlehem opened the scoring 15 minutes into the second half, when George McKelvey shot home after a free kick by James Wilson had been sent on to him by William Forrest and Fred Pepper. The second goal came with just two minutes left in the game. With Paterson pressing forward looking for an equalizer, McKelvey and Harry Ratican were given an opportunity for a breakaway that produced a goal for Ratican.

The same two teams, featuring 20 of the same 22 players, met again a week later in the AFA Cup final in Philadelphia. The score was the same, 2-0 for Bethlehem, and unsurprisingly the game apparently was an anti-climax, without the drama and desperate effort by Paterson that had been in evidence a week before. Bethlehem was in control throughout and prepared to head for Scandinavia as a triple champion.

Supposedly, the National Challenge Cup was the tougher competition of the two, but Bethlehem had not had the same sort of easy time in the early rounds of the AFA Cup that it had in the early rounds for the National Challenge Cup. The toughest test came in the semifinals on March 16 in Harrison, N.J., against Robins Dry Dock of Brooklyn, which was one of Bethlehem's rivals in the NAFBL, having taken over the Kearny Scots' franchise when that club dropped out of the league in January 1919.

"Rain fell during the greater part of the game," said the *Bethlehem Globe*, "and although the slippery conditions made the footing uncertain, the spectators were treated to a clever and hard fought exhibition of soccer. The Robins took the lead in the first five minutes of play and by valiant defense work were able to maintain it for the greater part of the game. With but twenty minutes to go in the second half, the Robins still in the lead, Bethlehem's superior condition began to tell."[45]

Robins' goal had come after a miskicked clearance by Fred Pepper in the Bethlehem goalmouth allowed the ball to fall to Ed Duffy for a point-blank shot. Whitey Fleming finally tied the game in the 70th minute after a long pass from Jock Ferguson set him free in front of the Robins goal. After a Robins goal had been called back for offside a few minutes after Fleming's goal, Harry Ratican put Bethlehem into the lead by converting a pass from Bob Millar. The lead didn't last long, as Duffy got his second goal after a clearance dropped at his feet for an unmarked shot.

With seven minutes left, after another offside goal, this time by Bethlehem, Harry Ratican scored the game winner. George McKelvey beat a Robins player to the ball on the right wing and centered to Ratican, who again put the ball into the net. Robins tried to tie the score again, but the closest there was to another goal was yet another goal called back for offside, again by Ratican.

It would be nice to say that Bethlehem got its third championship the same way it got the other two, with Paterson FC as the runnerup. This would be an exaggeration, however. Bethlehem ran away with the National Association Foot Ball League title, clinching with more than two months left in the season.

The Steelworkers started their NAFBL schedule with five victories in a row, outscoring those hapless victims by 25-0. They clinched the championship, their first league title in three years, on the first weekend of March. They needed a victory over New York FC on the Saturday followed by a Paterson FC loss to Merchant Ship on the Sunday to wrap up the title. They got both, which left them with an unassailable lead. They finished the season with 19 points in the standings, to 11 each for Paterson and Merchant Ship. They did sort of complete the circle by beating Paterson in the final game of the season, but the score was 2-1 this time, not 2-0.

With its three championships, Bethlehem Steel sailed off to Scandinavia as the champion of American soccer, unquestioned in most places. There had been talk the previous December of a trip to California for a game against the team from the Union Iron Works shipyard in San Francisco, which was owned by Bethlehem Steel and had easily been San Francisco's best in the 1917-18 season.[46] California teams were still 40 years away from beginning to compete in the U.S. Open Cup, but Union Iron Works proposed a meeting with Bethlehem's National Challenge Cup winners,which it said would decide the soccer championship of the United States. It seems likely that the claim by Union Iron Works, which had never played eastern competition, to be worthy of challenging Bethlehem Steel would have met the same dismal fate as did the Bethlehem Football Club's venture against West Hudson in 1907, although the possibility of an upset did exist. The trip was called off, however, for what were called financial reasons, probably meaning that Bethlehem Steel decided not to take on the expense of a trip on which its team would have had nothing to gain and everything to lose. And thus, there was one corner of American soccer that did not feel that its champion was being sent to face the Scandinavians.

Bethlehem Steel was the first American soccer club ever to undertake an overseas tour. However, this was not unplowed ground. In fact, the Scandinavian destination of this tour was chosen specifically because that route had been pioneered by the United States national team, playing under the name of the All-American Football Club, when it toured Sweden and Norway in 1916. That 1916 tour had been undertaken in the midst of World War I. Sweden and Norway both were neutrals in that war, as was the United States in 1916, the year before it entered the war on the allied side. By 1919, the war was over and there no longer was a need to find neutral opponents as there had been in 1916. Still, the success of the 1916 tour and the contacts established during it made the decision to return to Scandinavia a natural one. Rumors of the tour had been heard in Bethlehem for several months before it was officially announced on April 19, after Bethlehem had retained its national championship by beating Paterson in the National Challenge Cup final.

The majority of the 1916 Bethlehem Steel team had not been eligible for the 1916 tour, as they were British citizens, although some of them did later become naturalized Americans. There were two Bethlehem players on that tour, however, midfielders Tom Murray and Neil Clarke. Clarke was no longer with Bethlehem Steel by the time of the 1919 tour, but Murray was, having just returned from serving in the army during the war, and went on this tour. The 17 players in the Bethlehem party that sailed from New York on July 23, 1919 included six who were not regular Bethlehem players but were invited on this tour as guests. Four of those six had been on the 1916 tour: Albert Blakey and George Tintle, both just out of the army, John "Rabbit" Heminsley of Merchant Shipyard and James Robertson of Robins Dry Dock in Brooklyn. The other two guests were Archie Stark and Davey Brown, both of the Paterson team that Bethlehem had beaten in both cup finals a few months before. The inclusion of those two enabled Bethlehem Steel to field a forward line twice in the 14-game tour that included four future Hall of Famers, Stark, Brown, Harry Ratican and Whitey Fleming. That may have been the most powerful group of forwards ever to play for the same club team in American soccer history. In the days when the normal soccer formation included five forwards, the only other club to include four future Hall of Famers in its forward line was the 1930 Fall River Marksmen team that had forwards Alex McNab, Billy Gonsalves, Bert Patenaude and Werner Nilsen.[47]

Besides the six guest players, the touring team included 11 Bethlehem players: Fleming, Ratican (who had already announced that he was leaving), Murray, Bill Duncan, Fred Pepper, Jimmy Wilson, Jock Ferguson, Jim Campbell, George McKelvey, William Forrest and Sam Fletcher. The four officials were Thomas W. Cahill of the U.S. Football Association, who served as manager of the team; Billy Sheridan, manager of Bethlehem's athletic programs and the trainer of this team; Ernest Viberg, a New York soccer official who had been born in Sweden and served as interpreter and business manager, and Sune Stearn, a Swedish-born masseur from New York.

This was Cahill's second time leading an American team to Scandinavia. The fact that he had been manager of the 1916 team was a significant factor in why he was chosen to be manager of this one even though he had no regular connection with Bethlehem Steel.

Among the many hats that Cahill wore in American soccer at this time, the most important was as secretary of the U.S. Football Association, an organization in whose formation six years earlier he had been a prime mover.[48] Cahill had grown up in St. Louis, been an outstanding runner and soccer player there in his younger days and formed the Shamrocks soccer team that won city championships in 1899 and 1900. He and another St. Louis man, Winston Barker, were instrumental in organizing and financing the Pilgrims tours of 1905 and 1909 that did much to advance soccer in the United States.[49]

In 1910, Cahill moved east as part of his job with the Spalding sporting goods company, and two years later was the man who attended the FIFA Congress in Stockholm on behalf of the newly-formed American Amateur Football Association, seeking FIFA membership and eventually brokering the United States' entry into that body. Cahill was the first secretary of the USFA and served three times in that post, 1913-21, 1922-24 and 1929-31.

He also was editor of the annual *Spalding Guide*, a huge compilation of information on the sport published annually in the early decades of the 20th century, and secretary and chief organizer of the American Soccer League, which began play in the fall of 1921. James Robinson noted in his 1966 doctoral dissertation, *The History of Soccer in the City of St. Louis*, that Cahill's time with the USFA was not always placid, saying: "When Mr. Cahill was ousted [in 1924] as national secretary from the United States Football Association for what Mr. Peter J. Peel, its president, called insubordination, incompetency and tyrannical rule, Cahill devoted himself to the American Soccer League. He had organized this circuit and its rapid growth, he felt, had in part caused his removal from office by the National Commission."[50]

As manager of the Bethlehem team on the 1919 tour, Cahill's duties were roughly similar to what now is performed by the general manager of a professional sports team. The duties of what we today call the coach were performed more by trainer Sheridan. The line of demarcation between the two jobs was a bit vague, however.

Today, traveling soccer teams cross the Atlantic in a few hours. In 1919, the Bethlehem team's Swedish-American Line ship left New York on July 23 and didn't dock in Goteborg until 12 days later.

The opening of the tour involved a lot of speech-making: tributes from the guests to the hosts, tributes from the hosts to the guests, declarations about the brotherhood of man and declarations about the wholesomeness of international sports. Eventually, on Aug. 10, they got around to playing soccer.

The first game, between Bethlehem Steel and the Stockholm club Allmanna Idrottsklubben, popularly known as AIK, produced a 2-2 tie that seems to have been disappointing to the Swedish fans. Not disappointing because the local team failed to win, but rather because the visitors failed to be as entertaining as expected. It seems that the Swedes viewed Bethlehem Steel more as a Scottish team than as an American one, and expected more from it than a tie, especially after Bethlehem had scored the opening goal in less than a minute.[51] Eventually, they did get more. Bethlehem Steel finished the tour, which included 13 games in Sweden and one in Denmark, with a record of seven victories, two defeats and five ties. It outscored its opponents, but not overwhelmingly, 22-14. The games drew a total of 154,000 spectators, including 23,000 for that opening game in Stockholm, the largest crowd Bethlehem Steel had ever played in front of.

Perhaps Bethlehem Steel's best game of the 14 came near the middle of the tour, a 4-0 victory over the All-Skane picked team in Helsingborg on Aug. 27 (Skane is the southernmost province of Sweden, and includes the cities of Malmo and Helsingborg). That game was one of the two in which Bethlehem fielded its most star-studded set of forwards, and it showed. Davey Brown and Archie Stark scored in the opening minutes, Harry Ratican got the third goal just before halftime and William Forrest scored the fourth in the second half. The *Spalding Guide* said of the game:

> Bethlehem won its most decisive victory of the tour in the Helsingborg Stadium when it surprised the football followers of all Europe by defeating All-Skane, a strong and carefully selected representative eleven, by 4 goals to 0. In the Helsingborg triumph the tourists played in the best form yet displayed on the tour . . . .
>
> The Bethlehem forwards at once wrested the offensive from the Swedes and pressed hard until it could be seen, as was demonstrated in 1916, that American speed was too great for the Swedish combination football to overcome ["combination" play referred to emphasis on interpassing among players rather than on individual dribbling]. The pace was too stiff for the home team and Bethlehem soon found opportunity to show its own excellent combination work . . . .
>
> The entire Bethlehem forward line played unexcelled football.[52]

The two defeats came in consecutive games, in Malmo on Sept. 3 and Goteborg on Sept. 7. After that, the Steelworkers righted themselves and outscored the Swedes by 7-2 over the last five games of the tour. The tour ended on Sept. 24 the same way it had begun, with a tie at the Olympic Stadium in Stockholm. This time, the opponent was Hammarby, another top Stockholm club. Bethlehem made some unusual innovations to its lineup for the scoreless draw. Archie Stark, eventually to become one of the greatest goalscorers in American soccer history, played center half. George Tintle, perhaps the greatest American goalkeeper of his day, played forward. Surprisingly, Bethlehem's two leading scorers on the tour did not come from among its four superstar forwards, but rather were Rabbit Heminsley with eight goals and William Forrest with five.

Stark, who played very well on the tour, had been with Paterson FC for only one season after returning from serving in the army during the war. He been expected to stay with Bethlehem after the Scandinavian tour. Just a few days before Bethlehem opened its 1919-20 season with a friendly against the University of Pennsylvania team in late October, it still was expected that he would be in the Bethlehem lineup. But he changed his mind at the last minute, and the next time Bethlehem saw him he was in an opposing uniform, playing for Erie AA of Kearny against the Steelworkers.

The tour had been perhaps the highlight of Bethlehem's reign at the top of American soccer. Disappointments, at least by Bethlehem standards, were ahead, and the loss of Archie Stark to Erie was only one of them.

Steel Field, now Moravian College's football stadium, still looked much the same in 2008 (bottom photo) as it had when the Bethlehem Steel team was playing there in 1918 (top photo). (*Courtesy of Dan Morrison*)

Leaders of their teams on the field and off, and sometimes both, included (clockwise from top left) Edgar Lewis, Clive Toye, Archie Stark, and Giorgio Chinaglia. (*All photos courtesy of National Soccer Hall of Fame*)

Giants Stadium, part of the Meadowlands sports complex in East Rutherford, N.J., was the Cosmos' home from 1977 to 1985 and the scene of their greatest glory years. *(Courtesy of the National Soccer Hall of Fame)*

Giorgio Chinaglia joined two of his bosses, Steve Ross (right) and Cosmos president Rafael De la Sierra, to watch a practice from the bench at Giants Stadium. *(Courtesy of the National Soccer Hall of Fame).*

Pelé attempts to dribble between a pair of Dallas Tornado defenders during his debut game with the Cosmos in 1975. Pelé scored one of the Cosmos goals in a 2-2 tie. *(Courtesy of the National Soccer Hall of Fame)*

Bethlehem Steel's works in South Bethlehem around 1910. The main visible thing that is no longer there is the forest of smoke stacks rising from the open-hearth furnaces. *(Courtesy of Bethlehem Steel Collection, National Canal Museum, Easton, Pa.)*

Bethlehem's team, already including future Hall of Famers Edgar Lewis, Bobby Morrison, Whitey Fleming and Ned Donaghy, was a rugged-looking bunch in 1913. *(Courtesy of Dan Morrison)*

Meeting in Brazil during the negotiations in the spring of 1975 that
brought Pelé to the Cosmos were (from left) Pelé, Nesuhi Ertegun, Clive
Toye and Pelé's brother Zoca. *(Courtesy of National Soccer Hall of Fame)*

A celebration in the Cosmos' locker room after Pelé's 1,250th goal in 1975
included (from left) Clive Toye, Jay Emmett, Pelé, Julio Mazzei, Steve
Ross and Gordon Bradley. *(Courtesy of Clive Toye)*

Frantz Mathieu of the Chicago Sting, the Cosmos' most difficult opponent, dives in front of Giorgio Chinaglia to head the ball away from danger during a 1981 game. *(Courtesy of National Soccer Hall of Fame)*

Pelé walks onto the field at Randall's Island before the start of his first game with the Cosmos in June 1975. Clive Toye, at lower left, looks immensely pleased by it all. *(Courtesy of National Soccer Hall of Fame)*

The Bethlehem Steel team and officials, a traveling party that included no fewer than seven future Hall of Famers, posed for a group photograph in Sweden in 1919. *(Courtesy of Dan Morrison)*

The Steelworkers were backed by Bethlehem Steel officials and surrounded an impressive collection of silverware on the steps of a company building in 1915. *(Courtesy of Dan Morrison)*

Pelé, who was still without an NASL championship going into his final season with the Cosmos, hoisted the trophy after the Cosmos' victory in the 1977 NASL final in Portland. *(Courtesy of National Soccer Hall of Fame)*

Clive Toye casts a skeptical eye on the proceedings at Randall's Island. Beside him are Gordon Bradley (right), the Cosmos first coach, and Jorge Siega, their first player. *(Courtesy of National Soccer Hall of Fame)*

Archie Stark wore a Bethlehem Steel uniform for the first time as a guest player during the 1919 Scandinavian tour, but didn't join the team full-time until five years later. *(Courtesy of National Soccer Hall of Fame)*

Pelé attempts, with only moderate success, to teach President Ford how to juggle a soccer ball during his White House visit shortly after signing with the Cosmos in 1975. *(Courtesy of National Soccer Hall of Fame)*

FIVE

The Greatest Show
on Earth

In the summer of 1976, the New York Cosmos had moved out of the low-rent district of Randalls Island to Yankee Stadium, which they shared with another famous team. Despite being in different sports, there were a fair number of similarities between the Cosmos and the New York Yankees. One of those was that both had owners who loved the spotlight and meddled constantly in on-the-field affairs that should have been the province of players, coaches and managers.

The more famous of those two owners was the Yankees' George Steinbrenner, who was to become perhaps the most legendary "meddling owner" in American sports history. But, as strange as it may seem to those who have watched Steinbrenner in amazement over the years, he may have been the more laid back of the two at Yankee Stadium that summer. When it came to the Cosmos, Steve Ross didn't know when to quit.

While Ross had been constrained by the funeral-home business and the parking-lot business, getting into movies with the purchase of Warner Brothers in 1969 enabled his outsized personality to break free. But despite the opportunity to rub shoulders with the likes of Frank Sinatra and Cary Grant, he was a movie mogul second and a sports fan first. Warner's purchase of the Cosmos in 1970 got him into the sports business through a side door, although he would have preferred an NFL team. The Cosmos' signing of Pelé in 1975 projected him into the big time. Suddenly the NASL was no longer a backwater. By 1976, when Pelé was joined by Giorgio Chinaglia in the Cosmos' lineup, Ross had a front-page team at his command.

There seem to be three main characteristics of "meddling own-ers." One is feuding with referees and league officials in the manner of Mark Cuban, who has owned the Dallas Mavericks of the NBA since 2000. Another is getting involved in players' personal lives in the manner of Steinbrenner and Charles O. Finley, who bought the Kansas City Athletics baseball team in 1960, moved it to Oakland in 1968 and finally sold it in 1980. The third is taking a hand in game decisions in the manner of Ted Turner, who owned the Atlanta Braves from 1976 to 1996.

Cuban, who made his money in high-definition television, sits in a seat behind the Mavericks' bench at games and keeps up a constant barrage of yelling at the referees. Not only do the referees not like it, it has bothered Cuban's own players as well. In 2006, Mavericks star Dirk Nowitzki talked to the *Dallas Morning News* about the owner's courtside behavior. "He's got to learn how to control himself as well as the players do," Nowitzki said. "We can't lose our temper all the time on the court or off the court, and I think he's got to learn that, too. He's got to improve in that area and not yell at the officials the whole game."[1]

Finley was particularly good at irritating his players. Ken Harrelson called Finley "a menace to baseball" and was released by the A's after leading a player rebellion over a fine against one of them.[2] Reggie Jackson said that "Finley takes all the fun out of winning" after the 1973 World Series, which the A's won despite Finley's attempt to force second baseman Mike Andrews onto the injured list after he had made two errors.[3] Pitcher Vida Blue said after a 1972 salary dispute that Finley "has soured my stomach for baseball" and "treated me like a damn colored boy."[4] Politicians got into the act, too. In 1967, Sen. Stuart Symington of Missouri called Finley "one of the most disreputable characters ever to enter the American sports scene."[5] Later, after Finley had succeeded in moving his team from Kansas City to Oakland, Symington said that by getting Finley, Oakland had become "the luckiest city since Hiroshima."[6]

Turner once did what many other owners might have liked to. In 1977, he appointed himself "acting manager" of the Braves and took to the dugout for a game.[7] Most of the time, however, he merely gave orders from the owner's box.

Cuban, Finley and Turner are only three of the many obstreperous owners spread across all sports. Baseball has had the lion's share, with Steinbrenner, Finley and Turner being joined by the likes of Marge Schott of the Cincinnati Reds, Peter Angelos of the Baltimore Orioles and Wayne Huizenga of the Florida Marlins. The NFL has some, such as Dan Snyder of the Washington Redskins and Jerry Jones of the Dallas Cowboys. The NASL had Ross and a few others. And foreign soccer has had the likes of Bernard Tapie in France, Silvio Berlusconi in Italy and Vladimir Romanov in Scotland.

Steve Ross really came into his element with the arrival of Pelé in 1975. He was able to bask in the glow of a bigger international celebrity than any of Warner's movie stars, and the show of which he was ringmaster with the Cosmos was getting bigger and bigger. Still, the center of attention in 1975 was Pelé, and Ross remained somewhat in the background that year.

After the famous press conference at 21, Pelé's career with the Cosmos began with a quickly arranged friendly five days later against the Dallas Tornado (Lamar Hunt's team) at Randall's Island. That the game was an exhibition didn't really seem to matter, something that was repeated when David Beckham made his Los Angeles Galaxy debut in 2007. One thing that many Americans have been slow to realize about soccer is that there often are standings involved and that many games have significance beyond that day's score, so the fact that this was only a somewhat meaningless friendly went almost unnoticed. All that mattered was Pelé making his Cosmos debut, and there were 21,278 spectators at Downing Stadium that day, more than triple what the Cosmos had averaged in their five previous games at Randall's Island in 1975.

Any attempt to make the field more presentable to TV viewers via cosmetic means was a failure. The field still looked bizarre. Some areas, particularly in the center circle, were a distinctly darker shade of green than the rest of the field, and those dark areas contained spots that were clearly bare dirt, albeit rather odd-colored dirt.

Still, the game was a public-relations success for the Cosmos. They came from two goals down at halftime to gain a 2-2 tie. Pelé was involved in both of those second-half goals, setting up the first for Mordechai Speigler and scoring the second on a header. That the Tornado tired in the second half is understandable, since they had played a league game in Texas less than 18 hours before.

Pelé was not the only new, Brazilian face in the Cosmos locker room in June of 1975. Julio Mazzei, who was Pelé's closest advisor and had played such a large part in Pelé's decision to sign with the Cosmos, was the number-one figure in the superstar's entourage when he arrived in New York. Mazzei, who was often dubbed Professor Julio Mazzei, a reference to his background as a physical training educator, was to stay with the Cosmos, sometimes in unofficial capacities and twice as coach of the team, for considerably longer than Pelé himself did.

Pelé's first weeks with the Cosmos included some TV appearances, but those were much less glamorous than what was coming. Pelé was invited to the White House to meet President Ford in late June, when the Cosmos were scheduled to play the Washington Diplomats in an NASL game. Pelé and three Cosmos officials flew to Washington the day before the game for the White House meeting. Pelé and the president kicked a ball around the Rose Garden. The cameras clicked for a photo opportunity that may have scored more publicity points for Ford around the world than among American voters. Likely unmentioned at the Republican White House that day was the fact that Pelé's new boss, Steve Ross, was that most unusual creature among corporate tycoons, a significant Democratic Party fundraiser.

The Cosmos' trip to Washington was a landmark one. It included the visit to the White House, the largest crowd of Pelé's first season with the Cosmos (35,620 at RFK) and a 9-2 victory that was the Cosmos' high-water mark of the season, evening their record at 6-6. A lesser occasion had been the previous weekend's visit to Boston, which produced the most dangerous mob scene to which Pelé was subjected in his three seasons with the Cosmos. The game was a clash between Pelé and Portuguese superstar Eusebio, who by then was playing for the Boston Minutemen, and must have been reminiscent to Pelé of the riot-marred meeting between the two in New York in 1966.

The game between the Cosmos and the Boston Minutemen was played at the Boston team's usual home, Nickerson Field, which was the Boston University football stadium and had once been the Boston Braves' baseball stadium. Overselling that 12,500-seat stadium by about 8,000, instead of moving to a larger one, was the first mistake made by the Boston team's management. The second was not providing enough security officers. The third was allowing about 5,000 spectators to line up on the sidelines, within a few steps of the players.

The first signs of trouble came in the first half, after Pelé nearly scored on a free kick and the crowd ringing the field erupted. It got much worse in the second half, as Peter Bodo and Dave Hirshey related in *Pelé's New World*:

> Another roar bursts forth from the crowd, this one tremendous and scratchy-throated as Eusebio strikes, curling a direct kick into

the upper left for Boston. An avalanche of fans spills immediately onto the field to embrace their hero, but Eusebio never stops long enough to give them a chance, running in and out of the developing mob. It takes ten minutes to clear the field, and the game resumes. Immediately, Pelé goes on the attack . . . .

Pelé takes a pass in the Boston end near midfield, ducks and bobs by two defenders and slips the ball to [Mark] Liveric, who unloads a hard one that Messing [once and future Cosmo Shep Messing was playing for Boston this season] barely deflects to the left and right to the feet of Pelé, who pushes the ball into the goal. It appears to be the tying score. As he begins the traditional goal salute, high-leaping, yellow and green uniform thrust into the air, a mob is already forming around him, the first splashings of a monstrous wave about to break over the field.

Here they come now. All 5,000 of those who have been standing along the sidelines, waiting for the exact moment. They are roaring, ranting, waving Brazilian flags . . . . As yet, there is nothing particularly frightening in this demonstration. Then the referee signals that the goal has been disallowed because of a pushing penalty. That's when it becomes grotesque.

The fans come pouring down from every corner of the stadium, an army of soldier ants swarming over their wronged general . . . . Pelé is moving backwards as the sweep of the crowd closes on him, clutching, shouting, grabbing, eyes glazed with exultation and various stimulants. Pelé's shorts are shredded, his jersey torn to tatters, his right shoe ripped off . . . .

Pelé is lifted onto a stretcher and carried out. Toye orders the rest of the Cosmos off the field. They huddle in the locker room, Pelé lying on the stretcher, looking okay in the corner, but rubbing and holding his right ankle.[8]

The Cosmos eventually came out of the locker room (without Pelé, of course) and finished the game (the league later voided Boston's 2-1 victory), but Toye was furious the next day, saying "Unless our security demands are met, I will not allow Pelé to play again."[9]

Those demands carried a lot of weight, because the other teams knew that a visit from the Cosmos could be a huge gate attraction, but only if it included Pelé.

"If our advance men report to us that they are not satisfied with the security arrangements, we will play the game—but without Pelé," Toye said. "In the past, we requested that certain security be set up.

Now we are demanding it . . . . We will not allow this to happen again in any league city where we are to play. It's simple. This is now our mandate to the other teams and to the league."[10]

Toye's demands were met. The melee in Boston was the last serious crowd trouble the Cosmos faced during their Pelé years.

The rest of that 1975 season was pretty mundane, with the possible exception of the 9-2 victory in Washington. The Cosmos had a 3-6 record in NASL play when Pelé arrived in June. They were 8-10 in late July before Pelé missed the last four games of the season because of an injury. Two teams in each of the NASL's four divisions made the playoffs. The Cosmos finished third in their five-team division, but so far behind second-place Toronto that they might have won all four of those games and still not made the playoffs. As it was, they won two of them, and finished the season with a 10-12 record. Attendance at those last four games, two at home and two on the road, was back to pre-Pelé levels.

The Cosmos' mediocre play even after they added the world's most famous player to their lineup was a demonstration of the fact that soccer is a team game. Surrounding a great player with ordinary ones is not a recipe for success. By the start of the 1976 season, 21 of the 28 players who played for the Cosmos in 1975 were gone. Unhappily, so was the coach, Gordon Bradley, kicked upstairs into an ill-defined front-office position with the Cosmos.

After the season, and with Pelé recovered from his injury, the Cosmos made their first foreign tour, playing 10 games in Europe and the Caribbean. Pelé feared that the Cosmos might be embarrassed against European competition, and the team was reinforced with two Santos players, Ramon Mifflin and Nelsi Morais, who both ended up playing for the Cosmos in subsequent seasons.[11] The tour was a respectable one. In the 10 games, the Cosmos gained four victories and a tie, and outscored their opponents by 26-19 (although nearly half of those goals came against one weak opponent). The tour showed the start of a trend that was to display itself many times in Cosmos friendlies in the next few years, both in their postseason and preseason tours and in the games that they played at home against touring foreign teams: That teams in midseason form in their own leagues have such a tremendous advantage over visiting offseason teams that the results are often not to be taken very seriously.

Many things were different about the Cosmos in 1976, but two stood out: Yankee Stadium and Giorgio Chinaglia.

The Cosmos had never planned on moving back to Yankee Stadium, which they left after the 1971 season. But in 1976, the new stadium in the New Jersey Meadowlands was still under construction and Randall's Island did not seem a fitting stage for Pelé. Yankee Stadium, which was built in the early 1920s, was being reopened after having been closed for several years for a $100 million refurbishing project financed by the city of New York. The move back to the Bronx was an expensive one for the Cosmos, who paid a percentage of their gate receipts rather than a flat rental fee. Under the contract that they signed with the city and the Yankees, it was estimated that each game of their 12-game home season would cost them about the same as an entire season at Randall's Island had cost.[12]

"Maybe we won't make any money," said Toye, "but my job was to find a decent place for Pelé to play."[13]

In addition to the cost, the move left the Cosmos with something of a sword dangling over their heads, in the form of a contract clause that gave both the city and the Yankees the right to order a Cosmos game postponed up to four hours before kickoff if they felt that wet weather and soccer cleats posed a threat to the condition of the baseball playing field.[14] This wasn't just a theoretical worry for the Cosmos. A soccer game between the United States and England at Yankee Stadium in 1953 had been postponed for a day for exactly that reason, to the stupified frustration of the English. In the end, the clause never had to be invoked, but when the Cosmos did reach the NASL playoffs in 1976, they had to move their one home playoff game across the East River to Shea Stadium because of a schedule conflict with the Yankees.

The arrival of Chinaglia had been brewing for a while, as part of the Cosmos' efforts to surround Pelé with a better set of teammates than he had in 1975. Chinaglia and his American wife had been talking about a move to America for several years. In 1975, they bought a house in New Jersey and Chinaglia played his first game in an NASL uniform, as a guest player for the Hartford Bicentennials against the Polish national team the day after the Pelé mob scene game in Boston.

Clive Toye says that Chinaglia "fell into our lap,"[15] but it doesn't seem quite so simple when viewed from the perspective of Lazio, the Italian team Chinaglia had played for since 1969. In 1975, Lazio president Umberto Lenzini resisted allowing his team's icon, the man who had led Lazio to the Italian Serie A championship in the 1973-74 season, to depart after the Cosmos had shown interest in him. Probably the main reason why Lenzini was willing to consider the matter at all was that Chinaglia had gotten a bad name with many Italian fans because of an incident at the 1974 World Cup in West Germany. In that incident, Chinaglia swore at the Italian coach and broke some bottles in the dressing room after being taken out of a game against Haiti.[16]

By 1976, Lazio was no longer on top of Italian soccer and was struggling to avoid relegation to the second division. In March of that year, says Mario Risoli in his 2000 biography of Chinaglia, *Arrivederci Swansea*, the Cosmos renewed the effort to sign Chinaglia that Lenzini had resisted the year before. "Chinaglia needed no persuading," Risoli says. "His desire to join the Cosmos was as great as it was the previous summer. He issued Lenzini with an ultimatum. This would be his last season at Lazio. Either they sold him to the Cosmos and made some money or, if they refused to do that, he would quit football .... Realizing he was going to lose the striker anyway, Lenzini decided to cash in [to the tune of $750,000] and agreed to the sale."[17]

Even so, Chinaglia's departure from Italy was not a smooth one, partly due to the fact that the NASL played a spring-to-fall season while European leagues played a fall-to-spring season. When Chinaglia left to join the Cosmos, Lazio had three games left in its season. Many Lazio fans were distraught over losing their star goalscorer while going down to the wire in a relegation battle, so rather than flying directly to New York from Rome, where there had been reports that fans planned to block his plane from taking off, Chinaglia slipped out of town to Genoa and flew to America from there.[18] The fact that on Cosmos visits to Rome in the next few years Chinaglia's popularity among Lazio fans seemed undiminished may be attributed to the fact that Lazio survived that relegation battle. If Chinaglia's departure had precipitated a descent to Serie B, it might have been different.

Chinaglia joined the Cosmos five games into the 1976 NASL season. With Chinaglia in the fold, they won five of their next seven, improving their record to 8-4. Then there was a disaster, from the Cosmos' standpoint. In a game in Washington on June 27, goalkeeper Bob Rigby suffered a broken collarbone that put him out for the season. By the next game, there was a familiar face in the Cosmos' goal. Shep Messing, who had left the Cosmos in acrimonious circumstances in 1973, after posing for some nude magazine photos, had been reacquired by the Cosmos from Boston. After the magazine incident in 1973, Messing had been very quickly shown the door by both the Cosmos and the Long Island high school where he had been teaching, but by 1976 Messing and Clive Toye had buried the hatchet ("Buried it and laughed about it a lot," says Toye[19]). The return of Messing (and a coaching change) sparked a surge by the Cosmos. They won their next six games in a row and coasted into the playoffs, as Chinaglia finished the regular season with 19 goals in the 19 games he played.

Those playoffs lasted only two games. After a 2-0 victory over the Washington Diplomats in the first round (in the game played at Shea), the Cosmos traveled to Tampa and were eliminated by the Rowdies, 3-1. The second of Pele's three NASL seasons had ended without a championship for him and the Cosmos.

By the time the Cosmos reached the playoffs, Gordon Bradley was back coaching them again, partly because this was the year when Steve Ross turned into a Cosmos fanatic. At the start of the 1976 season, the Cosmos' manager was Englishman Ken Furphy, who had been brought in as a replacement for Bradley. The English playing style that Furphy favored and the English players he brought in didn't sit well with many Cosmos fans. While they were getting frustrated with Furphy, Furphy was getting frustrated with Steve Ross, whom Paul Gardner said decades later "knew very little about soccer and learned almost nothing."[20] That situation came to a head a few days after the Cosmos were beaten, 5-1, by the Tampa Bay Rowdies in early June. Furphy was summoned to a meeting at Ross' office in New York to discuss the heavy defeat. In addition to Furphy and Ross, those in attendance included Clive Toye, Gordon Bradley, Ahmet Ertegun, Nesuhi Ertegun, Julio Mazzei, Peppe Pinton and three players, Pelé, Giorgio Chinaglia and Ramon Mifflin.[21]

Gavin Newsham recounts the meeting in *Once in a Lifetime*: "What followed was a six-hour postmortem as to why the team had suffered such a humiliating defeat. Ross produced a video tape of the match, demanding explanations as to why each goal was conceded, whose fault it was and what was going to be done to arrest the team's erratic form . . . . Furphy was livid. While he had no problem explaining the team's performance to Ross [before the loss to Tampa, the Cosmos had won their three previous games by a total of 11-1], he felt that the presence of three of his players at the meeting had undermined his position as team coach, especially as Ross had repeatedly asked the opinions of Pelé, Mifflin and Chinaglia as to where the team was going wrong."[22]

Three weeks later, after a loss to the Washington Diplomats, the same one in which Rigby was injured, Ross called another meeting. Furphy refused to attend, and quit the next day.

According to Ross biographer Connie Bruck, there were two sides to Ross' absorption in the Cosmos:

> Ross was immensely supportive; he was in the Warner box for every home game, and travelled in the company jet to most games that were played away. Once, the Cosmos were in Florida, preparing for a game and staying at a Marriott adjacent to an airport. When Ross overheard one of the players complaining that he had not been able to sleep because of the noise of the planes, Ross immediately ordered that the team be moved to the Americana Hotel in Bal Harbour, where a chef, too, was personally assigned to the players.
>
> The price of such solicitude, however, was Ross's frequent interference. There were furious debates between Ross, the Erteguns, [Jay] Emmett and Toye about who should play key positions in each upcoming game. And following the games, Toye often had to contend with a very different Ross from the generous, thoughtful person who was so upset at a player's losing a night's sleep. "I'd get a call to come look at a tape of a game, where we'd maybe lost by a goal," Toye recalled. "The camera angle wouldn't be conclusive, so that, from the tape, it was impossible to tell. But Ross would go into a tirade, ranting, 'Protest the game! This is wrong!' "[23]

Toye did not find Ross' good side to be completely positive, either, as he makes clear in his version of the switching-hotels incident. "We were booked into the Marriott," said Toye in his autobiography, "not far from Miami airport, a perfectly acceptable team hotel, with proper meals booked and the team under control. One of them mentioned in Steve's hearing that he had heard a plane fly overhead and before you could say 'spoiled brats,' everyone was moved into the Fontainebleau on Miami Beach with suites for all and instructions to eat whatever they liked and just sign for it. The first crack in the breakdown of discipline was upon us."[24]

The next incident that put a serious strain on relations between Ross and the soccer men who worked for him took place at another game against Tampa Bay, three weeks after Furphy's departure. It resulted in Toye being forced to make a statement over the Yankee Stadium public-address system of which he says, "Not even George Steinbrenner has said anything as silly as this."[25] At halftime, the Cosmos were trailing, 3-1, and had had two goals disallowed by the referee. Says Gavin Newsham:

> As Toye sat in his chair, an exasperated Jay Emmett appeared at

his side, and demanded that he come down to the locker room immediately. When he arrived downstairs, Toye found Steve Ross pacing up and down with 'fire coming from his nostrils.' Ross, it transpired, had been so incensed by the refereeing decisions that he had instructed his players to remain in the locker room and not go out for the second half. Toye pleaded with Ross not to carry out his protest, arguing that it was against the interests of the team and its fans to abandon the game. Eventually, Ross relented, but only on the proviso that Toye make an announcement on the stadium's public address system informing the crowd (and the media) that the Cosmos would not just be playing the second half under protest but the remainder of the season. An incredulous Toye agreed. "Sillier things I have not said and I think sillier things I may not have heard."[26]

Ross was quieted—sort of. After the game, which the Cosmos rallied to win, 5-4, as Pelé played a dazzling second half, Ross complained about the refereeing and said, "Unless the league or somebody does something about officials, the Cosmos will not play in this league next year."[27] He didn't explain what league they would play in. As always, Ross was sure he wanted only the best for the Cosmos but not as sure of the realities of professional soccer. "Like all rich owners, he felt his team should always win. When they didn't, the referees were the villains," Paul Gardner wrote in a 2007 magazine article. "Before one game, he summoned the entire press corps to the 'multimedia' room. He stood gravely in front of us, with a long pointer. Television clips were shown, halted, re-run, while Ross indicated with his pointer all the anti-Cosmos referee errors. It was, of course, absurd. Ross' sidekick, Jay Emmett . . . . took a similarly childish line whenever Cosmos lost."[28]

While all this turmoil was going on, Giorgio Chinaglia was edging closer and closer to the seat of power. In the long run, the growing influence of Chinaglia may have been the most significant thing that happened to the Cosmos in 1976. It is quite possible that Chinaglia had Steve Ross' ear to a greater degree than any player has had an owner's ear in the history of professional sports. There have been other instances of players exerting control over teams and influencing personnel decisions far beyond their playing status. Perhaps the most famous is the case of basketball player Magic Johnson, who was widely believed in 1981 to have forced Paul Westhead out as coach of the Los Angeles Lakers, although Johnson denies that that was his intention.[29] Chinaglia trumps that, however. Chinaglia appears to have had a hand in bringing about the departures of no fewer than *four* Cosmos coaches: Ken Furphy, Gordon Bradley, Eddie Firmani and Hennes Weisweiler.

Two of Chinaglia's teammates had sharp memories of his position of influence.

Werner Roth says: "They [Chinaglia and Ross] related right away and I think Giorgio was also the type of person that tends to focus on individuals that have a certain amount of power and befriend them and he has this natural instinct to get into a position of power. So I think it was that natural instinct and his compatibility with Steve that eventually provided Giorgio with that platform to wield a lot of power in and around the Cosmos."[30]

Keith Eddy remembered an instance of Chinaglia using that power in 1977, after Bradley was released as coach: "I had a call from him, asking 'Would you like to coach the team?' I said, 'One, I don't want to and, two, you are not in a position to ask me.' He said 'Oh yes, I am. And if you don't do it I will get [Eddie] Firmani.' A few days later, Eddie was in the job. Whatever Giorgio wanted, he got."[31]

The Cosmos made another postseason tour after the 1976 NASL season, but this was a relatively abbreviated one. A month after the tour, it was announced that the Cosmos would be hitting the road again in a sense in 1977, moving their home base for the third time in four years, from Yankee Stadium to the now-completed Giants Stadium in New Jersey.

In addition to being the year when Pelé finally won an NASL championship, 1977 also was the year when soccer and the Cosmos became a New York phenomenon (or more correctly, a New Jersey one). The largest home crowd the Cosmos had ever drawn in their six seasons at Yankee Stadium, Hofstra and Randall's Island was 28,436, for their home opener at Yankee Stadium in 1976. They failed to match that in their home opener at Giants Stadium in 1977, drawing 26,752, and their next four home games all were below 25,000, but things started to take off in June. On June 5, they set a franchise record of 31,208 at a 6-0 win over Toronto. That game was the start of an amazing streak for the Cosmos, the first of 70 consecutive home games in NASL play, extending into 1981, at which they drew crowds of 30,000 or more. (During that streak, they also played 14 friendlies at Giants Stadium, of which 12 drew 30,000 or more.) The next game, a week later, attracted 36,816 and on June 19, Father's Day, the crowd was a breathtaking 62,394 for a game against Tampa Bay, the largest that had ever seen a soccer game in the United States. That record lasted less than two months. On Aug. 14, 77,691 were at a playoff game against Fort Lauderdale. That crowd remained the largest that ever saw an NASL game (helped by the fact that the Cosmos stopped selling standing-room tickets), but the greatest attendance epitaph that the Cosmos left was not the one-game record but that monumental streak of large crowds.

Helping a great deal to fuel that attendance surge was the arrival of the next great Cosmos signing, Franz Beckenbauer. The Cosmos' 1977 season, probably the most dramatic they ever played, was all about arrivals (Beckenbauer, Steve Hunt, Carlos Alberto) and departures (Gordon Bradley, Clive Toye, Pelé). The most important of those arrivals was Beckenbauer, the greatest player after Pelé that the Cosmos ever signed. He certainly was not in any way over the hill, even though he had been playing at the top levels of the sport for more than a decade. He still was the captain and star of both Bayern Munich, which had won the European Cup in 1974, '75 and '76, and the West German national team, which had won the World Cup in 1974. As had been the case with Chinaglia the year before and Pelé the year before that, Beckenbauer arrived in midseason. His first game, on May 29, 1997, was the Cosmos' 11th of the season, and it was just after his arrival that the attendances began to soar.

According to Gavin Newsham, the Cosmos had been making overtures in Beckenbauer's direction for a while, regarding him as a logical successor to Pelé, but Beckenbauer didn't want to consider leaving Germany until after the 1978 World Cup.[32] What changed his mind and brought him to New York in the spring of 1977 was the fact that the public obsession in Germany over rumors of his possible future departure turned his life there into a nightmare.[33]

Not everybody in the Cosmos' camp was thrilled about the arrival of Beckenbauer, who signed a four-year contract for $2.8 million. Toye, who was nearing the end of his days with the Cosmos, managed to sign Beckenbauer over the protestations of the Ertegun brothers, an event he refers to as a "battle won with wounds not recognized at the time."[34] Giorgio Chinaglia's displeasure over the arrival of Beckenbauer was well known, although Chinaglia claimed that it was not for the oft-cited reasons of jealousy. Rather, he told the *New York Times*, it was because he thought a subtle player like Beckenbauer, who didn't score many goals, couldn't draw crowds in America and wouldn't be of much help to the Cosmos at the gate.[35] The fact that Chinaglia had clashed frequently with none other than Pelé over their respective shares of the limelight didn't help to give Chinaglia's stated selfless reasons for opposing Beckenbauer the ring of reality.

The dispute with the Erteguns over the signing of Beckenbauer was another nail in Clive Toye's coffin. There had been many others, including a disagreement between Toye and Ross over leaving Yankee Stadium and moving to Giants Stadium, a move that Ross did not want to make. To this day, Toye and others are not in full agreement over whether he quit or was fired, although the fact that he was offered only a three-year consulting contract rather than a renewal of his contract as president of the Cosmos makes the latter seem likely, even if there was no shouting of "you're fired." His departure was announced at a press conference on June 13, 1977, just a little over two years since his triumphant signing of Pelé.

It appears that the most serious breach in the relations between Toye and the upper management of the Cosmos, at least from Toye's standpoint, came over interference in the running of the club by the Ertegun brothers. The clearest example of that was the endless discussions over who was to play in goal for the Cosmos, Shep Messing or the Turkish goalkeeper signed in 1977, Erol Yasin. The Turkish-born Erteguns favored Yasin. Toye also remembers an instance in which he was urged by Nesuhi Ertegun to sign four particular players, despite the fact the fact that three of the four played the same position.[36] The interference of the Erteguns was not making life at the Cosmos any more pleasant for Toye.

Paul Gardner minced no words in writing about the departure of Toye for *World Soccer* magazine later that year: "Toye did not resign. He was ousted, fired if you like, as the result of a power struggle within Warner Communications, the huge business conglomerate that is the owner of the Cosmos . . . . At the press conference it was announced that he would continue to work for the Cosmos in an advisory role. Evidently a smokescreen, another way of saying that he had been given a generous financial settlement. I have no reason to believe that Toye left the Cosmos with anything other than bad feelings. Certainly when I spoke to him a month later, he had the air of a very embittered man."[37]

With Toye, the only other Englishman among the Cosmos' leaders, now gone, Gordon Bradley's days were numbered. That number got a lot smaller after Bradley benched Giorgio Chinaglia for a June 26 game at Giants Stadium, and drew the ire of Steve Ross for that decision. Disharmony within the team, particularly coming from

Bobby Smith, who was upset about repeatedly being left out of the lineup, didn't help Bradley's situation.[38]

Bradley finally gave up the ghost a few games later, ironically after a victory on July 6, being kicked upstairs to the front office a second time. The Cosmos tried to promote the idea that Bradley had recommended the hiring of new coach Eddie Firmani himself,[39] but when Bradley departed from the Cosmos a few months later to become coach of the NASL's Washington team, the *New York Times* made no bones about the fact that he had been "forced out as coach of the Cosmos in midseason this year to make room for Eddie Firmani."[40] The selection of Firmani, supposedly a favorite of Giorgio Chinaglia, was as controversial as the demise of Bradley. Until about a month before taking the Cosmos job, Firmani had been the highly successful coach of the Tampa Bay Rowdies, who remained bitter about his sudden resignation there. Rowdies owner George Strawbridge said a year later that Firmani "ran out on this organization, the Rowdies team and the Rowdies fans. I weary of reading the righteous platitudes and convenient rationalizations that Eddie Firmani continues to make public and that he apparently uses to whitewash his conscience."[41]

Bradley harbored no illusions about the causes of his fall from grace. "No question he [Chinaglia] had a hand in what happened," Bradley said in Mario Risoli's 2000 biography of Chinaglia. "That's why I was bitter toward him and also Steve Ross for allowing it to happen. I thought Steve listened to Giorgio too much and allowed him to do too much."[42]

In a further irony, Bradley's last game was one that many people, including Ross, cited as a crucial step in the Cosmos' attendance surge. A crowd of 31,875 came to Giants Stadium on a rainy night to see a Cosmos team that did not include the injured Pelé rout the San Jose Earthquakes in a game that they could have seen on television.[43]

The Cosmos clinched a place in the 1977 NASL playoffs fairly early, but by the time those playoffs grew near, they were starting to look shaky again—and this year was the last chance for Pelé to win an NASL championship. On July 14, the Cosmos had a record of 12-9, but three of their last four games had been defeats. That day they signed Carlos Alberto, another of Pelé's former Santos teammates and the captain of Brazil's legendary 1970 World Cup champions. That acquisition, with which the Cosmos became the first team in soccer history to field the captains of the previous two World Cup winners, made the difference. With Carlos Alberto in the lineup, they won nine of their last 10 games and swept to the NASL title. Chinaglia, who scored 15 goals in 24 regular-season games, got his first NASL scoring championship that season, and Carlos Alberto got something of a name change. In New York, he was often called Alberto, as though that were his last name. Actually, it's the second half of his two-word nickname. His real last name is Torres. (Americans often had trouble with Brazilian nicknames. In the ABC telecast of Pelé's debut game with the Cosmos in 1975, his wife, Rose Nascimento, was referred to in an on-screen graphic as "Rose Pelé.")

Carlos Alberto was used to playing right back, but the Cosmos used him as a sweeper, because that enabled them to move Beckenbauer up to midfield (something Beckenbauer didn't necessarily like). Carlos Alberto was able to accomplish miracles back there. Wrote Paul Gardner in 1982: "The sight of Carlos Alberto trotting into the melee [in front of the goal] and swiftly emerging with the ball under control—without seeming to have made any particular effort to get it—is one that continues to delight Cosmos fans."[44] George Best was similarly amazed at how Carlos Alberto was able to do what he did when he said: "You know, Alberto is not a good tackler, he can't head the ball properly, he's not fast, he's not rugged and he can't mark man-to-man, so I keep asking myself—why does he always end up with the bloody ball?"[45]

There were two highlights to that playoff run. The first was the astounding scene on Aug. 14, 1977, when a crowd of 77,691 jammed into Giants Stadium to see the Cosmos score an 8-3 rout of the Fort Lauderdale Strikers in the first leg of a quarterfinal playoff series. The Cosmos had high hopes for this one, particularly because they knew that fans were aware that, theoretically, this could be the last game (excepting a postseason farewell exhibition) that Pelé would play at Giants Stadium. The Cosmos were worried nevertheless. They had an advance ticket sale of 47,500,[46] but a 1947 game in New York involving a Jewish team from Palestine had an advance sale of more than 61,000 before rain held the crowd down to 43,177. And it drizzled all day on Aug. 14, 1977, until about two hours before the start of the Cosmos game.

This time, the weather did not hold down the numbers, either at the turnstiles or on the field. By the time the last of those 77,691 fans had squeezed into Giants Stadium, sometime during the first half, the Cosmos were well on their way to victory, thanks to early goals by Steve Hunt, Franz Beckenbauer and Giorgio Chinaglia. "It was all over after the first quarter of an hour," said Cosmos midfielder Terry

Garbett. "We were pretty sharp tonight. Steve Hunt got that early goal, and it released all the tension."[47]

The other highlight, of course, was the final, and Hunt again scored the opening goal as the Cosmos gained a 2-1 victory over the Seattle Sounders. The game was played at Civic Stadium in Portland, on a field so bad, in the words of Alex Yannis of the *New York Times*, "that Charlie Brown would probably refuse to let his baseball team play on it."[48] Hunt's opening goal in the 19th minute of play was a freak one, either a horrible blunder by goalkeeper Tony Chursky or an excellent piece of opportunism by Hunt, depending on your perspective. After collecting the ball, Chursky rolled it a few feet in front of him, toward the goal, preparatory to kicking it to a teammate. Hunt was closer behind Chursky than the Seattle goalkeeper apparently realized, leaped past him, stole the ball and pushed it into a wide-open net.

The Sounders equalized not long after that, and the dramatic game flowed back and forth for more than an hour before Chinaglia scored the game winner on a header 13 minutes before the end. The Cosmos were as delirious after the game as any newly-crowned champion team, but they had something extra, an American championship for Pelé. Perhaps the most emotional of them was Shep Messing, who had made one of the greatest saves of his life just moments before Chinaglia's goal. "Right now, I don't even care that I won a championship, or that the Cosmos won a championship, but just that Pelé did . . . . It's such an honor to be part of giving him this championship."[49] For his part, Pelé said that: "I can stop now, as a champion. I have everything that I have wanted from my life in soccer."[50]

With a championship in hand, the waning days of an icon on the field and some exotic destinations, the 1977 postseason tour turned into a glamorous, celebratory procession, even if it was not a terribly long tour. The fact that it was due to end back at Giants Stadium with the final game of Pelé's career made it all the more poignant. Asian crowds were delighted to see a collection of stars like Pelé, Beckenbauer, Carlos Alberto and Chinaglia. The Cosmos drew crowds of 72,000 in Tokyo, 80,000 in Beijing, 50,000 in Shanghai and 60,000 in Calcutta. They began their tour on Sept. 1 and returned to New Jersey at the end of the month, having won four, lost none and tied three. Good soccer, and even more so, good diplomacy. The Cosmos also may have realized something in the course of this Asian visit that was useful knowledge for trying to build a team's reputation, and thus its gate receipts, back home. Victories were a lot easier to come by on tours to the Third World than on tours to Europe, but many American fans didn't realize the difference. For instance, the Cosmos knew that Japan was a soccer backwater, but to some of their fans, a victory over the Furukawa Electric Company was just as impressive as one over Manchester United or Real Madrid would have been.

Plans for the Pelé Farewell Game on Oct. 1 had been on the drawing board for a long time. Since before Pelé joined the Cosmos, actually. Clive Toye told about the start of that planning, a conversation with Santos president Modesto Roma more than two years before in Brazil, in his autobiography: "It was spring time in 1975 and the signing of Pelé looked by now as if it really was going to happen. 'I envy you,' he [Roma] said. 'I wish he was staying.' So, on the spur and emotion of the moment, I said I would give him back to Santos at the very end, for one half, the last half of his life. We scribbled the agreement there and then, on the back of an envelope, resting on the top of a very dusty car late one night outside the stadium in Santos. A fee of $20,000, travel and expenses and a final game at Giants Stadium, Cosmos vs. Santos, with Pelé changing shirts at half time."[51]

And that's how it happened, with a crowd of 75,646 watching in the rain at Giants Stadium. There had been a brief flap when the Cosmos found that they had accidentally oversold the stadium by about 5,000, but on the day, everything was joy and happiness.

The Cosmos might have preferred that all this joy be expressed at a later time. As the *New York Times* put it: "All this is not to suggest that Warner Communications and the Cosmos players did not do everything they could to get Pelé to reconsider and play again. According to Shep Messing, the goalie, Warner put tremendous pressure on him to unretire, probably in the form of millions of dollars. The other players tried to talk him out of retiring throughout the North American Soccer League playoffs."[52]

If Toye had a vision while writing that agreement on the back of the envelope in Santos in 1975 of what this game might be like, the reality exceeded it, with the possible exception of the rain. The crowd was filled with celebrities, from Muhammad Ali to Mick Jaggar to Robert Redford to Henry Kissinger to Bobby Moore. Pelé scored the last goal of his career, for the Cosmos, on a wicked 30-yard free kick just before halftime. Then, in a speech after the game from the center of the field, he called it "the greatest moment of my life."[53] The Cosmos won the game, 2-1, but appropriately, the *New York Times'* story on the game didn't mention the final score until the 10th paragraph and never said who scored the winning goal. Those facts weren't what the day was about.

The Cosmos actually weren't quite through for 1977. They had three more games, albeit anticlimactic ones. One of them, however, was interesting enough to draw another 33,712 fans to Giants Stadium a week after the Pelé Farewell Game, to see a 1-1 tie between the Cosmos and the Chinese national team, which was repaying the visit that the Cosmos had made to China a month before. It was an interesting occasion for the Cosmos. It gave them a chance to feel what the rest of their lives, post-Pelé, would be like.

By the next summer, the Cosmos knew that there very definitely was life after Pelé. If anything, the Cosmos were better in 1978 than they had been in 1977, and their status as the NASL's dominant team was only in serious doubt once. The Cosmos' new signings of foreign stars weren't quite the marquee names of the previous few years, but Vladislav Bogicevic of Yugoslavia, Dennis Tueart of England and Giuseppe Wilson of Italy ended up making huge contributions to the Cosmos. They played a combined total of 88 NASL games for the Cosmos in 1978. Tueart scored 33 goals in his two years with the Cosmos, including two of their three goals in the 1978 championship-game victory over Tampa Bay. Wilson, a former teammate of Giorgio Chinaglia with several Italian teams, was the defensive player of the game that day. And Bogicevic, famed for his pinpoint passes, was to become perhaps the greatest midfielder in the history of the NASL.

The Cosmos opened the 1978 NASL season with seven consecutive victories and completed the regular season with a 24-6 record and a runaway championship of their division. Giorgio Chinaglia scored 34 goals in the regular season, his best mark ever, and then added five more goals in the playoffs.

Even in the most dominant season the Cosmos ever played, there were glitches, however. The relationship between Chinaglia and Eddie Firmani began to deteriorate after the Italian star was taken out of a game against the Memphis Rogues in late May (shades of the 1974 World Cup). A 9-2 loss to Minnesota in the first leg of their quarterfinal playoff series temporarily shook up the Cosmos, although in the end it didn't derail their championship express. And some disappointing results in Europe on a postseason tour knocked the high-flying Cosmos down a peg. Still, 1978 was a banner year for the Cosmos.

1978 may have been the high-water mark of the NASL. The league-wide attendance average that season was 14,064, down a few hundred from the surge of 1977, but still strong. The surge prompted the league to expand to 24 teams, the arrival of foreign star players continued and the league signed a national television contract for the 1979 season. The 2001 *Encyclopedia of American Soccer History* talked about the long-term results of all that growth:

> All this influx of superstars cost big money, which was unquestionably a large factor in the NASL's eventual end. A decade and more later, when blame was being handed out, there was plenty of finger-pointing at the Cosmos. The claim was that they had started the spending race, forcing it on other teams that didn't have pockets as deep as they did, thus bankrupting the league. The argument may have some truth, but may also be a vast oversimplification. Still, whoever was to blame for the overspending, there is no question that wild overspending it was.
>
> The NASL was in paradise at this point, and to say that it was a fool's paradise would be 20-20 hindsight. It really did appear that soccer was making the grade in the United States. Maybe someone with access to the NASL's balance sheets might have thought otherwise, but the public picture was more than just positive, it was ecstatic. After the attendance burst of 1977, the expansion from 18 teams in 1977 to 24 in 1978 seemed logical, not the misstep that it would appear in retrospect to have been.[54]

It seems quite possible that the rift between Giorgio Chinaglia and Eddie Firmani could easily have been avoided, but Chinaglia was someone inclined to shoot first and ask questions later. If Chinaglia, sitting on the bench in the latter stages of that May 24 game in Memphis, had asked Firmani the reasons for the substitution, he would have learned that it had to do with the way other players were playing, not Chinaglia. But Chinaglia wasn't sitting on the bench. After being substituted, he had stormed straight into the locker room, the same way he had done at that World Cup game in West Germany in 1974.

Mario Risoli detailed Firmani's view of the day's events in *Arrivederci Swansea*:

> Firmani remembers the incident well. He believes his decision to replace Chinaglia with Fred Grgurev in the second half cost him his friendship with Chinaglia and made him a vulnerable target at the Meadowlands. "After that," says Firmani, "my relationship with him was absolutely zero. That was the beginning of the end."

Cosmos were a goal down with a quarter of an hour left when Firmani made that substitution. "We started pumping balls into the box and Giorgio was not the best in the air," explains the former coach. "Their defenders were just knocking the balls out, so I decided to put on Grgurev, who was very good in the air. As Giorgio came off the field he pointed at me and said, 'You've had it.' He immediately went to the phone in the dressing room and called Steve Ross.". . .

Before he made the switch Firmani intended to castigate his players in the dressing-room after the game for not playing to Chinaglia's strengths, but after Chinaglia made that remark he changed his mind. "I wanted to save Giorgio's face. Because he had something to do with bringing me to New York, I felt I owed him something. I was going to hammer the team for playing the way they did. I taught them how to play to Giorgio. I was going to say, 'If you don't play with him, I'm not going to put him in the bloody team!' But after Giorgio behaved like he did, I said nothing."[55]

Gordon Bradley had lasted less than two weeks as coach of the Cosmos after benching Chinaglia in 1977. Firmani lasted more than a year after the substitution incident in 1978. But, as Firmani noted, the incident was the beginning of the end of his time as coach of the Cosmos.

The Cosmos swept easily into the 1978 playoffs, but that quarterfinal against Minnesota gave a bad jolt to the foundations of their NASL dominance. If the home-and-home series had been decided by total goals, as most such series in soccer around the world are, they would have been eliminated. As it was, they barely escaped.

The 9-2 defeat on Aug. 14 stunned the Cosmos, who had been outscoring their opponents by an average of about 3-1 per game that season. Alan Willey scored five of the Minnesota goals. But a 4-0 Cosmos victory in the return game two days later at Giants Stadium forced a "mini-game" overtime to decide the issue, then a shootout when there were no goals in the mini-game. (The shootout was the NASL's version of postgame penalty kicks, with players dribbling in from 35 yards out and given five seconds to shoot.) It took six rounds for the Cosmos to overcome the Kicks in the shootout, but the key was in the fifth, as Carlos Alberto kept the Cosmos alive with a surprise move.

"Although the records show that Franz Beckenbauer scored the winning goal in that shoot-out, it was Carlos Alberto's audacious effort that not only kept the Cosmos in the game but revealed the true talent of the man," says Gavin Newsham. "Whereas most players in the shoot-out dribble the ball towards the goalkeeper and wait for him to commit himself to a save or tackle, Alberto simply waited for the referee's whistle and scooped the ball up into the air. As it bounced ahead of him, the Minnesota keeper Tino Lettieri advanced off his line, but was clearly confused by Alberto's intentions. With the keeper stranded outside his area, Alberto then calmly lobbed it up and over Lettieri's head and into the empty net."[56]

It may have been the most striking individual effort in the Cosmos' history (albeit in a shootout). Without it, the Cosmos would not have retained their NASL title.

The final, after Portland had been beaten in the semifinals, was not an anticlimax, but it was not the sort of pitched battle the Cosmos and the Tampa Bay Rowdies had been playing repeatedly for several years, becoming easily the NASL's most heated rivals. The Cosmos were in control most of the way, helped greatly by the fact that Tampa Bay's biggest star, Rodney Marsh, was unable to play, sidelined by an injury that created what television commentator Paul Gardner called "a huge vacuum in the midfield."[57] Goals by Tueart and Chinaglia gave the Cosmos a 2-0 halftime lead. Tampa Bay closed the margin a bit with a goal in the 73rd minute, and gave the game a few minutes of tension, but Tueart soon got an insurance goal and the Cosmos coasted home. It was a triumphant occasion for the Cosmos and the fans who packed Giants Stadium to see it, but not nearly as dramatic a one as the 1977 final.

The Cosmos' year ended with a considerably more extensive post-season schedule than in previous years, one that included a flirtation with the only man who could rival Franz Beckenbauer for the title of the world's greatest player, Dutchman Johan Cruyff.

The Cosmos had been holding talks with Cruyff since early in the summer, and Cruyff was scheduled to play for the Cosmos in a three-game series at Giants Stadium in late August and early September. The figuring was that he would be in a Cosmos uniform fulltime by the 1979 season. In the end, he played only the first game of that series, between the Cosmos and a World All-Star team, before returning to Europe with an injury, although he did play for the Cosmos in a game in London later in September. Those two were his only games for the Cosmos, and he was with the Los Angeles Aztecs by the start of the 1979 NASL season.

The Greatest Show on Earth

The three games at Giants Stadium were the start of a 19-game marathon through 12 countries on three continents. By the time the tour was over, it was late November and the next NASL season was almost as close as the last one. The Cosmos results on that tour were decidedly mixed. They finished it with five victories, nine defeats and five ties. The low point was probably three games that they played in West Germany in mid-September. A 7-1 loss to Bayern Munich was followed by a 6-1 loss to VFB Stuttgart and a 2-0 loss to Freiburg, a lesser team than the first two opponents. But if the tour showed that the Cosmos weren't ready to take on the best of European and South American soccer, it also showed that they were becoming a prominent international brand name, to be marketed by Warner all over the world. In 1974, the last pre-Pelé year, they played 24 games, of which the only one outside the United States was an NASL road game in Toronto. In 1978, they played 59, including 20 outside the United States, and that was only the beginning. In each of the following three years they were to play more than 60 games.

For the Cosmos, 1979 began where 1978 had ended, on the road. In addition to three games in the Bahamas, where they conducted their preseason training camp, they played two games in Trinidad (one of them against a Brazilian team) and two in Colombia, their first preseason venture into South America.

The trip to South America was much shorter than the preseason tours the Cosmos made there in 1980 and '81, but one of the games in Colombia was fateful for them. In a 2-0 victory over America Cali on March 15, Werner Roth, the last of the 1972 NASL champion team still with the Cosmos and captain of the 1978 squad, suffered a knee injury that initially was reported would sideline him for three to six weeks.[58] It did a lot more than that. Roth came on as a substitute in the Cosmos' next-to-last game of the 1979 NASL regular season, but those 18 minutes were his only appearance of what proved to be his final season with the Cosmos. It's not as though there was no one to replace him, however. Turnover is a constant with professional sports teams, and it may have been even more pronounced with the Cosmos. As always, there were new foreign stars arriving. The most notable ones during 1979 included Johan Neeskens and Wim Rijsbergen of Holland, Francisco Marinho of Brazil, Andranik Eskandarian of Iran and Seninho of Portugal.

Roth wasn't the only big name with the Cosmos whose time ran out that year. The other was Eddie Firmani, who had been skating on thin ice ever since getting on the wrong side of Giorgio Chinaglia a year before. The axe fell on Firmani on June 1, 1979. Chinaglia does not seem to have been directly involved in Firmani's demise, except for the difference his influence with Steve Ross might have had if he had not been abstaining from supporting Firmani ever since the substitution incident. Firmani thinks that Chinaglia's silence was involvement enough. "I had a good relationship with all the players—all except Giorgio and he had such pull with Steve Ross and the board," Firmani told Mario Risoli. "Have I forgiven Giorgio? Not really. If I see him again I'll say hello, but that's it."[59]

The official reason given by Cosmos vice president Rafael de la Sierra for Firmani's dismissal, the team's poor play, seemed quite surprising. Firmani had a remarkably good record for a supposedly unsuccessful coach. He had won NASL championships in 1977 and 1978, and his 1979 team was off to a 9-2 start.

The real reasons may have been Firmani's continuation of Clive Toye's dispute with the Erteguns over Erol Yasin, his reluctance to use Francisco Marinho as much as the higher-ups wanted him to and his unhappiness over the heavy schedule of tours and in-season friendlies the Cosmos were playing.[60]

One of those friendlies, perhaps the biggest one the Cosmos ever played, was just a few days away when the Cosmos dismissed Firmani. That was against the Argentine national team, which had won the World Cup a year before.

The Argentinians were not the usual in-season visitor. This was not a club playing vacation games in its offseason and maybe fielding a team of reserves. Argentina was getting ready for the opening round of the 1979 South American championships, in which it was to face Brazil and Bolivia, and had just completed a European tour with a 3-1 victory over Scotland in Glasgow (this was at a time when Scotland was still among the world's best). The lineup that Argentina fielded against the Cosmos four days after the victory in Glasgow contained six of the 11 who had started in the World Cup final against Holland in 1978, goalkeeper Ubaldo Fillol; defenders Daniel Passarella, Alberto Tarantini and Jorge Olguin; midfielder Americo Gallego and forward Leopoldo Luque. Among the replacements was an 18-year-old midfielder named Diego Maradona, who had been left out of the World Cup team the year before because he was so young.

The Cosmos, who certainly were not at full strength, quite surprisingly held their own against the world champions. Argentina's 1-

0 victory came on a header by Passarella, the Argentine team's captain, in the 88th minute of the game. The Cosmos' injured regulars included Beckenbauer, Bogicevic, Roth, Seninho, Rijsbergen and Terry Garbett. For the last 12 minutes of the game, the Cosmos' lineup included six Americans (plus Canadian goalkeeper Jack Brand).

Ike Kuhns of the *Newark Star-Ledger* wrote that the Cosmos had played Argentina to a standstill. "Giorgio Chinaglia had a goal nullified by offside," Kuhns noted, "and the Cosmos had at least three other good scoring chances and Argentina, struggling on the Astroturf, never were able to take charge of the game."[61]

Then it was back to NASL competition, and victory after victory. Firmani had been replaced by Ray Klivecka, a former college coach who had been a Cosmos assistant, but then Julio Mazzei was named technical director, supervising Klivecka, and while Klivecka was the coach in name, Mazzei was the coach in reality.[62] As if the Cosmos didn't have enough foreign stars, a few days after the game against Argentina, they were augmented by yet another, Neeskens. He had been playing second fiddle to his countryman Cruyff for a succession of teams for years, but he was a world superstar in his own right, known both for his tremendous skill and for being a fearless tackler and ballwinner. The fact that Neeskens joined the Cosmos shortly after Cruyff joined the Los Angeles Aztecs, making it definite that he would not be coming to the Cosmos, may not have been a coincidence. In addition to getting Neeskens, the Cosmos did get something out of their brief association with Cruyff. Because the Cosmos held the NASL rights to Cruyff, the Aztecs had to pay the Cosmos $600,000 in order to sign the Dutch superstar.[63]

With Neeskens in the fold, Beckenbauer and most of the others back after injuries, and Chinaglia and Carlos Alberto performing well, the Cosmos swept to the same regular-season record as the year before, 24-6. That put them easily into the playoffs and helped to set up a semifinal meeting with the Vancouver Whitecaps that was one of the classics of NASL history. Once again, Carlos Alberto, who had revived the Cosmos from a late-season slump in 1977 and saved them from elimination with his unorthodox shootout goal in 1978, played a major role in determining their championship fate.

The semifinal against Vancouver wasn't the first difficult hurdle the Cosmos faced in the 1979 playoffs. In the quarterfinals, the Tulsa Roughnecks won the first game of their series against the Cosmos, 3-0, in Tulsa. Once the series got back to the Meadowlands, it was a different story. The Cosmos took the return game by 3-0 and then the tie-breaking mini-game by 3-1 to advance to their meeting with Vancouver.

There had been bad blood between the Cosmos and the Whitecaps all season, including a fight that saw four players sent off during a game in July, and it continued into the first game of the semifinal series, a 2-0 victory for Vancouver at Empire Stadium in Vancouver. The spark that set off the trouble was the second Vancouver goal, on a breakaway by Trevor Whymark. The Cosmos felt that the goal should have been disallowed for offside. Carlos Alberto led the Cosmos' futile protest against the goal, and the atmosphere wasn't helped any when Andranik Eskandarian was red carded after taking a run at a Vancouver player. Then, in the tunnel leading to the locker rooms after the game, Carlos Alberto got into an altercation with an official that, according to the league reports, included spitting on the man.

The first leg was played on Wednesday, Aug. 29. The second leg was three days later at Giants Stadium. In between, the Cosmos learned that they would have to play that second leg without either Eskandarian, suspended by the league for the game as a result of his red card, or Carlos Alberto, suspended for the rest of the season because of the tunnel incident. Cosmos protests of the action were in vain. Ironically, the absence of Carlos Alberto forced the Cosmos to move Franz Beckenbauer back from midfield to sweeper. Beckenbauer was the most famous sweeper in the history of the sport but, since the arrival of Carlos Alberto in 1977, Beckenbauer had been playing in midfield for the Cosmos, somewhat unhappily.

The Cosmos took a 2-1 lead into the locker room at halftime of that second leg game on Sept. 1. Chinaglia scored both Cosmos goals, after short passes from Vladislav Bogicevic and then Seninho had found him wide open in front of the net. The Whitecaps had tied the game after Chinaglia's first goal, and they did so again in the second half, with Whymark scoring on a sharp header. It wasn't the first time Chinaglia and his teammates had been burned by Whymark. In 1973, Chinaglia had watched Whymark, then playing for Ipswich Town of England, put four goals into Lazio's net in a UEFA Cup game.

NASL rules dictated that because Vancouver had won the first leg, if the Whitecaps won this second leg, the series would be over, and if the Cosmos won it, then a 30-minute mini-game would be played to settle the issue. Neither won the second leg, at least not in the usual manner. After Whymark's goal, the game ended in a 2-2 tie, and there were no further goals during the 15 minutes of sudden-death overtime (although Kevin Hector of the Whitecaps did force

Giants Stadium to hold its breath by hitting the far post with a long-range shot). A shootout did break the tie, however, giving the second-leg victory to the Cosmos and forcing the mini-game.

The second-leg game had been 105 minutes of end-to-end action, and the mini-game was more of the same, but with no scoring. Carl Valentine came very close for Vancouver with a shot that ricocheted down after hitting the crossbar but was ruled not to have crossed the goalline. Mark Liveric thought he had won the game for the Cosmos with a goal in the final minute, but it was disallowed for a foul, so a second shootout was needed to decide which of the two exhausted teams would advance. Vancouver won that honor, and began making preparations to return to Giants Stadium a week later for the final, while the Cosmos, licking wounds both mental and physical after a marathon afternoon, began making preparations for yet another foreign tour.

The Cosmos were not particularly sporting about it all. The day before the game, De la Sierra had commented on the league's rejection of their protests by saying of the second-leg game: "So we'll lose. Isn't that what the commissioner wants?"[64] After the game, Julio Mazzei said that Vancouver had won because that was what the league wanted, adding that "the officials were against us in the playoffs."[65]

The postseason tour was to Asia this time. In six weeks on tour, the Cosmos played 13 games, two each in Hong Kong, South Korea, Indonesia and Japan, one each in Singapore and Malaysia and three in Australia. The fact that none of those places was a soccer power was not lost on the Cosmos. The Cosmos did better on this tour than they had done in Europe the year before, finishing it with six wins, three losses and four ties. Their minds were already on 1980 and retribution, however.

The Cosmos got that retribution—and some more controversy, of course—in 1980. They repeated their regular-season success of the previous two years, winning their division with a 24-8 record. In the first round of the playoffs, they dispatched the Tulsa Roughnecks far more easily than they had in 1979, winning by 3-1 in Tulsa and 8-1 at the Meadowlands. They then stumbled a bit against the Dallas Tornado in the quarterfinals. A 3-2 victory in the first leg in Dallas was followed by a stunning 3-0 defeat at Giants Stadium four days later. The Cosmos regrouped in time to win the mini-game by 3-0. A semifinal victory over the Los Angeles Aztecs then put the Cosmos into the final against the Fort Lauderdale Strikers at RFK Stadium in Washington.

The final was not the cakewalk that the 3-0 final score would imply, but it was not as difficult a victory as many other big games that the Cosmos had won in the past. After a scoreless first half, Julio Cesar Romero, a 20-year-old Paraguayan who was one of the Cosmos' main foreign signings for 1980, opened the scoring. At that point, at least one of Fort Lauderdale's stars saw the handwriting on the wall. "We let them off the hook by not scoring the first half," said Ray Hudson after the game. "I knew at halftime the team that scored first would win. Once they scored we didn't have the guns or the players to respond or come back. The enthusiasm drained right out of us. We were done."[66]

According to Ike Kuhns of the *Newark Star-Ledger*, "The Cosmos seemed more determined to play despite the intense heat [it was 97 in Washington that day], while the Strikers played ultra conservatively."[67] One Cosmos player described Fort Lauderdale's strategy in words that sound funny today. "Their tactics were kind of silly for a final game," said Angelo DiBernardo. "When you get this far you come to attack. It's do or die. They were very cautious."[68] But this was 1980, and the era of boringly cautious finals of major tournaments was still in the future.

DiBernardo's words also highlighted one thing that had been endearing the Cosmos to American soccer fans ever since the arrival five years before of skillful Latin players like Pelé and Ramon Mifflin. The Cosmos in their heyday were always noted for flair, never for caution. Their defense was solid, but the thing that made them such a spectacular success was their relentless attack.

Giorgio Chinaglia scored the last two Cosmos goals, his 49th and 50th of the NASL season. The league only counted regular-season goals in its official statistics, so Chinaglia, who caught fire during the playoffs, officially was credited by the league with only 32 goals.

As so often was the case after big victories, not all the Cosmos were happy. The main one who wasn't was Carlos Alberto, benched by coach Hennes Weisweiler, who had replaced Julio Mazzei at the helm of the Cosmos a few months before. "The coach benched me in Dallas and I accepted that," Carlos Alberto said, "but not today. I want to tell you right now that I won't play for this coach again."[69] That last turned out to not really be true, but the fighting between Carlos Alberto and Weisweiler did continue, and Carlos Alberto was gone before the start of the 1981 NASL season.

Weisweiler, who had coached several top clubs in West Germany and Spain, was the first foreign superstar coach the Cosmos had ever hired to go with their galaxy of foreign superstar players. The man he succeeded, Mazzei, became the first Cosmos coach to depart from that job with a smile on his face.

"I'm extremely happy that he's coming sooner than expected," Mazzei said in April when it was announced that Weisweiler would be leaving FC Cologne and ending Mazzei's caretaker status a month before the end of the West German season.[70]

Of course, Mazzei's happiness was related to the fact that while he was relinquishing the coaching duties to Weisweiler, he retained his position as technical director. And there had been icing on the cake for the Brazilian coach, who had been such a close associate of Pelé. Mazzei had had the pleasure of coaching the Cosmos in a 2-1 victory over Santos as part of the Cosmos' preseason South American tour. That game on March 14 was played at the Vila Belmiro Stadium in Santos, and Franz Beckenbauer and Rick Davis got the Cosmos goals.

About two months after that game in Santos, the Cosmos said that Beckenbauer, whose four-year contract was due to expire in October, had agreed to sign for an additional two seasons. The contract never was signed, however, and in early July Beckenbauer announced that he would be returning to Germany in the fall, to play for SV Hamburg. Salary was not an issue. Reportedly, the new Cosmos contract that was never signed had been for more money per year than the Cosmos paid Pelé.[71] What was an issue, it seemed, was Beckenbauer's endorsement status in Germany. Sporting goods manufacturer Adidas, unhappy with the drop in Beckenbauer's value to the company while he was playing in the United States, refused to renew its contract with Beckenbauer beyond its 1985 expiration unless he returned to Germany.[72]

The Cosmos held a farewell game for Beckenbauer after the season, just as they had for Pelé in 1977. Unfortunately, the softspoken Beckenbauer was not the star attraction that day. That role went to the magnetic Pelé, who agreed to put on a Cosmos' uniform again for the game, scored a goal and thoroughly upstaged Beckenbauer.[73] Actually, Beckenbauer was back with the Cosmos a few years later, playing the 1983 season at Giants Stadium despite his well known dislike for playing on Astroturf, something that may have been a factor in his decision to return to Germany.

Beckenbauer had never really inherited the mantle of Pelé as the man who symbolized the Cosmos the way the team had hoped he might, but Giorgio Chinaglia was glad to fill that vacuum, and 1980 was his banner season.

Chinaglia scored two goals or more in a game 14 times in the 1980 NASL season. The best was an incredible seven goals in a playoff game against Tulsa on Aug. 31. Of the Cosmos' seven playoff games, the only one in which Chinaglia didn't score was the 3-0 loss to Dallas on Sept. 7, and he scored two goals in the series overtime "mini-game" that followed the regular game that night. He finished the regular season with 32 goals in 32 games, his second best total ever, and then followed that with 18 more goals in the playoffs. His 50 NASL goals in 1980 were the third best season total ever in first-division United States soccer, topped only by Archie Stark's 67 goals for Bethlehem Steel in the 1924-25 American Soccer League season and Davey Brown's 52 for the New York Giants in the 1926-27 ASL season. The most that Chinaglia had ever scored in an Italian season with Lazio was 24, and he was in goalscoring heaven with the Cosmos.

Chinaglia kept right on scoring on the Cosmos' postseason tour. In 12 games in Europe and Africa, he had 12 goals, giving him a total in all games for the Cosmos in 1980 of 76 goals (better than Stark's 75 in all games during Bethlehem Steel's 1924-25 season). His teammates only had a combined total of eight goals on the tour, however, as the Cosmos won three games, lost five and tied four.

It didn't take too much longer for Chinaglia to become embroiled in a dispute with Weisweiler and start threatening to leave the Cosmos. That departure didn't happen, at least not until Chinaglia retired in 1983, but the Cosmos were starting to look a bit frayed, even with Chinaglia still on the field and their financial crises still a few years away. The loss of Franz Beckenbauer and Carlos Alberto between the 1980 and 1981 seasons marked the end of an era for the Cosmos, who already had seen stars like Pelé, Werner Roth and Terry Garbett retire. The Cosmos still had one more NASL championship in their future, but by the end of 1980, their greatest years were now past.

SIX

Second Fiddle

Bethlehem Steel's Scandinavian tour in the summer of 1919 may have been a triumph, but the fashion in which the players came home to Pennsylvania was a bit more ragged. A majority of the team arrived back in Bethlehem together, but some stayed overseas longer to visit their families in England or Scotland and some never arrived back at all, having decided to move to other clubs.

This was not a sign of the imminent demise of the Bethlehem Steel team. The Steelworkers still had 11 years to go, and in those 11 years they would win four league championships and three major cup titles. But they would never again reach the heights of dominance they had between 1915 and 1919, and they would spend much of those 11 years watching other teams, particularly Robins Dry Dock of Brooklyn, Scullin Steel of St. Louis and the Fall River Marksmen, take the largest share of the honors in American soccer.

Bethlehem Steel got off to a very slow start to the 1919-20 season, thanks to its straggling and tardy return from Europe. The Steelworkers played their final game in Sweden on Sept. 24 and most of them sailed from Stockholm on Sept. 27. Two players who had left earlier arrived back in Bethlehem on Oct. 2, followed a week later by the main group, although several players remained in Europe for nearly another month. The National Association Foot Ball League schedule had begun on Sept. 28, but Bethlehem Steel didn't play its

149

first league game until Dec. 6, by which time some teams had played as many as seven league games.

Once the Steelworkers did get going, they did so in a stumbling fashion that served warning that the post-Scandinavia version of Bethlehem Steel might not be as dominant as the earlier one. They lost two of their first three league games, to the New York FC on Dec. 14 and Erie AA of Kearny on Dec. 21. Eventually, they righted themselves, won their last eight league games and took the NAFBL championship by a single point over Erie. A 4-0 win over Erie on May 15 got them back in the middle of the race, and then victories over Robins in their final two games, 6-1 on May 22 and 2-0 on June 6, put them across the finish line barely in front.

Bethlehem won the NAFBL again in 1921, its third straight championship in that league, and did so in more decisive fashion than a year before. It was tied for first place with New York FC going into a game with that team on Jan. 15, 1921. Bethlehem won, 4-0, that day, with newcomer Harold Brittan scoring the first two goals, and was never headed that season. The following week, the Steelworkers beat Robins Dry Dock, 3-2, with Brittan getting another goal, to strengthen their position still more. By the end of the season, which was the NAFBL's last, Bethlehem Steel had pulled six points ahead of the pack.

However, Bethlehem Steel's record in cup competition during those last two NAFBL seasons indicated more of a downturn in the Steelworkers' fortunes. A landmark event in that slide happened in October 1919, when Harry Ratican signed to play for Robins Dry Dock. Ratican had said the previous spring that he planned to leave. Bethlehem officials had hoped that he might change his mind during the Scandinavian tour, but the opposite may have occurred. According to the *Bethlehem Globe*: "Ratican refused to comment on the reason for his desiring a change of scene, but it is believed that his action was prompted by friction with some of the players. It is understood that for some time he had not been getting along any too well with certain members of the team."[1]

At Robins, Ratican joined several other former Bethlehem Steel players, most notably Bob Millar, who still held the Bethlehem record for goals in a single season with 59 in the 1914-15 season, and Neil Clarke, who had starred on Bethlehem's National Challenge Cup winners in 1915 and 1916. Millar, Clarke and Ratican were a large part of the foundation that made Robins quickly into a very strong team.

Bethlehem had been in the final of the National Challenge Cup five years in a row, but in the 1919-20 competition they didn't even reach the semifinals. Their opponents in the first four rounds had all been from the Philadelphia area, and the Steelworkers got past them fairly easily, winning the four games by a total of 21-3. In the quarterfinals on April 4, 1920 at Todd Field in Brooklyn, the opponent was Robins Dry Dock, and Bethlehem's run ended there. As the 30-minute overtime was winding down, it appeared the game was likely to end in a 0-0 tie, a result that favored Bethlehem, since the game was on Robins' home field and a replay would be in Bethlehem. But Robins had Bethlehem's defenders at full stretch, and the pressure finally paid off, with Robins forward Jack McGuire putting the ball past Bill Duncan off a corner kick for the deciding goal. After that victory, Robins was riding about as high as could be, with its record for the 1919-20 season consisting at that point of 22 victories and a tie.

Bethlehem wasn't ousted as early in the AFA Cup. The Steelworkers' run got them past the two leading teams from the West Hudson region at that point, Federal Ship of Kearny by 5-0 in the quarterfinals and then Erie AA by 5-1 in the semifinals. In the latter game, Bethlehem looked for a day like its old self, as it "displayed the form that has made the team famous from one end of the country to the other" according to the *Newark Evening News*.[2] Whitey Fleming scored three goals, all within a space of 15 minutes in the first half.

However, waiting in the final was Robins Dry Dock, and another 1-0 defeat, which the *New York Times* said "completed the dethronement of the famous steelmakers."[3] Fleming, who had missed the National Challenge Cup quarterfinal against Robins because of laryngitis, was back, but he wasn't enough. Bethlehem's Tommy Murphy put the ball into his own net during a goalmouth scramble midway through the second half and that was all the scoring. The Robins players added insult to injury by crowding around Murphy and shaking his hand after the own-goal.[4] The fact that Bethlehem was no longer the champion of either cup may have influenced the Brazilian government's thinking when it cancelled a Brazilian tour by Bethlehem Steel just before the team was to board its ship in New York on Aug. 14, 1920.

At least Bethlehem had extended its 1920 cup efforts into the spring. The next season, it didn't get that far. By the second day of January 1921, the NAFBL title was all it had left to play for that year.

Bethlehem's National Challenge Cup bid ended first, in a second-round loss to Erie in Harrison on Nov. 7, 1920. "The score was 4 goals to 3, but the score doesn't indicate in any degree the superiority of the

West Hudson outfit [referring to the West Hudson region, not the West Hudson AA, which no longer existed] over the crack Pennsylvanians," the *Newark Evening News* said. "Bethlehem was afforded very few opportunities to score. For fully three-quarters of the game the ball was in the territory of the Bethlehem team, and the Eries kept raining kick after kick in the direction of the Penn Staters' goal."[5]

They only got a bit farther in AFA Cup, into the fourth round. Then they met Robins again on Jan. 1, 1921, and suffered yet another 1-0 defeat. This loss was a bit more biting than the other two, because it took place at Steel Field and was the first game Bethlehem had ever lost there, after 53 victories and two ties since the field was opened in 1916. The irony of those three consecutive 1-0 eliminations by Robins in cup games is that in the same two seasons, 1919-20 and 1920-21, Bethlehem played Robins four times in the National Association Foot Ball League and won all four.

By the fall of 1921, Bethlehem Steel, Robins Dry Dock and Erie AA all were playing in the original American Soccer League, which had supplanted the National Association Foot Ball League. Bethlehem Steel had moved its base of operations (temporarily, it turned out) to Philadelphia and was playing under the name of Philadelphia FC. Robins had changed its name to Todd Shipyards and Erie AA had changed its name to Harrison FC.

The birth of the American Soccer League had been rumored for a while before it took place in May 1921. The first inklings came in late November 1920, when it was reported that Thomas W. Cahill, the only secretary the U.S. Football Association had ever had, planned to resign from that post. When Cahill confirmed this a week later, the *Bethlehem Globe* said Cahill "intended to devote his time to organizing a national league of professional soccer teams."[6] This would not be the first time such an attempt had been made. In the fall of 1894, the American League of Professional Football Clubs lasted only three weeks, leaving behind a pile of errors that constituted a manual of how not to do it. That league was centered on Eastern cities. An attempt in 1909 centered on the Midwest and was led by Chicago baseball interests, but it never got off the ground.

The 1921 *Spalding Guide* (edited by Cahill, of course), made it clear that the new league was Cahill's baby, saying: "The American Soccer League was conceived and organized by Thomas W. Cahill . . . . It has been Cahill's dream to place soccer on a plane in this country comparable to its place in Scandinavian sporting life and eventually to bring the sport to be recognized as the national game of the of the fall-to-spring months. After many years of direction of the National Challenge Cup competition, or national championships, he concluded that the only means of winning general public interest was through the medium of professional leagues playing regular schedules much as the major leagues of baseball operate."[7]

Both the 1894 and 1909 attempts, organized by baseball people, had been efforts to put major-league baseball stadiums to more profitable use in the offseason than just sitting empty. They failed, but leagues with lesser objectives didn't, and as the plans for the new pro league took shape in the spring of 1921, it became apparent that the league would be a combination of two of those lesser leagues, the National Association Foot Ball League in New York, New Jersey and Pennsylvania, and the Southern New England Soccer League in Massachusetts and Rhode Island.

The *Spalding Guide* hoped that this would be only the start: "Unquestionably, if the American League venture meets with marked success, similar leagues will be operated within another year or two in the Middle West, where the sport already has a strong grip, and possibly also on the Pacific Coast, where a high grade of soccer has been played for years under USFA supervision. Eventually, then, would come an annual national title series in which would clash the pennant winners in several sectional big leagues, a series which, it is anticipated, will come in time to be as popular, or nearly, so, as the world series of baseball."[8] This may have been the start of soccer's status as the perennial "sport of the future" in America.

Bethlehem Steel was the dominant member of the National Association Foot Ball League, at that point on the way to its third straight league championship. But as the planning for the new league continued, it became apparent that Bethlehem, Pa.'s place in the league wasn't guaranteed. Two significant reasons were the chronic attendance problems in Bethlehem and the desire of Philadelphia to get a team, if necessary by kidnapping Bethlehem's.

The first public acknowledgement of this situation came on Jan. 17, 1921, when the *Philadelphia Inquirer* reported that "it is the intention of Mr. Cahill to have one strong team in this city, probably the Bethlehem club."[9] Philadelphia interests continued promoting the idea of moving the Bethlehem Steel team there, and Bethlehem officials continued denying that this could happen. When the league was officially formed on May 7, 1921 and the lineup of teams was announced, both Bethlehem Steel and a team called "Philadelphia FC" were listed. But while most of the teams in the league were existing clubs, the Philadelphia FC was just a shell, and the rumors that Bethlehem Steel would be moved into that shell persisted.

By the time the first season began in mid-September 1921, the fears of fans in Bethlehem had come true. "As originally planned, the league was to have included Bethlehem Steel Football Club," the 1921 *Spalding Guide* said, "but at the last moment the Falco team of Holyoke [Mass.] replaced Bethlehem and a majority of the Bethlehem team's stars were berthed on the Philadelphia club."[10] The name on the uniforms said Philadelphia, not Bethlehem, but few fans were fooled, despite the fact that there was an amateur team still playing in Bethlehem that was called Bethlehem Steel. There was no question that Philadelphia FC was the real Bethlehem Steel, moved to the big city where attendance might be greater. During Philadelphia FC's 1921-22 ASL season, 13 players appeared in 10 or more games. Of those 13, all but two were former Bethlehem Steel players.

Philadelphia FC, which played some of its home games at the Baker Bowl, a big-league baseball park, made even quicker work of its opposition in the first ASL season than Bethlehem Steel had in the last NAFBL season. By the end of the third weekend of the season, on Oct. 2, it had eight points from four games, while no one else in the league had more than three points. The ersatz Quakers won 10 of their first 12 games (the other two were ties) and had nearly blown the race open by Christmas. On Jan. 1, 1922, they had 22 points and a five-point lead over their closest pursuers. Three months later, New York FC had closed the gap to three points, but Philadelphia FC closed strongly. It ended the season with 38 points from its 24 games, to 33 points for second-place New York FC. Todd Shipyard, the former Robins Dry Dock, was third with 29, but Todd/Robins maintained its dominance of Philadelphia/Bethlehem on the cup scene. There was no AFA Cup that season, but in the National Challenge Cup, Todd once again was the Steelworkers' nemesis, eliminating them by 4-1 in a fourth-round game on Dec. 26, 1921.

Bethlehem Steel drew no better in Philadelphia than it had in Bethlehem, and the ruse that had resulted in the Steelworkers playing in false colors in the 1921-22 season lasted only a year. By the start of the 1922-23 season, they were back in Bethlehem. Still, that was a dismal season for them, the first since they began regular league competition in 1911 that they had failed to win either their league championship or one of the major cup titles.

Second Fiddle

The news in April 1922 that the team would be returning to Bethlehem was followed in subsequent months by word of various key players who had become free agents that summer and would not be among the returning Steelworkers. In July, it was revealed that Whitey Fleming and Jock Ferguson, two of the leading players of Bethlehem Steel's great teams of the 1915-19 era, had left for J&P Coats of Pawtucket, R.I. Before the start of the new season in September, Harold Brittan, Bethlehem's leading scorer the previous two seasons, departed for the new Fall River Marksmen team in Massachusetts.

Bethlehem Steel had been without a serious rival from Fall River for several years. The Fall River Rovers faded after 1918 and the Fall River United team that played in the 1921-22 ASL season was not a worthy successor to Fall River's great soccer tradition, finishing sixth in the seven-team league. For the 1922-23 season, Fall River United was taken over by sports promoter Sam Mark, who renamed the team the Marksmen; built a stadium just across the state line in North Tiverton, R.I., so the Massachusetts Blue Laws wouldn't prevent it from playing home games on Sunday, and set about signing some star players. Among the luminaries who played for Fall River in that 1922-23 season were former Bethlehem stars Harold Brittan, Bob Millar, Neil Clarke and Fred Pepper. The four games that Bill McPherson played for Fall River that season were the first of 370 games in his ASL career, the most by any ASL player.

Whitey Fleming, who had scored 15 goals for Philadelphia FC in the 1921-22 season, had 22 for J&P Coats in 1922-23 as he led the team from Rhode Island to a narrow victory over Bethlehem for the second ASL title. Bethlehem led the ASL standings throughout the fall and winter, but couldn't hold on. Starting in late January, Coats won 14 games in a row to barely overhaul the Steelworkers. The key game was one in Pawtucket on April 14, 1923 that Bethlehem entered with a three-point lead. Coats won, 1-0, that day, closing the gap to one point, and moved past Bethlehem a few weeks later. A second crucial homestretch defeat was a loss to Paterson FC on May 6. A month after that, Coats captured the title by beating that same Paterson team in its final game of the season, finishing with 44 points to Bethlehem's 42. The Fall River Marksmen, improving considerably over Fall River United's performance a season before, were third with 35 points.

Fleming and Brittan were replaced as Bethlehem's top scorers by Daniel McNiven, a young import from Scotland who led the ASL with 28 goals in his only Bethlehem season.

Bethlehem got through the first three rounds of the National Challenge Cup with victories over Philadelphia teams before it ran up against New York FC in the fourth round and was sent home with a 4-1 defeat on Dec. 24, 1922. Imitating the trend of the Bethlehem-vs.-Robins rivalry of previous seasons, Bethlehem had three wins and a tie in league competition that season against New York FC, but couldn't get past it in cup competition.

One of the Philadelphia teams that Bethlehem beat in the early rounds of the National Challenge Cup was Fleischer Yarn, a 1-0 victim in Bethlehem on Nov. 4, 1922. A week later in Philadelphia, Fleischer got its revenge, a 3-2 victory over Bethlehem that eliminated the Steelworkers in the very first round of the AFA Cup. Between the cup defeats, the runnerup finish in the ASL race and the departures of Fleming, Ferguson and Brittan, it was not a season to remember for Bethlehem, despite its return to the banks of the Lehigh River.

The 1923-24 season was the one in which Bethlehem Steel's rivalry with the Fall River Marksmen really began to grow into something comparable to its rivalry with the Fall River Rovers in the previous decade. The two met six times in competitive games that season, as they battled for honors in the ASL and both cups, plus one friendly.

Once again, a big name on Bethlehem's forward line had departed, as had happened in the past with Millar, Ratican, Fleming and Brittan. This time it was Daniel McNiven, who never repeated the big season he had with 28 goals in 1922-23. In his last three ASL seasons, at New York FC, New York Giants and Indiana Flooring, McNiven had a combined total of 14 goals. Once again, however, there were new names to fill the gap. This time, it was Walter Jackson and Alex Jackson, a pair of Scottish brothers. Walter was the one with the established reputation, made in several seasons with Kilmarnock in the Scottish first division, but it was Alex, several years younger than Walter, who eventually became an international star in Scotland and England, after the brothers left Bethlehem a year later.

During the years of Bethlehem Steel vs. Fall River Rovers clashes, a measure of the intensity of the rivalry between the two cities had been the sniping between newspapers. That battle broke out anew in 1923, after a disagreement about the percentage of the gate the visiting Bethlehem team was to be paid for a preseason friendly between Bethlehem and the Marksmen. According to the *Fall River Herald*, the only difference between Bethlehem Steel and highway robbers of the 19th century was that "the Jesse James boys used a horse and a pistol while the Bethlehem Steel management uses the telephone and tele-graph wires."[11]

The first of those six competitive games was an ASL meeting on Dec. 15, 1923, in Bethlehem. For both teams it was the 10th game of the ASL season. Fall River went into it with a one-point lead in the standings, but Bethlehem's 1-0 victory put it into first place with 16 points, to Fall River's 15. Three weeks later, the two met again in North Tiverton, and this time the situation was reversed. Fall River's Bill McPherson scored the only goal of a 1-0 game that lifted the Marksmen into a tie with the Steelworkers, each team with 20 points.

The race was still very close, with Fall River one point ahead, when the two met in early March in a semifinal of the National Challenge Cup. Bethlehem's route to that semifinal meeting with Fall River had included its usual easy passage through the early rounds. For the third year in a row, it played Philadelphia teams in the first three rounds, and beat them by a combined 19-0. It got tougher in late December. After a 2-2 tie with New York FC in the fourth round, Bethlehem won the replay by only 4-3. A goal by Daniel McNiven gave New York FC a 2-1 lead in the middle of the first half, but Walter Jackson tied it just before halftime and scored two more goals in the first six minutes of the second half. A month later, another replay was required after Bethlehem and Newark tied their quarterfinal, but this time Bethlehem didn't have such a struggle in the rematch, winning by 4-0. That set up the semifinal against Fall River on March 9 at Dexter Park in Brooklyn.

Fall River's 2-0 victory that day was the most significant the Marksmen had yet accomplished in their two seasons. Beating Bethlehem wasn't like beating the powerhouse of five years before, but Bethlehem was starting to regain its strength. Former Bethlehem player Dougie Campbell was involved in both Fall River goals, which came just before halftime. He crossed to a wide-open Johnny Reid for the first and put the second into the net himself. After the intermission, Fall River went into a defensive shell for the rest of the game.

Both the *New York Times* and the *Bethlehem Globe* said that the crowd that day in Brooklyn was 20,000, which would make it the largest that had ever seen a soccer game in the United States at that time. The *Newark Evening News* said 15,000, just below the record set in 1905 in St. Louis. The fact that all three papers cited very round numbers implies that they were just guesses.

The *Times* described a scene in which the enthusiasm of the crowd contrasted sharply with the condition of the field:

The contest was witnessed by more than 20,000 persons, who were kept at a fever pitch of excitement throughout the battle . . . . Probably never before has the dilapidated park near Brooklyn Manor witnessed such a classic. Every seat in the grand stands and the bleachers was occupied, spectators crowded the aisles and exits, while others stood along the side lines through the hour and a half of play. Others were forced to watch the game from near-by hills and roofs of buildings.

Overhead the sky was clear and a sharp tang in the air made the weather ideal for the playing of the game, but underfoot the ground was a sea of mud . . . . However, despite the condition of the playing surface, the contest was fast throughout and dexterous footwork marked the performances of many.[12]

The *Evening News* may have disagreed about the size of the crowd, but it agreed about the playing conditions, saying: "Dexter Park was an unhappy selection as a neutral battleground for a contest of such importance and was unworthy of the crowd that journeyed to it from all parts of the East. The south end of the field presented a layer of oozy mud about a foot deep. The entrances to the stands also were aisles of mud."[13]

In the weeks after that game, Fall River sharply widened its one-point lead in the ASL standings. The next time that Bethlehem and Fall River met was in the AFA Cup final two months later. In between those two games, each played six ASL games. Bethlehem had a dismal record of one win, two ties and three defeats in that stretch. Fall River had six straight victories as it broke the ASL race open.

Perhaps Bethlehem Steel did have an excuse for that record. At least some of its concentration was elsewhere in those two months, on a trip that showed both that the glamour of its name was undiminished and that the reality was looking up again as well. In between the two cup games against Fall River, Bethlehem made a trip to St. Louis for three games, and won all three this time. Victories of 3-2 and 2-1 over St. Louis all-star teams on consecutive days were followed a day after that by a 4-0 rout of the team from Gillespie, Ill., a coal-mining town across the Mississippi River where soccer was king.

The AFA Cup final on May 11 was not a classic, but the game in Jersey City did provide Bethlehem Steel with its first championship since 1919 in either of the two big cup competitions. Jack Rattay, not a regular with Bethlehem Steel, got the only goal of the game 30 minutes in, when the ball came to him in a goalmouth scramble after a free kick and he shot home.

Bethlehem and Fall River met twice more after the AFA Cup final, although one of them was a meaningless game. The more significant of the two took place in Bethlehem on May 17, with Bethlehem Steel still clinging to the barest of chances in the ASL standings. The *Bethlehem Globe*, despite doing calculations that showed Bethlehem Steel still holding a mathematical chance of winning, seemed to have given up hope, referring to Fall River in its story about the AFA Cup final as "a team that is destined to win the honors in the American Soccer League race."[14] That was an accurate assessment. A look in retrospect shows that in order for Bethlehem to have won the ASL title, it would have had to win all five of its remaining games while Fall River was losing all three it had left.

Fall River rendered the mathematical calculations moot on May 17, scoring a 3-0 victory at Steel Field in which Harold Brittan had two of the goals. The victory did more than clinch the ASL title for the Marksmen. It also made them the first ASL team to win the "double," taking the United States' top league and cup titles in the same year. They had followed their victory over Bethlehem in the National Challenge Cup semifinals by beating a St. Louis team in the final three weeks later. Whether Fall River was the first team to win an American double was open to debate. West Hudson won the National Association Foot Ball League and the AFA Cup in 1912, while Bethlehem won the NAFBL and the National Challenge Cup in 1919, but there could be arguments that those were lesser achievements and Fall River's was the first "real" American double.

With its double, Fall River proved that, Bethlehem Steel's experience notwithstanding, a successful economic climate wasn't absolutely necessary as a background to success on the soccer field. In 1924, the city of Fall River was in a desperate downturn as the textile industry that had sustained southeastern New England for half a century moved elsewhere.[15] That doesn't seem to have slowed the Marksmen, at least not in 1924.

Bethlehem Steel finished fast in the ASL. Once it was mathematically eliminated, it went on a winning streak that enabled it to finish with 40 points to Fall River's 44. It ended the season on June 8 with a 4-1 victory over New York FC that gave it second place in the final standings. The Jackson brothers each scored goals in what was to be the last game that they ever played in tandem for Bethlehem Steel.

Even more significantly for Bethlehem Steel, it also was the last game that Archie Stark ever played for New York FC. By the start of the 1924-25 ASL season, Stark was back in the uniform he had last worn on Bethlehem Steel's Scandinavian tour in 1919.

The summer of 1924 marked some big changes for the ASL generally. In late June, the league voted to add four new teams to the eight it already had. Those teams, in Boston, New Bedford, Providence and New York, went out and signed a lot of new players. "Boston, in particular, made all the clubs take notice by signing a number of well-known Scottish players," according to soccer historian Colin Jose. "At the start of the season, the team was coached by a well-known Scottish international, Tommy Muirhead of Glasgow Rangers, and included in the lineup was another Scottish international, outside right Alex McNab, while the rest of the team included a number of players with experience at the highest levels of Scottish soccer."[16]

In previous seasons, ASL clubs had played each of the others four times, for a 28-game season. Expanding to 12 teams while keeping the same four-games rate meant extending the schedule to 44 games. That precipitated a dispute with the United States Football Association over the participation of ASL teams in the National Challenge Cup. At its annual meeting in Detroit in mid-July, the USFA accepted a system under which 14 eastern clubs could make application to be exempted from the early rounds of the National Challenge Cup. This, as the *Bethlehem Globe* pointed out, would have the effect of enabling some ASL teams to play league games against strong league opponents in beautiful autumn weather that would otherwise be used up on early-round cup mismatches against amateur opponents. Still, it wasn't enough for the ASL, which wanted all of its teams automatically exempted from the early rounds. The league voted in early August to boycott the National Challenge Cup and was joined in this action by the St. Louis Soccer League, foreshadowing the all-out "Soccer War" that began four years later. There quickly was talk that the boycott was the brainchild of Thomas W. Cahill, seeking revenge after being ousted as secretary of the USFA in April 1924, but Cahill denied that he had had any part in the boycott decision.

In those days, cup games were the highlights of the schedule for most ASL clubs, and the boycott, coming in the same season that the AFA Cup was finally discontinued, caused a void. Five months after withdrawing from the National Challenge Cup, the ASL decided to fill that gap by starting a cup competition of its own. The particular incentive in this competition, which later became known as the Lewis Cup after the donation of a trophy by Bethlehem Steel's Edgar Lewis, was that the winner would meet the champions of the St. Louis Soccer League for the title of professional soccer champion of the United States. However, the 12 ASL clubs ended up playing a combined total of only 11 games in what that season was called the American Soccer League cup. It wasn't much of a diversion from the ASL schedule, in which those same clubs played 252 games.

Bethlehem Steel lasted only two games in that first Lewis Cup. A 3-1 victory over Indiana Flooring in the first round on Jan. 24, 1925, was followed three weeks later by a 1-0 elimination at the hands of the New Bedford Whalers. In the final on March 29, the Boston Wonder Workers beat Fall River, and then went on to defeat Ben Millers of St. Louis the following month for the U.S. professional title, which was held for the only time in 1925. ASL and St. Louis teams were back in the National Challenge Cup by the 1925-26 season. However, the Lewis Cup, even without its stepping-stone status, thrived for years, until 1963. In the last final, Ukrainian Sitch of Newark beat Ukrainian Nationals of Philadelphia, and the trophy that Edgar Lewis donated now sits in a museum in Kiev.

Bethlehem Steel's sibling stars of the 1923-24 season, Walter and Alex Jackson, sailed from New York for their Scottish vacation on Aug. 9. By the end of the month, Bethlehem fans had realized that the vacation was a charade and the brothers weren't going to be returning. The pain of this realization was eased very suddenly, however. On Saturday, Sept. 6, Archie Stark played in an intrasquad game in Bethlehem. The following Wednesday, the team announced that he had signed with Bethlehem for the 1924-25 season, and on Sept. 13 he played his first ASL game for the Steelworkers, against Philadelphia FC.

What a debut it was. Stark got two goals in the opening minutes, first poking a cross by Neil Turner into the Philadelphia net and then heading home a cross by Malcolm Goldie. Before halftime, he had made it a hat trick, converting a cross from Turner. In the middle of the second half, a pass from Tommy Maxwell set up another goal for Stark as Bethlehem completed its 7-1 victory. This was the 70th ASL game Stark had played, but his first four-goal outburst.

Archie Stark, who had been born in Scotland in 1897 but moved with his parents to New Jersey when he was 12 years old, in that season became the biggest star American soccer had yet produced.

His initiation into big-time soccer had come in 1915, when he was

17 years old and the hero of the Kearny Scots team that won the AFA Cup, scoring the winning goal in the final against Brooklyn Celtic. Subsequently, he served in the U.S. Army in France during World War I, played for Bethlehem on its Scandinavian tour in 1919, for Erie AA in the last two seasons of the National Association Foot Ball League and for New York FC in the first three seasons of the ASL. The four goals he scored against Philadelphia FC in his Bethlehem debut on Sept. 13, 1924 brought his total of ASL goals to 49 at that point, and started him on a dizzying 1924-25 season.

Stark had often tormented Bethlehem Steel as an opponent. In both 1920, playing for Erie AA, and 1922, playing for New York FC, he scored goals in games that knocked Bethlehem out of the National Challenge Cup . During the 1923-24 ASL season, he scored four goals in four games against Bethlehem Steel, including the lone goal of New York FC's 1-0 victory on April 26, 1924, which virtually ended Bethlehem's ASL hopes that season.

Between the 1923-24 and 1924-25 ASL seasons, New York FC's franchise was taken over by the Indiana Flooring Company, but few of New York FC's players were included in the transaction. Stark, perhaps feeling that he had made a mistake when he signed with Erie rather than Bethlehem in 1919, made no secret of his wish to play for the Steelworkers and the deal was arranged, with the approval of the ASL. After the season began, several teams protested the deal, and the ASL was forced to ratify it a second time on Oct. 18.

Bethlehem Steel and the Fall River Marksmen engaged in another tremendous battle during the 1924-25 ASL season, although Fall River, the eventual champion, had the upper hand most of the way. On the opening day of the season, Bethlehem gained its 7-1 rout of Philadelphia FC and Fall River played a 2-2 tie with J&P Coats. That was the only time all season that Bethlehem led the standings. The next day, Bethlehem didn't play, and Fall River beat Coats to take a lead it never lost.

Bethlehem trailed by a few points most of the season, but in the last two months of the schedule it pulled nearly level. The two teams went into the month of May with 60 points each, but Fall River had four games left and Bethlehem only three. On the weekend of May 2-3, Bethlehem had a tie and Fall River a win and tie as the Marksmen opened a 63-61 lead over the Steelworkers. The games of May 10, played 40 miles apart in Rhode Island, decided the issue. Bethlehem, playing in Providence, suffered a 1-0 loss to the Clamdiggers, with Tom Florie scoring the only goal on a penalty early in the first half.

Meanwhile, Fall River went wild on its home field in North Tiverton, burying Fleischer Yarn of Philadelphia by 9-0 to clinch the title. A week later, the season ended with Fall River holding a 66-63 lead.

While Bethlehem Steel was involved in its season-long pursuit of Fall River, Archie Stark was piling up the goals. The ASL record for goals in a season was 28, set by Bethlehem's Daniel McNiven in the 1922-23 season. Stark broke that record by mid-December, when he scored his 29th and 30th goals in Bethlehem's 20th game of the season, a 3-0 win over J&P Coats. He seemed almost reluctant on the record-breaker, a disputed penalty on which he sent a soft shot straight at the goalkeeper that was bobbled into the net anyway. No. 30 was a stunning goal however, perhaps the greatest that Stark ever scored.

"It was a play heralded as one of the finest ever witnessed on the Steel Field, rivaling anything probably ever seen on any other American field, and a bit of classical soccer play that was a rare treat for the spectators," the *Bethlehem Globe* said. "Getting possession of the ball in midfield, Stark came down the center, taking charge after charge as he dribbled through the Coats defenses and then wound up his effort with a shot that completely beat Schoefield, the visitors' goalie."[17]

Stark's first five-goal game ever, in an 8-1 win over Fleischer Yarn on Jan. 17, lifted him to 43 goals. On the last day of the season, with Bethlehem already mathematically eliminated, he scored five more against Philadelphia FC, giving him 11 goals in four games against the last-place Philadelphians and 67 for the ASL season.

Those 67 more than doubled the old record. The most that any U.S. player has had in a first-division season since then is 52, by Davey Brown of the New York Giants in the 1926-27 ASL season. Giorgio Chinaglia's 50 for the New York Cosmos in 1980 is left well behind. Stark did have a little advantage over Chinaglia in the length of his season, but not all that much of one. Bethlehem Steel played 44 ASL games in 1924-25; the Cosmos played 39 NASL games in 1980.

In addition to his 67 ASL goals, Stark scored three in a Lewis Cup game against Indiana Flooring in January, and five in two friendlies against an Ohio all-star team in late May. Those 75 in all 51 games that Bethlehem Steel played during its 1924-25 schedule easily beat Bob Millar's Bethlehem record of 59, but they were eclipsed years later by Chinaglia's 76 in all 68 games that the Cosmos played in their 1980 schedule (the difference in the way the seasons are numbered results from the fact that Bethlehem played fall-to-spring schedules and the Cosmos played spring-to-fall schedules).

The argument can be made that the longevity of Stark's first-division record owes a lot to the fact that soccer was a more attacking game in 1925 than it became later. However, there also was an important factor working against Stark, as David Wangerin explains in *Soccer in a Football World*. "The achievement was all the more remarkable," Wangerin says, "in that it came in the last season before the offside rule was changed to undermine the stifling defensive tactics that had developed in Britain, a move that immediately produced a deluge of goals."[18]

Bethlehem Steel's number-one hero had established himself on the banks of the Lehigh. The Steelworkers had quite a few other heroes over the years, most notably Jock Ferguson, Whitey Fleming and Harry Ratican, but Archie Stark was clearly greater than any of them.

Bethlehem Steel's 1925-26 season could be counted as a disappointment if one looked only at the ASL standings, in which it suffered the first third-place finish in its history. But to the Steelworkers, this was the season in which they returned to the top in the National Challenge Cup, winning their first championship since 1919 in the event they had once dominated.

That season demonstrates the difficulty of winning the double, of the pressure on a team in trying to give its all in both events. For by the time Bethlehem started its efforts in the National Challenge Cup on Jan. 17, 1926, the ASL race was virtually decided. At that point, the Steelworkers trailed the Fall River Marksmen by 44 points to 32 and had very little hope left. Bethlehem had started the season well, and held a one-point lead over Fall River after the first three weeks. Then the Marksmen went on a streak of 29 consecutive ASL games without a defeat that turned the league into a runaway. This had the effect on Bethlehem of enabling it to concentrate its sights on the National Challenge Cup, with happy results.

Thanks to the ASL boycott of the previous season, Bethlehem was spared the preliminary-round meetings with local opponents this time. It reached the final by means of a steady march through ASL opposition, beating four league rivals by a total of 12-4. Newark Skeeters, a 5-1 loser in the first round, and J&P Coats, ousted by 3-1 in the semifinals, were not difficult struggles, but the second round and quarterfinals were tighter. Philadelphia FC, which finished next-to-last in the ASL that season, proved unexpectedly tough in the second round on Feb. 13, surrendering only to a late goal by Archie Stark after tying the game at 1-1 in the middle of the second half. In the quarterfinals on March 13 at Hawthorne Park in Brooklyn, Andy

Stradan, an amateur who two years later captained the United States team at the Amsterdam Olympic Games, put the New York Giants in front just six minutes into the game. Bethlehem rallied later in the first half, however, and goals by Stark and Malcolm Goldie gave it the victory.

The final, against Ben Millers of St. Louis, the 1920 champion, was played at Ebbets Field in Brooklyn, and this time everybody seems to have been in agreement on the attendance, 18,000, although that soon became a moot point. The crowd was a record for a soccer game in the United States, but one that lasted only a few weeks, until 27,000 and then 46,000 saw games played in New York by the touring Austrian team Hakoah.

As had been the case with several previous finals between St. Louis teams and eastern teams, the game presented a contrast in styles of play that seems ironic now. Bethlehem Steel, whose players were mostly British, played in the intricate short-passing style favored by British teams at the time and Brazilian teams today, keeping the ball on the ground in what was known as the "carpet system." Ben Millers and other St. Louis teams, primarily fielding native players, played in the direct, long-ball style so prevalent in Britain in recent years but once thought by some to be an American improvement on the British short-passing style. Levi Wilcox of the *Philadelphia Inquirer* summed up the feeling of betting fans by saying: "Those who have learned to admire the game abroad largely place their faith in Bethlehem, which resorts to the scientific, accurate passing game that has made Great Britain's elevens powerful in the soccer world. But the native-born element—and they are legion—have great confidence in the smashing youngsters from the West."[19]

Those youngsters didn't look quite as smashing after Bethlehem's 7-2 victory, which included three goals by Archie Stark. The writers in attendance competed with each in heaping praise on Bethlehem, which for the day looked as good as the Bethlehem juggernaut of 10 years before.

From the *Newark Evening News*: "The Bethlehem soccerites outclassed their Western opponents in ridiculously easy fashion."[20]

From the *New York Times*: "They [the spectators] saw the Bethlehem team, exponents of the carpet system, clean up the Ben Millers with all the efficiency of a vacuum cleaner .... The victors were better on the offense, superior on the defense and even outspeeded the Ben Millers, who were known as the Greyhounds of the West."[21]

From the *Philadelphia Inquirer*: "From the kickoff until the final whistle, Bethlehem exhibited wonderful form and proved so far superior to their younger opponents that there was never the least doubt as to which was the better team."[22]

The first two of Stark's three goals about settled the issue. The first came on a header from a corner kick by Goldie in the sixth minute. Fourteen minutes later, Stark got another after Johnny Grainger slipped a deft pass to him in the goalmouth. Bethlehem was already two goals up and its goalkeeper, Dave Carson, had yet to even touch the ball.

Goldie made the score 3-0 before halftime. Stark's third goal, in the 53rd minute, made it 4-1. The last three Bethlehem goals, from Johnny Rollo (twice) and John Jaap, were icing on Stark's cake. As Levi Wilcox put it: "What made Bethlehem's victory possible was the deadly toe, the cunning and the uncanny ability of Archie Stark." [23]

Stark didn't score goals in the 1925-26 season at his 1924-25 pace, but still did well. He finished second in the ASL scoring race that season, with 43 goals to 44 for Andy Stevens of the New Bedford Whalers. In addition to those 43, he also had 12 more for Bethlehem in cup games and friendlies, but his only four-goal game didn't come in a Bethlehem uniform. On Nov. 8, 1925, he scored four times for the United States in a 6-1 victory over Canada in New York, setting a single-game record for the U.S. national team that still stood more than 80 years later, although it had been tied twice.

A week after winning the National Challenge Cup, Bethlehem began its efforts in the Lewis Cup. Again, as in the first edition of this tournament, the Steelworkers failed to reach the final, although for a while things seemed to be going well for them. Victories over Philadelphia FC and Newark Skeeters in the first two rounds were followed by a 2-0 win over the New York Giants in the first leg of the two-game, aggregate-score semifinals. After that came the deluge, in more ways than one. The second leg, just a day after the first, was played in a driving rain on a quagmire of a field in New York. Bethlehem trailed by 6-1 at halftime. Early in the second half, goals by Rollo and Bob McGregor cut the margin to 6-3, and left Bethlehem trailing by only a single goal on aggregate. Survival was in sight, but three more New York goals in the remaining time put an end to that.

Bethlehem fared even more poorly in the Lewis Cup in the 1926-27 season, losing to Newark in the opening round on Feb. 13, 1927. But that 4-2 defeat, against a team Bethlehem dominated in league games that season, did help to clear the decks for other successes.

Second Fiddle

Bethlehem didn't repeat as National Challenge Cup champion in 1927, but it did have a good run, although one that ended in a disappointing loss to the Fall River Marksmen. That run, which took only a month in the spring of 1927, began with victories over Philadelphia FC (3-1), Trenton FC (6-0) and Newark Skeeters (1-0), to set up a semifinal meeting on April 24 with Fall River in Providence, R.I., supposedly neutral but much closer to Fall River than to Bethlehem.

The unhappy *Bethlehem Globe-Times*, a newspaper not given to much enthusiasm about Bethlehem Steel defeats, referred to the semifinal as "a game of wasted chances and ill designed strategy."[24]

Indeed, there were a few mishaps. Bethlehem Steel scored the opening goal five minutes into the game after Fall River defender Charlie McGill fell while attempting to clear a shot and Bethlehem's Tom Gillespie rushed in to capitalize. The Steelworkers held the lead until just before halftime. In the 40th minute, Bethlehem goalkeeper Dave Edwards came out to collect a long ball into the goalmouth, changed his mind, backtracked, slipped and fell, barely brushed the ball with a fist as it sailed by him, and watched Dougie Campbell collect it and put it easily into the open net. Four minutes later, Edwards seemed frozen as Dave McEachran rose to a cross by Bill McPherson and headed it past him.

The following week, Fall River beat Holley Carburetor of Detroit, 7-0, in the final. It seems very likely that if Bethlehem had been Holley's opponent instead of Fall River, the Steelworkers would have won easily. They were well aware of that fact, and very frustrated by it, for by this point, they had already clinched the ASL championship, and the disappointing effort on April 24 seemed to be the only thing that stood between them and winning the double.

Bethlehem had taken charge of the 1926-27 ASL race fairly early in the season. By the time they suffered their first defeat of the season, against Indiana Flooring in New York on Oct. 10, they had already collected 13 points from their first eight games. Fall River, which was aiming for its fourth straight title, had only eight points from nine games.

By late November, Fall River had caught up a bit. It handed Bethlehem a 2-1 defeat in North Tiverton on Oct. 17, and came into a Nov. 27 game in Bethlehem trailing by only 28 points-to-26 in the standings, although it had played 20 games by this point, to Bethlehem's 18. The Boston Wonder Workers, Bethlehem's closest pursuer in the opening weeks, had lost their last three games in a row and fallen back a bit in the standings, with only 22 points.

Bethlehem didn't clinch the title for almost five months after that Nov. 27 game, but it was the decisive day nevertheless. Fall River left the field in Bethlehem a demoralized 4-0 loser, and Bethlehem was on the way. The Steelworkers had expanded their lead in the standings to four points, and they still had two games in hand. By the end of the season in May, Bethlehem Steel had piled up 66 points, to 57 for runnerup Boston. Then came Fall River with 56, New Bedford with 54 and the New York Giants with 49. The standings also included percentages, designed to compensate for differences in the number of games played, but they proved unnecessary in this case. Each of the five leading contenders played full schedules of 44 games. Bethlehem won so easily that it was able to field a diluted lineup in the clinching game, a 3-3 tie with the New York Giants on April 17. It rested more than half of its regulars in anticipation of two big games in the following week, the National Challenge Cup semifinal against Fall River and an international friendly against Hakoah of Austria.

By the 1926-27 season, ASL teams had adjusted to the changes in the offside rule that had been introduced worldwide a year before, but ASL play that season included several striking innovations, as Colin Jose recounts in *American Soccer League, 1921-31*:

> For the first time, substitutes were permitted, each team being allowed to substitute two players up to 15 minutes from the end of the game. In addition, goal judges were used, one at each end of the ground, and had two functions, the first and obvious one being to assist the referee in deciding when the ball had passed over the line and into the goal. The second was much more controversial . . . . the introduction of the penalty box. In 1926, the ASL goal judges were required to keep the time of the penalties and players penalized were required to stand behind their respective goals with the goal judge.[25]

Bethlehem ended up a winner, but Archie Stark had a disappointing season, at least compared to his previous two. Injuries caused him to miss more than a third of Bethlehem's league games, and he finished only seventh among ASL goal scorers, with 23, far behind the 52 scored by Davey Brown of the New York Giants. Stark, whose last goal of the season came on March 20, with two months to go, wasn't even the top scorer on the Bethlehem team. Tom Gillespie scored 33 goals.

The National Challenge Cup victory of 1926 was the last of Bethlehem Steel's five triumphs in that event, but the Steelworkers showed in 1928 that they weren't quite through hoisting cups, for that year brought them their only Lewis Cup title. It also brought them some controversy of a sort that they weren't accustomed to.

The ASL played its first split season in 1927-28. The first half was scheduled to run from September through December and the second half from February through May, with the first-place and second-place finishers from each half playing off for the championship.

Bethlehem had held a slight lead going into the final three games of the first half, and it appeared that it might qualify for the playoffs without difficulty. On the morning of Dec. 31, 1927, the Steelworkers had 40 points in the standings, to 39 for New Bedford and 38 for Boston. Bethlehem couldn't close the deal, however. Those final three games were a tie and two defeats and Boston slipped past, finishing with 43 points to 41 apiece for Bethlehem and New Bedford.

The system for determining who would make the playoffs was fairly straightforward, but it didn't work without some glitches. First, that tie between Bethlehem and New Bedford for second place in the first half necessitated a tie-breaking playoff. Second, the team that won that playoff, New Bedford, also finished first in the second half, so it qualified for the postseason playoffs from both halves along with the Boston Wonder Workers (first in the first half) and the Fall River Marksmen (second in the second half). Yet another tiebreaker, between the two third-place teams, Bethlehem and the New York Nationals, was needed to determine who the fourth team in the postseason playoffs would be.

The Steelworkers fared better in the playoff against New York Nationals than they had in the earlier one against New Bedford, winning by 2-1 at home on June 4 and 4-0 in New York on June 6. That advanced them into the playoffs proper, where they met the Boston Wonder Workers in the semifinals. This was where the controversy happened. Protested games, particularly in single-elimination cup tournaments, were far more common in American soccer early in the 20th century than they are today, but until June 1928, Bethlehem Steel had generally avoided such complications.

Boston won the first game of the playoff, on June 9 in Boston, by 3-1, and Bethlehem came out of the game with a string of injuries, including one to goalkeeper Dave Edwards. The second game, three days later on a neutral site in Brooklyn, produced a 4-0 victory for Bethlehem, with Archie Stark scoring two goals, and the Steelworkers seemingly were on the way to the final against New Bedford. The second-leg victory had been difficult to achieve, as the *Bethlehem*

Globe-Times said the following day: "Bethlehem went into that game leaving a flock of cripples behind and at the same time being forced to press into service players who were not sound. So acute was the situation that an outside goalie had to be procured to make it possible to field a complete team. The score of 4 to 0 is self-explanatory of the Steelmen's gallant fight in overcoming a two-goal handicap."[26]

The same day that those words appeared in print, the Boston team filed a protest with the league against the use of that "outside goalie," Steve Smith of the Brooklyn Wanderers, whom Bethlehem thought it had received permission to use. The next day, ASL president Bill Cunningham voided Bethlehem's victory and sent Boston to the final, in which it defeated New Bedford, 4-2.

The decision was upheld at a league meeting the following week, by which time it was all academic, since the final already had been held. The partisan *Bethlehem Globe-Times* said of the meeting: "It is understood that the league secretary, Dave Scott, confessed that the entire proceedings eliminating Bethlehem from the playoffs was due to his mistake . . . . When pointing out that the rules provided for a replay where a game was declared no contest because of an ineligible player, the league executives explained that the forfeit was declared due to the lateness of the season and the little time remaining to include a replay . . . . it was generally understood that to overrule the decision would mean the resignation of the president."[27]

The Steelworkers began their cup efforts, in both the Lewis Cup and the National Challenge Cup, in January. The National Challenge Cup produced an early exit. After a first-round victory over a lesser team, Philadelphia Centennial, the Steelworkers met the Brooklyn Wanderers in the second round. A 1-1 tie in Brooklyn on Jan. 29 was followed by a 3-2 defeat in the replay a week later in Bethlehem.

By this time, Bethlehem had ousted the New York Nationals by a 3-2 aggregate over a two-game series in the first round of the Lewis Cup. Next in that tournament came the Newark Skeeters in the semifinals on March 3 and 4. The Steelworkers were again suffering their chronic attendance problems in Bethlehem, and ended up playing eight "home" games in March, April and May of 1928 not at Steel Field but at Northeast High School Field in Philadelphia.

Bethlehem played well in Philadelphia on March 3, beating Newark by 3-1, with Archie Stark scoring the last two goals. A day later in Newark, the Steelworkers finished the job with a 4-0 victory that put them into the final. Tom Gillespie had two of the Bethlehem goals in the second leg.

Bethlehem's opponent in the Lewis Cup final on April 7 and 14 was the Boston Wonder Workers, the same team the Steelworkers later met controversially in the ASL playoffs. Boston had a strong lineup. In addition to former Bethlehem star Whitey Fleming, who by this time was 37 years old, the "Woodsies" featured a cast of Scottish import stars such as Alex McNab, Barney Battles and Johnny Ballantyne. Nevertheless, Bethlehem won the first leg, 3-2, with Archie Stark scoring the first and last Bethlehem goals. A week later, a 2-2 tie in Boston gave Bethlehem the cup on aggregate. Again, Stark was on the scoresheet, with a goal in the middle of the first half that put Bethlehem up by 2-1. Battles scored both Boston goals, and also hit the crossbar twice, but it wasn't enough.

Although Bethlehem played a league game against the New York Nationals at Steel Field a week after its Lewis Cup game in Philadelphia on March 3, the move to Philadelphia resumed the week after that, with strong indications that the team's departure from Bethlehem might become a permanent one.

Team official Luther Lewis, who was the brother of Edgar Lewis, stated the problem in clear and perhaps threatening terms at a Kiwanis Club meeting in Bethlehem in mid-March:

> "We are merely seeking moral support and some financial support from Bethlehemites. We never did and never will expect to make money on the game. In fact, we expect to lose some, but what we do need and want is moral support.
>
> "Every team likes to play before a crowd, and we are no exception. In other cities, we are greeted by salvos of cheers for the other team, but in this city the stands are always quiet. It is getting so bad that many teams are objecting to playing in this city because of the [poor] gate receipts. If it were not for the reputation achieved by our team in its past campaigning, we would be without games.
>
> "We at present have invitations from Philadelphia, Newark and Trenton to move our team to those cities, and we are at present seriously contemplating doing so. Unless we can be assured of moral support and some financial assistance in this city, I am afraid that the Bethlehem Steel soccer team has played its last game here."[28]

The fact that Bethlehem Steel stayed on in Bethlehem, resuming regular play there in September 1928, may have had something to do with the failure of an attempt by Edgar Lewis to buy the land in Harrison, N.J., where Bethlehem Steel had played its first game back in 1907, and which had been unused as an athletic field since the baseball park there had burned down in 1923. According to an obituary of Lewis in the 1949 edition of the *U.S. Annual Soccer Guide and Record*: "Lewis offered to buy the site and erect a stadium for soccer that would do credit to the sport . . . . This generous plan hit many snags in legislature halls and other places."[29]

In the summer of 1928, a storm broke over the ASL, in the form of a series of demands by New York Nationals owner Charles Stoneham that started what became known as the Soccer War.

Stoneham also was the owner of the New York Giants baseball team, and much of his proposals had to do with his desire to see big-league American soccer run more along the lines of big-league baseball. The fact that much of Stoneham's plan had to do with displacing the National Challenge Cup as the premier championship of American soccer might seem ironic considering that Stoneham's own team had won that championship just a few months before, but it doesn't seem as ironic if you look at the New York Nationals' 1927-28 season in detail. Stoneham's team played a very heavy schedule. Between the ASL, the National Challenge Cup and the Lewis Cup, the Nationals played 65 games over a period of 38 weeks. Perhaps even more important, the nine games that the Nationals played en route to winning the National Challenge Cup came in the midst of the ASL season, and during a stretch in which it won only twice in 10 ASL games and dropped out of contention in the ASL standings.

Stoneham's proposals included the idea that within a few years, a midwestern division of the ASL be founded, centered on St. Louis and Chicago, and that a final between the winners of the two divisions replace the National Challenge Cup as the true championship of American soccer.

It wasn't just about the National Challenge Cup, however. In fact, that may have been just a symptom. As *The Encyclopedia of American Soccer History* puts it: "Although the issue over which the two organizations [the ASL and the U.S. Football Association] chose to lock horns was the participation by ASL teams in the U.S. Open Cup tournament, the stake for which they were fighting really was the question of which of the two was to be the controlling organization of soccer in the United States."[30]

The Encyclopedia continues:

> In 1927, the United States got into hot water with FIFA over the matter of the signing of European professional players by Ameri-

can Soccer League teams. The USFA managed to avoid expulsion from FIFA, but the USFA's bowing to foreign authority inspired in some ASL owners the desire to free themselves from the various limitations imposed on them by the USFA and by FIFA's European leaders.

As a result, in the summer of 1928, New York Nationals owner Charles Stoneham proposed to other ASL owners that the league withdraw its teams from the U.S. Open Cup. On the surface, the reason was the overcrowding of the schedule, but control of the sport was the real issue.

The ASL accepted Stoneham's proposal and ordered that the teams be withdrawn from the cup. Three of them who had opposed the proposal, Bethlehem Steel, New York Giants and Newark Skeeters, refused to withdraw and were suspended by the league. The league was then suspended by the USFA.[31]

Bethlehem Steel's decision to stay with the National Challenge Cup didn't get it very far in that tournament. After victories in the first two rounds over Canton of Baltimore and Walsh Chevrolet of Fall River, the Steelworkers met up with another pro club, New York Giants, in the quarterfinals.

The game in Brooklyn on March 3, 1929 ended with a 2-2 tie and Bethlehem lucky to still be alive. A penalty by Jock Marshall in the 75th minute and a goal by John Jaap a few minutes after that enabled the Steelworkers to come back after New York had taken a 2-0 lead early in the second half. In the replay on March 9 at Frankford Stadium in Philadelphia, Bethlehem was not as lucky. After Bethlehem had led at halftime, a five-goal second half by the New Yorkers settled the issue by a 6-3 count.

Bethlehem still managed to win a championship, of a sort, in 1929. That came in the Eastern Soccer League, a makeshift circuit built around the three teams that had been suspended by the ASL. In addition to those three, it also included several semipro teams that had been members of the Southern New York State Association. Bethlehem won both halves of the season, and thus the league championship. Archie Stark had a strong season. Between the ASL and the ESL, Bethlehem Steel played 44 league games, in which Stark scored 48 goals. He had another six in four National Challenge Cup games.

A month into the 1929-30 season, with Bethlehem Steel still suspended from the ASL and playing in the weaker ESL, the Soccer War was settled. Support for the USFA from national federations in other countries gradually wore down the ASL and convinced it to give in and Stoneham to give up his demands. The rump ASL and the ESL ended their seasons, and the old ASL was put back together, using the name Atlantic Coast League but quite obviously the full ASL once again. By whatever name, it was to be Bethlehem Steel's final season.

Bethlehem Steel had gotten off to a fast start in the ESL when the Soccer War was settled and that league came to a halt. The Steelworkers had played 10 games and won eight of those, scoring 30 goals along the way. A month later, when they began play in the reconstituted ASL, they had cooled off considerably. Their first five games in the Atlantic Coast League produced one victory, one tie and three defeats. Bethlehem was never really in the running in its final "ASL" season, and finished seventh in the 10-team league, with the only losing record it ever suffered.

A lot had changed in between the settling of the Soccer War on Oct. 9 and Bethlehem's first ACL game on Nov. 9. One of the most famous events of the 20th century had taken place, the Stock Market Crash of October 1929. The crash probably had more immediate effect on the league than on Bethlehem, which temporarily was somewhat sheltered from its effects. The Bethlehem Steel Corp. didn't begin to badly feel the effects of the Depression until orders slowed dramatically in 1931. In 1930, Bethlehem produced 5.9 million tons of steel, which only six years before would have been its best year ever.[32] It actually earned more in the first quarter of 1930 than it had in the first quarter of 1929.[33] As the Depression deepened over the next year or two, its main effect on ASL teams was indirect. Would-be spectators had no money for optional purchases like tickets to a soccer game.

The ASL season was already well under way at the time of the Soccer War settlement. The season had begun earlier than usual, in the second week of August, and most teams had been playing at a frantic pace, completing more than 15 games. The Fall River Marksmen were in first place, and when the league resumed in early November, they continued to flourish, not losing a game until their 18th of the new season, on Jan. 26. The 1929-30 Marksmen were one of the greatest teams in American soccer history, and featured a forward line that included four future Hall of Famers, Billy Gonsalves, Alex McNab, Bert Patenaude and Werner Nilsen. They won the league easily that season, and became the first team ever to win the ASL championship, the National Challenge Cup and the Lewis Cup all in the same season. This was their last full season in Fall River, however, as they moved to New York in early 1931.

Edgar Lewis left the Bethlehem Steel Corp. on Feb. 28, 1930, about six weeks before the disbanding of the soccer team was announced. The conventional wisdom concerning the end of the team is that the Soccer War left Lewis disillusioned about the sport, or at least about the politicking on the administrative side of it. He surely had also become discouraged by the perennial attendance problems in Bethlehem, and perhaps also by the frustration of his own efforts to buy land for the team elsewhere. In addition, there likely was some corporate belt-tightening at Bethlehem Steel in the wake of the Stock Market Crash, which would have limited the spending available for soccer.

Nevertheless, while those things may well have been factors in Lewis' thinking, the most simple explanation behind his willingness to break his ties to soccer, and thus behind the disbanding of the team, has more to do with steelmaking than with soccer. The most often stated reason for Lewis' departure from the Bethlehem Steel Corp. was the one repeated by *Time Magazine* in 1936 after Lewis was named chairman of Jones & Laughlin Steel in Pittsburgh. *Time* said that Lewis had left Bethlehem Steel in 1930 "because Bethlehem was not big enough for both Eugene Grace and himself."[34] The obituary of Lewis in the 1949 edition of the *U.S. Annual Soccer Guide and Record* adds cryptically that Lewis quit "on a matter of policy, his stand being on the humane side."[35]

Was the problem between Lewis and Grace a case of simple rivalry, two ambitious men and only one presidency, or was there a particular disagreement? The latter possibility exists. Grace was famous as a hard-liner on the labor issues that rocked the steel industry in the 1920s and '30s. Lewis, the "up-from-the-mill steelman," was much more conciliatory toward unions. Events in 1937 at the companies the two men then headed illustrate the contrast. Jones & Laughlin, where Lewis had been in charge for about a year, became the first of the "independent" steelmakers to reach a contract settlement with the Steelworkers Organizing Committee, the union that later changed its name to United Steelworkers. In that same year, according to the *Allentown Morning Call's* 2003 history of the company, Grace "armed Bethlehem Steel to keep the union out by force. The company supplied its policemen with tear gas, pistols, revolvers, rifles, shotguns, machine guns and submachine guns, and hired undercover agents to spy on union organizers."[36] (Bethlehem eventually settled with the SWOC in 1941, after it was threatened with the loss of government contracts for violating federal labor-relations law.) After the 1937 settlement at Jones & Laughlin, Lewis said that J&L was "gratified that such an important issue has been so amicably settled by peaceful and democratic methods,"[37] a quite different statement from the fire one can imagine Grace breathing in the same situation. Two months later, an article in *The Nation* magazine referred to Lewis as "one of those paragon steel executives who want to produce steel in a state of industrial peace."[38] Lewis and Grace were very different men, who may have clashed on labor issues, so it seems quite possible that it was corporate matters, not soccer matters, that were most important in causing the disbanding of the Bethlehem Steel soccer team.

While Lewis may have gotten on well with ordinary workers, that didn't mean that he got paid like them. Later in 1930, after Lewis had left, Bethlehem Steel attempted to buy the Youngstown Sheet & Tube Co., a leading specialty steelmaker. A group of Youngstown stockholders objected fiercely to the takeover, and in the course of their fight to block it, they obtained and publicized a list of the bonuses paid in 1929 to 15 leading Bethlehem Steel executives. It already was well known that Charles M. Schwab rewarded his executives primarily through a system of bonuses rather than their modest salaries, but the public still was surprised by the size of the bonuses, about $3.5 million to the 15 men. Lewis' bonus for 1929 was $375,784.[39]

By the time Edgar Lewis left Bethlehem, it wasn't just Bethlehem that was struggling. It was the entire American Soccer League. Maybe without the Stock Market Crash, the ASL could have survived the effects of the Soccer War. Maybe without the Soccer War, it could have survived the effects of the Stock Market Crash. The double-whammy was too much, and the league outlasted the Bethlehem Steel team by only a year or two. The league sputtered to a close in stages during 1931 and 1932. In the fall of 1933, a new ASL began, with spending scaled way back, and without either Bethlehem Steel or a team in Fall River. This second ASL is the one that more American soccer fans remember, the ASL of Brookhattan and Kearny Scots and Walter Bahr. It lasted until 1983.

Bethlehem Steel may have had a disappointing final league season, but it did have one last good cup run, which ended in a final clash with Fall River. At this point, Bethlehem was paying the price for its poor attendance at home, as the USFA forced it to play all five of its cup games on the road.

That run began with a relatively easy victory, 8-1 on Feb. 9, 1930 over Newark Portuguese, an amateur team, at Ironbound Stadium in Newark. Archie Stark, Tom Gillespie and John Jaap each scored two goals. In the second round, two weeks later at Starlight Park in the Bronx, the Steelworkers faced a more difficult task, but came out with a 2-1 win over the New York Giants. They trailed by 1-0 at halftime thanks to a shot by George Moorhouse that was deflected into the net by Bethlehem's Bill Finleyson. Fifteen minutes into the second half, Stark finally beat New York goalkeeper Jock Brown, who had been stonewalling Bethlehem until then, after a fine pass from Jaap. Five minutes later, according to the *New York Times*, "Stark, Jaap and [Sandy] Dick swept right through with some dazzling combinations, which resulted in the last named sending in a crashing shot which entered the far top corner of the net to put Bethlehem in the lead, where it stayed to the final whistle."[40]

The quarterfinal opponent was Brooklyn Wanderers, at Hawthorne Field in Brooklyn on March 2, and the game was a less tense one than the struggle with the New York Giants had been. Bethlehem won by 2-0 on two early goals. Both came on counterattacks that victimized Brooklyn goalkeeper Steve Smith, the "outside goalie" who had caused Bethlehem's disqualification in the ASL playoffs two years before. Twice, the counterattacks forced Smith to rush out to meet them and twice the ball ended up in the net behind him, put there by Jaap in the 15th minute of the game and Dick in the 17th.

That victory set up the semifinal meeting with Fall River, which had played what was to be its last league game against Bethlehem back on Jan. 11. The semifinal was played on March 16 on a neutral site, the Polo Grounds in New York, and was worthy of the many great Bethlehem-Fall River battles of previous years.

Marksmen goalkeeper Johnny Reder was flawless in the first half, but Bethlehem got the game's first goal 10 minutes after intermission. Stark brought the ball up the center, avoided a tackle by Charlie McGill and slipped a pass to Dick in the left side of the penalty area. Fall River defender Bob McAuley nearly headed Dick's shot clear, but it skimmed off McAuley's head into the net.

A short while later, Bethlehem had a chance to raise its lead to 2-0, after Stark was brought down by McAuley inside the penalty area. Strangely, Bethlehem chose the injured Bill Carnihan to take the penalty kick, and Carnihan put his shot two feet wide. On two other occasions in the second half, Bethlehem appealed for penalties, but to no avail, and with eight minutes left in the game, Fall River's Alex McNab tied the score.

Thirty minutes of scoreless overtime were played, after which it was announced that the replay would be held a week later at Battery Park in New Bedford. Just before the end of the overtime, Stark put the ball into the net after a pass from Jaap, but what would have been the winning goal was disallowed for handling.

On March 23, the Steelworkers and the Marksmen produced another classic in front of 13,000 fans, the most ever at Battery Park, alternating goals through the second half as Fall River scored a 3-2 victory. This time, Carnihan's injuries kept the Bethlehem captain, who also was the heart of the Steelworkers' defense, on the sideline, but Fall River also had to replace an injured defender, Charlie McGill, early in the game. When McGill was injured, Fall River put Billy Gonsalves into the game, replacing a fullback with a forward, and making various other adjustments. Gonsalves then opened the scoring five minutes after halftime. Fall River's Tec White appeared ready to shoot, and drew the Bethlehem defense toward him, before slipping the ball to the unmarked Gonsalves in front of the goal. In the 64th minute, Stark matched that, collecting a loose ball that had escaped Reder in a goalmouth scramble and shooting home. Three minutes later, Dave Priestly had put Fall River in front again, shooting through a forest of legs, but five minutes after that, Stark tied it a second time, again scoring after the ball had fallen to his feet in a goalmouth scramble.

The winning goal came in the 71st minute. Fall River's Bobby Ballantyne brought the ball upfield, lost to it Bethlehem's Bill Gibson, got it back after Gibson failed to clear it and scored with a shot to the far post.

Fall River and Bethlehem had produced a rousing finish to their long rivalry. Over the years, Bethlehem played teams from Fall River a total of 50 times, most of which were against the Fall River Rovers before 1920 or the Fall River Marksmen after 1920. Sam Mark, a man who knew a profitable thing when he saw one, tried to lure Bethlehem Steel to Fall River for one last game after the team's disbanding had been announced. Bethlehem declined, on the grounds that it would have meant playing three games in three days on the team's final weekend.

The disbanding of the team was announced about three weeks after the last Bethlehem-Fall River game, but there had been substantial straws in the wind well before that. Reports started to come from Philadelphia in January that Bethlehem Steel was poised to once again finish its season there as a result of the poor attendance in Bethlehem. On Feb. 6, Levi Wilcox reported in the *Philadelphia Inquirer* that "there is a possibility that on account of the Bethlehem team not playing to capacity crowds on their home grounds, that the franchise will be transferred to this city, and the players now sporting their colors released to the Phillies, who will be granted permission to finish out Bethlehem's schedule."[41] The theme was picked up a few weeks later by the *Bethlehem Globe-Times*, which said: "Although advices confirming the announcement have not been forthcoming from officers of the Bethlehem soccer club, it is publicly declared in Philadelphia that the Steel City booters will make their first appearance in that city in a league game on March 1."[42]

However, the *Globe-Times* article went on to note, as Wilcox also had, that there were some objections to the plan, coming from Philadelphia amateur clubs whose gate receipts might be badly damaged by the arrival of a pro team in town. The March 1 starting date came and went, but on March 15, Wilcox wrote: "Bethlehem Steel will play their first Atlantic Coast Soccer League match in this city, Saturday, March 22. While this statement is not definite, Manager W. Luther Lewis has complied with the financial request of the Football Association of Eastern Pennsylvania and District, and everything is now complete."[43] Five days later, in between the two Bethlehem-Fall River games, Wilcox reversed field, declaring that "Bethlehem Steel will not play in this city next Saturday and, for that matter, any other Saturday. For it came to pass last night that Manager W. Luther Lewis of the Steelmen announced that his application to transfer the franchise to this city has been turned down flat by the officers and delegates of the Football Association of Eastern Pennsylvania and District."[44]

That rejection was a serious blow to the team's future, and by the time the disbanding of the team was announced on April 14, its imminent demise was an open secret. On April 11, the *Bethlehem Globe-Times* said that "The close of the present soccer season will perhaps be the swan song for the Bethlehem soccer team if rumor which daily becomes more persistent means anything. As yet no official announcement has been made, but since players are [talking] about the doleful tidings, it is taken for granted that such action is probably contemplated."[45] On April 14, the *Globe-Times* said that the end was near: "Rumor that has been persistent hereabouts for the past several weeks and is now gossiped throughout the Atlantic Coast Soccer League circuit, that when Bethlehem concludes its present season the team will disband and the city no longer be represented by a major club, will probably be officially verified at the league meeting to be held tonight in Providence, R.I."[46] It was verified, but the New York Times hadn't been waiting for any announcement. In its story on the morning of April 14 about the previous day's league game between Bethlehem Steel and the New York Giants, the Times said: "It was the steelmen's last appearance in New York, for the famous club, after nearly twenty years in competition, will be disbanded at the end of the month."[47]

Never in any of the Bethlehem Globe-Times stories about the team's disbanding is there any mention of the departure of Edgar Lewis, and the possible effect that may have had. This is not surprising, however. The Globe-Times was controlled by the Bethlehem Steel Corp., and discussion of internal corporation matters was off limits. The names of Bethlehem Steel executives usually only appeared in the newspaper in connection with charitable donations and events.

Actually, the April 13 game against the New York Giants proved to be not Bethlehem Steel's last appearance in New York. The Steelworkers played two more games there, the second of which, against the Hakoah All-Stars on April 27 in Brooklyn, was Bethlehem Steel's final game. The Hakoah team, which included a number of players who had stayed in New York after the American visits a few years before by the Austrian team of the same name, won by 3-2. Archie Stark had the last goal ever scored by Bethlehem Steel.

On the morning of that final game, the demise of the Steelworkers sent one New York newspaper to amazing heights of both handwringing and eulogizing. After saying that "the disbanding of the Schwab booting aggregation is little short of calamitous," the New York News went on to state that "they have set, in their long and noble history, an example that is destined to shine, beacon-like, for athletic organizations in many fields, and the club's history, in and out of the record books, is one not likely to be surpassed in any field of sport."[48]

Thomas W. Cahill, back once again as secretary of the USFA, was only a bit more restrained in his report to that organization later in the year, in which he called the passing of the Steelworkers "a stunning blow to soccer football."[49]

After that game, the players scattered to the winds, including a few who returned home to Scotland. There had been some overtures from other cities for transfer of the entire team, but these apparently were never seriously considered. The largest number of former Bethlehem Steel players ended up with a new ASL club called the Newark Americans in the fall of 1930. Ten former Bethlehem Steel players played for the Newark Americans in 1930 and 1931, among them such luminaries as Archie Stark, Bill Carnihan, Sandy Dick, John Jaap and Tom Gillespie. The Americans fared well in the fall of 1930, but faded in 1931. In those two years, Stark got 18 more ASL goals, bringing his total to 260, still the most ever in first-division American soccer.

What Stark did not do in 1930 is play for the United States in the first World Cup in Uruguay. At first glance, this seems particularly surprising considering that he did accompany the Fall River Marksmen as a guest player on their tour of Austria, Hungary and Czechoslovakia later that summer. Passing up a chance to play in the World Cup would be unthinkable today. But the demise of Bethlehem Steel and the struggles of the ASL did have Stark and the rest of the Bethlehem players wondering where their future income was going to come from. In the early summer of 1930, Stark was involved in starting an automotive business in his hometown of Kearny, N.J. By the time of the Fall River tour in August and September, that business was up and running, and Stark was free to play some more soccer. Also, the World Cup was not the huge event in 1930 that it was to become. It was not even referred to by that name. Newspaper articles early in 1930 generally referred to it as a world championship tournament or simply as the U.S. all-star team's tour of Uruguay.

No former Bethlehem Steel players were among the 16 American players at that World Cup in Montevideo. Besides Stark, the one who had been most often mentioned in speculation about the makeup of the team earlier in the year was Jaap, but he didn't go either. There was a Bethlehem Steel presence in that United States delegation, however. The team was coached by Bob Millar, the Bethlehem star of more than a decade earlier, who had been coaching the Indiana Flooring and New York Nationals ASL teams since retiring as a player.

At the time of the disbanding of the Bethlehem Steel team, Stark was 32 years old, and he continued playing for only a few more years. In 1933 the second, semipro, American Soccer League was started. Stark played in the first season of the new league, but not for Kearny Scots, the team with which he had started his soccer career as a teenager. Instead, he played in the 1933-34 ASL season for Kearny Irish, helping them to win the league championship and tying for the scoring title with 22 goals.

For 15 years before 1930, the biggest corporate name in American soccer had been that of a team owned by one of the world's industrial giants. By 1933, the biggest was that of a team sponsored by a St. Louis department store, and the Bethlehem Steel team was quickly becoming just a memory.

SEVEN

... the Harder They Fall

No other defeat was as ominous a landmark in the decline of the Cosmos from their former heights as the loss to the Chicago Sting in the 1981 NASL championship game. The Cosmos had won three of the previous four NASL titles, but they seemed diminished in 1981, and there was no escaping that fact after the loss in the final.

The Cosmos and their fans weren't terribly shocked by the defeat. The Sting had won both of the two regular-season meetings between the teams and the handwriting was on the wall, even though the Cosmos did come back to win a final NASL title in 1982. Expected or not, the defeat in 1981 brought home the idea that the Cosmos' run of success and glamour might not be destined to go on forever.

The Sting had been gradually creeping up on the Cosmos for several years. They entered the league in 1975 and, in their first six seasons, they had made the playoffs four times, including the last three in a row. Still, they had gotten past their first playoff opponent only once. Their best effort had come in 1979, when they beat the San Diego Sockers in the first round of the playoffs, but then were eliminated by the Fort Lauderdale Strikers in the quarterfinals. In 1980, they won their division, but lost to San Diego in the first round of the playoffs.

Clive Toye became president of the Sting a few months after departing from the Cosmos in the summer of 1977, but he only stayed in Chicago through the 1979 season. Although Toye was gone from the Sting by 1981, a number of the players whom he had signed were still there. Of the 13 players the Sting used in the 1981 NASL final against the Cosmos, five arrived there during Toye's two seasons as president of the Sting. Those included the team's two biggest stars, Karl-Heinz Granitza and Arno Steffenhagen, who both arrived in 1978.

While Toye did good work for the Sting, as did coach Willie Roy, the driving force behind the team was its owner, Chicago commodities broker Lee Stern, who founded the team in 1975 and became one of the NASL's leading executives. Ted Howard, who was executive director of the NASL in 1981, cites Stern's "incredible passion"[1] as the number-one attribute that he brought to the team.

"He believed in his team and was totally absorbed by it," Howard says of Stern. "Good or bad, he was a hands-on owner who was involved and who produced a very competitive team . . . . While Lee could be abrasive and combative, you had to respect what he did for the sport in Chicago. He made sure, under difficult circumstances [the team was constantly forced to switch stadiums during the baseball season] that he put out an attractive, attacking team."[2]

Those stadium problems in Chicago seriously bedeviled the Sting, as Toye tells in his memoirs:

> The Chicago Sting in the '80s had a unique problem. Soldier Field, the previous home, was not available, so the Sting played at home at Comisky Park, home of the White Sox, on the south side, and played at home at Wrigley Field, home of the Cubs, on the north side. Not simultaneously, you understand, but at one or the other, depending on when the baseball teams were away and let us in. It's one thing to look at the schedule to see whether you are playing at home or on the road; another entirely to see where you are playing at home from game to game. Although when I went there Mayor [Michael] Bilandic had said, unequivocally, that there would be a domed stadium in the Windy City within three years, the wind still whistles through whatever they have there and it whistled so uncomfortably that even Lee Stern was ready to give up . . . . He had me research every other possible landing place for the Sting, Jacksonville, Florida; Nashville, Tennessee, and mostly Milwaukee, Wisconsin. We had a deal on the table from Milwaukee, from a group ready to buy and play in County Stadium. But Lee's heart, as always, ruled his head, and as his heart was in the Sting and in Chicago, he finally turned it down. And won two championships for his efforts."[3]

Efforts by Granitza, who by 1981 was the undisputed star of the Sting, had a lot to do with those championships as well. The German

184

forward was chosen as a first-team NASL all-star only once, in 1984, by which time Giorgio Chinaglia was retired and no longer in the way. But in his seven seasons with the Sting, Granitza played 225 games and scored 141 goals, making him the NASL's third-highest career goalscorer. Granitza was unusual among the NASL's leading foreign stars in that he had not been a big star in his own country, playing largely for minor teams in West Germany. He hit stardom in the United States, however, and was inducted into the National Soccer Hall of Fame on the same evening in 2003 as both Lee Stern and Clive Toye.

With Granitza leading the way, scoring 19 goals in the 31 games that he played, the Sting had their strongest regular season yet in 1981, and entered the playoffs as a serious threat to the Cosmos, perhaps even as the favorite. Unfortunately for the Sting, their emergence came at a time when the NASL as a whole was starting to struggle.

The television contract that the NASL had signed with ABC after its booming 1977 season had been severely cut back in 1980. In the 1978 and 1979 seasons, ABC had televised an NASL game of the week. The ratings were poor, however, and by 1981, ABC was showing only the NASL championship game, one of the most serious blows the league had received, and even it was on tape delay rather than live.

In addition, the league was in trouble with FIFA over the rules. In 1973, FIFA had granted permission for the NASL to experiment with a change in the offside rule, adding a line across the field 35 yards out from the goal, outside which a player couldn't be called offside. By 1981, FIFA had become very impatient with the NASL, and by extension with the USSF, for allowing the experiment to continue beyond the time FIFA had allotted for it. With the USSF threatened with expulsion from FIFA, the league agreed to discontinue the 35-yard offside rule at the end of the 1981 season.

Toye (and many others) also believe that the NASL's rapid expansion of the late 1970s was a major factor in its later struggles. From its low of five teams in 1969, the NASL had been expanding gradually and stood at 18 teams in 1977, when the Cosmos began attracting huge crowds at Giants Stadium. That success sparked a major additional round of expansion, and in 1978 the league was up to 24 teams. Toye discusses those events in some detail, saying:

> We spent an entire year [1977], of one week-end a month, to work
> on the Long Term Strategic Plan, which at the end said, among

many other things: We have 18 clubs. Six are doing well. Six are okay and can be improved. Six either have to be moved to better markets or taken over by new owners or dumped.

Lamar Hunt was part of that Long Term group, so were Lee Stern and Jim Ruben of Minnesota and Steve Danzansky from DC and myself. As Lee Stern put it: "So many weekends. We put together a great package and Phil [Woosnam] never paid any attention to it . . . . We talked about not expanding and Phil was always wanting to expand to get more revenue from the sale of expansion teams. The other thing was to concentrate on regional television, not national television. Nobody cared whether Tulsa played Fort Lauderdale."

Thus, outside that committee, Phil Woosnam was working on new franchises, at $3 million a pop, and when it came to a vote at the annual meeting, the idea of six new clubs coming in, with $18 million to be divided, was too strong a lure . . . .

In the main the new owners, to put it mildly, did not have a clue . . . . lured by the sight of crowds packing Giants Stadium and believing that all they needed was a franchise, a big stadium, some players and the way ahead would be golden.[4]

Actually, there were seven NASL expansion teams in 1978, six completely new ones and one replacing the Connecticut Bicentennials, who had folded. By 1981, every one of those seven had either folded or moved to a new city, and the NASL's downward spiral was gaining momentum.

To a considerable degree, the Cosmos had created an illusion of success that has fooled others besides the new NASL owners that it attracted. Many American soccer fans today are puzzled by how a league drawing crowds of 70,000 could have foundered. They don't realize that those big crowds at Giants Stadium were the tip that appeared above the surface, but that the iceberg below was very thin. The Cosmos' attendance in 1981 averaged 34,784 per game, down from their high of 50,684 in 1978. Even with that decrease, the Cosmos' numbers still dwarfed the 1981 leaguewide average of 14,674. Those new owners were entranced by the NASL record crowd of 77,691 that the Cosmos drew on Aug. 14, 1977, but they may not have been aware that the same day, an NASL playoff game between the Los Angeles Aztecs and Dallas Tornado at the cavernous L.A. Coliseum drew 5,295.

Giorgio Chinaglia was still scoring plenty of goals in 1981, at almost his frantic pace of 1980. He had started the season like a house afire, with 15 goals in the Cosmos' first 10 regular-season games. He couldn't maintain that rate, but he did finish the regular season with 29 goals in 32 games. It was enough to gain his fourth NASL scoring title in six seasons and the only NASL most valuable player award he ever won.

Inevitably, or so it seems in retrospect, Chinaglia also was starting to come into conflict with Hennes Weisweiler. And why not? Both were strong-willed men, and Chinaglia had clashed with three previous Cosmos coaches.

A rift between Weisweiler and Chinaglia also was the logical next step after one between Weisweiler and Carlos Alberto, which had opened after Carlos Alberto was benched for the 1980 NASL title game and which had healed only temporarily. Contrary to what he had said after that game, Carlos Alberto did play for the Cosmos on their postseason tour in the fall of 1980, but Weisweiler suspended him for leaving the team during the 1981 preseason tour (Carlos Alberto said it was with permission) and Carlos Alberto announced in April that he was quitting the Cosmos. Four months later, the strain between Weisweiler and Chinaglia was starting to show, with a key reason being that Weisweiler had the Cosmos playing in a conservative fashion that didn't sit well with a goalscorer like Chinaglia. "I'm complaining about the style of play," Chinaglia told the *New York Times* just before the start of the NASL playoffs. "We should attack more. This guy is very conservative. We won only one game comfortably. We never blew anyone out except Dallas."[5]

The *Times* noted further that "Weisweiler is known as 'the professor of coaches,' but he hasn't given a single clinic since he arrived in the United States 15 months ago. What is worse, officials of the Cosmos say, is that Weisweiler hasn't made a single public appearance on behalf of the team."[6]

The Cosmos didn't exactly storm into those playoffs. They lost four of their last six regular-season games, and followed that with a loss to a Brazilian team in a friendly in between the regular season and the playoffs. In mid-season, they had surprisingly failed to win the Trans-Atlantic Challenge Cup, a tournament that had to be rearranged a bit at the last minute after a Soviet team refused to play in protest of the fact that the Cosmos' roster included a South African player, Steve Wegerle.

The Cosmos righted themselves somewhat in the playoffs. They needed a tie-breaking third game to defeat the Tampa Bay Rowdies in the quarterfinals, but in the semifinals they beat the Fort Lauderdale

Strikers by 4-3 on the road and 4-1 at home to sweep into the final, which was played at Exhibition Stadium in Toronto. Opposing the Cosmos there, however, was Chicago, their "bogey" team.

The Cosmos and the Sting had met twice in the regular season. Chicago won by 3-2 in overtime at Giants Stadium in May, and by 6-5 after a shootout in Chicago in June. Those two victories brought the Sting's all-time record against the Cosmos to six victories and one defeat, an impressive mark considering that it was achieved during the Cosmos' peak years. The scores of those two games earlier in the season may have been above average, but they were not out of character for the Cosmos and Sting. Going into the final, the Cosmos had averaged 2.62 goals a game and the Sting 2.46 goals a game in NASL play in 1981. The day before the game, coaches Weisweiler and Roy both promised to play in an attacking manner.

So, it was quite a letdown when the game was still 0-0 after 90 minutes of regulation and 15 minutes of overtime. In the shootout, Chicago got goals from its third shooter, Granitza, and its fifth, Rudy Glenn. Only Vladislav Bogicevic, the third shooter, scored for the Cosmos, and when Bob Iarusci missed the Cosmos fifth shot, Chicago took home the trophy.

With the championship lost, the glue really came apart between Weisweiler and Chinaglia, who vowed never to play for Weisweiler again and to boycott the Cosmos' postseason tour.[7] As had happened a year before with Carlos Alberto, the boycott was avoided when a temporary truce was arranged between the coach and player, but the 1981 final did prove to be the last competitive game Chinaglia ever played for Weisweiler, who either quit or was fired by the Cosmos (accounts vary) in February 1982.

The postseason tour was a pallid thing compared with some of the processions of previous years. At least the preseason tour seven months before had included one spectacular crowd. The 105,000 who saw the Cosmos play Club America at the Estadio Azteca in Mexico City in March were the largest Cosmos crowd ever. The autumn tour had none of that glamour. The only victory in six games was against an Icelandic team, in sub-freezing weather in Reykjavik. There also were two ties, but the tour concluded with an embarrassing 7-1 defeat against French club Lille.

Things looked up a bit for the Cosmos in 1982, at least on the surface. The new coach, hired on an interim basis a few days after the Cosmos and Hennes Weisweiler parted company, was Julio Mazzei, who was both Weisweiler's predecessor and now his successor as well. He was the second Cosmos coach to have a return engagement in that position, after Gordon Bradley, but he would not be the last.

Not only was Mazzei back, soon Carlos Alberto was, too. The Brazilian had played for the California Surf in the 1981 season, but became a free agent when that team folded, and was playing for the Cosmos' indoor team, in which Weisweiler wasn't involved. Mazzei quickly induced him to stay with the Cosmos for the 1982 outdoor season as well. "With Weisweiler gone and his old friend back at the helm, it hadn't taken much persuasion to lure Carlos Alberto back to New York for a final season," Gavin Newsham notes in *Once in a Lifetime*.[8]

The defeat in the 1981 final certainly had had an effect, however. In March, the *New York Times* preview of the 1982 season said, under the headline "Cosmos Era Could End" that "for the first time in five seasons, the league's most glamorous team may have difficulty winning its division."[9] The morning of the final in September 1982, the *Newark Star-Ledger* said: "There is a lot riding on this game, no matter who you talk to. Nobody is predicting that Warner Communications would scrap the Cosmos if they failed to win the Soccer Bowl for a second year in a row, but there would be massive changes."[10]

In the end, neither of the feared results, the failure to win the division or the failure to win the NASL final, happened. Still, because the NASL's problems were becoming undeniable (a status in which they would soon be joined by Warner's problems), the 1982 season had something of a bittersweet feel about it. This was sharpest at the biggest event of the summer at Giants Stadium, which wasn't actually a Cosmos game. The event was a world all-star game organized by FIFA and featuring a European all-star team against a Rest of the World all-star team. According to the *Encyclopedia of American Soccer History*, the game "could have been a magnificent occasion for American soccer. The trouble was that when it was played, the North American Soccer League was on the downslide, and FIFA's mission in bringing the game to the Meadowlands clearly was to try to rescue American soccer rather than to celebrate it."[11] The game was in early August and the NASL had indicated in June that it recognized its difficult situation by shoving Phil Woosnam to the side. He retained his title of commissioner but became subordinate to Howard Samuels, hired as president and chief executive officer of the league.[12]

A rescue mission it may have been, but the FIFA game was a spectacular evening of soccer. The European team, which featured the likes of England's Kevin Keegan, Poland's Zbigniew Boniek and

Italy's Paolo Rossi, won by 3-2 from the Rest of the World team, which was built around Brazilians Zico, Socrates, Junior, Oscar and Falcao.

Despite the dark clouds, it was a good season for the Cosmos, although they didn't know that it was to be their last such. They started very fast. Through the end of May, they had compiled a record of 9-2 in NASL play and Giorgio Chinaglia (who also was in his last good season) had scored 10 goals in those 11 games. The only serious blemish was a 4-3 loss to the Chicago Sting, a team they certainly would have preferred to beat, in the deciding game of the Trans-Atlantic Challenge Cup at Giants Stadium. The Trans-Atlantic Challenge Cup was a tournament that the NASL had started in 1980 in a bid to give its top teams some meaningful competition against foreign teams. Like other such attempts, most notably the International Soccer League of the 1960s, the foreign teams were in their offseason and may not have found it as meaningful as did their hosts.

Actually, by the time of the Trans-Atlantic Cup meeting on May 31, the Cosmos had already broken their Sting jinx. They had beaten the Sting in their first two league meetings of the season, 3-1 on April 24 in Chicago and by the same score on May 16 in Giants Stadium. They would gain additional victories over the Sting in July and August. The Sting were quite a different team in 1982 than they had been in the championship run of 1981, despite the fact that every one of the players who had beaten the Cosmos in the 1981 final was back. The Sting started the season miserably, losing seven of their first eight games, and never got untracked. They finished the season 13-19, last in their division and a long way from the playoffs.

The Cosmos finished 23-9 and outdistanced the rest of the league by a good margin. They compiled 203 points under the NASL system, which gave teams six points for a victory and additional points for goals scored. The closest to them was the Seattle Sounders with 166.

The 5-0 victory with which the Cosmos opened the playoffs against the Tulsa Roughnecks on Aug. 25 was deceptive. Tulsa didn't go down easily. The Roughnecks came back with a 1-0 victory three days later in Tulsa, forcing a third game. Back at Giants Stadium on Sept. 1, the Cosmos took nearly the entire 90 minutes to secure their place in the next round. Steve Hunt scored the only goal with 1 minute, 38 seconds left in the game.

Because the NASL had contracted to 14 teams, only eight made the playoffs in 1982, so the victory over Tulsa put the Cosmos into the semifinals against the San Diego Sockers. This time they didn't need a third game, beating San Diego by 2-1 both times, but they looked poor anyway. "I don't know why we don't play good," said Vladislav Bogicevic after a first leg in which the losing Sockers had been the more impressive team. "We looked like 11 different pieces in various parts of the field. We looked like elephants."[13] Both coaches were upset, Mazzei at the way his team had played and Ron Newman over the fact that his team had lost. San Diego came close to winning the return leg three days later, but a goal by Giorgio Chinaglia in the second minute of overtime put the Cosmos into the Soccer Bowl for the fifth time in six seasons.

The troubles besetting the NASL were on display for all to see at the championship game in San Diego a week later, which matched the Cosmos against the Seattle Sounders. The glitz of the Cosmos' glory years was gone, as George Vescey noted in the *New York Times*.

> There are few corporate jets lined up at the airport; there are few lines at the restaurants; there is no trace of crowds chanting team slogans in the streets.
>
> The most emotion at the 1982 Soccer Bowl so far has been Howard J. Samuels, the recently appointed president of the North American Soccer League, terming his first championship game "a disaster"...soccer has fallen a long way from the mobs that greeted Pelé in 1975 and the peak of 24 teams in 1978. Samuels, who was named president above the present commissioner, Phil Woosnam, last June, freely admits that attendance is down 20 percent from last year and that four of the surviving 14 clubs are in trouble; the other 10 ownerships are merely losing their shirts.[14]

Frank Coluccio, the owner of the Sounders, agreed with Samuels' desire to turn the neutral-site NASL title game into a best-of-three series in front of the two teams' home fans. "It really makes me sick," Coluccio said before the game about the San Diego site. "I believe this is very poor marketing when they brought this game here in San Diego. I don't think they'll draw 25,000 people."[15] He hit the nail on the head about the attendance, which was 22,634, the lowest for the NASL championship game since 1975.

In the regular season, the Cosmos had split a pair of 3-2 games with Seattle. The final was not as high scoring. Giorgio Chinaglia got the only goal of the Cosmos victory in the 31st minute, his 24th goal of a year in which he won yet another NASL scoring title. This was the third Soccer Bowl in which he had scored the winning goal. To many, however, the hero of the night was Carlos Alberto, on the brink of retirement and playing his final NASL game, hobbled by injuries, on his last legs both figuratively and literally, rarely venturing upfield, but still marshalling the defense that held the Sounders scoreless.

Ten days later, the Cosmos treated Carlos Alberto to a farewell game, as they had done in previous years for Pelé and Franz Beckenbauer. The opponent was Flamengo from Rio de Janeiro, the reigning South American champion. The Cosmos, fielding a team that included Beckenbauer and Brazilian national team captain Socrates as guest players, rallied from a 3-0 halftime deficit with three goals by Chinaglia to gain a tie. Carlos Alberto said at halftime that "I don't want to say goodbye"[16] but conceded after the game that "I prepared for this game a year ago, so I am not so sad. It was time for me to stop."[17] In the course of his NASL seasons, Carlos Alberto had raised his total of career games to more than 1,600, the most of any active player in the world.[18]

With that, the Cosmos set off on their traditional postseason tour. After a stop in Los Angeles for a loss to a Mexican team, it was off to Australia, Asia and six consecutive victories, a departure from the Cosmos' usual mediocre fall results. The tour ended in Tokyo on Nov. 10, a few weeks before things turned seriously sour for Warner Communications.

The crowd of celebrities in the Cosmos' locker room after their NASL title game victory in San Diego on Sept. 18, 1982 had included one new face, movie director Steven Spielberg, whose most recent picture, *E.T.*, had been the smash hit of the year. The fact that Spielberg had become a member of Steve Ross' inner circle is symbolic of the woes that were to overtake Warner Communications, and thus the Cosmos, before the end of the year.

Spielberg's locker-room visit resulted from the fact that Ross had agreed two months before to pay a huge sum in order to gain for Warner's Atari division the right to make an E.T. video game. Throughout 1980, 1981 and 1982, Atari had been the division that was providing the bulk of Warner's profits and fueling its spending on the Cosmos. The E.T. game was to be part of the reason why that gravy train suddenly derailed.

The Cosmos had not been built on a foundation of Atari. The signings of Pelé, Chinaglia, Beckenbauer and Carlos Alberto, the move to the Meadowlands, the attendance surge of 1977 and the NASL titles in 1977 and 1978 all happened before Atari took off. But by the early 1980s, Atari, a maker of home computers and video games that Warner had bought in 1976 for $28 million, had become the founda-

192

tion that was keeping the Cosmos' pockets deep while the rest of the NASL was struggling. Says Ross biographer Connie Bruck: "In 1979, Atari made a profit of $6 million; for 1980, it would escalate ten-fold, to nearly $70 million. And the people running Atari were convinced there was no plateau in sight . . . . there probably had not been another company in the history of American business that grew as large, as fast, as Atari."[19] The plateau certainly wasn't reached in 1981, when Atari profits grew to $287 million.[20]

Indeed, for a while Atari was threatening to become larger than Warner itself. In mid-October 1982, when Warner made its last quarterly earnings report before the December Atari crash, it reported that its Consumer Electronics Division, a formal name for Atari, had contributed more than half of the company's revenues for the third quarter, $528.9 million out of $1.03 billion.[21]

Despite numbers like that, the Atari crash cannot—or at least should not—have been completely a surprise to Warner. Even Steve Ross himself had occasionally indicated uncertainty about the division that was sending his company soaring, telling people that it was too good to be true or that video games were apt to prove a passing fad.[22] Ironically, Ross apparently was not paying attention when signs began to appear that he might be correct. Richard M. Clurman, a former *Time Magazine* reporter, wrote about those signs in *To the End of Time*, his 1992 history of Time Inc.:

> By early 1982, intoxicated by the success of its Pac-Man cartridge, Atari kept shipping more video games than the stores were selling. Inventory control was close to nonexistent. Overproduction, long-term credit, discounts and a freewheeling return policy created tons of oversupply . . . .
> When a *Wall Street Journal* "Heard on the Street" column asked in May 1982, "Is the home video game market close to saturation?" Warner's public relations staff went to work. It was a plot by short sellers, said Warner's flacks, to drive the price of the stock down. Although warning signals were flashing in Sunnyvale [Atari's headquarters in Sunnyvale, Calif.], with cancellations mounting as fast as orders, in June of 1982 an inattentive and always upbeat Ross reported to the stockholders on "Atari's excellent performance," "another record quarter," "unprecedented rate of sales of Pac-Man."
> But even before then, there were forecasts of a devastating storm darkening the skies over Sunnyvale. And by July executive memos reported "cancellation activity almost doubled, three times greater

than in recent weeks." The fall sales reports warned of the "frightening realization that inventory levels are dangerously high." Atari's chief of operations urged that "we take a very hard look, quickly, to devise further cut-backs, possibly take some involuntary vacation." Marketing analysts at Atari wrote with dismay "We have run out of answers, foresee major cancellations in November and December." Meanwhile, in New York at a board meeting, Ross was predicting that Atari was "heading for a good Christmas."[23]

Some outside the company were aware of the danger signs, too. Gordon Crawford, a California stock analyst whose firm at one time was among Warner's largest shareholders, later said: "We started selling our $200 million stake in Warner in January of 1982. In June, after the CES [the Consumer Electronics Show, a major trade show] and hearing Steve's optimism, I told our people to accelerate our getting rid of the stock. By the fall we didn't own a share."[24] In September 1982, *Business Week* said that "Atari is facing a growing number of competitors in home video games—at a time when many industry watchers believe this phenomenon is peaking," and quoted investment banker Richard P. Simons of Goldman, Sachs as saying that "Atari's period of mega growth is behind it."[25]

In July, Ross had agreed to pay $23 million for the E.T. rights. The deal, which was $22 million more than Atari had ever paid for game rights before, included acceptance of Spielberg's condition that the game be out by the Christmas shopping season, an astonishingly short development time.

"What Atari had bought," wrote Connie Bruck, "was the right to use the title 'E.T.,' and also its image; engineers at Atari, with Spielberg's input, were now to design a game. The project, however, was blighted from inception."[26] Of the four million E.T. games that Atari shipped, about 3.5 million were returned. Atari executive Skip Paul comments that "It wasn't a game. It was a thing waddling around on a screen."[27]

On Nov. 17, Atari lowered its projection of earnings for the fourth quarter of 1982, a projection intended primarily to assist stock analysts in making their recommendations to investors, by $81 million. On Dec. 8, it made an additional reduction of $53 million in that projection, and Warner was forced to issue a statement in which it conceded, among other things, that it now expected dramatic decreases in the corporation's profits for the quarter and the year.[28] The stock market reacted. The huge influx of sell orders in the hours after the statement meant that trading in Warner Communications on Dec. 9 didn't open until 3:32 p.m. Warner stock, which had closed the day before at 51⅞, closed on Dec. 9 at 35⅛, a brutal one-day plunge of more than 32 percent. Within the next year, it dipped as low as 19⅞. Downturns in the rest of the video-game industry, in which competition had been increasing sharply in a field that Atari once dominated, soon followed.[29]

The drop set off a flood of red ink at Warner, which lost $417 million in 1983 and $586 million in 1984.[30] The Cosmos' spending on new players virtually disappeared. The only additions to the roster in the 1983 NASL season were Franz Beckenbauer, who actually had come out of retirement and returned to the Cosmos during their postseason tour in September 1982, and American Mike Fox, who played only two NASL games in 1983. Coach Julio Mazzei talked of adding Brazilian midfielder Falcao, one of the stars of the 1982 World Cup, but Warner's financial straits made that only a pipedream.

The video-game industry has long since recovered from the crash of 1982 and 1983, when other companies besides Atari suffered, and now includes makers of games played on computers as well as on TV sets. By the 1990s, Nintendo was as big a name as Atari once had been. Atari, which was sold by Warner in 1984 and 1985, never did truly recover, however.

The Atari crash was not the only bad news for Warner Communications and Steve Ross in the fall of 1982. The other particularly upsetting things were two federal investigations, one of Warner's involvement in the fraudulent Westchester Premier Theatre nearly 10 years before and the other of possible insider-trading violations by Warner executives around the time of the Atari crash. Neither ended up touching Ross personally, but both caused him a huge amount of worry.

Writing about the Westchester Premier Theatre business, Richard Clurman said in *To the End of Time* in 1992 that "To this day, the involvement of Ross and Warner—then a $2 billion company—in a piddling $250,000 investment scam makes no sense and probably never will."[31]

The Westchester Premier Theatre was a joint venture of several "soldiers" from New York's Gambino, Colombo and Genovese organized crime families.[32] The 3,500-seat theater, designed for Las Vegas-style show biz acts, operated for only a few years in the mid-1970s, and quickly went bankrupt despite a lineup of attractions that included major stars like Johnny Carson, Frank Sinatra and Diana

Ross. It was doomed largely by the illegal activities that surrounded it, particularly the skimming of box-office receipts.[33]

Federal prosecutors later alleged that in 1973, when the theater's founders were trying to sell stock in the venture to satisfy start-up legal requirements, Warner assistant treasurer Solomon Weiss had overseen the receiving of $170,000 in kickbacks given in return for arranging Warner's purchase of $250,000 of the stock.[34] Three Warner officers were indicted in connection with the scheme. Jay Emmett, who was Steve Ross' closest friend, and Leonard Horwitz accepted plea bargains. Weiss resisted and went to trial in November 1982.

Prosecutor Nathaniel Ackerman charged in his opening statement at Weiss' trial that Ross had been fully aware of the fund into which the kickbacks were placed.[35] During the several weeks of the trial, that allegation was repeated under oath by Emmett, who had agreed to testify against Weiss as part of his plea bargain, and was denied in statements issued by Ross. Although Emmett had pleaded guilty nearly two years before, his sentencing was delayed until after he testified at the Weiss trial (Emmett got a five-year suspended sentence). At Emmett's sentencing in December 1982, just four days after the Warner stock plunge, Ackerman stated that: "In our view, the real culprit has not yet been brought to justice. The real culprit in this instance is the chairman of the board of Warner Communications, and the investigation of him is continuing."[36]

Ross never was indicted. The Justice Department ended its investigation of Ross in 1985 with a statement that there had been "insufficient evidence to bring charges."[37] Nevertheless, it had been a very uncomfortable episode for Ross, who felt that Ackerman had "smeared his name with no proof of wrongdoing."[38]

Ross, who decided in late 1981 to sell 360,000 shares of Warner Communications stock, and who did sell that much and more between late August and early November of 1982, also had a narrow escape in the Atari insider-trading matter. Connie Bruck elaborates:

> Only a month before the Atari news broke, Ross had finished selling his WCI stock for roughly $21 million—something he had done while he and his executives had been zealously touting the stock to securities analysts. Had the [Securities and Exchange Commission] commenced an investigation of Ross for stock manipulation and insider trading at the same time that he was under threat of indictment in the Westchester scandal, the odds of his prevailing on all fronts—against the U.S. Attorney's office, the SEC, and the most cat-

aclysmic crisis of his business career—would have been significantly diminished.

As it happened, however, there was a far more clear-cut (albeit comparatively insignificant) case of abuse for the SEC to focus on. Raymond Kassar [the Atari CEO] had sold 5,000 WCI shares on December 8, before the public announcement was made [only 23 minutes before], and Dennis Groth, Atari's chief financial officer, had sold some 6,000 shares on December 1. There also had been selling by four other high-ranking Atari executives in the weeks before December 8.[39]

The SEC investigation, in which Warner cooperated, zeroed in on and forced restitution and other concessions from Kassar and Groth, who had sold only 11,000 shares between them. Ross, who shortly before had sold 479,000 shares, slipped out a side door.

The Atari collapse, the Solomon Weiss trial and the start of the insider-trading investigation all happened within a few weeks of each other, making it quite an unhappy time for Warner Communications and for Ross. For the Cosmos, who had plenty of troubles of their own at this point, Warner's difficulties were yet another worry that they didn't need.

When the Cosmos took the field for their first game of the 1983 NASL season, their lineup included not a single player who hadn't played for them in 1982. Even without any new faces, it wasn't a bad lineup. Giorgio Chinaglia was still there, as were Vladislav Bogicevic, Johan Neeskens, Hubert Birkenmeier, Andranik Eskandarian, Rick Davis, Roberto Cabañas and Julio Cesar Romero. Franz Beckenbauer, who had retired at the end of the 1981-82 West German season but had been lured back onto the field a few months later by the Cosmos, also was on the roster, as was Wim Rijsbergen. With no turnover, however, the team was starting to get long in the tooth. The average age of that opening-day starting 11 was 29.3 years.

Chinaglia had considered retiring in the offseason after receiving an offer from Rome to become chief executive of Lazio,[40] but he got off to another very fast start with the Cosmos. He scored 16 goals in the Cosmos' first 13 NASL games, and in the same stretch had five more goals in four nonleague games. He didn't get much farther than that, however. Chinaglia was 36, not young for a forward, and the injuries he had been avoiding for years finally caught up with him in his final season.

"The thought of retirement is the furthest thing from my mind,"[41] Chinaglia said after scoring three goals against Tulsa on May 15 in the sixth game of the NASL season, but it can't have been all that distant. In mid-June, it was announced that Chinaglia had bought a part interest in Lazio and was becoming president of the club after all while continuing to play for the Cosmos.[43] In late June, he missed three games, the first NASL games he had missed since the 1979 season, because of a trip to Italy to look after his business interests there.

In his first game back after the trip, on July 6, he suffered a severe tear of his left hamstring.[43] He was sidelined for five weeks by what was the first serious injury of his professional career.[44] Between July 6 and the Cosmos' elimination from the playoffs two months later, he played only five of their 15 games, scored only three goals and decided to retire at the end of the season. Both the injury and his growing involvement with Lazio were factors keeping him out of the Cosmos lineup. Fortunately for the Cosmos, they already had been grooming a successor in Cabañas and he took over now, finishing the season as the NASL's leading goalscorer with 25 goals.

Nevertheless, Chinaglia was a major participant in one final grand occasion for the Cosmos. Such occasions had become frequent since the Cosmos moved to the Meadowlands in 1977. They had included the record crowds and the Pele farewell in 1977, the 1978 Soccer Bowl against Tampa Bay, the friendly with Argentina and the classic semifinal against Vancouver in 1979, the Beckenbauer farewell in 1980 and the Carlos Alberto farewell in 1982. The last such occasion was a game against SV Hamburg of West Germany on June 15, 1983.

Hamburg was the reigning European champion, having beaten Juventus Turin of Italy for that honor the month before. The game was only a friendly, and had the inherent disadvantage of friendlies between touring teams in their off-season and home teams in mid-season form. The Cosmos had played 45 friendlies against European teams, either at home or in Europe, in the years since they went bigtime after the arrival of Pelé in 1975. Of those, 23 had been won by the in-season team and only seven by the touring team.

Still, Hamburg general manager Gunter Netzer downplayed that factor before the game. "People around the world will be watching for the result," he said, "because the Cosmos just won the Trans-Atlantic Cup on top of being the league champions here, and we just won the European Cup."[45] Netzer, a great German star of 10 years before, continued that theme after the Cosmos' 7-2 victory, saying:

"They'll find excuses for us in Germany, but the truth is that we were embarrassed."[46]

Some observers called the second half, in which the Cosmos outscored the Germans by 6-0, the best 45 minutes of soccer the Cosmos had ever played. Cosmos midfielder Wim Rijsbergen wasn't so sure. "People are going to make us world champions all of a sudden," he said. "One day we can't beat Golden Bay and the next we do this. Sure, we played well, but 7-2 is not a realistic score."[47]

Hamburg did have excuses. They weren't used to the artificial turf and the Cosmos were; they were jet-lagged from the flight over the Atlantic; they were missing a few of their stars. Most of all, they were on vacation and the Cosmos were at work. However, Chinaglia had flown across the ocean even more recently than the Hamburg players, having gotten off a flight from Rome just a few hours before the game. That didn't stop him from scoring two goals, including a spectacular volley early in the second half that tied the game at 2-2. As impressive as it was, however, it may have been the last great hurrah for both Chinaglia and the Cosmos.

The rout of Hamburg capped a spring that had been an eventful one for the Cosmos and the NASL. Not only had Chinaglia bought his interest in Lazio, FIFA had decided not to award the 1986 World Cup to the United States.

Colombia had been designated way back in 1974 as the host of the 1986 World Cup, but it was not the most stable country in Latin America, and doubts began to arise even before FIFA decided to expand the tournament from 16 teams to 24. Colombia eventually decided that it couldn't handle the job and announced in November 1982 that it was pulling out as host.

The NASL was eager for the United States to step into the void, and perhaps bolster American interest in soccer.[48] For that reason, FIFA's decision on May 20, 1983 to choose Mexico, rather than the United States, as Colombia's replacement, has sometimes been cited in exaggerated fashion as having been what killed the NASL. British authors John Sugden and Alan Tomlinson included a good account of that day, on which the decision apparently was reached privately before the meeting had begun, in their 1998 book, *FIFA and the Contest for World Football*. "There was indeed deep disappointment among the US delegation when its serious bid lost out to a barely documented Mexican bid," they said. "Whilst Dr. Henry Kissinger was making an hour-long sophisticated presentation incorporating detailed commercial analyses, the Mexican delegation was in the lobby of the Stockholm hotel, already following up its eight-minute presentation with preparations for a celebration and victory reception . . . . The FIFA decision, and the manner in which it was reached, were both disappointing and humiliating to the US soccer establishment, including Warner, the financial backers of the NASL."[49] However, Sugden and Tomlinson overinterpret the impact of the decision when they add that after the snub, "it was hardly surprising that Warner withdrew its support."[50]

They also quote former Cosmos star Carlos Alberto repeating the same theme with the statement that "Very few people know why soccer in the United States finished . . . . If FIFA makes the 1986 World Cup in the USA, this was the best market. When FIFA decided on Mexico, Warner Communications say 'I finished. I don't put money in.' "[51]

Gavin Newsham notes in *Once in a Lifetime* that "Any sense that the good times were returning to the Cosmos and the NASL [because of the return of Franz Beckenbauer] was soon quashed, though, by the news that the USSF had failed in their bid to bring the 1986 World Cup Finals to the United States."[52] David Tossell in *Playing for Uncle Sam* includes "the failed American World Cup bid" in his list of eight reasons why the NASL folded.[53] Mario Risoli in *Arrivederci Swansea* says of the demise of the NASL: "some blamed the rising costs, others blamed FIFA's decision not to award the 1986 World Cup to the United States."[54]

But the FIFA decision should be viewed in the light of the fact that at the time, Warner was in the midst of a quarter in which it lost an appalling $283.4 million, a reversal of more than a third of a billion dollars from the $68.2 million profit in the same quarter a year before.[55] Compared to losing money at a rate of more than $3 million a day, the FIFA snub was small potatoes.

A more accurate assessment of the FIFA decision's effect comes from soccer historian David Wangerin in *Soccer in a Football World*, when he says that "Falling at the start of the 1983 NASL season, the blow sent the league reeling"[56] but stops far short of blaming it for the NASL's ills.

Chinaglia was back from his torn hamstring and his Italian adventures in time for the start of the playoffs in early September. Even with their greatest marksman out for half the season, the Cosmos still had led the NASL regular-season standings for the sixth year in a row, and won their division by a runaway margin. They finished the regular season in fine style, winning their last eight games in a row. Their opponent in the first round of the playoffs, the Montreal Manic, had finished last in that same division, but snuck into the playoffs anyway, because the top eight teams in point totals made the playoffs, regardless of their division finish, and the Manic were eighth in points out of the 12-team league. The Cosmos had won all four regular-season meetings between the two, by a combined score of 15-3.

Chinaglia may have been over his injury, but not everybody was happy with him. He had returned to the lineup on Aug. 14, a few weeks earlier than had been expected, but during his absence he had been devoting a lot of time to Lazio, and that continued. He missed the last game of the regular season because of a trip to Italy, and then, unexpectedly, missed the Cosmos' final practice before the playoff opener. "We haven't heard from him for the last three days," Julio Mazzei told the *New York Times* the day before the game. "He was supposed to be here at 3 o'clock [the previous day]. If he comes back, he'll be a plus for us and I will use him if he tells me he is in physical and mental condition. If he's not here, we proved that we can do it without him."[57]

"George has always been in a position where he could do these things," said one teammate. "People shouldn't be surprised."[58] Mazzei and his players weren't the only ones upset about Chinaglia's absences. Before his latest trip to Italy, Chinaglia had been asked about the reason for his mid-October farewell game being scheduled for Rome rather than Giants Stadium and said: "I have a right to choose my own things and I don't think the majority of fans like me here . . . . they should all shut up."[59]

The day after the missed practice, the Cosmos didn't have to play without Chinaglia, but they still couldn't beat the Manic. Montreal pulled off a 4-2 upset of the Cosmos at Giants Stadium. Alan Willey broke a 1-1 halftime tie with a goal for Montreal in the 61st minute, and Brian Quinn made it 3-1 a few minutes later. Chinaglia, who had scored the Cosmos' first-half goal, missed a penalty late in the game, but not one that would have made a difference in the game. Chinaglia's goal, on a header in the 41st minute, would turn out to be the last one he ever scored for the Cosmos.

"The Manic didn't look like a team that made the playoffs by gaining the last wild-card," Alex Yannis wrote in the *New York Times*. "The visitors played harder, ran more and faster, and yielded little space to the Cosmos, who captured first place in the overall point standing. The Cosmos never got into their rhythm and missed numerous opportunities."[60]

Adding emphasis to the way that the Cosmos were no longer the spectacle of their glory years was the fact that the weeknight game drew only 17,202 fans, the Cosmos' smallest home playoff crowd since the 1972 NASL final against St. Louis at Hofstra.

Six days later in Montreal, needing a victory to avoid elimination, the Cosmos had the better of the play, but couldn't hit the net. After a scoreless tie, the shootout went seven rounds before Montreal's Dragan Vujovic scored the winning goal. "Luck was against us," said Franz Beckenbauer, who played his final NASL game for the second time. "We played much better tonight, but we lost the series in the first game, when we played so bad in Giants Stadium."[61]

The Manic advanced to the playoff semifinals, where they lost to Tulsa. The Cosmos advanced to 1984, which Montreal didn't. The Manic, who had moved from Philadelphia after the 1980 season, had built up a loyal following in their first two seasons in Montreal. Then Molson Brewery, their owner, decided to emulate the Team America idea being used (unsuccessfully, it turned out) in Washington and before the 1983 season, announced that the Manic would be turned into a Canadian national team for the 1984 season. Attendance nosedived in 1983, and the team folded in November 1983.[62] Stumbles of that sort were piling up throughout the NASL.

The Cosmos' postseason tour was abbreviated this time. The last three games, in the Ivory Coast and Cameroon, were really just an afterthought. The one that mattered was the first, a Giorgio Chinaglia Farewell Game, between the Cosmos and Lazio at the Olympic Stadium in Rome on Oct. 16. As Pelé had done at his farewell game six years before, Chinaglia played the first half for the Cosmos and the second for his earlier team. Like Pelé in 1977, he scored a goal. Unlike Pelé, he was now the owner of that earlier team. And unlike Pelé, his goal came against the Cosmos, in the 77th minute of Lazio's 3-1 victory.[63]

Chinaglia finished his career with 397 goals for the Cosmos, counting all games, NASL regular-season, NASL playoffs and internationals.[64] He was more than 300 goals ahead of second place, and his 397 goals were more than the next seven players on the list combined. His days of involvement with the Cosmos were not over, however.

It seemed in 1983 that the financial underpinnings that supported the Cosmos couldn't possibly get more precarious. Events in 1984 proved that they could. Actually, those events began in December 1983, when Australian billionaire Rupert Murdoch announced that over the previous few months he had purchased 6.7 percent of the stock in Warner Communications.

Murdoch's new Warner ownership was above the five-percent threshold that required him to report his investment to the Securities and Exchange Commission, but he insisted that it was not the precursor of a takeover bid.[65] Steve Ross wasn't so sure that Murdoch's intentions were benign (he was soon proved right about that), and by January, Warner had engineered a complicated "White Knight" deal with Chris-Craft Industries in which Chris-Craft became a 19-percent owner of Warner and Warner became a 42.5-percent owner of BHC, a Chris-Craft subsidiary that included a string of television stations. The deal effectively blocked Murdoch from taking over Warner, because he was still an Australian citizen at the time, and federal law barred foreign citizens from owning more than 20 percent of an American television station. After a series of legal maneuvers in which Murdoch attempted to have Warner's Chris-Craft strategem ruled illegal, he gave up his bid in March 1984 and allowed Warner to buy his shares from him.

Via the deal between Warner and Chris-Craft, the Cosmos escaped the clutches of Murdoch, but they were delivered into the clutches of Herb Siegel, Chris-Craft's owner. That was not necessarily bad. It's not as though Siegel had anything remotely comparable to Murdoch's reputation as a yellow journalist. But Siegel definitely was a no-nonsense cost-cutter, and the deal with Chris-Craft put someone into a position of great influence at Warner who was dedicated to eliminating Warner's frills. The Cosmos clearly had become a frill.

Richard Clurman referred to some of Siegel's pet cost-cutting projects in *To the End of Time*:

> Siegel says he didn't "object to indulging the people in the core businesses." But did a company with Warner's huge losses need to invest $48 million more to tone up its air force of two Gulfstreams (later upped to four), a Hawker Siddely, plus three helicopters. "This company," Siegel told the board, "is not an airline."...
>
> And what about the "$8 million in decorative paintings and $700,000 to redo one executive's office"; a $950,000 fee to Ross's pal, Warner director...Bill vanden Heuvel for a negligible role in the sale of their Ralph Lauren cosmetics company? A $500,000 contribution to director Beverly Sills's New York City Opera? Five company apartments in Trump Tower?[66]

Shortly after making the deal with Warner in January 1984, Siegel told the *New York Times* that "I'm a major investor, but I'm not looking to run Warner."[67] That changed in the following months. "Given what was at stake for him, he could hardly afford to be passive," wrote Connie Bruck in *Master of the Game*. "When Ross and Siegel had made their deal, they had agreed to what was later announced as the 'asset redeployment program;' personnel would be reduced, expenses cut, non-core divisions sold .... But by the summer of 1984, Siegel felt that what he often referred to as the 'clean-up' of the company was running much too slowly."[68]

In 2000, *Business Week*, writing about Siegel's involvement in a more recent boardroom fight at another company, said of his early days at Warner: "Siegel was hardly a passive investor, launching withering attacks on Warner's lavish spending and Ross's propensity for expensive acquisitions."[69]

The axe may or may not have fallen on the Cosmos, who were no longer really an instance of lavish spending by this time, in the summer of 1984. The reason for the doubt has to do with the fact that while the official story was that Warner did sell a majority interest in the team to Giorgio Chinaglia, there are those who don't believe that any such transaction ever happened, and feel that Warner remained in control.

Chief among those doubters is Clive Toye, who said in his memoirs that "None of us worked out how, and certainly not why, the Cosmos franchise was transferred from Warner Communications, a major public company, to Chinaglia. The league office had no documentation, the lawyers were in the dark, it just happened and remains murky to this day. In retrospect, it is obvious that no legal transfer ever took place."[70]

The official story, that the sale did happen, or was going to, started to be heard in early June, when Chinaglia and his business mananger, Peppe Pinton, began talking about it. "Ross had wanted [Chinaglia] to run the team," the *New York Times* reported. "But Chinaglia said he had insisted on being a part-owner as well, and that Ross had agreed."[71]

It wasn't until July 26 that the deal was announced. Warner would receive no payment for the 60 percent it was turning over to a group of investors headed by Chinaglia, who would instead provide an unspecified amount of working capital.[72] Working capital in this instance apparently meant a contribution toward meeting the team's current expenses. The deal that gave Chinaglia control of the team was approved by NASL owners during a conference call on Aug. 22, 1984.[73]

Gavin Newsham says in *Once in a Lifetime* that the working capital involved was a "reported $1.5 million."[74] That's a good bit less than the supposed value of the club, which had been reported in the previous six months at various figures ranging between $7 million and $15 million.[75] But at this point, the Cosmos were not a property that had suitors lined up eager to buy.

Those bills that Chinaglia's group would face were a little less thanks to some salary cuts that the Cosmos had made a few months earlier. In late May, they released four players who had refused to accept pay cuts. The four, who had played a combined total of 21 NASL seasons, included three who had won NASL championships with the Cosmos, Hubert Birkenmeier, Angelo DiBernardo and Jeff Durgan (the fourth was Steve Moyers). The largest of the cuts was the 45 percent asked of Birkenmeier, who was making $175,000 a year.[76] By early July, all four had returned to the team after accepting the cuts, which did a lot more to satisfy new NASL salary cap requirements than to make any significant difference in Warner's losses, which reached an astonishing $437.5 million in the second quarter of 1984.[77]

Unlike 1983, the Cosmos' roster did include quite a few new faces in 1984, but these were not the big-name international acquisitions of past years. Instead, they were mostly inexpensive young Americans like Dan Canter and Kaz Tambi, some of them brought in because they could aid the Cosmos' indoor team. Of the 27 players who appeared in NASL games for the Cosmos in 1984, 13 were American citizens, the highest percentage of Americans fielded by the Cosmos in any of their 14 NASL seasons.

While Warner's losses were mounting, other numbers were going down, specifically the Cosmos' attendance figures. Their streak of 70 NASL home games at which they had drawn crowds of 30,000 or more had ended in 1981, but they did show in 1984 that they were still capable of drawing big crowds on certain occasions. They had five crowds of over 30,000 at Giants Stadium in 1984. The trouble was that none of those were for NASL games.

The Cosmos drew 32,653 for a game in early May against a Cosmos Alumni team that featured such luminaries as Pelé, Franz Beckenbauer and Carlos Alberto and such stars of the Cosmos' early years as Randy Horton, John Kerr and Jorge Siega. They drew 37,629 in late May for a game against Barcelona of Spain and Diego Maradona, 34,158 in June for the Trans-Atlantic Challenge Cup final against Udinese of Italy, 37,318 in July for a game against a World All-Star team, and 36,724 in August for a friendly against Juventus of Italy. However, their largest crowd for an NASL game in 1984 was only 21,385, the number who saw their home opener against Tampa Bay on May 13. It was not unlike the first New York Generals season in 1968, when their ordinarily mediocre attendance went through the roof the day Santos and Benfica played in the second game of a doubleheader. It may have had an effect on the Cosmos' actions in 1985, pushing them toward the decision that they could get along better playing friendlies than playing in the NASL.

The Cosmos had hit their peak in attendance at NASL games in 1978, averaging 50,684 for 19 games. Since then, that average had dropped to 48,167 in 1979, 42,727 in 1980, 34,784 in 1981, 28,538 in 1982, and 26,614 in 1983. The starkly obvious trend took an even deeper dip in 1984, with an average of only 12,817. In both 1983 and 1984, the largest NASL crowds the Cosmos played in front of were on the road. Their last two home crowds of the 1984 season were 8,736 and 7,581, the first time they had fallen below 10,000 at home since they played at Yankee Stadium.

Despite the attendance troubles, the Cosmos, who by now were being coached once again by Eddie Firmani, appeared for a while as though they might be headed for their fifth NASL title in eight seasons. They trailed the Chicago Sting in the standings for most of the season, but pulled ahead in late August and went into their final three games with a comfortable lead as they attempted to qualify for the four-team playoffs. Then came a horrendous late-season collapse, one of the worst in American pro sports history. After beating the Toronto Blizzard by 2-1 on Sept. 5, thanks to a goal by Ricky Davis and a victory in the shootout, the Cosmos had a commanding 115 points in the standings, with three games left. They held a five-point lead over the Toronto Blizzard, who had only one game left, and an 11-point lead over Chicago, which had two games left.

Because of the NASL's unusual system of standings points and the fact that the three teams each had played different numbers of games, it is extremely hard to express the standings situation in easily understood numbers. The situation for the Cosmos was clear, however. In order for them to fail to make the playoffs, they had to lose all three of their remaining games, while Toronto was winning its game and Chicago was winning both of its two. All six of those results had to go against the Cosmos.

Not only did the Cosmos lose all three of their games, they were shut out in all three, the only time in the club's history that they were blanked three times in a row. They lost to the Tulsa Roughnecks by 2-0 on Sept. 8, to the Golden Bay Earthquakes by 1-0 on Sept. 12, and to the Chicago Sting by 1-0 on Sept. 15. Chicago, which won that final NASL title, was the only good team of the three. Golden Bay had an 8-16 record that season and finished last in the five-team Western Division. Tulsa was 10-14 and finished one place ahead of Golden Bay. Both Golden Bay and Tulsa had long since been eliminated from playoff contention when they faced the Cosmos in what were meaningless games for them.

At least the Cosmos had Davis, one of their best American players ever, in the lineup for those two games. The fact that they didn't have him for the deciding game against Chicago is another example of the way the Cosmos were trying to cut costs. Davis had played for the Cosmos from 1978 through 1983, but in the fall of 1983, they made and then withdrew an offer to pay him the same $150,000 in 1984 that they had in 1983. Davis then signed with the St. Louis Steamers of the Major Indoor Soccer League. In the summer of 1984, he did sign two 15-day contracts with the Cosmos as a replacement for injured Jeff Durgan. The NASL only allowed teams to sign players to two 15-day contracts, and the second one expired with the Golden Bay game on Sept. 12.[78]

The season came down to the last game, between the Cosmos and Chicago at Comisky Park in Chicago. Toronto had finished its season a few days before with 117 points. The Cosmos still had 115 and Chicago had 113. There was a very slim mathematical chance that both the Cosmos and Sting might advance to the playoffs, but the overwhelming likelihood was that the winner would go to the playoffs and the loser would go home. Karl-Heinz Granitza's goal for Chicago in the final minute of the game determined that it would be the Cosmos who would go home. There was no Cosmos overseas tour after this season, which the NASL didn't yet know was to be its last. Given the state of the Cosmos' finances at this point, putting 20 men on a plane to go anywhere farther than Staten Island might have been too expensive.

Between the end of the 1984 season in September 1984 and the end of the Cosmos in June 1985, the Cosmos' existence was a funeral procession. First, there was the unexpected death of NASL president Howard Samuels on Oct. 25, 1984. Then there was the impoverished Cosmos' withdrawal from the MISL on Feb. 22, 1985, the demise of the NASL on March 28, 1985 and finally the last breath of the Cosmos on June 21, 1985.

Whether he actually owned the Cosmos or not, there was no question by the fall of 1984 that Giorgio Chinaglia was running the team. Peppe Pinton, Chinaglia's business manager since 1976 and briefly a vice president of the Cosmos when Warner was still in charge, also was deeply involved in the operation of the team, party because Chinaglia had to split his time between Lazio and the Cosmos. While he continued to live in New Jersey, Chinaglia was making frequent trips to Italy.

In their glory years, the Cosmos had never paid very much attention to indoor soccer. As their outdoor attendance waned in the 1980s, their involvement with the indoor game increased. In 1979, the NASL started an indoor league, in competition with the Major Indoor Soccer League, but in some years, the Cosmos hadn't bothered to field an indoor team. The Cosmos reached the championship game of the indoor NASL in the 1983-84 season, losing to the San Diego Sockers, who were to become the perennial champions of American indoor soccer. Even with a winning record, attendance was poor for the Cosmos indoor team, which played some of its home games at the Meadowlands Arena and some at Madison Square Garden in New York. In a step eerily similar to the dying Bethlehem Steel team's attempts to move to Philadelphia in 1930, the Cosmos talked in March 1984 of moving their indoor team to Hartford because of low attendance and high costs where they were playing.[79]

In the winter of 1984-85, the NASL did not have an indoor league, but by then permission had been given by both leagues for four NASL teams to join the MISL. The Cosmos were one of the four, but they struggled on both the field and the balance sheet. As the MISL season progressed, the Cosmos stumbled from one financial crisis to another. There was renewed talk of moving the team out of town, to Hartford or Buffalo. On Feb. 22, 1985, the Cosmos announced that while they still were going ahead with outdoor plans for 1985, they were folding their indoor team and withdrawing from the MISL. Their record in the 1984-85 MISL season at that point was 11-22 and they had suffered losses reported as high as $2 million.[80] "We have no obligation if the fans don't support us," Pinton, by this time the managing director of the Cosmos, had said two weeks earlier. "If you sell ice cream and nobody buys ice cream, there is no sense in going to the corner and ringing your bell all day."[81]

The next negative milestone was the end of the NASL. Clive Toye, who had been president of the Toronto Blizzard in the last several NASL seasons, was now running the league as a result of the death of Samuels in 1984 and the firing of Phil Woosnam the year before. Several of the 1984 NASL teams had folded or switched their membership to the MISL, and only three teams, the Cosmos, the Minnesota Strikers (formerly the Fort Lauderdale Strikers) and the Toronto Blizzard were still lined up to play in the 1985 NASL season. The situation was not unlike the one that the NASL had faced in early 1970, when it was down to four teams before Washington and Rochester joined. Toye hoped to attract a few more, but that hope went down the drain after the Cosmos announced that they were not going to post the $250,000 performance bond that would have committed them to playing in the 1985 season. Toye says that he recalls vividly being in a meeting in Vancouver at which he seemed to be succeeding in convincing a group of businessmen to join the league when one of their staff came in with a wire-service report that Chinaglia intended not to post the bond and the entire project dissolved.[82]

Toye tells in his memoirs about what followed:

> Formal and legal to the end, we followed the League Constitution and held a formal hearing at which the Cosmos were charged with failing to post a performance bond—a charge which, if proven, and that was simple enough, carried a penalty of expulsion from the League. Mark Beinstock, the League counsel, conducted the hearing, as he should, and I sat there, giving evidence, fully conscious of the irony. Here was this club that I had started 14 years before, before it was born, before it had a name, or a coach, or a stadium, or a player, and here I was, being part of its death. President Chinaglia, whom I blamed, and still blame, for many of the Cosmos' ills, had not, of course, posted his performance bond. But his performance was true to form. He threatened to throw Mark Beinstock out the window.[83]

The Cosmos were drummed out of the league in a vote taken that day, March 13.[84] Fifteen days later, after trying without success to add to the two teams it had left, the NASL announced that it was suspending operations. "We simply ran out of time," Toye said.[85]

Toye has since noted that "When Chinaglia failed to put up his money, that led to others not putting up their money. It affected the league enormously. I was trying to interest some people in staying and some people coming in, and the fact the Cosmos failed to post their bond was very significant."[86] He also has said of Chinaglia that "Giorgio had a malign influence on the Cosmos. I would say he was almost single-handedly responsible for the death of the Cosmos."[87]

The Cosmos were not yet fully dead at this point, but they might be compared to an actor who doesn't want to leave the stage and prolongs his character's death scene. What they had left was plans to play a series of 11 international exhibitions at Giants Stadium in the summer of 1985. They had to clear a few hurdles first, however. They had to pay some fines that they owed to the U.S. Soccer Federation and, since they had to be a member of a league affiliated with the USSF before the USSF could sanction the international games, they joined the Italian-American League of New Jersey, an amateur league.[88]

The Cosmos opened that summer series at Giants Stadium against Independiente of Argentina on May 27, which happened to be the same day that 87-year-old former Bethlehem Steel superstar Archie Stark died six miles away in Kearny, N.J. A goal by Vojislav Vuckevic with 4 seconds left enabled them to gain a 2-2 tie in front of 16,556 spectators. "The tie makes me extremely pleased," said coach Ray Klivecka. "The players responded well in the first game of what you can call a new chapter for us."[89]

The Cosmos looked pretty good in their next game 13 days later, a 2-0 win over Sporting Lisbon of Portugal that showed off some of the team's new Latin American talent and prompted that "Cosmos Are For Real"[90] headline. A crowd of 15,724 saw Roberto Figueroa of Honduras and Carlos Caszely of Chile score goals. Peppe Pinton was exultant, saying: "I think the Cosmos fans are still there and they aren't going to like waking up and reading in their newspaper that the Cosmos shut out Sporting Lisbon and they weren't there to see it."[91]

The Cosmos were already publicizing their next three games at Giants Stadium, with the rest of the summer's schedule still on the drawing board. The three were on June 16 against Lazio, Chinaglia's other club, which had just been relegated to the second division in Italy; on June 19 against a West German all-star team headed by the now-39-year-old Franz Beckenbauer, and on July 7 against Red Star Belgrade of Yugoslavia .

The Lazio game proved a disaster, a 2-1 defeat that may or may not have had the crowd of 8,677 scrambling for the exits, but seemed to have the leaders of the Cosmos doing so. In the *Newark Star-Ledger*, Ike Kuhns said:

> The Cosmos may have died last night in the very stadium where a few years ago fans fought over tickets.
>
> And if it was the final game for America's most famous soccer club, the record will show that they dropped a 2-1 verdict to Lazio of Rome in a fight-marred, controversial clash which ended with both teams in a free-for-all melee on the field.

The events on the field were only incidental in the wake of what followed. Cosmos' president Giorgio Chinaglia and managing director Peppe Pinton admitted that they would recommend today that the rest of this summer's international schedule be canceled and the club be disbanded.[92]

"It seems that we're fighting a losing proposition," Chinaglia told the *New York Times*. "It's probable we won't continue. We'll decide that in a meeting tomorrow."[93] The next day, Pinton resigned, but the meeting wasn't held, and Chinaglia departed for Rome, leaving Warner Communications and the other owners to try to settle the issues. Those owners struggled on for a few more days, but by June 21, the jig was up. The *Newark Star-Ledger* reported the next day that "The Cosmos officially folded yesterday after meetings aimed at saving the financially ailing soccer club failed to produce a plan to keep it going . . . . the Cosmos, once one of the most famous soccer teams in the world, came to an end in a board room in the Warner Communications building, the same building where it was born."[94] The *New York Times* story on the events of June 21 was written by the same reporter, Alex Yannis, who had covered the press conference on Dec. 10, 1970 at which the team's birth was announced.

The Cosmos issued a statement on June 21 that implied that there was a possibility that the team could return at some point, but that was a forlorn hope. For them, this was really the end.

EIGHT

The End . . . or Not?

The Bethlehem Steel soccer team came to an end in 1930, and the New York Cosmos did the same in 1985, but the corporations that owned them lived on. While the Bethlehem Steel Corp. did eventually succumb, both Bethlehem Steel and Warner Communications recovered from the downturns that helped to doom their soccer teams and went on to profitable years.

The most prominent symbol of Bethlehem Steel's recovery is the Golden Gate Bridge in San Francisco, built in 1937 by Bethlehem using steel from its own furnaces. World War II had the same sort of effect on Bethlehem Steel's financial position that World War I had, and the company's annual revenues topped $1 billion for the first time in 1942. Those revenues didn't dip after 1945 as much as they had after 1918, and they passed the $2-billion mark for the first time in 1953.[1]

It was particularly in the 1950s that Bethlehem Steel gained a reputation as a symbol of corporate extravagance. John Strohmeyer, a Bethlehem native who was editor of the *Bethlehem Globe-Times* for many years, quotes former Bethlehem Steel executive Donald Swan on that subject in his 1986 book, *Crisis in Bethlehem*: "Bethlehem at that time had the reputation that its hallways were lined with gold, and when you became employed there they gave you a pick to mine it."[2] Strohmeyer further notes that in 1959, when he was editor of the *Globe-Times*, the newspaper reprinted a *Business Week* list of the nation's highest paid corporate executives and that seven of the top 10 were from Bethlehem Steel.[3]

Perhaps the greatest symbol of Bethlehem Steel's self-indulgence was the $35-million Martin Tower building, built in 1972 as Bethle-

213

hem Steel's headquarters. The building is on the northwest side of the city of Bethlehem, about two miles from the plant on the south bank of the Lehigh River. The most striking thing about the Martin Tower, today a beautiful, empty white elephant, is that the 21-story building is in the shape of an X rather than the more usual rectangle. It was designed that way so that each floor would have eight corner offices rather than four.

Part of Bethlehem Steel's later problems was something often cited in the post mortems of dead industries and companies, that it had thought that the good times were never going to end. Those good times ended with a resounding crash in the summer of 1977, when nearly 10,000 employees in Bethlehem Steel's plants and offices were laid off.

"No one factor was to blame," the *Allentown Morning Call* wrote in its 2003 history of Bethlehem Steel. "Rather Black Friday [the day when 2,500 Martin Tower office workers were laid off]—and ultimately the demise of Bethlehem Steel—was the confluence of decades of mistakes that caused the former behemoth to collapse under the weight of its own corporate obesity."[4]

One of those mistakes was a corporate culture that valued conformity rather than innovative thinking. Strohmeyer labels that conformity as part of the legacy of Eugene Grace, the man who caused Edgar Lewis' exit from Bethlehem Steel in 1930. "Eugene Grace wanted corporate uniformity," he says in *Crisis in Bethlehem*. "He not only created an inbred board consisting only of officers employed within the company, but also established the precedent for board behavior: lunch together in the corporate dining room, golf together in the afternoon, socializing together in the evening. His word was law. It prevailed in all decisions from building new open hearths to installing a new sand trap on the tenth hole . . . . Many bright middle-management executives found the environment suffocating"[5]

The *Allentown Morning Call* history says that Grace "planted the seeds of doom" via his autocratic methods and his "smug and ultimately misguided belief that the world would always need Bethlehem's steel."[6]

Bethlehem Steel's main plant in Bethlehem closed in 1995. The company filed for bankruptcy in 2001 and its remaining assets were sold in 2003. The plant in Bethlehem now sits empty and rusting. A casino development has taken over a portion of the site, but much of the skeleton of Bethlehem Steel remains, including the 180-foot tall blast furnaces, towering over the rest like gigantic gravestones.

The End . . . or Not?

Warner Communications was not immune to extravagance either. Perish the thought. Steve Ross, referred to by Connie Bruck as "acquisitive, indulgent, pampered, grandiose"[7] and once by Rupert Murdoch as "living like Midas"[8] wouldn't have stood for penny-pinching. If the Martin Tower was the symbol of Bethlehem Steel's lavishness, the symbol of Warner's was Villa Eden, an estate near Acapulco, Mexico, that Warner bought in the early 1970s as a vacation home for its executives. One of the expenses that Herb Siegel objected to in his cost-cutting days was a bill for $25,999 for tennis balls and sneakers at Villa Eden.[9]

Ross had the distribution of perks, not only to himself but also to his friends and co-workers, down to a science. Bruck says: "By carrying the distribution of largesse to extremes, he had succeeded not only in engendering loyalty but in building himself up to mythic proportions. He had increasingly become defined by the extravagance of his generous gestures . . . . Who but a contemporary potentate, after all, could so afford to indulge every whim—sending the company plane across the country to bring [Stephen] Spielberg's dogs to East Hampton [Long Island], for example, or back to New York from the Caribbean, where he was vacationing with Quincy Jones, to get Nathan's hot dogs?"[10]

In 1979, Ross bought a massive apartment at 71st Street and Park Avenue in Manhattan, a three-story penthouse atop a landmark building that had been home to members of the Rockefeller and Vanderbilt families.[11] He also had a house in East Hampton. In 1901, Bethlehem Steel's Charles M. Schwab built a full-block mansion at 72nd Street and Riverside Drive in Manhattan, with 90 bedrooms, six elevators and a power plant that consumed 10 tons of coal a day.[12] He later added a 1,000-acre estate in Loretto, Pa. The two men were not very different from each other.

However, being the head of a movie studio was a perk in itself, one that Ross enjoyed but Schwab and his successors didn't. Allan Raphael, a New York investment broker, unwitting referred to that fact in 1984 when he said of the glamour of Hollywood: "If you are a businessman and you are president of Bethlehem Steel—who cares? But if you are head of a movie studio, it's 'Steve baby.' "[13]

Warner Communications recovered from its financial crises of the mid-1980s. In 1990, Ross engineered a merger with Time Inc. to create the TimeWarner conglomerate that exists today. Two years later, Ross died of prostate cancer. His sometime protégé, Giorgio Chinaglia, has not proven to be the businessman that Ross was. In addition to presiding over the death of the Cosmos in June 1985, Chinaglia six months later sold Lazio, which was facing the possibility of both bankruptcy and relegation to the Italian third division.[14] In November 2007, Chinaglia was fined 4.2 million Euros (about $6 million) in absentia by Italian authorities for his part in what they claimed was a scam involving a fake bid to buy Lazio. Chingalia contended the bid was real, despite the fact that he has called his earlier purchase of Lazio "the worst mistake of my life."[15] In July 2008, Chinaglia and the other seven men fined in November 2007 were charged with having used laundered money from organized crime in the Lazio bid. The other seven, all of whom were living in Italy, were arrested, but Chinaglia, who lives in the United States and had not yet paid the fine, remained a fugitive from Italian justice.

Chinaglia is among several of the foreign stars signed by the Cosmos who remained in the United States, at least part time, after the end of the Cosmos. The others who stayed included Vladislav Bogicevic, Andranik Eskandarian and Hubert Birkenmeier (as well as off-the-field names Gordon Bradley and Clive Toye). A few of Bethlehem Steel's Scottish imports stayed on this side of the Atlantic as well, most notably Jock Ferguson, Whitey Fleming and Bob Millar.

Soccer has struggled in the Lehigh Valley since the disbanding of the Bethlehem Steel team in 1930. There were two Lehigh Valley teams in the second American Soccer League, which was founded in 1933 as a scaled-down version of the original, with considerably less spending. A team called the Bethlehem Hungarians played one highly unsuccessful year, finishing last among 12 teams in the 1938-39 season. The Pennsylvania Stoners, founded in 1979 in Allentown, and carrying a name based on the fact that Pennsylvania is nicknamed the Keystone State, were much better. They reached the playoffs in each of their five seasons, won the ASL title in 1981, were runnerup in 1983 and were a semifinalist two other times. However, when the league folded after the 1983 season, the Stoners folded, too. In 2008, a new Pennsylvania Stoners team began play in the National Premier Soccer League, an amateur league that is part of the fourth division of American soccer (they had nearby competition from a new minor-league baseball team whose name, the Lehigh Valley IronPigs, reflected the area's industrial history).

The New York area had plenty of soccer activity before the Cosmos and has had more since their demise. That has included one team in Major League Soccer, the New York Red Bulls, playing at Giants

Stadium. There have been several others in lower divisions, including the New York Centaurs, the New Jersey Eagles and the Long Island Rough Riders.

There are many fans in the New York area who would like to see the name Cosmos revived in Major League Soccer, although the comments that they post on Internet bulletin boards sometimes make one wonder whether they understand that bringing back the name would not automatically bring back the 70,000 crowds and the rest of the hoopla. One who, quite naturally, would love to see the name revived is Peppe Pinton, whose involvement with the Cosmos did not end with his resignation in June 1985. Pinton now owns the rights to the Cosmos name and logo, and also is among those who deny that Giorgio Chinaglia's supposed 1984 purchase of the Cosmos from Warner Communications ever took place. "Giorgio never owned the Cosmos," Pinton said a few years ago. "It took me many years, bit by bit, to get it from Warner."[16] There has been talk of an MLS expansion team on the Queens-Long Island side of New York, away from the Red Bulls, but anybody who wants to name such a team the Cosmos would have to buy the right to do so from Pinton, whose office in Northvale, N.J., is decorated with trophies from the Cosmos' NASL days.[17] It wouldn't be cheap.

In the meanwhile, former Cosmos players have participated in reunion events a few times. Fifty-two former Cosmos players attended a Cosmos reunion held at Giants Stadium in 1991. None were at the NASL reunion held in 2005 in Dallas, but there were 12 at the National Soccer Hall of Fame in 2003 for the festivities surrounding the induction of 16 former NASL figures (including Ross, both Erteguns, Toye and Carlos Alberto).

The chances of a corporate-backed dynasty similar to Bethlehem Steel and the New York Cosmos happening in MLS seem uncertain. A major stumbling block is MLS' single-entity structure, under which the teams are owned by the league and investors buy the right to operate them from the league. There has been talk that this structure might be only a temporary thing, but more than a dozen years into the league's history, it doesn't seem to be changing anytime soon.

MLS has worked hard at trying to avoid the mistakes of the NASL. In particular, it has been very cautious about spending and expansion. Sunil Gulati, who was the deputy commissioner of MLS when it was launched in 1996, was very proud during that first season of having put together the playing roster for the entire 10-team league for only $15 million. Expansion has been equally cautious. By 2010, which will be MLS' 15th season, it is scheduled to expand to 16 teams. The NASL's 1978 explosion to 24 teams took place in its 11th season.

Spending and expansion are the two most frequently cited ways in which the NASL went astray and which MLS has sought to avoid. Clive Toye has often mentioned another, how in its early years, the NASL paid careful attention to missionary work in the American soccer community, but in its later years got away from that. Hennes Weisweiler's aversion to community work during his two seasons as coach of the Cosmos was well known. Less publicized is a stark example cited in a *New York Times* article about the woes of the NASL in November 1983. Writer Lawrie Mifflin detailed a 1981 incident in which the Seattle Sounders lost a game after their goalkeeper was sent off for shoving a referee. After the game, the coach declared that in the future, any player who hurt the team that way would be punished by having to do more youth clinics, a statement that can't have made the team any friends in the local youth soccer community.[18]

Said Toye in the same article: "A lot of these new owners [after the 1978 expansion] thought all the Cosmos did was spend a lot of money on players and that all they had to do was spend a lot of money on players, too, not realizing the seven years of hard work that went into the Cosmos before 1978...Until 1977 or '78, league people were intensely part of the community. But after that, most never went for so much as a cup of coffee with local soccer people."[19]

A second New York team may be a central item in MLS' thinking, but there are numerous other expansion candidates, and MLS is trying hard not to expand too fast, so a second New York team might not happen. Even if it does, it seems unlikely to become a dynasty of the Bethlehem/Cosmos sort very soon. The very definition of a dynasty includes the fact that it doesn't happen overnight. And there are a few much better dynasty candidates in MLS, such as the Houston Dynamo, D.C. United, the Chicago Fire and the Los Angeles Galaxy.

The Red Bulls, MLS' only corporate-owned team, could also be a candidate, despite their poor record over the years. Their owners seem eager to spend, although they have to deal with the MLS salary cap, one of the measures designed to help MLS avoid overspending of the NASL sort. The new Red Bulls stadium in Harrison, N.J., is being built a half-mile east of the site of Harrison Oval, where Bethlehem Steel played its first game in 1907 and subsequently played many other memorable games. It is seven miles south of Giants Stadium in East Rutherford, N.J., where the Cosmos played from 1977 to 1985. The area is loaded with soccer history, much of it related to either Bethlehem Steel or the Cosmos. With the advent of Red Bull Arena, there could someday be more history made nearby, but for it to be the equal of what has gone before would be a large order. People like Edgar Lewis, Clive Toye, Archie Stark and Giorgio Chinaglia have set the bar very high.

APPENDIX A

Some Bethlehem Steel and Cosmos Team Records

Bethlehem's teams in its six National Challenge Cup finals

May 1, 1915 vs. Brooklyn Celtic in South Bethlehem, Pa.—Bill Duncan, Sam Fletcher, Jock Ferguson, Jim Campbell, Neil Clarke, Bobby Morrison, James Ford, Tom Murray, Bob Millar, Fred Pepper, Whitey Fleming. Goals—Ford, Millar, Fleming

May 6, 1916 vs. Fall River Rovers in Pawtucket, R.I.—Bill Duncan, Sam Fletcher, Jock Ferguson, Tom Murray, Jim Campbell, Bobby Morrison, Sam McDonald, Fred Pepper, Neil Clarke, Paddy Butler, Whitey Fleming. Goal—Fleming

May 5, 1917 vs. Fall River Rovers in Pawtucket, R.I.—Bill Duncan, Sam Fletcher, Jock Ferguson, Tom Murray, Jim Campbell, William Kirkpatrick, George McKelvey, Fred Pepper, Jimmy Easton, William Forrest, Whitey Fleming.

April 27, 1918 vs. Fall River Rovers in Pawtucket, R.I.—Bill Duncan, Sam Fletcher, Jock Ferguson, Tom Murray, Jim Campbell, William Kirkpatrick, Jimmy Murphy, Fred Pepper, Harry Ratican, Jimmy Easton, Whitey Fleming. Goals—Ratican, Fleming.

May 19, 1918 replay vs. Fall River Rovers in Harrison, N.J.—Bill Duncan, Sam Fletcher, Jock Ferguson, Tom Murray, Jim Campbell, William Kirkpatrick, Jimmy Murphy, Fred Pepper, Harry Ratican, William Forrest, Whitey Fleming. Goals—Ratican, Ratican, Pepper.

April 19, 1919 vs. Paterson FC in Fall River, Mass.—Bill Duncan, James Wilson, Jock Ferguson, Fred Pepper, Jim Campbell, Sydney Brown, George McKelvey, William Forrest, Harry Ratican, Bob Millar, Whitey Fleming. Goals—McKelvey, Ratican.

April 11, 1926 vs. Ben Millers in Brooklyn, N.Y.—Dave Carson, Joe Berryman, Billy Allan, Robert McDonald, Bill Carnihan, Bob McGregor, John Jaap, Johnny Grainger, Archie Stark, Johnnie Rollo, Malcolm Goldie. Goals—Stark, Stark, Stark, Rollo, Jaap, McDonald, Goldie.

The Cosmos' teams in their six NASL championship finals

Aug. 26, 1972 vs. Dallas Tornado in Hempstead, N.Y.—Richard Blackmore, Karol Kapcinski, Werner Roth, Dieter Zajdel, Barry Mahy, John Kerr, Siggy Stritzl, Josef Jelinek (Gordon Bradley), Randy Horton, Willie Mfum (Everald Cummings), Roby Young. Goals—Horton, Jelinek.

Aug. 28, 1977 vs. Seattle Sounders in Portland, Ore.—Shep Messing, Paul Hunter, Werner Roth, Carlos Alberto, Nelsi Morais, Terry Garbett (Vito Dimitrijevic), Franz Beckenbauer, Steve Hunt, Tony Field, Giorgio Chinaglia (Jomo Sono), Pele. Goals—Hunt, Chinaglia.

Aug. 27, 1978 vs. Tampa Bay Rowdies in East Rutherford, N.J.—Jack Brand, Bob Iarusci, Werner Roth, Carlos Alberto, Giuseppe Wilson, Vito Dimitrijevic (Seninho), Franz Beckenbauer, Vladislav Bogicevic (Terry Garbett), Dennis Tueart (Garry Ayre), Giorgio Chinaglia, Steve Hunt. Goals—Tueart, Chinaglia, Tueart.

Sept. 21, 1980 vs. Fort Lauderdale Strikers in Washington, D.C.—Hubert Birkenmeier, Andranik Eskandarian (Rick Davis), Jeff Durgan, Franz Beckenbauer, Wim Rijsbergen, Angelo DiBernardo, Vladislav Bogicevic, Julio Cesar Romero, Francois van der Elst, Giorgio Chinaglia, Robert Cabanas. Goals—Romero, Chinaglia, Chinaglia.

Sept. 26, 1981 vs. Chicago Sting in Toronto, Ontario—Hubert Birkenmeier, Andranik Eskandarian, Bob Iarusci, Jeff Durgan, Wim Rijsbergen (Julio Cesar Romero), Johan Neeskens, Ivan Buljan, Vladislav Bogicevic, Seninho, Giorgio Chinaglia, Steve Wegerle (Chico Borja).

Sept. 18, 1982 vs. Seattle Sounders in San Diego, Calif.—Hubert Birkenmeier, Andranik Eskandarian, Jeff Durgan, Carlos Alberto, Boris Bandov, Rick Davis, Julio Cesar Romero, Vladislav Bogicevic, Steve Hunt, Giorgio Chinaglia, Robert Cabanas (Steve Wegerle). Goal—Chinaglia.

Bethlehem's two long undefeated streaks

41 games, between Jan, 31, 1914 and Feb. 27, 1915

1/31/14 – Bethlehem 4, West Hudson 1 (AFA Cup quarterfinal third replay in Philadelphia).

2/07/14 – Bethlehem 4, Philadelphia Peabody 0 (Allied American League in Philadelphia).

2/21/14 – Bethlehem 1, Allied League All-Stars 1 (friendly in Bethlehem).

2/28/14 – Bethlehem 9, Centenary 0 (Allied Amateur Cup first round in Bethlehem).

3/21/14 – Bethlehem 4, Philadelphia Disston 1 (Allied American League in Philadelphia).

3/29/14 – Bethlehem 2, Jersey City FC 2 (AFA Cup semifinal in Jersey City).

4/04/14 – Bethlehem 2, Jersey City FC 1 (AFA Cup semifinal replay in Bethlehem).

4/08/14 – Bethlehem 8, Reading 1 (Allied American League in Bethlehem).

4/11/14 – Bethlehem 3, Philadelphia Putnam 0 (Allied Amateur Cup second round in Bethlehem).

4/13/14 – Bethlehem 4, Philadelphia Smith 1 (Allied American League in Philadelphia).

4/13/14 – Bethlehem 2, Philadelphia Schuylkill Falls 0 (Allied American League in Philadelphia).

4/19/14 – Bethlehem 0, Philadelphia.Tacony 0 (AFA Cup final in Paterson, N.J.).

4/25/14 – Bethhelem 6, Philadelphia Smith 0 (Allied American League in Bethlehem).

5/03/14 – Bethlehem 1, Philadelphia Tacony 0 (AFA Cup final replay in Newark).

5/09/14 – Bethlehem 6, Philadelphia Kensington 1 (friendly in Philadelphia).

5/16/14 – Bethlehem 2, Allied League All-Stars 0 (friendly in Philadelphia).

8/01/14 – Bethlehem 5, Allied League All-Stars 0 (friendly in Philadelphia).

9/19/14 – Bethlehem 5, Philadelphia Disston 1 (friendly in Bethlehem)

9/26/14 – Bethlehem 3, Philadelphia Peabody 0 (friendly in Bethlehem).

10/04/14 – Bethlehem 7, Philadelphia Schuylkill Falls 1 (American League in Philadelphia).

10/10/14 – Bethlehem 2, Philadelphia Victor 2 (American League in Bethlehem).

10/17/14 – Bethlehem 1, Philadelphia Hibernian 1 (American League in Philadelphia).

10/24/14 – Bethlehem 2, Philadelphia Disston 2 (American League in Bethlehem).

10/31/14 – Bethlehem 6, West Philadelphia 0 (AFA Cup first round in Bethlehem).

11/07/14 – Bethlehem 7, Reading 2 (friendly in Kutztown, Pa.)

11/14/14 – Bethlehem 7, Philadelphia Putnam 1 (National Cup first round in Bethlehem).

11/21/14 – Bethlehem 4, West Philadelphia 0 (American League in Philadelphia).

11/26/14 – Bethlehem 7, Blue Mountain League Stars 1 (friendly in Bethlehem).

11/28/14 – Bethlehem 2, Clan McDonald 0 (AFA Cup second round in Brooklyn).

12/05/14 – Bethlehem 7, Philadelphia Rangers 0 (American League in Bethlehem).

12/12/14 – Bethlehem 16, Philadelphia Peabody 0 (National Cup second round in Bethlehem).

12/19/14 – Bethlehem 6, Camden Victor Talking Machine 2 (American League in Camden).

1/02/15 – Bethlehem 5, Blue Mountain League Stars 4 (friendly in Bethlehem).

1/09/15 – Bethlehem 6, Holyoke Farr Alpaca 1 (AFA Cup quarterfinal in Bethlehem).

1/16/15 – Bethlehem 5, Philadelphia Victor 2 (American League in Philadelphia).

1/31/15 – Bethlehem 1, Philadelphia Disston 0 (American League in Philadelphia).

2/06/15 – Bethlehem 7, Camden Victor Talking Machine 0 (American League in Bethlehem).

2/13/15 – Bethlehem 1, Philadelphia Victor 0 (National Cup third round in Philadelphia).

2/20/15 – Bethlehem 3, Allentown YMCA 1 (friendly in Bethlehem).

2/22/15 – Bethlehem 11, Philadelphia Rangers 0 (American League in Bethlehem).

2/27/15 – Bethlehem 5, Philadelphia Schuylkill Falls 1 (American League in Bethlehem).

41 games, between Nov. 25, 1915 and Dec. 23, 1916

11/25/15 – Bethlehem 4, Blue Mountain League Stars 3 (friendly in Bethlehem).

12/04/15 – Bethlehem 2, Philadelphia Rangers 0 (American League in Bethlehem).

12/11/15 – Bethlehem 1, Philadelphia Disston 1 (National Cup second round in Bethlehem).

12/25/15 – Bethlehem 3, Philadelphia Disston 0 (National Cup second round replay in Philadelphia).

1/08/16 – Bethlehem 6, Philadelphia Boys' Club 0 (American League in Philadelphia).

1/15/16 – Bethlehem 6, Philadelphia Hibernian 0 (National Cup third round in Bethlehem).

1/22/16 – Bethlehem 1, Philadelphia Hibernian 0 (friendly in Philadelphia).

1/29/16 – Bethlehem 2, Brooklyn Clan MacDonald 0 (AFA Cup second round in Bethlehem).

2/12/16 – Bethlehem 13, Philadelphia Rangers 0 (American League in Bethlehem).

3/12/16 – Bethlehem 5, Lehigh University 0 (friendly in South Bethlehem).

3/25/16 – Bethlehem 5, Blue Mountain League Stars 3 (friendly in Bethlehem).

4/03/16 – Bethlehem 1, West Hudson 0 (National Cup quarterfinal in Harrison, N.J.).

4/16/16 – Bethlehem 0, Chicago Pullman 0 (National Cup semifinal in Chicago).

4/22/16 – Bethlehem 2, Chicago Pullman 1 (National Cup semifinal replay in South Bethlehem).

4/24/16 – Bethlehem 4, Philadelphia Hibernian 1 (American League in Bethlehem).

4/30/16 – Bethlehem 5, Jersey City FC 0 (AFA Cup quarterfinal in Jersey City, N.J.).

5/06/16 – Bethlehem 1, Fall River Rovers 0 (National Cup final in Pawtucket, R.I.).

5/11/16 – Bethlehem 2, Philadelphia Disston 1 (American League in South Bethlehem).

5/13/16 – Bethlehem 7, Philadelphia Hibernian 0 (American League in Philadelphia).

5/20/16 – Bethlehem 3, Fall River Rovers 1 (AFA Cup semifinal in Fall River, Mass.).

5/27/16 – Bethlehem 0, Philadelphia Disston 0 (American League playoff in Philadelphia).

6/10/16 – Bethlehem 3, Kearny Scots 0 (AFA Cup final in South Bethlehem).

9/16/16 – Bethlehem 5, Froheim FC 1 (friendly).

9/23/16 – Bethlehem 7, West Hudson 0 (friendly in Bethlehem).

9/30/16 – Bethlehem 2, Allentown YMCA 0 (friendly in Allentown).

10/07/16 – Bethlehem 7, Blue Mountain League Stars 1 (friendly in Bethlehem).

10/12/16 – Bethlehem 3, New Bedford FC 0 (friendly in New Bedford, Mass.).

10/13/16 – Bethlehem 4, Fall River Pan-American 0 (friendly in Fall River, Mass.).

10/14/16 – Bethlehem 3, J&P Coats 2 (friendly in Pawtucket, R.I.).

10/21/16 – Bethlehem 2, Kearny Scots 0 (friendly in Bethlehem).

10/28/16 – Bethlehem 6, Philadelphia Putnam 1 (AFA Cup first round in Bethlehem).

10/29/16 – Bethlehem 2, Kearny Scots 0 (friendly in East Newark, N.J.).

11/04/16 – Bethlehem 4, Babcock & Wilcox 1 (friendly in Bethlehem).

11/07/16 – Bethlehem 3, New York FC 2 (friendly in New York).

11/11/16 – Bethlehem 5, Philadelphia Veteran 0 (National Cup first round in Bethlehem).

11/19/16 – Bethlehem 5, Paterson Dublin 0 (friendly in Paterson, N.J.).

11/25/16 – Bethlehem 7, New York IRT 0 (friendly in Bethlehem).

11/30/16 – Bethlehem 3, Babcock & Wilcox 2 (friendly in Bayonne, N.J.).

12/02/16 – Bethlehem 2, New Bedford FC 1 (friendly in Bethlehem).

12/09/16 – Bethlehem 2, Philadelphia Disston 0 (AFA Cup second round in Bethlehem).

12/23/16 – Bethlehem 2, Chicago All-Stars 1 (friendly in Chicago).

The Cosmos' streak of 30,000+ NASL crowds at Giants Stadium

70 games, between June 5, 1977 and May 3, 1981

6/05/77 – vs. Toronto Metros-Croatia (31,208)

6/12/77 – vs. Minnesota Kicks (36,816)

6/19/77 – vs. Tampa Bay Rowdies (62,394)

6/26/77 – vs. Los Angeles Aztecs (57,191)

7/06/77 – vs. San Jose Earthquakes (31,875)

7/17/77 – vs. Portland Timbers (41,205)

7/27/77 – vs. Washington Diplomats (34,189)

7/31/77 – vs. Connecticut Bicentennials (46,389)

8/10/77 – vs. Tampa Bay Rowdies (57,828)

8/14/77 – vs. Fort Lauderdale Strikers (77,691)

8/24/77 – vs. Rochester Lancers (73,669)

4/02/78 – vs. Fort Lauderdale Strikers (44,442)

4/16/78 – vs. Tulsa Roughnecks (41,216)

4/23/78 – vs. Dallas Tornado (50,127)

5/07/78 – vs. Detroit Express (45,321)

5/21/78 – vs. Seattle Sounders (71,219)

5/28/78 – vs. Rochester Lancers (41,305)

6/04/78 – vs. Vancouver Whitecaps (44,673)

6/11/78 – vs. Philadelphia Fury (42,385)

6/18/78 – vs. Washington Diplomats (47,700)

6/21/78 – vs. Colorado Caribou (32,476)

6/28/78 – vs. Los Angeles Aztecs (42,131)
7/02/78 – vs. California Surf (42,140)
7/12/78 – vs. New England Tea Men (62,497)
7/26/78 – vs. Toronto Metros-Croatia (50,178)
7/30/78 – vs. Tampa Bay Rowdies (60,032)
8/09/78 – vs. Seattle Sounders (47,780)
8/16/78 – vs. Minnesota Kicks (60,199)
8/23/78 – vs. Portland Timbers (65,287)
8/27/78 – vs. Tampa Bay Rowdies (74,901)
4/22/79 – vs. Fort Lauderdale Strikers (72,342)
4/29/79 – vs. Philadelphia Fury (46,375)
5/06/79 – vs. Houston Hurricane (50,142)
5/20/79 – vs. Tulsa Roughnecks (46,344)
6/03/79 – vs. Toronto Blizzard (38,762)
6/09/79 – vs. Dallas Tornado (45,031)
6/24/79 – vs. New England Tea Men (41,428)
6/27/79 – vs. Portland Timbers (33,271)
7/01/79 – vs. Rochester Lancers (40,379)
7/11/79 – vs. Seattle Sounders (40,207)
7/15/79 – vs. Vancouver Whitecaps (48,753)
7/25/79 – vs. Minnesota Kicks (57,223)
7/29/79 – vs. San Jose Earthquakes (35,450)
8/08/79 – vs. Tampa Bay Rowdies (70,042)
8/12/79 – vs. Washington Diplomats (34,599)
8/19/79 – vs. Toronto Blizzards (46,531)
8/26/79 – vs. Tulsa Roughnecks (76,031)
9/01/79 – vs. Vancouver Whitecaps (44,109)
4/13/80 – vs. Minnesota Kicks (51,225)
4/20/80 – vs. Tampa Bay Rowdies (46,182)
5/04/80 – vs. Dallas Tornado (41,378)
5/11/80 – vs. Memphis Rogues (31,458)
6/04/80 – vs. New England Tea Men (34,723)
6/08/80 – vs. Atlanta Chiefs (35,007)
6/22/80 – vs. Fort Lauderdale Strikers (70,132)
7/02/80 – vs. Toronto Blizzard (33,281)
7/06/80 – vs. Portland Timbers (41,260)
7/09/80 – vs. Philadelphia Fury (31,783)
7/20/80 – vs. Seattle Sounders (60,182)
7/23/80 – vs. San Diego Sockers (33,008)
8/03/80 – vs. Los Angeles Aztecs (48,019)
8/07/80 – vs. Edmonton Drillers (30,283)
8/17/80 – vs. Washington Diplomats (55,764)
8/24/80 – vs. Rochester Lancers (40,383)
8/31/80 – vs. Tulsa Roughnecks (40,285)

Appendix A

9/07/80 – vs. Dallas Tornado (45,153)
9/13/80 – vs. Los Angeles Aztecs (42,324)
4/12/81 – vs. Minnesota Kicks (40,378)
4/26/81 – vs. Tampa Bay Rowdies (40,238)
5/03/81 – vs. Washington Diplomats (34,189)

APPENDIX B

Record Goalscoring Seasons by Chinaglia and Stark

Giorgio Chinaglia's 76 goals for the Cosmos in 1980

2/24/80 – vs. Bahamas All-Stars in Nassau, Bahamas (1 goal)
3/16/80 – vs. Uberlandia in Uberlandia, Brazil (1)
3/21/80 – vs. Argentinos Juniors in Buenos Aires (2)
3/25/80 – vs. Tigres in Monterrey, Mexico (1)
3/28/80 – vs. Los Angeles Aztecs in Los Angeles (1)
4/09/80 – vs. Fort Lauderdale Strikers in Fort Lauderdale, Fla. (1)
4/13/80 – vs. Minnesota Kicks at Giants Stadium (1)
4/20/80 – vs. Tampa Bay Rowdies at Giants Stadium (2)
4/26/80 – vs. Tulsa Roughnecks in Tulsa, Okla. (1)
4/29/80 – vs. FC Cologne at Giants Stadium (2)
5/04/80 – vs. Dallas Tornado at Giants Stadium (1)
5/08/80 – vs. Toronto Blizzards in Toronto (1)
5/16/80 – vs. California Surf in Anaheim, Calif. (2)
5/21/80 – vs. Manchester City at Giants Stadium (2)
5/24/80 – vs. AS Roma at Giants Stadium (3)
5/26/80 – vs. Vancouver Whitecaps at Giants Stadium (1)
6/01/80 – vs. Washington Diplomats in Washington (1)
6/04/80 – vs. New England Tea Men at Giants Stadium (1)
6/08/80 – vs. Atlanta Chiefs at Giants Stadium (3)
6/14/80 – vs. Tampa Bay Rowdies in Tampa, Fla. (2)
6/22/80 – vs. Fort Lauderdale Strikers at Giants Stadium (1)
7/02/80 – vs. Toronto Blizzard at Giants Stadium (1)
7/06/80 – vs. Portland Timbers at Giants Stadium (3)
7/09/80 – vs. Philadelphia Fury at Giants Stadium (2)
7/20/80 – vs. Seattle Sounders at Giants Stadium (1)
7/23/80 – vs. San Diego Sockers at Giants Stadium (2)
8/03/80 – vs. Los Angeles Aztecs at Giants Stadium (2)
8/07/80 – vs. Edmonton Drillers at Giants Stadium (1)
8/13/80 – vs. Atlanta Chiefs in Atlanta (1)
8/17/80 – vs. Washington Diplomats at Giants Stadium (1)
8/24/80 – vs. Rochester Lancers at Giants Stadium (1)
8/28/80 – vs. Tulsa Roughnecks in Tulsa, Okla. (2)

8/31/80 – vs. Tulsa Roughnecks at Giants Stadium (7)
9/03/80 – vs. Dallas Tornado in Irving, Texas (1)
9/07/80 – vs. Dallas Tornado at Giants Stadium (2)
9/10/80 – vs. Los Angeles Aztecs in Pasadena, Calif. (1)
9/13/80 – vs. Los Angeles Aztecs at Giants Stadium (3)
9/21/80 – vs. Fort Lauderdale Strikers in Washington (2)
10/01/80 – vs. Hajduk Split in Split, Yugoslavia (1)
10/04/80 – vs. Sporting Lisbon in Lisbon, Portugal (1)
10/12/80 – vs. Napoli in Naples, Italy (1)
10/15/80 – vs. Fiorentina in Florence, Italy (2)
10/21/80 – vs. Al-Ahly in Cairo, Egypt (1)
10/28/80 – vs. Lazio in Rome (2)
10/30/80 – vs. Porto in Oporto, Portugal (1)
11/01/80 – vs. La Louviere in La Louviere, Belgium (2)
11/05/80 – vs. Real Betis in Seville, Spain (1)

Archie Stark's 75 goals in Bethlehem's 1924-25 schedule

9/13/24 – vs. Philadelphia FC at Steel Field (4 goals)
9/20/24 – vs. Boston Wonder Workers in Boston (2)
9/27/24 – vs. Fleischer Yarn in Philadelphia (1)
10/11/24 – vs. New Bedford Whalers in New Bedford, Mass. (3)
10/12/24 – vs. Indiana Flooring in New York (1)
10/18/24 – vs. Providence Clamdiggers at Steel Field (1)
11/01/24 – vs. Fall River Marksmen at Steel Field (1)
11/04/24 – vs. Newark Skeeters at Steel Field (2)
11/08/24 – vs. New Bedford Whalers at Steel Field (3)
11/15/24 – vs. Brooklyn Wanderers at Steel Field (2)
11/16/24 – vs. Brooklyn Wanderers in Brooklyn (1)
11/22/24 – vs. J&P Coats in Pawtucket, R.I. (2)
11/27/24 – vs. Newark Skeeters in Newark, N.J. (3)
11/29/24 – vs. Boston Wonder Workers in Boston (1)
12/06/24 – vs. New York Giants at Steel Field (1)
12/13/24 – vs. J&P Coats at Steel Field (2)
12/20/24 – vs. Indiana Flooring at Steel Field (2)
12/21/24 – vs. New York Giants in New York (1)
12/25/24 – vs. Fleischer Yarn at Steel Field (2)
12/27/24 – vs. Newark Skeeters at Steel Field (2)
1/01/25 – vs. Indiana Flooring in New York (1)
1/17/25 – vs. Fleischer Yarn at Steel Field (5)
1/24/25 – vs. Indiana Flooring at Steel Field (3)
1/31/25 – vs. Brooklyn Wanderers at Steel Field (4)
2/08/25 – vs. Fall River Marksmen in North Tiverton, R.I. (1)
2/21/25 – vs. Fall River Marksmen at Steel Field (1)

2/28/25 – vs. Boston Wonder Workers in Boston (1)
3/07/25 – vs. Providence Clamdiggers at Steel Field (1)
3/14/25 – vs. J&P Coats in Pawtucket, R.I. (2)
3/21/25 – vs. Philadelphia FC at Steel Field (2)
3/28/25 – vs. J&P Coats at Steel Field (1)
4/04/25 – vs. New York Giants at Steel Field (3)
4/18/25 – vs. Fleischer Yarn in Philadelphia (2)
4/26/25 – vs. New York Giants in New York (1)
5/16/25 – vs. Philadelphia FC at Steel Field (5)
5/30/25 – vs. Ohio All-Stars in Cleveland (4)
5/31/25 – vs. Ohio All-Stars in Cleveland (1)

Notes

Chapter One: A Matched Pair

1. E-mail from Jim Trecker, Oct. 14, 2006.
2. Michael Lewis. "30 years later, Pele legacy remains strong." *New York Daily News.* June 5, 2005.
3. Andrei Markovits and Steve Hellerman. *Offside: Soccer and American Exceptionalism.* (Princeton, N.J.: Princeton University Press, 2001), pp. 102 and 110.
4. David Wangerin. *Soccer in a Football World.* (London: WSC Books, 2006), p. 37.
5. Sam Foulds and Paul Harris. *America's Soccer Heritage.* (Manhattan Beach, Calif.: Soccer for Americans, 1979), p. 40.
6. John Arlott, ed. *The Oxford Companion to World Sports and Games.* (London: Oxford University Press, 1975) pp. 2, 88, 443, 643, 720 and 821.
7. Ron Borges. "In NFL's rich history, Modell did his share." *Boston Globe,* April 4, 2004.
8. Tim Tucker. "Braves players publicly prefer private owner." *Atlanta Journal-Constitution,* April 27, 2006.
9. Bill Virgin. "Sports teams break mold." *Seattle Post-Intelligencer,* Jan. 31, 2006.
10. Connie Bruck. *Master of the Game: Steve Ross and the Creation of Time Warner.* (New York: Simon & Schuster, 1994), p. 211.
11. http://www.forbes.com/lists/2006/33/334613.html
12. Andrew O'Toole. *Smiling Irish Eyes: Art Rooney and the Pittsburgh Steelers.* (Haworth, N.J.: St. Johann Press, 2004), pp. 53-4.
13. O'Toole, pp. 49-53.
14. Bruck, p. 89.
15. Rob Hughes. "Big Names Bubble Up in Real Madrid Election." *International Herald-Tribune,* May 31, 2006.
16. http://news.bbc.co.uk/sport2/hi/football/europe/3716251.stim
17. Alex Bello. *Futebol: Soccer, The Brazilian Way.* (New York and London, Bloomsbury, 2002). pp. 288-290.

18. Richard Goldstein. "Fred Saigh, who helped Cardinals stay put, dies at 94." *New York Times*, Jan. 2, 2000.
19. "Anheuser-Busch buys Cardinals stadium naming rights." *USA Today*, Aug. 4, 2004.
20. Robert Whiting. *You Gotta Have Wa*. (New York: Macmillan Publishing, 1989), p. 1.
21. "Financial Summary." *Bethlehem Review*, March 1955, p. 5.
22. Bruck, p. 105.
23. Alex Yannis. "Pele's Signing Crystallizes Unrest Among U.S.-Born Soccer Pros." *New York Times*, July 16, 1975.
24. Colin Jose. *NASL: A Complete Record of the North American Soccer League*. (Derby, England: Breedon Books, 1989). pp. 123-142, 239-262.
25. Clive Toye. *A Kick in the Grass: The Slow Rise and Quick Demise of the NASL*. (Haworth, N.J.: St. Johann Press, 2006), p. 141.
26. Jose, p. 30.
27. Colin Jose. *American Soccer League, 1921-31*. (Lanham, Md.: Scarecrow Press, 1998). pp. 470-492.
28. Jose, *American Soccer League*, p. 7.
29. Jose, *American Soccer League*, p. 7.
30. Jose, *American Soccer League*, p. 8.
31. "Jackson Brothers Go Abroad." *Bethlehem Globe*, Aug. 8, 1924.
32. Jose, *American Soccer League*, p. 13.
33. Jose, *American Soccer League*, p. 13.
34. Brian Glanville. "American threat to World Cup." *World Soccer*, March 1978.
35. Toye, p. 165.
36. Bruck, pp. 203, 211.
37. Robert Hessen. *Steel Titan: The Life of Charles M. Schwab*. (Pittsburgh: University of Pittsburgh Press, 1975), p. 170.
38. Interview with Don McKee, Jan. 8, 2007.
39. "Cosmos Are For Real," *Soccer Week*, June 13, 1985.

Chapter Two: Lehigh Valley Boys

1. Mark Assad, Mike Fassinelli, David Venditta and Frank Whalen. "Birth of a Giant." *Allentown Morning Call*, Dec. 14, 2003.
2. Lance Metz, Introduction to *Memoirs of a Steelworker* by David Kuchta. (Easton, Pa.: Canal History and Technology Press, 1995), p. 1.
3. Assad. "Birth of a Giant."
4. Gerald Eggert. *The Iron Industry of Pennsylvania*. (University Park, Pa.: Pennsylvania Historical Association, 1994), p. 52.
5. Stephen E. Ambrose. *Nothing Like It in the World: The Men Who Built the Transcontinental Railroad, 1863-69*. (New York: Simon & Schuster, 2000), p. 147.

Notes

6. Eggert, p. 79
7. Eggert, pp. 80-81.
8. Thomas J. Misa. *A Nation of Steel: The Making of Modern America, 1865-1925*. (Baltimore: Johns Hopkins University Press, 1995), p. 5.
9. Misa, pp. 19-20.
10. Assad. "Birth of a Giant."
11. Assad. "Birth of a Giant."
12. Assad. "Birth of a Giant."
13. Metz, p. 2.
14. Misa, pp. 97-98.
15. Misa, p. 98.
16. Misa, p. 102.
17. Misa, pp. 98-102.
18. Robert Hessen. *Steel Titan: The Life of Charles M. Schwab*. (Pittsburgh: University of Pittsburgh Press, 1975), pp. 24-25.
19. W. Ross Yates, ed. *Bethlehem of Pennsylvania: The Golden Years, 1841-1920*. (Bethlehem Pa.: Bethlehem Book Committee, 1976), pp. 117-118.
20. Misa, pp. 107-117.
21. William Manchester. *The Arms of Krupp*. (Boston: Little, Brown and Company, 1964), p. 221.
22. Assad. "Birth of a Giant."
23. Yates, pp. 192-193.
24. Hessen, p. 132.
25. Mark Assad, Mike Fassinelli, David Venditta and Frank Whalen. "The King of Steel." *Allentown Morning Call*, Dec. 14, 2003.
26. Hessen, p. 149.
27. Hessen, pp. 127-128.
28. Hessen, pp. 145-162.
29. Yates, p. 198.
30. Hessen, p. 16.
31. Hessen, pp. 16, 20, 29, 68, 123.
32. Assad. "The King of Steel."
33. Metz, p. 3.
34. Mark Assad, Mike Fassinelli, David Venditta and Frank Whalen. "Marvels of Steel." *Allentown Morning Call*, Dec. 14, 2003.
35. Hessen, pp. 173.
36. "Saucon – Yesterday." *Bethlehem Review*, July 1954, p. 8.
37. Yates, p. 206.
38. Arundel Cotter. *The Story of Bethlehem Steel*. (New York: Moody, 1916), p. 45
39. Roger Allaway, Colin Jose and David Litterer. *The Encyclopedia of American Soccer History*. (Lanham, Md.: Scarecrow Press, 2001). p. 235.
40. Roger Allaway. *Rangers, Rovers and Spindles*. (Haworth, N.J.: St. Johann Press, 2005), p. 50.

41. "A Swing Along Athletic Row." *Bethlehem Globe*, June 2, 1925.
42. "Testimonial Dinner to Bethlehems Team" *Bethlehem Globe*, June 25, 1915.
43. Allaway. *Rangers, Rovers and Spindles,* p. 50.
44. "Easy Win for West Hudsons." *Newark Evening News*, Nov. 18, 1907.
45. "Family's Fourth," *Time Magazine*, April 13, 1936, p. 76.
46. "Jones & Laughlin: Depressions and Mutations of a Mighty Dynasty Work Change in Steel's 4th Largest" *Pittsburgh Bulletin Index*, April 9, 1936.
47. "H. Edgar Lewis, Former Steel Executive, Dies at 66." *Bethlehem Globe-Times*, Dec. 5, 1948.
48. "Financial Summary." *Bethlehem Review*, March 1955, p. 5.
49. "Banquet to Soccer Player." *Bethlehem Globe*, July 22, 1919.
50. "The Allied Amateur Football Association," *Spalding's Official Association Foot Ball Guide*, 1912-13, p. 138
51. "Soccer." *South Bethlehem Globe*, Sept. 23, 1912.
52. Sam Foulds and Paul Harris. *America's Soccer Heritage.* (Manhattan Beach, Calif.: Soccer for Americans, 1979), p. 25.
53. Richard Henshaw, *The Encyclopedia of World Soccer.* (Washington: New Republic Books, 1979), p. 733.
54. Oliver Hemingway. "Soccer Foot Ball in Philadelphia." *Spalding's Official Soccer Foot Ball Guide, 1914-15,* p. 85.
55. "Bethlehems 3; Braddock 2." *South Bethlehem Globe*, Dec. 8, 1913.
56. "Braddock Loses at Soccer After Sensational Game." *Pittsburgh Post*, Dec. 7, 1913.
57. "Braddock Loses at Soccer After Sensational Game." *Pittsburgh Post*, Dec. 7, 1913.
58. "Soccer Cup Teams Wallow in Slush." *Newark Evening News*, Jan. 5, 1914.
59. "Annual Report of the Secretary," *Spalding's Official Soccer Foot Ball Guide, 1915-16,* p. 17
60. William Serrin. *Homestead: The Glory and Tragedy of an American Steel Town.* (New York: Random House, 1992), pp. 139-140.
61. "Bethlehem Lowers Homestead Colors." *Philadelphia Inquirer*, April 6, 1915.

Chapter Three: Gothamites

1. Roger Allaway. *Rangers, Rovers and Spindles.* (Haworth, N.J.: St. Johann Press, 2005), p. 44.
2. Colin Jose. *American Soccer League, 1921-31.* (Lanham, Md.: Scarecrow Press, 1998). p. 9.
3. Allaway, p. 62.
4. Roger Allaway, Colin Jose and David Litterer. *The Encyclopedia of American Soccer History.* (Lanham, Md.: Scarecrow Press, 2001), pp. 192-193.

Notes

5. David Wangerin. *Soccer in a Football World.* (London: When Saturday Comes, 2006), p. 122.
6. Wangerin, pp. 122-123.
7. Clive Toye. *A Kick in the Grass: The Slow Rise and Quick Demise of the NASL.* (Haworth, N.J.: St. Johann Press, 2006), p. 24.
8. www.ncaa.org/library/
9. Alex Yannis. *Inside Soccer.* (New York: McGraw-Hill, 1980), p.80.
10. Mike Woitalla. "U.S. mix better than ever." *Soccer America,* May 2008, p. 16.
11. Yannis, p. 46.
12. Paul Gardner, NASL championship game broadcast on TVS, Aug. 27, 1978.
13. Toye, pp. 33-34.
14. Gavin Newsham. *Once in a Lifetime.* (New York: Grove Press, 2006), pp. 16-17.
15. Connie Bruck. *Master of the Game: Steve Ross and the Creation of Time Warner.* (New York: Simon & Schuster, 1994), p. 61.
16. Marilyn Bender. "From Caskets to Cable." *New York Times,* Aug. 13, 1972.
17. Bruck, p. 26.
18. Bender. "From Caskets..."
19. Nekesa Mumbi Moody. "Rock, R&B titan Ahmet Ertegun dies." *Philadelphia Inquirer,* Dec. 15, 2006.
20. www.rockhall.com
21. Tim Weiner. "Ahmet Ertegun, Founder of Atlantic Records, Dies." *New York Times,* Dec. 14, 2006.
22. Newsham, , p. 20.
23. Bruck, p. 84.
24. Newsham, p. 21.
25. Newsham, p. 22.
26. Bruck, p. 93.
27. Bender. "From Caskets..."
28. Alex Yannis. "New York and Toronto Get Soccer Franchises." *New York Times,* Dec. 11, 1970
29. Toye, pp. 7.
30. Colin Jose. *NASL: A Complete Record of the North American Soccer League.* (Derby, England: Breedon Books, 1989). p. 19.
31. Toye, p. 49.
32. Toye, pp. 51-52.
33. Interview with Bruce Arena, Nashville, Tenn., Jan. 17, 1997.
34. "Cosmos and Darts in Soccer Revival." *New York Times,* May 5, 1971.
35. Alex Yannis. "Bangu Trounces Cosmos in Soccer." *New York Times,* Aug. 21, 1971.

36. Yannis. "Bangu Trounces..."
37. Newsham, p. 29.
38. Alex Yannis. "Cosmos, Stars Vie for N.A.S.L. Title Tonight at Hofstra," *New York Times*, Aug. 26, 1972.
39. Alex Yannis. "Cosmos Conquer Stars for Title." *New York Times*, Aug. 27, 1972.
40. Yannis. "Cosmos, Stars Vie..."
41. Toye, p. 59.
42. Joe Gergen. "Cosmos Gained Much In Losing to Dynamo." *Newsday*, Aug. 31, 1972.
43. Gergen. "Cosmos Gained..."
44. Gergen. "Cosmos Gained..."
45. Toye, p. 95.
46. Toye, p. 95.
47. Newsham, p. 63.
48. Newsham, p. 64.
49. E-mail from Frank Litsky, Jan. 27, 2007.
50. Toye, pp. 97-98.
51. E-mail from Walt Murphy, Feb. 23, 2007.
52. E-mail from Frank Litsky, Jan. 27, 2007.
53. Yannis, *Inside Soccer*, p. 53.
54. Richard Henshaw. *The Encyclopedia of World Soccer*. (Washington: New Republic Books, 1979), p. 609.
55. Harry Harris. *Pelé: His Life and Times*. (London, Robson Books, 2001), p. 128.
56. Peter Bodo and David Hirshey. *Pelé's New World*. (New York: W.W. Norton, 1977), pp. 82-84, 88-90.
57. Bodo, p. 91.
58. Harris, p. 139-140.
59. Pele, with Robert L. Fish. *My Life and the Beautiful Game*. (London: New English Library, 1977), p. 221.
60. Pele, pp. 221-224.
61. Pele, p. 224.
62. Toye, p. 86.
63. Joe Marcus. *The World of Pele*. (New York: Mason/Charter, 1976), p. 146.
64. Bodo, p. 106
65. Marcus, p. 148.
66. Gerald Eskenazi. "Prospects for Cosmos Take a Bullish Turn." *New York Times*, June 5, 1975.
67. David Tossell. *Playing for Uncle Sam: The Brits' Story of the North American Soccer League*. (Edinburgh: Mainstream Publishing, 2003), p. 75.
68. Marvine Howe. "Pele Out To Sway U.S. Fans." *New York Times*, June 5, 1975.
69. "The Toes That Bind." *Time Magazine*, June 4, 1973, p. 45.

Notes

Chapter Four: Men of Steel

1. "Financial Summary." *Bethlehem Review*, March 1955, p. 5.
2. John Steele Gordon. *An Empire of Wealth: The Epic History of American Economic Power*. (New York: HarperCollins, 2004), p. 289.
3. "Soccer Outlook Bright." *South Bethlehem Globe*, Sept. 1, 1915.
4. Mark Assad, Mike Frassinelli, David Venditta and Frank Whalen. "The King of Steel." *Allentown Morning Call*, Dec. 14, 2003.
5. Robert Hessen. *Steel Titan: The Life of Charles M. Schwab*. (Pittsburgh: University of Pittsburgh Press, 1975), pp. 214-215.
6. Assad. "The King of Steel."
7. Gordon, p. 289.
8. Hessen, p. 216.
9. Mark Ruetter. *Sparrows Point: Making Steel—The Rise and Ruin of American Industrial Might*. (New York: Summit Books, 1988), p. 115.
10. W. Ross Yates, ed. *Bethlehem of Pennsylvania: The Golden Years, 1841-1920*. (Bethlehem Pa.: Bethlehem Book Committee, 1976), p. 313.
11. "Bethlehem A.F.C. Notes." *South Bethlehem Globe*, March 18, 1915.
12. Robert Creamer. *Babe:The Legend Comes to Life*. (New York: Simon and Schuster, 1974), p. 159.
13. Seymour L. Wolfbein. *Decline of a Cotton Textile City: A Study of New Bedford*. (New York, Columbia University Press, 1944). p. 11.
14. E-mail from Hank Steinbrecher, March 13, 2007.
15. "Soccer." *South Bethlehem Globe*, Oct. 1, 1915.
16. "Goal from Penalty Kick Eliminates West Hudsons." *Newark Evening News*, April 3, 1916.
17. "Mob Referee at Big Soccer Game." *New York Times*, May 7, 1916.
18. "Bethlehem Retains U.S. Soccer Title." *South Bethlehem Globe*, May 8, 1916.
19. "Bethlehem Eleven Wins from Fall River Rover, 3-1." *South Bethlehem Globe*, May 22, 1916.
20. "Scots Beaten at Soccer." *New York Times*, June 11, 1916.
21. "Bethlehem Takes Soccer Trophy from Scots' Team," *Newark Evening News*, June 12, 1916.
22. William Sheridan. "Bethlehem Steel Company F.C." *Spalding's Official Soccer Football Guide, 1918-19*, p. 49.
23. "American Champions' Tour of Sweden and Denmark." *Spalding's Official Soccer Football Guide, 1919-20*, p. 33.
24. Interview with Paul Moyer, Bethlehem, Pa., Oct. 30, 2006.
25. "Bethlehems Swamp West Hudsons." *Newark Evening News*, Sept. 25, 1916.
26. Lance Metz, Introduction to *Memoirs of a Steelworker* by David Kuchta. (Easton, Pa.: Canal History and Technology Press, 1995), p. 3-4.
27. "Bethlehem Beats Hibs for Third Time, Score, 6-0." *South Bethlehem Globe*, Jan. 17, 1916.

28. "Beth. Soccerites Conquer Leading New England Teams." *South Bethlehem Globe*, Oct. 17, 1916.
29. "Beth. Loses and Draws with St. Louis Soccer Teams." *South Bethlehem Globe*, Dec. 26, 1916.
30. "Beth. Loses and Draws with St. Louis Soccer Teams." *South Bethlehem Globe*, Dec. 26, 1916.
31. "Swords Clinches Title for Rovers." *Newark Evening News*, May 7, 1917.
32. "Swords Clinches Title for Rovers." *Newark Evening News*, May 7, 1917.
33. "Bethlehem Steel Loses Championship." *South Bethlehem Globe*, May 7, 1917.
34. "Bethlehem Steel Lands the American Championship." *South Bethlehem Globe*, May 14, 1917.
35. "Bethlehem is Over Anxious in Game at Pawtucket, R.I." *Bethlehem Globe*, May 6, 1918.
36. "Bethlehem Outkicks Fall River Rovers in Final of Soccer Championship Play." *Newark Evening News*, May 20, 1918.
37. "Jabbing the Great Soccer Battle With the Ol' Ink Javelin." *Newark Evening News*, May 20, 1918.
38. "Are Disstons a Stumbling Block?" *Bethlehem Globe*, April 25, 1918.
39. "Bethlehem Steel Soccer Team Wins American Cup and for Second Time in Career a Double Championship." *Bethlehem Globe*, May 27, 1918.
40. "Championship Soccer Team Will Remain Intact." *Bethlehem Globe*, July 24, 1918.
41. Creamer, pp. 158-159.
42. Leigh Montville. *The Big Bam: The Life and Times of Babe Ruth* (New York: Doubleday, 2006), pp. 78-79.
43. Yates, p. 311.
44. "Another Soccer Championship for This City." *Bethlehem Globe*, April 21, 1919.
45. "Bethlehem Enters Finals for American Cup." *Bethlehem Globe*, March 17, 1919.
46. "San Francisco Soccer League." *Spalding's Official Soccer Football Guide, 1918-19*, p. 103.
47. Roger Allaway. *Rangers, Rovers and Spindles*. (Haworth, N.J.: St. Johann Press, 2005), pp. 76-77.
48. James Robinson. *The History of Soccer in the City of St. Louis*. (dissertation, St. Louis University, 1966), p. 94.
49. Robinson, pp. 88-89.
50. Robinson, p. 98.
51. "The Game with Allmanna Idrottsclubben." *Spalding's Official Soccer Football Guide, 1919-20*, pp. 35-37.
52. "All-Skane Team Overwhelmed by Bethlehem." *Spalding's Official Soccer Football Guide, 1919-20*, pp. 43-45.

Notes

Chapter Five: The Greatest Show on Earth

1. Eddie Sefko. "Dirk to Cuban: Chill Out." *Dallas Morning News*, July 1, 2006.
2. Nick Acocella. "Finley Enraged and Entertained." www.espn.go.com. Sept. 23, 2005.
3. Nick Acocella. "More Info on Charles Finley." www.espn.go.com. Aug. 20, 2006.
4. www.sabr.org.
5. "Nay for Quality." *Time Magazine*, Oct. 27, 1967, p. 69.
6. Nick Acocella. "More Info on Charles Finley." www.espn.go.com. Aug. 20, 2006.
7. "With Turner in Dugout, Braves Lose 17th in a Row." *New York Times*, May 12, 1977.
8. Peter Bodo and David Hirshey. *Pelé's New World*. (New York: W.W. Norton, 1977), p. 140-141.
9. Alex Yannis. "Cosmos Demand More Security for Pele." *New York Times*, June 22, 1975
10. Joe Marcus. *The World of Pele*. (New York: Mason/Charter, 1976), p. 167.
11. Pele, with Robert L. Fish. *My Life and the Beautiful Game*. (London: New English Library, 1977), p. 228.
12. Alex Yannis. "Cosmos Will Play In Yankee Stadium." *New York Times*, Feb. 13, 1976.
13. Yannis. "Cosmos Will Play..."
14. Yannis. "Cosmos Will Play..."
15. Gavin Newsham. *Once in a Lifetime*. (New York: Grove Press, 2006), p. 82.
16. Mario Risoli. *Arrivederci Swansea*. (Edinburgh: Mainstream Publishing, 2000). p. 145.
17. Risoli, pp. 167-168.
18. Newsham, p. 83.
19. E-mail from Clive Toye, June 15, 2007.
20. Paul Gardner. "NASL in wonderland." *World Soccer*, July 2007.
21. Newsham, p. 88.
22. Newsham, pp. 88-89.
23. Connie Bruck. *Master of the Game: Steve Ross and the Creation of Time Warner*. (New York: Simon & Schuster, 1994), p. 92-93.
24. Clive Toye. *A Kick in the Grass: The Slow Rise and Quick Demise of the NASL*. (Haworth, N.J.: St. Johann Press, 2006), p. 68.
25. Toye, p. 103.
26. Newsham, p. 91.
27. Alex Yannis. "27,892 See Cosmos Top Rowdies, 5-4." *New York Times*, July 15, 1976.
28. Paul Gardner. "NASL in wonderland." *World Soccer*, July 2007.

29. Earvin Johnson, with William Novak. *My Life.* (New York: Random House, 1992), p. 140.
30. Newsham, p. 113.
31. David Tossell. *Playing for Uncle Sam: The Brits' Story of the North American Soccer League.* (Edinburgh: Mainstream Publishing, 2003), p. 124.
32. Newsham, p. 105.
33. Newsham, p. 106.
34. Toye, p. 116.
35. Alex Yannis. "Beckenbauer of Little Value to Cosmos, Chinaglia Says." *New York Times,* April 24, 1977.
36. Tossell, pp. 122-123.
37. Paul Gardner. "Strange Goings on at the Cosmos." *World Soccer,* August 1977.
38. Newsham, p. 117.
39. Lawrie Mifflin. "Firmani Cosmos' Coach; Bradley Still VP." *New York Daily News,* July 8, 1977.
40. Alex Yannis. "Cosmos' Bradley Resigning Today; Likely to Become Diplomats' Coach." *New York Times,* Oct. 25, 1977.
41. Alex Yannis. "Firmani Case Sparks Cosmos-Rowdies Game." *New York Times,* April 30, 1978.
42. Risoli, pp. 179-180.
43. Alex Yannis. *Inside Soccer.* (New York: McGraw-Hill, 1980), p. 39.
44. Paul Gardner. "Carlos the Great." *New York Daily News Sunday Magazine.* July 27, 1982.
45. Gardner. "Carlos..."
46. Tony Kornheiser. "Despite Forecast, Brightest Cosmos Day." *New York Times,* Aug. 15, 1977.
47. Alex Yannis. "Cosmos Triumph at Giants Stadium Before Record Soccer Crowd of 77,691." *New York Times,* Aug. 15, 1977.
48. Alex Yannis. "Cosmos Going for Title No. 2 Today." *New York Times,* Aug. 28, 1977.
49. Lawrie Mifflin. "Cosmos Champs, 2-1." *New York Daily News,* Aug. 29, 1977.
50. Lawrie Mifflin. "Pele Makes a Foe Feel Like a Winner." *New York Daily News,* Aug. 29, 1977.
51. Toye, p. 120.
52. Tony Kornheiser. "Love! Love! Love! Cries Pele to 75,646 in Farewell." *New York Times,* Oct. 2, 1977.
53. Kornheiser. "Love..."
54. Roger Allaway, Colin Jose and David Litterer. *The Encyclopedia of American Soccer History.* (Lanham, Md.: Scarecrow Press, 2001). p. 202.
55. Risoli, pp. 186-187.
56. Newsham, pp. 159-160.

57. Paul Gardner, NASL championship game broadcast on TVS, Aug. 27, 1978.
58. "Roth of Cosmos Sidelined." *New York Times*, March 19, 1979.
59. Risoli, p. 190.
60. Alex Yannis. "Cosmos Dismiss Firmani as Coach." *New York Times*, June 2, 1979 and Thomas Rogers, "Official Asserts Firmani Failed to Get the Most Out of Cosmos." *New York Times*, June 3, 1979.
61. Ike Kuhns. "70,134 see late goal edge Cosmos, 1-0." *Newark Star-Ledger*, June 7, 1979.
62. Newsham, pp. 191-172.
63. Alex Yannis. "Cosmos to Get $600,000 for Releasing Cruyff." *New York Times*. May 24, 1979.
64. Alex Yannis. "Alberto of Cosmos Suspended for Rest of '79." *New York Times*, Sept. 1, 1979.
65. Newsham, p. 178.
66. Alex Yannis. "Cosmos Capture Soccer Bowl, 3-0." *New York Times*, Sept. 22, 1980.
67. Ike Kuhns. "Cosmos take Soccer Bowl." *Newark Star-Ledger*, Sept. 22, 1980.
68. Kuhns. "Cosmos take..."
69. Yannis. "Cosmos Capture..."
70. Alex Yannis. "Weisweiler to Join Cosmos on April 27." *New York Times*, April 18, 1980.
71. Alex Yannis. "Beckenbauer Agrees To Sign for 2 Years," *New York Times*, May 23, 1980.
72. Alex Yannis. "Beckenbauer to Leave Cosmos," *New York Times*, July 2, 1980.
73. Newsham, p. 194.

Chapter Six: Second Fiddle

1. "A Swing Along Athletic Row." *Bethlehem Globe*, Oct. 14, 1919.
2. "Bethlehems Down Eries in Cup Tie." *Newark Evening News*, March 29, 1920.
3. "Robins Again Beat Bethlehem Eleven." *New York Times*, May 3, 1920.
4. "Fluke Goal Decides Soccer Match." *Newark Evening News*, May 3, 1920.
5. "Eries Eliminate Bethlehem Soccer Eleven In Second Round of National Cup Tourney." *Newark Evening News*, Nov. 8, 1920.
6. "Cahill's Resignation is a Big Surprise in Soccer World." *Bethlehem Globe*, Dec. 7, 1920.
7. Charles A. Lovett. "First Big Professional League Launched." *Spalding's Official Soccer Football Guide, 1921-22*, p. 38.
8. Lovett. "First. Big..." p. 38.
9. Levi Wilcox. "Plan Inter-City Soccer Circuit." *Philadelphia Inquirer*, Jan. 17, 1921.

10. Lovett. "First Big..." p. 37.
11. "Bethlehem Team Will Show at Stadium Sunday." *Fall River Herald*, Sept. 26, 1923.
12. "Fall River Beats Bethlehem, 2-0." *New York Times*, March 10, 1924.
13. "Fall River Winner In Eastern Final." *Newark Evening News*, March 10, 1924.
14. Fred S. Nonnemacher. "Speaking of Champs, Steel Soccer Team Joins That Class." *Bethlehem Globe*, May 14, 1924.
15. Roger Allaway. *Rangers, Rovers and Spindles*. (Haworth, N.J.: St. Johann Press, 2002). pp. 65-66, 71-72.
16. Colin Jose. *American Soccer League, 1921-31*. (Lanham, Md.: Scarecrow Press, 1998). p. 66.
17. "A Swing Along Athletic Row." *Bethlehem Globe*, Dec. 15, 1924.
18. David Wangerin. *Soccer in a Football World*. (London: WSC Books, 2006), p. 59.
19. Levi Wilcox. "Cup and League Tilts Feature Layout Today on Local Soccer Fields." *Philadelphia Inquirer*, April 10, 1926.
20. "Stark Features Bethlehem Win." *Newark Evening News*, April 12, 1926.
21. "Bethlehem Wins, 7-2; Takes Soccer Title." *New York Times*, April 12, 1926.
22. "Bethlehem Booters Defeat Ben Millers." *Philadelphia Inquirer*, April 12, 1926.
23. "Bethlehem Booters Defeat Ben Millers." *Philadelphia Inquirer*, April 12, 1926.
24. "Bethlehem Steel Loses Cup Classic." *Bethlehem Globe-Times*, April 25, 1927.
25. Jose, p. 124.
26. "A Swing Along Athletic Row." *Bethlehem Globe-Times*, June 13, 1928.
27. " 'Left Hand' Decision in Soccer Squabble." *Bethlehem Globe-Times*, June 21, 1928.
28. "Poor Support of Soccer Blamed." *Bethlehem Globe-Times*, March 15, 1928.
29. Edward P. Duffy. "Horace Edgar Lewis." *U.S. Annual Soccer Guide and Record, 1949*.
30. Roger Allaway, Colin Jose and David Litterer. *The Encyclopedia of American Soccer History*. (Lanham, Md.: Scarecrow Press, 2001). p. 268.
31. Allaway. *Encyclopedia*, p. 268.
32. "Operating Data." *Bethlehem Review*, March 1995, p. 6.
33. "Bethlehem Steel Earnings Gain in First Quarter." *Philadelphia Inquirer*, April 25, 1930.
34. "Family's Fourth." *Time Magazine*, April 13, 1936, p. 76.
35. Duffy.
36. Mark Assad, Mike Fassinelli, David Venditta and Frank Whalen. "The Grace Period." *Allentown Morning Call*, Dec. 14, 2003.
37. "Steel Job Done." *Time Magazine*, May 31, 1937.

Notes

38. Benjamin Stolberg. "Big Steel, Little Steel and C.I.O." *The Nation*, July 31, 1937.
39. "Bethlehem Bonuses." *Time Magazine*, Aug. 11, 1930.
40. "Bethlehem Beats Soccer Giants, 2-1." *New York Times*, Feb. 24, 1930.
41. Levi Wilcox. "Up to Steelmen to Satisfy State Body." *Philadelphia Inquirer*, Feb. 6, 1930.
42. "A Swing Along Athletic Row." *Bethlehem Globe-Times*, Feb. 20, 1930.
43. Levi Wilcox. "Steel Soccermen Ready to Play Here." *Philadelphia Inquirer*, March 15, 1930.
44. Levi Wilcox. "Bethlehem Booters Barred." *Philadelphia Inquirer*, March 20, 1930.
45. "A Swing Along Athletic Row." *Bethlehem Globe-Times*, April 11, 1930.
46. "Rumor Grows That Bethlehem Soccer Team Will Disband." *Bethlehem Globe-Times*, April 14, 1930.
47. "Soccer Giants Top Bethlehem, 3-2." *New York Times*, April 14, 1930.
48. C.A. Lovett, "Bethlehem Leaves Soccer Void." *New York Sunday News*, April 27, 1930.
49. Thomas W. Cahill, "Annual Report of the Secretary." *Reports of Officers and Committees, United States Football Association, Season 1929-30*, p. 12.

Chapter Seven: ...the Harder They Fall

1. E-mail from Ted Howard, Nov. 11, 2007.
2. E-mail from Ted Howard, Nov. 11, 2007.
3. Clive Toye. *A Kick in the Grass: The Slow Rise and Quick Demise of the NASL*. (Haworth, N.J.: St. Johann Press, 2006), pp. 98-99.
4. Toye, pp. 153-154.
5. Alex Yannis. "Chinaglia-Weisweiler Split Widening." *New York Times*, Aug. 30, 1981.
6. Yannis. "...Split Widening."
7. Mario Risoli. *Arrivederci Swansea*. (Edinburgh: Mainstream Publishing, 2000). p. 193.
8. Gavin Newsham. *Once in a Lifetime*. (New York: Grove Press, 2006), pp. 214-215.
9. Alex Yannis. "Cosmos Era Could End." *New York Times*, March 28, 1982.
10. Ike Kuhns. "NASL's future on Soccer Bowl?" *Newark Star-Ledger*, Sept. 18, 1982.
11. Roger Allaway, Colin Jose and David Litterer. *The Encyclopedia of American Soccer History*. (Lanham, Md.: Scarecrow Press, 2001), p. 429.
12. Lawrie Mifflin. "Samuels is Named to Head N.A.S.L." *New York Times*, June 26, 1982.
13. Alex Yannis. "Cosmos Defeat Sockers." *New York Times*, Sept. 6, 1982.

14. George Vecsey. "The Soccer Bowl Not a Super Bowl." *New York Times*, Sept. 19, 1982.
15. Frank Coluccio, interview on KIRO-TV, Seattle, Sept. 17, 1982.
16. Ike Kuhns. "Giorgio 'tricks' Flamengo in Alberto's Farewell, 3-3." *Newark Star-Ledger*, Sept. 29, 1982
17. Kuhns. "Giorgio 'tricks'..."
18. Alex Yannis. "Final Salute to Carlos Alberto." *New York Times*, Sept. 28, 1982.
19. Connie Bruck. *Master of the Game: Steve Ross and the Creation of Time Warner.* (New York: Simon & Schuster, 1994), p. 165.
20. "Pac-Man and Beyond." *New York Times*, June 4, 1982.
21. Andrew Pollack. "RCA Posts a Profit; Warner, Tandy Up." *New York Times*, Oct. 19, 1982.
22. Bruck, pp. 165, 169.
23. Richard M. Clurman. *To the End of Time: The Seduction and Conquest of a Media Empire.* (New York: Simon & Schuster, 1992), pp. 116-117.
24. Clurman, p. 119.
25. "Atari's Struggle to Stay Ahead." *Business Week*, Sept. 13, 1982.
26. Bruck, p. 179.
27. Bruck, p. 180.
28. Bruck, p. 180
29. "The Video-Game Shakeout." *Newsweek*, Dec. 20, 1982.
30. Clurman, pp. 119-120.
31. Clurman, pp. 107-108.
32. Bruck, p. 110.
33. Clurman, p. 110.
34. Arnold H. Lubasch. "Prosecutor Links Chief At Warner to Bribe Plan." *New York Times*, Nov. 4, 1982.
35. Lubasch. "Prosecutor Links..."
36. Arnold H. Lubasch. "Ex-Warner Aides Put on Probation." *New York Times*, Dec. 14, 1982.
37. Clurman, p. 114
38. Alex S. Jones. "The 3 Protagonists." *New York Times*, Jan. 4, 1984.
39. Bruck, p. 183
40. Risoli, p. 195.
41. Risoli, p. 196.
42. "Chinaglia Moonlighting." *New York Times*, June 14, 1983.
43. Lawrie Mifflin. "Cosmos Turn Back Team America, 4-0." *New York Times*, July 7, 1983.
44. Risoli, p. 196.
45. Alex Yannis. "A Match of Soccer Champions." *New York Times*, June 15, 1983.
46. Alex Yannis. "Cosmos Trounce Europe Champions." *New York Times*, June 16, 1983.

Notes

47. Yannis. "Cosmos Trounce..."
48. David Wangerin. *Soccer in a Football World.* (London: WSC Books, 2006), p. 214.
49. John Sugden and Alan Tomlinson, *FIFA and the Contest for World Football.* (Cambridge, England: Polity Press, 1998), pp. 207-208.
50. Sugden, p. 208.
51. Sugden, p. 207.
52. Newsham, p. 230.
53. David Tossell. *Playing for Uncle Sam: The Brits' Story of the North American Soccer League.* (Edinburgh: Mainstream Publishing, 2003), p. 239.
54. Risoli, p. 197.
55. Andrew Pollack. "Warner Posts a $283.4 Million Loss." *New York Times,* July 22, 1983.
56. Wangerin, p. 215.
57. Alex Yannis. "Chinaglia Misses Cosmos Workout." *New York Times,* Sept. 6, 1983.
58. Phil Mushnick. "Giorgio's trip to Italy makes Cosmos bitter." *New York Post,* Sept. 3, 1983.
59. " 'Shut up.' Giorgio tells booing fans." *New York Daily News,* Aug. 28, 1983.
60. Alex Yannis. "Cosmos Shocked in Playoff Opener." *New York Times,* Sept. 7, 1983.
61. Alex Yannis. "Cosmos Ousted in Playoffs." *New York Times,* Sept. 13, 1983.
62. Colin Jose. *NASL: A Complete Record of the North American Soccer League.* (Derby, England: Breedon Books, 1989). pp. 15.
63. "A Farewell to Chinaglia." *New York Times,* Oct. 16, 1983.
64. "Cosmos Career Goal Scoring—All Games." *New York Cosmos Media Guide 1984,* p. 65.
65. Alex S. Jones. "Murdoch Buys 6.7% Of Warner." *New York Times,* Dec. 3, 1983.
66. Clurman, pp. 127-128.
67. Alex S. Jones. "Chris-Craft's Feisty Chairman – He's Relishing the Intense Battle Over Warner." *New York Times,* Jan. 22, 1984.
68. Bruck, p. 211.
69. Ronald Grover. "Herb Siegel: The Fly in Viacom's Ointment." *Business Week,* Feb. 11, 2000.
70. Toye, p. 165.
71. Alex Yannis. "Cosmos Win, 4-1, to Gain Challenge Cup." *New York Times,* June 4, 1984.
72. Robert McG. Thomas Jr. "Chinaglia Purchases Control of Cosmos." *New York Times,* July 27, 1984.
73. Alex Yannis. "Cosmos Said to Join M.I.S.L." *New York Times,* Aug. 23, 1984.
74. Newsham, p. 244.
75. Rupert Murdoch's High-Stakes Gamble on Warner," *Business Week,* Jan.

23, 1984 and Alex Yannis. "Cosmos Win, 4-1, to Gain Challange Cup." *New York Times*, June 4, 1984.

76. Alex Yannis. "Cosmos Waive 4 Over Pay." *New York Times*, May 23, 1984.
77. Lee A. Daniels. "Warner Loses Over $400 Million." *New York Times*, Aug. 3, 1984.
78. Lawrie Mifflin. "The Cosmos' Fall Brings Down Davis." *New York Times*, Sept. 13, 1984.
79. Alex Yannis. "Hartford Shift Seen For Indoor Cosmos." *New York Times*, March 8, 1984.
80. Alex Yannis. "Cosmos Fold Indoor Squad." *New York Times*, Feb. 23, 1985.
81. Michael Goodwin. "Cosmos Face Deep Problems." *New York Times*, Feb. 13, 1985.
82. E-mail from Clive Toye, Dec. 8, 2007.
83. Toye, p. 165.
84. Newsham, p. 250.
85. "Season Off for N.A.S.L." *New York Times*, March 29, 1985.
86. Risoli, p. 197.
87. Newsham, p. 258.
88. "Cosmos Pay $19,223 in Fines." *New York Times*, April 18, 1985.
89. Alex Yannis. "Goal with 0:04 Left Gives Cosmos Tie." *New York Times*, May 28, 1985.
90. "Cosmos Are For Real," *Soccer Week*, June 13, 1985.
91. Ike Kuhns. "Cosmos top Lisbon, 2-0." *Newark Star-Ledger*, June 10, 1985.
92. Ike Kuhns. "Cosmos may scrap slate." *Newark Star-Ledger*, June 17, 1985.
93. Alex Yannis. "Cosmos Lose, 2-1; May Cancel Games." *New York Times*, June 17, 1985.
94. Ike Kuhns. "Cosmos fold as late efforts fail." *Newark Star-Ledger*, June 22, 1985.

Chapter Eight: The End . . . or Not?

1. "Financial Summary." *Bethlehem Review*, March 1955, p. 5.
2. John Strohmeyer. *Crisis in Bethlehem: Big Steel's Struggle to Survive* (Bethesda, Md.: Adler & Adler, 1986). p 29.
3. Strohmeyer, p. 29.
4. Mark Assad, Mike Fassinelli, David Venditta and Frank Whalen. "The Bitter End." *Allentown Morning Call*, Dec. 14, 2003.
5. Strohmeyer, p. 30.
6. Mark Assad, Mike Fassinelli, David Venditta and Frank Whalen. "The Grace Period." *Allentown Morning Call*, Dec. 14, 2003.
7. Connie Bruck. *Master of the Game: Steve Ross and the Creation of Time Warner.* (New York: Simon & Schuster, 1994), p. 213.
8. Bruck, p. 202.
9. Bruck, p. 212.

Notes

10. Bruck, p. 213.
11. Michael Gross. *740 Park.* (New York: Broadway Books, 2005), pp. 441-442.
12. Robert Hessen. *Steel Titan: The Life of Charles M. Schwab.* (Pittsburgh: University of Pittsburgh Press, 1975), pp. 132-133.
13. Leslie Wayne. "The Battle for Survival at Warner." *New York Times,* Jan. 8, 1984.
14. Mario Risoli. *Arrivederci Swansea.* (Edinburgh: Mainstream Publishing, 2000). p. 203.
15. Risoli, p. 198.
16. Clive Toye. *A Kick in the Grass: The Slow Rise and Quick Demise of the NASL.* (Haworth, N.J.: St. Johann Press, 2006), p. 165.
17. E-mail from Peppe Pinton,, Dec. 12, 2007.
18. Lawrie Mifflin. "Why N.A.S.L. Is in Trouble." *New York Times,* Nov. 13, 1983.
19. Mifflin. "Why...."

Bibliography

Books

Allaway, Roger. *Rangers, Rovers and Spindles*. Haworth, N.J.; St. Johann Press, 2005.

Allaway, Roger, Colin Jose and David Litterer. *The Encyclopedia of American Soccer History*. Lanham, Md.: Scarecrow Press, 2001.

Ambrose, Stephen E. *Nothing Like It in the World: The Men Who Built the Transcontinental Railroad, 1863-1869*. New York: Simon & Schuster, 2000.

Arlott, John ed. *The Oxford Companion to World Sports and Games*. London: Oxford University Press, 1975.

Bello, Alex. *Futebol: Soccer, The Brazilian Way*. New York and London: Bloomsbury, 2002.

Bodo, Peter and David Hirshey. *Pelé's New World*. New York: W.W. Norton, 1977.

Bruck, Connie. *Master of the Game: Steve Ross and the Creation of Time Warner*. New York: Simon & Schuster, 1994.

Clurman, Richard M. *To the End of Time: The Seduction and Conquest of a Media Empire*. New York: Simon & Schuster, 1992.

Cotter, Arundel *The Story of Bethlehem Steel*. New York: Moody, 1916.

Creamer, Robert *Babe: The Legend Comes to Life*. New York: Simon & Schuster, 1974.

Eggert, Gerald. *The Iron Industry of Pennsylvania*. University Park, Pa.: Pennsylvania Historical Association, 1994.

Foulds, Sam T.N. and Paul Harris. *America's Soccer Heritage*. Manhattan Beach, Calif.: Soccer for Americans, 1979.

Gordon, John Steele. *An Empire of Wealth: The Epic History of American Economic Power*. New York: HarperCollins, 2004.

Gross, Michael. *740 Park*. New York: Broadway Books, 2005.

Harris, Harry. *Pelé: His Life and Times*. London: Robson Books, 2001.

Henshaw, Richard. *The Encyclopedia of World Soccer*. Washington: New Republic Books, 1979.

Hessen, Robert. *Steel Titan: The Life of Charles M. Schwab.* Pittsburgh: University of Pittsburgh Press, 1975.

Johnson, Earvin, with William Novak. *My Life.* New York: Random House, 1992.

Jose, Colin. *American Soccer League 1921-31.* Lanham, Md.: Scarecrow Press, 1998.

Jose, Colin. *NASL: A Complete Record of the North American Soccer League.* Derby, England: Breedon Books, 1989.

Jose, Colin. *North American Soccer League Encyclopedia.* Haworth, N.J.: St. Johann Press, 2003.

Kuchta, David. *Memoirs of a Steelworker.* Easton, Pa.: Canal History and Technology Press, 1995.

Manchester, William. *The Arms of Krupp.* New York: Little, Brown and Company, 1964.

Marcus, Joe. *The World of Pelé.* New York: Mason/Charter, 1976.

Markovits, Andrei and Steve Hellerman. *Offside: Soccer and American Exceptionalism.* Princeton, N.J.: Princeton University Press, 2001.

Misa, Thomas J. *A Nation of Steel: The Making of Modern America, 1865-1925.* Baltimore: Johns Hopkins University Press, 1995.

Newsham, Gavin. *Once in a Lifetime: The Incredible Story of the New York Cosmos.* New York, Grove Press, 2006.

Nelson, Cordner and Roberto Quercetani. *Runners and Races: 1500m./Mile.* Los Altos, Calif.: Tafnews Press, 1973.

O'Toole, Andrew. *Smiling Irish Eyes: Art Rooney and the Pittsburgh Steelers.* Haworth, N.J.: St. Johann Press, 2004.

Pelé, with Robert L. Fish. *My Life and the Beautiful Game.* London: New English Library, 1977.

Ruetter, Mark. *Sparrows Point: Making Steel—The Rise and Ruin of American Industrial Might.* New York: Simon & Schuster, 1988.

Risoli, Mario. *Arrivederci Swansea.* Edinburgh: Mainstream Publishing, 2000.

Serrin, William. *Homestead: The Glory and Tragedy of an American Steel Town.* New York: Random House, 1992.

Smith, Melvin I. *Evolvements of Early American Foot Ball: Through the 1890/91 Season.* Bloomington, Ind.: AuthorHouse, 2008.

Strohmeyer, John. *Crisis in Bethlehem: Big Steel's Struggle to Survive.* Bethesda, Md.: Adler & Adler, 1986.

Sugden, John and Alan Tomlinson. *FIFA and the Contest for World Football.* Cambridge, England: Polity Press, 1998

Tossell, David. *Playing for Uncle Sam: The Brits' Story of the North American Soccer League.* Edinburgh: Mainstream Publishing, 2003.

Toye, Clive. *A Kick in the Grass: The Slow Rise and Quick Demise of the NASL.* Haworth, N.J.: St. Johann Press, 2006.

Wangerin, David. *Soccer in a Football World.* London: WSC Books, 2006.

Whiting, Robert. *You Gotta Have Wa.* New York: Macmillan Publishing, 1989.

Wolfbein, Seymour L. *Decline of a Cotton Textile City: A Study of New Bedford.* New York: Columbia University Press, 1944.

Yannis, Alex. *Inside Soccer.* New York: McGraw-Hill, 1980.

Yates, W. Ross, ed. *Bethlehem of Pennsylvania: The Golden Years, 1841-1920.* Bethlehem, Pa.: Bethlehem Book Committee, 1976.

Newspapers

Allentown Morning Call, Dec. 14, 2003.

Atlanta Journal-Constitution, Apr. 27, 2006.

Boston Globe, April 4, 2004.

Dallas Morning News, July 1, 2006.

Fall River Herald, Sept. 26, 1923.

International Herald-Tribune, May 31, 2006.

New York News, April 27, 1930; July 8, 1977; Aug. 29, 1977; Aug. 28, 1983; June 5, 2005.

New York Post, Sept. 3, 1983.

New York Times, May 7, 1916; June 11, 1916; May 3, 1920; March 10, 1924; April 12, 1926; Feb. 24, 1930; April 14, 1930; Dec. 11, 1970; Aug. 13, 1972; Aug. 26, 1972; Aug. 27, 1972; June 5, 1975; June 22, 1975; July 16, 1975; Feb. 13, 1976; July 15, 1976; April 24, 1977; May 12, 1977; Aug 15, 1977; Aug. 28, 1977; Oct. 2, 1977; Oct. 25, 1977; April 30, 1978; March 19, 1979; May 24, 1979; June 2, 1979; June 3, 1979; Sept. 1, 1979; April 18, 1980; May 23, 1980; July 2, 1980; Sept. 22, 1980; Aug. 30, 1981; March 28, 1982; June 4, 1982; June 26, 1982; Sept. 6, 1982; Sept. 19, 1982; Sept. 28, 1982; Oct. 19, 1982; Nov. 4, 1982; Dec. 14, 1982; June 14, 1983; June 15, 1983; June 16, 1983; July 7, 1983; July 22, 1983; Sept. 6, 1983; Sept. 7, 1983; Sept. 13, 1983; Oct. 16, 1983; Nov. 13, 1983; Dec. 3, 1983; Jan. 4, 1984; Jan. 8, 1984; Jan. 22, 1984; Feb. 23, 1984; March 8, 1984; May 23, 1984; June 4, 1984; July 27, 1984; Aug. 3, 1984; Aug. 23, 1984; Sept. 13, 1984; Feb. 13, 1985; Feb. 23, 1985; March 29, 1985; April 18, 1985; May 28, 1985; June 17, 1985; Jan. 2, 2000; Dec. 14, 2006.

Newark Evening News, Jan. 5, 1914; April 3, 1916; June 12, 1916; Sept. 25, 1916; May 20, 1918, March 29, 1920; May 3, 1920; Nov. 8, 1920; March 10, 1924; April 12, 1926.

Newark Star-Ledger, June 7, 1979; Sept. 22, 1980; Sept. 18, 1982; Sept. 29, 1982; June 10, 1985; June 17, 1985; June 22, 1985.

Newsday, Aug. 31, 1972.

Philadelphia Inquirer, April 6, 1915; Jan. 17, 1921; April 10, 1926; April 12, 1926; Feb. 6, 1930; March 15, 1930; March 20, 1930; April 25, 1930; Dec. 15, 2006.

Pittsburgh Bulletin Index, April 9, 1936.

Pittsburgh Post, Dec. 7, 1913.

Seattle Post-Intelligencer, Jan. 31, 2006.

Soccer Week, June 13, 1985.

South Bethlehem Globe/Bethlehem Globe/Bethlehem Globe-Times, Sept. 23, 1912;
Dec. 8, 1913; March 18, 1915; Oct. 1, 1915; May 8, 1916; May 22, 1916;
April 25, 1918; May 6, 1918; Oct. 14, 1919; Dec. 7, 1920; May 14, 1924;
Aug. 8, 1924; Dec. 15, 1924; March 15, 1928; April 25, 1928; June 13, 1928;
June 21, 1928; Feb. 20, 1930; April 11, 1930; April 14, 1930; Dec. 5, 1948.
USA Today, Aug. 4, 2004.

Articles in periodicals

Cahill, Thomas W. "Annual Report of the Secretary." *Reports of Officers and Committees, United States Football Association, Season 1929-30.*
Duffy, Edward P. "Horace Edgar Lewis," *U.S. Annual Soccer Guide and Record,* 1949.
Gardner, Paul. "Carlos the Great," *New York Daily News Sunday Magazine.* June 27, 1982.
Gardner, Paul. "NASL in wonderland," *World Soccer,* July 2007.
Gardner, Paul. "Strange Goings On at the Cosmos," *World Soccer,* August 1977.
Glanville, Brian. "American threat to World Cup," *World Soccer,* March 1978.
Hemingway, Oliver. " Soccer Foot Ball in Philadelphia," *Spalding's Official Soccer Foot Ball Guide,* 1914-15.
Lovett, Charles A. "First Big Professional League Launched," *Spalding's Official Soccer Football Guide,* 1921-22.
Grover, Ronald. "Herb Siegel: The Fly in Viacom's Ointment," *Business Week,* Feb. 11, 2000.
Sheridan, William. "Bethlehem Steel Company F.C.," *Spalding's Official Soccer Football Guide,* 1918-19.
Stolberg, Benjamin. "Big Steel, Little Steel and C.I.O." *The Nation,* July 31, 1937.
Woitalla, Mike. "U.S. mix better than ever." *Soccer America,* May 2008.

"Annual Report of the Secretary," *Spalding's Official Soccer Foot Ball Guide,* 1915-16.
"Atari's Struggle to Stay Ahead," *Business Week,* Sept. 13, 1982.
"Bethlehem Bonuses," *Time Magazine,* Aug. 11, 1930.
"Cosmos Career Goal Scoring—All Games," *New York Cosmos Media Guide 1984.*
"Family's Fourth," *Time Magazine,* April 13, 1936.
"Financial Summary," *Bethlehem Review,* March 1955.
"Murdoch Builds the Suspense at Warner," *Business Week,* Jan 16, 1984.
"Nay for Quality," *Time Magazine,* Oct. 27, 1967.
"Operating Data," *Bethlehem Review,* March 1955.
"Rupert Murdoch's High-Stakes Gamble on Warner," *Business Week,* Jan. 23, 1984.

Bibliography

"Saucon – Yesterday," *Bethlehem Review,* July 1954.
"Steel Job Done," *Time Magazine,* May 31, 1937.
"The Allied Amateur Football Association," *Spalding's Official Association Foot Ball Guide,* 1912-13.
"The Toes That Bind," *Time Magazine,* June 4, 1973.
"The Video-Game Shakeout," Newsweek, Dec. 20, 1982.

Television broadcasts

TVS, NASL championship game, Aug. 27, 1978.
KIRO-TV Seattle, interview with Frank Coluccio, Sept. 17, 1982.

Internet Websites

British Broadcasting Corp.: www.bbc.co.uk
Bethlehem Steel soccer team: www.geocities.com/bethlehem_soccer/
ESPN: www.espn.go.com
Forbes Magazine: www.forbes.com
National Soccer Hall of Fame: www.soccerhall.org
National Collegiate Athletic Association: www.ncaa.org
Rock 'n' Rock Hall of Fame: www.rockhall.com
Society for American Baseball Research: www.sabr.org
Track and Field News: www.trackandfieldnews.com

Index

Aberdeen FC, 30
Abramovich, Roman, 17
AC Milan, 7
Ackerman, Nathaniel, 196
Adidas, 147
Agar, Nat 17, 64
Agnelli, Gianni, 17-9
AIK Stockholm, 82, 115
Akron Goodyear, 110
All-Skane, 116
Albritton, Joe, 71
Allentown, Pa., 47-48, 216
Allianz Arena (Munich), 24
Allied Amateur Cup, 50, 51, 54, 55, 60
Allied American FA, 53, 92
Allied American League, 51, 54-6, 59, 93
America Cali, 141
American Amateur Football Association,
    52, 53, 115
American Broadcasting Co., 185
American Football Association, 52-4, 58, 63,
    93
American Football Association Cup, 3, 45,
    52, 54-6, 58, 60, 62, 63, 87, 92, 93, 97-9,
    104, 105, 107, 111, 112, 151, 152, 154, 156,
    158, 159, 162
American League of Philadelphia, 60, 92-4,
    98
American League of Professional Football
    Clubs, 152
American Shipbuilding Company, 15
American Soccer League, 1,7, 9, 10, 13, 17,
    29, 30, 32, 33, 66, 69, 70, 92, 100, 111, 115,
    148, 155, 157-9, 161-4, 167-71, 180, 181
formation of, 93, 152-4
1924 expansion, 160
role in Soccer War, 160, 172-4
demise of, 176

"second" ASL, 8, 65, 176, 181, 216
Anaheim Angels 20
Anaheim Mighty Ducks 20
Andrews, Mike, 120
Anheuser-Busch, 19-21, 31
Arcelor-Mittal, 8
Arena, Bruce, 26, 76
Argentine national team, 142, 143
Armstrong, W.G. and Co., 40
artificial turf, 77, 147, 199
Ashley, Ted, 73
Astor House, 53
Atari, 5, 25, 192-4, 196, 197
Atlanta Braves, 21, 120
Atlanta Chiefs, 68, 76
Atlanta Falcons, 14
Atlanta Hawks 21
Atlanta Thrashers 21
Atlantic Coast League, 174, 179
Atlantic Records, 72
Atletico Madrid 18

Babcock & Wilcox FC (Bayonne), 46, 107
Baker Bowl (Philadelphia), 154
Baker, Newton, 108
Ballantyne, Bobby, 178
Ballantyne, Johnny, 29, 171
Baltimore Bays, 68, 74, 75
Baltimore, Md., 173
Bangu AC (Rio de Janeiro), 67, 76, 79
Banks, Gordon, 27
Barcelona, FC, 86, 205
Barker, Winston, 114
Battery Park (New Bedford), 178
Battles, Barney, 171
Bayer AG, 22
Bayer Leverkusen, 22
Bayern Munich, 4, 131, 141

Bayonne, N.J., 46, 107

Beardsley, Peter, 28

Beckenbauer, Franz, 6, 10-12, 27, 30, 31, 77, 131, 132, 134, 135, 139, 140, 143, 144, 147, 148, 192, 195, 197, 198, 200, 202, 205, 210

Beijing, China, 135

Beinstock, Mark, 209

Bell, Bert, 16

Belfast Celtic, 66

Ben Millers FC (St. Louis), 24, 102, 161, 165

Benfica SL (Lisbon), 70, 206

Bernabeau, Santiago 18

Bessemer, Henry, 37

Bessemer process, 37, 38, 40

Best, George, 27, 84, 85, 134

Bethlehem Hungarians, 216

Bethlehem Iron Co., 36, 38-41

Bethlehem, Pa. 4, 46, 47, 50, 51, 56, 58, 61, 93, 95, 99, 110, 149, 153-7, 159, 167, 168, 171, 214

Bethlehem Rolling Mill and Iron Co., 36

Bethlehem Steel Corporation, 4, 7, 14, 27, 32, 46-9, 60, 99, 100, 108, 113, 174, 175, 176, 180, 215

pre-1904 history, 35-42

rebirth under Schwab, 42-4

World War I and, 25, 62, 87-9

grants to soccer team, 62, 98

baseball league, 90, 91, 109

post-soccer years, 8, 213, 214

downfall of, 214

Bethlehem Steel FC, 1-3, 5-7, 13, 22, 25, 28-32, 39, 48, 50, 53, 61, 77, 87-94, 101, 108, 148, 151, 161, 164, 169, 171, 173, 174, 210, 216, 217, 219

beginnings of, 35, 44, 46, 47, 58, 218

1913-14 breakout season , 51, 54-9

undefeated streaks, 54, 57, 59, 60, 62, 102, 104

1915 National Challenge Cup final, 62, 64

1916 National Challenge Cup final, 95-7

1917 National Challenge Cup final, 103, 104

1918 National Challenge Cup final, 105, 106

Triple 1919 championship, 107, 110-2

1919 Scandinavian tour, 4, 9, 10, 98, 111-7 , 149, 150, 160, 162

role in start of American Soccer League, 152-4

1921-22 Philadelphia FC season, 152-4

attendance problems, 98, 100, 153, 154, 170, 171, 175, 178, 179

rivalry with Fall River teams, 33, 62, 96, 97, 103, 105, 106, 155-9, 162, 167, 168, 176-8

1926 National Challenge Cup final, 165-6

folding of , 8, 33, 175, 178-81

BHC Communications Inc., 203

Bidwill, Charlie, 16

Bilandic, Michael, 184

Birkenmeier, Hubert, 197, 205, 216

Blakey, Albert, 114

Blank, Arthur, 14

blue laws, 100, 155

Blue Mountain League, 95

Blue, Vida, 120

Bogicevic, Vladislav, 11, 27, 137, 143, 144, 188, 191, 197, 216

Booth, William, 97

Boston Braves, 49, 122

Boston Celtics, 7, 17

Boston, Mass., 45, 122, 123, 125

Boston Minutemen, 122, 123, 126

Boston Red Sox, 17, 109

Boston University, 122

Boston Wonder Workers, 29, 32, 161, 167-71

Braddock FC, 50, 56, 57, 61

Braddock, Pa., 42, 56

Bradley, Gordon, 11, 70, 74-6, 79, 124, 127, 130-3, 139, 189, 216

Brand, Jack, 143

Brazilian national team, 82

Bristol, Pa., 46, 110

Brittan, Harold, 9, 150, 155, 156, 159

Brookhattan FC (New York), 13, 14, 24, 176

Brooklyn Celtic FC, 60-2, 64, 94, 103, 162

Brooklyn Dodgers, 17, 67

Brooklyn Field Club, 57, 60, 62, 64

Brooklyn Hispano, 65

Brooklyn, N.Y., 10, 46, 57, 59, 60, 62, 64, 66, 97, 104, 149, 151, 157, 164, 165, 173, 177, 180

Brooklyn Wanderers, 17, 65, 170, 177

Brown, Andrew M., 30

Brown, Davey, 9, 111, 114, 116, 148, 163, 168

Brown, Jock, 177

Brown, Walter, 17

Bryan, William Jennings, 88

Buffalo, N.Y., 54, 93, 101, 208

Burns, Charlie, 96

Busch, Gussie, 20

Cabanas, Roberto, 197, 198

Cablevision Systems, 20, 23

Cahill, Thomas W., 9, 53, 98, 114, 115, 152, 160, 180

Cambria Steel Co., 36, 91

Canal Plus, 22

Index

Canter, Dan, 205
Calderon, Ramon, 18
California Surf, 189
Camden, N.J., 46, 50, 60, 110
Camden Rovers, 50
Campbell, Dougie, 157, 167
Campbell, James, 60, 107, 111, 114
Canadian national team, 202
Canton FC (Baltimore), 173
Cardington FC (Upper Darby), 51
Carlos Alberto, 6, 11, 27, 70, 131, 133-5, 139,
    140, 143, 144, 146, 148, 187, 189, 191, 192,
    198, 200, 205, 217
Carnegie, Andrew, 5, 39, 42
Carnegie Steel Co., 39-42, 48, 49, 56, 61
Carnihan, Bill, 177, 178, 181
Carroll College, 45
Carson, Dave, 166
Cassidy, Jack, 47
Caszely, Carlos, 210
Celtic FC (Glasgow), 66
Centenary FC (Philadelphia), 54
Centennial AA (Philadelphia), 51, 170
Chelsea FC (London), 4, 7, 9, 17
Chester, Pa., 50
Chicago Bricklayers FC, 110
Chicago Cubs, 16, 20, 184
Chicago Fire, 32. 35, 218
Chicago, Ill., 45, 46, 54, 93, 95, 98, 102, 152,
    172, 188, 190, 207
Chicago Slovak, 13, 69
Chicago Sting, 2, 183-5, 188, 190, 206, 207
Chicago White Sox, 17, 109, 184
Chinaglia, Giorgio, 1, 11, 13, 27, 31, 77, 119,
    124, 126, 127, 131-3, 135, 137, 140, 143,
    144, 147, 185, 186, 191, 192, 215, 217, 219
and Lazio, 125, 126, 148, 197-202, 208, 216
move to Cosmos, 125, 126
behind-the-scenes influence, 11, 129, 130,
    133, 142
goalscoring feats, 127, 134, 137, 146, 148,
    163, 187, 190, 197, 202
disputes with coaches, 126, 132, 133, 137-9,
    142, 148, 187, 188
injuries, 198, 200, 201
running the Cosmos after retiring, 11, 204,
    205, 207-11, 216
Chinese national team, 137
Chris-Craft Industries, 203
Chunichi Dragons, 23
Churchill, Winston, 88
Chursky, Tony, 135
Civic Stadium (Portland), 135

Clan McDonald FC (Brooklyn), 60, 97, 104
Clark AA (Kearny), 46
Clark Thread Mill, 45, 46
Clarke, Neil, 60, 95, 96, 97, 102, 113, 150, 155
Cleveland Browns, 14, 73
Cleveland, Ohio, 15, 54, 93
Club America (Mexico City), 23, 78, 188
Cologne, FC, 147
Coluccio, Frank, 191
Columbia Broadcasting System, 20, 31
Comcast Corporation, 20, 23
Comisky, Charles, 17, 21
Comisky Park (Chicago), 184, 207
Connecticut Bicentennials, 186 (see also
    Hartford Bicentennials)
Corinthians (England), 66
Cosmopolitans (New York), 64
County Stadium (Milwaukee), 184
Cox, Bill, 66, 67
Crowder, Enoch, 108, 109
Cruyff, Johan, 27, 86, 140, 143
CSKA Moscow, 18
Cuban, Mark, 120
Cubillas, Teofilo, 27, 31
Cunningham, Bill, 170
Cunningham, Stan, 80
Crawford, Gordon, 194

Daewoo Royals, 24
Dalei Corporation, 23
Dallas Cowboys, 121
Dallas Mavericks, 120
Dallas Tornado, 17, 77, 121, 145, 148, 187
Davis, Rick, 11, 147, 197, 206, 207
Dazansky, Steve, 186
D.C. United, 2, 59, 92, 218
de Brito, Sergio, 84
de la Sierra, Rafael, 142, 145
Depression, The, 7, 79, 174
Detroit Cougars, 70
Detroit, Mich., 45, 54, 93, 160, 167
Detroit Pistons, 16
Dexter Park (Brooklyn), 157, 158
Deyna, Kazimierz, 27
DiBernardo, Angelo, 146, 205
Dick, Sandy, 177, 181
DiNolfo, Pat, 70
Disston AA (Philadelphia), 46, 56, 60, 93,
    94-95, 98, 105-7
Disston & Sons Saw Works, 94
Donaghy, Ned, 9, 56, 59
Downing Stadium (New York), 79-81, 121
    (see also Randall's Island)

draft (military), 90, 91, 106-9
Dravosburg, Pa., 49
Duffy, Ed, 112
Dukla Prague, 18, 67, 78
Duncan, Bill, 103, 106, 111, 114, 151
Duquesne Works (Carnegie Steel), 48
Durgan, Jeff, 205, 207
Durham, England, 75
Dynamo Moscow (*see* Moscow Dynamo)

East End Field (Bethlehem), 51, 58, 90, 94, 100
East Hampton, N.Y., 215
East Newark, N.J., 104
East Rutherford, N.J., 219
Eastern Pennsylvania League, 50, 93
Eastern Soccer League, 173, 174
Ebbets Field (Brooklyn), 165
Eddy, Keith, 130
Edgar Thompson Steel Works, 39, 42, 56
Edwards, Dave, 167, 169
Emirates Stadium (London), 24
Emmett, Jay, 73, 128, 129, 196
Empire Stadium (Vancouver), 144
English Premier League, 17
Erie AA (Kearny), 117, 150-2, 162
Ertegun, Ahmet, 11, 72, 73, 127
Ertegun brothers, 73, 128, 131, 132, 142, 217
Ertegun, Neshui, 12, 72, 73, 127, 132
Eskandarian, Andranik, 141, 144, 197, 216
Estadio Azteca (Mexico City), 23, 78, 188
E.T., 192, 194
European Cup, 131, 198
Eusebio, 122, 123
Exhibition Stadium (Toronto), 188

FA of Philadelphia, 53
Falcao, 190, 195
Fall River, Mass., 4, 10, 45, 62, 63, 64, 97, 100, 101, 110, 159, 167, 173, 175, 176
Fall River Marksmen, 2, 32, 33, 114, 149, 155-9, 161-4, 167-9, 174-8, 181
Fall River Pan-American, 101, 105
Fall River Rovers, 2, 62, 96, 97, 103, 105, 106, 110, 155, 156, 178
Fall River United, 155
Farr Alpaca (Holyoke), 46, 58, 60, 154
Federal League, 106
Federal Shipyard AA (Kearny), 46, 91, 151
Ferguson, Jock, 6, 9, 106, 111, 112, 114, 155, 156, 164, 216
Fiat Group, 17

FIFA (Federation Internationale de Football Association), 30, 52, 53, 54, 68, 115, 172, 173, 185, 189, 199, 200
Figueroa, Roberto, 210
Fillol, Ubaldo, 142
Finlayson, Bill, 177
Finley, Charles O., 120
Fiolax, 83, 84
Firmani, Eddie, 130, 133, 137-9, 142, 206
Flamengo (Rio de Janiero), 192
Fleischer Yarn (Philadelphia), 156, 163
Fleming, Whitey, 6, 9, 51, 56, 57, 59, 61, 62, 95, 96, 101, 105-7, 112, 114, 151, 155, 156, 164, 171, 216
Fletcher, Sam, 114
Florie, Tom, 162
Football Association (England), 53
Football Association of Eastern Pennsylvania and District, 179
Football League (England), 66, 68
Forbes Field (Pittsburgh), 56
Ford, Gerald, 122
Ford, James, 60-2
Fore River Shipbuilding Co., 44, 88, 109
Fore River Shipyard FC, 46, 91
Forrest, William, 111, 114, 116
Fort Lauderdale Strikers, 1, 31, 131, 134, 145, 146, 183, 186, 187, 209
Fort Wayne Pistons, 16
Fox, Mike, 195
Foxboro, Mass., 59
Francis, Trevor, 28
Frankel, William, 71
Frankford Stadium (Philadelphia), 173
Frankfurt, West Germany, 83
Franklin Field (Philadelphia), 32, 77, 105
Freemasons Tavern (London), 54
Freiburg, SC, 141
Fritz, John, 36, 38, 39
Fulton County Stadium (Atlanta), 68
Furphy, Ken, 127, 128, 130
Furukawa Electric Co., 136
Fuschl am See, Austria, 26

Galbraith, John, 17
Gallego, Americo, 142
Garbett, Terry, 134, 135, 143, 148
Gary, Elbert, 41-2
Gazprom, 23
Genoa, Italy, 126
German-American Soccer League, 66, 69, 75, 76

Index

Giants Stadium (East Rutherford), 1, 80,
  125, 130, 132, 134, 136, 137, 139, 140, 141,
  144, 145, 186, 188-190, 201, 202, 205, 210,
  216 217, 219
Gibson, Bill, 178
Gil, Jesus, 18
Gilchrist-Thomas, Sidney, 40
Gillespie, Ill., 158
Gillespie, Tom, 167, 170, 177, 181
Glenn, Rudy, 188
Golden Bay Earthquakes, 199, 206, 207
Goldie, Malcolm, 161, 165, 166
Goldman Sachs Group, 194
Gonsalves, Billy, 65, 114, 174, 178
Goteborg, Sweden, 115, 116
Gotham Soccer Club, 73
Gottleib, Eddie, 17
Grace, Eugene, 32, 49, 98, 175, 176, 214
Grainger, Johnny, 166
Granitza, Karl-Heinz, 184, 185, 188, 207
Greater Los Angeles Soccer League, 69
Greek-Americans (New York), 92
Grey beam, 25, 43, 44, 87
Grey, Henry, 43, 44
Green Bay Packers, 7
Grgurev, Fred, 138, 139
Grobelaar, Bruce, 28
Groth, Dennis, 197
Gulati, Sunil, 217

Hakoah (Vienna), 30, 66, 165, 168, 180
Hakoah All-Stars (Brooklyn), 180
Halas, George, 16, 17
Hamburg, SV, 147, 198, 199
Hammarby IF (Stockholm), 116
Hankyu Braves, 23
Hanshin Tigers, 23
Hapoel (Palestine), 66
Harlan & Hollingsworth Corp., 44, 109
Harlem Field (New York), 104
Harrelson, Ken, 120
Harrisburg, Pa., 48
Harrison FC, 152
Harrison, N.J., 27, 45, 47, 58, 95, 104, 106,
  111, 151, 171, 218
Harrison Oval, 47, 58, 218
Hartford Bicentennials, 125 (see also Con-
  necticut Bicentennials)
Hartford, Conn., 74, 208
Harvey, Hayward A., 40
Harvey United Steel Co., 40
Hawthorne Park (Brooklyn), 164, 177

Heart of Midlothian FC, 30
Hector, Kevin, 144
Hellenic FC (New York), 69
Helsingborg, Sweden, 116
Hemingway, Oliver, 55, 59
Heminsley, Rabbit, 114, 116
Hempstead, N.Y., 77
Hermann, Robert, 17
Hibernian FC (Philadelphia), 51, 60, 95
Hiroshima Carp, 23
Hofstra Stadium (Hempstead), 77, 79, 80,
  130, 202
Holley Carburetor FC (Detroit), 167
Holyoke Falcos (see Farr Alpaca)
Homestead Steel FC, 46, 61, 62, 103, 110
Homestead Steel Works, 40, 42, 61, 91
Horton, Randy, 6, 76, 77, 205
Horwitz, Leonard, 196
Hota SC (New York), 75
Howard, Ted, 184
Howard & Bullough FC (Pawtucket), 46
Houston Dynamo, 218
Hudson, Ray, 146
Hudson River, 63
Hunt, Lamar, 17, 68, 69, 121, 186
Hunt, Steve, 131, 134, 135, 190
Hunter, Catfish, 86
Hyde Park Blues FC, 95

Iarusci, Bob, 188
Independiente, FC (Buenos Aires), 210
Indiana Flooring Company FC (New York),
  24, 64, 156, 161, 162, 167, 181
Inland Steel Co., 91
Innisfails FC (St. Louis), 110
International Soccer League (New York), 67,
  78, 190
Ipswich Town FC, 144
Ironbound Stadium (Newark), 176
Ironton Structural Steel Co., 43
Italian-American League of New Jersey, 210

J-League, 23
J&P Coats (Pawtucket), 46, 96, 101, 155,
  162-4
Jaap, John, 9, 166, 173, 177, 178, 181
Jackson, Alex, 30, 156, 161
Jackson brothers, 159
Jackson, Reggie, 120
Jackson, Shoeless Joe, 109
Jackson, Walter, 30, 156, 157, 161
Jeffrey Manufacturing Co., 50

Jelinek, Joseph, 6, 77, 78
Jersey City AC, 59, 97
Jersey City, N.J., 59, 158
John F. Kennedy International Airport, 83
Joe Simpkins Ford (St. Louis), 24
Johnson, Magic, 129
Johnstown, Pa., 36
Joliet Steel Works FC, 46, 91, 103, 105
Jones, Jerry, 121
Jones & Laughlin Steel Co., 48, 50, 91, 175, 176
Justice Department, U.S., 196
Juventus FC (Turin), 18, 198, 205

Kansas City Athletics, 120
Kashima Antlers, 23
Kasser, Raymond, 197
Kearny Irish, 181
Kearny, N.J., 1, 45, 46, 52, 63, 64, 65, 150, 151, 181, 210
Kearny Scots, 13, 14, 46, 61, 65, 93, 97, 111, 162, 176, 181
Kelly, William, 37, 38
Kensington AA (Philadelphia), 51
Kerr, John Sr., 70, 78, 205
Kilmarnock FC, 67, 156
Kinney National Services, 12, 47, 71-3
Kintetsu Braves, 23
Klivecka, Ray, 143, 210
Kluge, John, 25, 26
Krupp, Friedrich AG, 40, 89
Kutis FC (St. Louis), 24

Lancaster, Pa., 50
Lance, Jack, 59
Landy, Francis, 103
Lawson, Duncan, 58
Lazio, SS (Rome), 125, 126, 144, 148, 210
Lebanon, Pa., 91, 109
Leccese, Joe, 14
Lehigh River, 36, 89, 98, 156, 164, 214
Lehigh University, 49, 51, 62, 94, 98
Lehigh Valley, 47, 48, 50, 95, 216
Lehigh Valley Railroad, 35
Lennox, Bob, 99
Lenzini, Umberto, 125, 126
Leonard, Dutch, 109
Lettieri, Tino, 140
Leverkusen, Germany, 22
Lewis Cup, 65, 161, 166, 169-72, 174
Lewis, Edgar, 6, 10, 46, 47, 65, 161, 176, 219
    pre-Bethlehem background, 48, 49
    playing years, 48-51, 56, 57

attempt to buy land in Harrison, 171, 172, 175
    departure from Bethlehem Steel, 7, 33, 50, 175, 176, 180, 214
Lewis, Luther, 171, 179
Lille OSC, 188
Lipton Tea Co., 21
Litsky, Frank, 80, 81
Liveric, Mark, 123, 145
Liverpool FC, 66
Lokomotiv Moscow, 18
Long Island Rough Riders, 217
Lonsdale Avenue Ground (Pawtucket), 96
Loretto, Pa., 42, 215
Los Angeles Aztecs, 32, 140, 143, 145
Los Angeles, Calif., 192
Los Angeles Dodgers, 21
Los Angeles Galaxy, 35, 59, 92, 121, 218
Los Angeles Lakers, 17, 129
Louisiana-Pacific Co., 21
Lucky Goldstar Bulls, 24
Luque, Leopoldo, 142

Maccabi (Los Angeles), 14
Mack, Connie, 17
Madison Square Garden, 208
Madison Square Garden Corp., 21
Mahy, Barry, 70, 78
Major Indoor Soccer League, 207, 208
Major League Soccer, 17, 25, 26, 28, 32, 33, 59, 92, 216-8
Malmo, Sweden, 116
Manchester United FC, 4, 7, 83
Manhattan Beer (Chicago), 24
Mara, Tim, 16
Maradona, Diego, 142, 205
Marinho, Francisco, 141, 142
Mark, Sam, 155, 178
Marquette Oval (Brooklyn), 57, 60
Marsh, Rodney, 140
Marshall, George Preston, 16
Marshall, Jock, 173
Martin Tower, 99, 213-5
Martin's Ferry, Ohio, 48, 49
Masnik, Juan, 6
Mateschitz, Dietrich, 26
Mazzei, Julio, 83, 84, 121, 122, 127, 143, 145-7, 188, 189, 191, 195, 201
McAuley, Bob, 177
McEachran, Dave, 167
McGill, Charlie, 167, 177, 178
McGregor, Bob, 166
McGuire, Jack, 151

Index

McHolland, Jimmy, 58
McKee, Don, 32
McKeesport FC, 105
McKelvey, George, 97, 102, 104, 111, 112, 114
McNab, Alex, 29, 114, 160, 171, 174, 177
McNiven, Daniel, 155-7, 163
McPherson, Bill, 155, 157, 167
Meadowlands Arena (East Rutherford), 208
"meddling" owners, 15, 119-21
Memphis Rogues, 137
Merchant Shipbuilding FC (Bristol), 46, 110, 112, 114
Messing, Shep, 28, 123, 126, 127, 132, 135, 136
Metropolitan Oval (New York), 66
MetroStars, 26, 27
Mexico City, 188
Miami, Fla., 22
Midvale Steel Co., 44, 91
Mifflin, Ramon, 124, 127
Millar, Bob, 10, 57, 60-2, 112, 150, 155, 156, 163, 181, 216
Millwall FC (London), 28
Milwaukee, Wisc., 184
Minnesota Kicks, 70, 137, 139
Minnesota Strikers, 209
Miranda, Eurico, 18, 19
Mitsubishi Motors, 23
Modell, Art, 14
Molson Brewery Ltd., 21, 31, 202
Montreal Canadiens, 21, 31
Montreal Manic, 21, 200-2
Moore, Bobby, 27, 136
Moorhouse, George, 177
Morais, Nelsi, 124
Moravian College, 90, 98, 99
Morgan, J. Pierpont, 5, 41
Morgan Stanley, 22
Morgan-Strasser FC, 13, 14, 24
Morrison, Bobby, 10, 56, 95
Morrison, Dan, 49
Morse Dry Dock FC (Brooklyn), 46, 64
Moscow Dynamo, 18, 78, 79
Moyer, Paul, 99
Moyers, Steve, 205
Muirhead, Tommy, 160
Muller, Gerd, 27
Murdoch, Rupert, 202, 203, 215
Murphy, Jimmy, 107
Murphy, Tommy, 151
Murphy, Walt, 81
Murray, Tom, 113, 114

Nairn Linoleum Co., 45
Nankai Hawks, 23
Napoli, SSC, 24
Nascimento, Rose, 134
Nashville, Tenn., 184
National Association Foot Ball League, 45, 46, 64, 93, 99, 100, 102, 104, 105, 107, 111, 112, 149-54, 159, 162
National Basketball Association, 16, 20, 21, 54, 120
National Car Rental Co., 22
National Challenge Cup, 3, 9, 10, 31, 54-7, 60-2, 64, 65, 87, 91-3, 95, 98, 102-6, 110, 111, 113, 150-4, 156-62, 164-8, 170, 172-4
National Football League, 14, 16-7, 121
National Hockey League, 20, 21
National Professional Soccer League (outdoor), 68, 69, 74
National Slug Rejectors, 13, 24
National Soccer Hall of Fame, 5, 6, 8, 13, 49, 72, 185, 217
National Soccer League of Chicago, 69
NCAA (National Collegiate Athletic Association), 101
Necaxa, Club, 23
Neeskens, Johan, 6, 27, 141, 143, 197
Netzer, Gunter, 198
New Bedford FC 56, 101
New Bedford, Mass., 33, 56, 64, 101, 178
New Bedford Whalers, 33, 161, 166, 168, 169
New England Tea Men, 21
New Jersey Eagles, 217
New York Americans, 17, 65
New York Centaurs, 217
New York Cosmos, 1-8, 11-5, 18, 19, 21, 25-8, 31-3, 67, 69-71, 74, 77-82, 84-5, 119, 123-7, 129-34, 137, 138, 140, 141, 143, 145 , 147, 148, 163, 183, 185-7, 189, 190, 195, 197, 200, 201, 203, 217-9
    founding of, 12, 47, 70, 72-4
    preparations for first season, 74-6
    1972 NASL final, 77, 202
    debut of Pelé, 80, 121
    1977 NASL final, 135
    1978 NASL final, 137, 140
    controversial 1979 defeat, 143-5
    1980 NASL final, 145, 146
    1981 NASL final, 183, 188
    1982 NASL final, 189, 191
    sale to Chinaglia, 204
    1984 late-season collapse, 206, 207
    1985 final struggles, 8, 34, 206-11, 216

attendance, 130, 131, 133, 134, 186, 192, 202, 205, 206
in-season friendlies, 130, 142, 143, 198, 199
overseas tours, 3, 124, 130, 135, 136, 137, 141, 145, 148, 188, 192, 202, 207
indoor team, 189, 207, 208
New York Continentals, 104
New York FC, 64, 65, 93, 104, 107, 112, 150, 154, 156, 157, 159, 160, 162
New York Generals, 63, 70, 75, 76, 206
New York Giants (baseball), 17, 65, 67, 172
New York Giants (football), 16, 139
New York Giants (soccer), 64, 65, 156, 163, 165, 166, 168, 173, 177, 180
New York IRT, 106
New York Jets, 74
New York Knicks, 20
New York Nationals, 64, 65, 169-73, 181
New York, N.Y., 45, 47, 53, 54, 57, 63-7, 70, 76, 79, 82-5, 115, 121, 122, 125, 127, 131, 161, 165, 167, 177, 180, 215, 216, 218
New York Rangers, 20
New York Red Bulls, 26, 27, 216, 217, 218 (*see also* MetroStars)
New York Shipbuilding FC (Camden), 46, 110
New York Yankees, 7, 15, 16, 20, 31, 119, 125
Newark Americans, 180
Newark Caledonian, 46
Newark, N.J., 47, 52, 59, 63, 104, 171, 177
Newark Peppers, 106
Newark Portuguese, 177
Newark Skeeters, 157, 164, 166, 167, 170, 173
Newman, Ron, 191
News Corporation, 21
Nickerson Field (Boston), 122
Nilsen, Werner, 114, 174
Nintendo, 21, 195
Nippon Ham Fighters, 23
North American Soccer League, 1,3, 6, 7, 11, 12, 17, 21, 26-8, 30-4, 63, 69-73, 75, 77-9, 81, 92, 124-6, 131, 133, 134, 136-8, 140-4, 148, 183-5, 187, 189, 190, 192, 195, 198, 204-7, 217
formation of, 67, 68
early crisis years, 68, 69, 74
attendance surge and expansion, 137, 138, 185, 186, 218
decline of, 33, 138, 185, 186, 189, 191, 193, 199, 200, 202
folding of, 8, 208, 209

North Tiverton, R.I., 155, 157, 163, 167
Northeast High School Field (Philadelphia), 170
Nowitzki, Dirk, 120

Oakland Athletics, 120
Oakland, Calif., 120
Olaff, Gene, 65
Olguin, Jorge, 142
Olympic Games, 165
Olympic Stadium (Rome), 202
Olympic Stadium (Stockholm), 116
Olympique Marseilles, 4
O'Malley, Walter, 17
Oneida Football Club, 45
ONT (Kearny), 46, 52, 63
O'Reilly, John, 79
Orient Leasing Co., 23

Packer, Asa, 39
Pan-American Exposition, 101
Panic of 1893, 45
Panic of 1907, 44
Paris Saint-Germain, 22
Parma FC, 23
Parmalat SpA, 23
Passaic River, 47, 63
Passaic Steel Co., 49
Passarella, Daniel, 142, 143
Partick Thistle, 29
Patenaude, Bert, 114, 174
Paterson FC, 91, 93, 107, 110-4, 117, 155
Paterson, N.J., 59
Paterson Silk Sox, 65 (*see also* Paterson FC)
Paterson True Blues, 46, 64, 110
Pawtucket, R.I., 46, 64, 95-8, 101, 103, 105-7, 155
Paul, Skip, 194
Peabody FC (Philadelphia), 61
Peel, Peter J., 115
Pelé, 3, 6, 12, 27, 28, 31, 66, 70, 75, 76, 85, 119, 121, 122, 124, 125, 127, 129, 131, 133, 135, 137, 146-8, 192, 205
pre-Cosmos career, 82, 83
pursued by Cosmos, 75, 81-5
arrival with Cosmos, 12, 80, 85, 86, 121, 122
1975 mob scene in Boston, 122, 123, 125
1977 NASL championship, 130, 135
Farewell Game, 136, 137, 198
Pennsylvania Stoners, 216
Pepper, Fred, 61, 97, 107, 111, 112, 114, 155

Index

Peugeot SA, 22
Philadelphia 76ers, 20
Philadelphia Atoms, 32
Philadelphia Electric FC, 56
Philadelphia FC, 10, 152-4, 161-4, 166, 167
Philadelphia Flyers, 17, 20
Philadelphia Nationals, 33, 35
Philadelphia, Pa., 45, 46, 50, 52, 56, 59, 61, 65, 66, 76, 77, 93, 105, 111, 152-4, 156, 170, 171, 173, 178, 179
Philips Electronics Co., 22
Pilgrims, 45, 66, 114
Pinton, Peppe, 127, 204, 208, 210, 211, 217
Pittsburgh, Pa., 38, 48, 54, 56, 57, 91, 93, 175
Pittsburgh Pirates, 17, 21
Pittsburgh Steelers, 16
Pohang Steelers, 23
Polish national team, 125
Polo Grounds (New York), 66, 67, 177
Ponta Delgada (Fall River), 13
Ponte Preta, AA, 83
Portland, Ore., 135
Portland Timbers, 21, 140
Pontardulais, Wales, 48
Priestley, Dave, 178
Providence Clamdiggers, 162
Providence, R.I., 167, 180
PSV Eindhoven, 22
Pullman FC (Chicago), 61, 95
Putnam AA (Philadelphia), 55, 61

Quincy, Mass., 44, 46, 91, 109
Quinn, Brian, 201

Ramos, Tab, 12
Randall's Island, 79-81, 119, 121, 125, 130
Rangers FC (Glasgow), 66, 160
Raphael, Allan, 215
Ratican, Harry, 9, 10, 101, 102, 106, 107, 111, 112, 114, 116, 150, 156, 164
Rattay, Jack, 158
Reading, Pa., 48, 50
Real Madrid, 4, 6-7, 18, 86
Red Bull Arena, 219
Red Bull GmbH, 25-7
Red Bull Salzburg, 26
Reder, Johnny, 177, 178
Red Star (Belgrade), 210
Reid, Johnny, 157
Republic Steel Co., 91
Reykjavik, Iceland, 188
Rigby, Bob, 126, 127
Rijsbergen, Wim, 141, 143, 197, 199

Rio de Janiero, Brazil, 82, 192
Robert F. Kennedy Stadium (Washington), 145
Robertson, James, 114
Robins Dry Dock FC (Brooklyn), 46, 64, 91, 93, 111, 112, 114, 149-52, 156 (see also Todd Shipyards)
Rochester Lancers, 70, 76, 209
Rogers Communications Inc., 21
Rollo, Johnny, 166
Roma, Modesto, 136
Rome, Italy, 126, 201, 202
Romero, Julio Cesar, 146, 197
Rooney, Art, 16, 19
Ross, Steve , 7, 12, 32, 74, 130, 132, 133, 134, 139, 142, 215, 217
    pre-Cosmos background, 71-3, 119
    involvement in founding of Cosmos, 71, 73
    obsession with Cosmos in peak years, 119, 121, 127-9
    role in Warner's 1980s troubles, 192-7, 203, 204
Roth, Werner, 12, 130, 141, 143, 148
Roy, Willy, 184, 188
Ruben, Jim, 186
Ruppert, Jacob, 20
Ruth, Babe, 15, 108, 109

Saigh, Fred, 19, 20
St. Louis Cardinals, 19, 20, 31
St. Louis, Mo., 4, 24, 45, 46, 54, 63, 91-3, 101-4, 110, 114, 149, 157-9, 161, 165, 172
St. Louis Professional League, 92, 160, 161
St. Louis Shamrocks, 114
St. Louis Stars, 17, 77, 202
St. Louis Steamers, 207
Salcedo, Fabri, 65
Samuels, Howard, 189, 191, 207, 208
San Diego, Calif., 191, 192
San Diego Sockers, 28, 183, 190, 191, 208
San Francisco, Calif., 44, 88, 113, 213
San Jose, Calif., 26
San Jose Earthquakes, 133 (see also Golden Bay Earthquakes)
San Luis FC, 23
Sanchez, Hugo, 28
Santos, Brazil, 82, 83, 147, 206
Santos FC, 66, 70, 75, 76, 82, 83, 124, 133, 136, 147
Sao Paulo state league, 82
Saucon Creek, 35
Saucon plant (Bethlehem Steel), 44

Saucona Iron Company, 35, 36
Scaife, Robert, 90
Schiano, Charlie, 70
Schneider Ironworks, 40
Schoefield, Tommy, 163
Schuylkill Falls FC (Philadelphia), 56, 60
Schwab, Charles M., 32, 41-4, 48, 49, 56, 61, 62, 88, 89, 176, 215
Schwaben (Chicago), 14, 69
Schwarcz, Erno, 17
Scott, Dave, 170
Scottish Football Association, 29
Scullin Steel FC (St. Louis), 24, 46, 91, 92, 149
Seattle Mariners, 21
Seattle Sounders, 28, 135, 190-2, 218
Securities and Exchange Commission, 196, 197, 203
Seibu Lions, 23
Seninho, 141, 143, 144
Shanghai, China, 135
Shea Stadium, 125, 127
Sheridan, Billy, 108, 114, 115
Siega, Jorge, 76, 205
Siegel, Herb, 32, 203, 204, 215
Siemens, Charles, 40
Simmons, Richard P., 194
Smethurst, Derek, 28
Smith AA (Philadelphia), 51, 56
Smith, Bobby, 12, 28. 133
Smith, Steve, 170, 177
Snider, Ed, 17
Soccer Bowl, 189, 191, 198
Soccer War, 7, 33, 160, 172-6
Sochaux, FC, 22
Socrates, 190, 192
Soldier Field (Chicago), 184
Souness, Graeme, 28
South Bethlehem, Pa., 35-6, 49, 51, 61, 95, 100
Southern New England Soccer League, 64, 153
Southern New York State Association, 53, 173
Spalding, A.G. & Bros., 114, 115
Spanish influenza, 108-110
Spartak Moscow, 18
Speigler, Mordechai, 6, 121
Spielberg, Steven, 192, 194, 215
Sporting CP (Lisbon), 210
Stark, Archie, 1, 6, 10, 61, 110, 117, 148, 159, 165, 166, 168-71, 173, 177, 178, 180, 210, 219

early background, 161, 162
1919 Bethlehem tour, 114, 116
1924 move to Bethlehem, 65, 161
1924-25 record season, 60, 161-4
after Bethlehem, 181
Starlight Park (New York), 24, 65, 80, 177
Starzell, Stan, 77
Stearn, Sune, 114
Steel Field (Bethlehem), 25, 90, 91, 94, 98-100, 105, 110, 152, 159, 163, 170, 171
Steelworkers Organizing Committee, 175
Steffenhagen, Arno, 184
Steinbrenner, George, 15-7, 19, 20, 119, 120, 128
Stern, Lee, 184-6
Stevens, Andy, 166
Stix, Baer & Fuller (St. Louis), 2, 24
Stock Market Crash, 7, 25, 31, 33, 174-6
Stockholm, Sweden, 53, 115, 116, 149
Stoneham, Charles, 17, 65, 172-4
Stradan, Andy, 165
Strawbridge, George, 133
Stritzl, Siggy, 76
"submarine deal," 88
Sullivan, "Sinker," 96, 103
Sumimoto Metal Industries, Ltd., 23
Sunnyvale, Calif., 193
Swan, Donald, 213
Swansea, Wales, 48
Swedish-American Line, 115
Swords, Thomas, 103, 110
Symington, Stuart, 120

Tacony FC (Philadelphia), 51, 59, 60, 93, 94
Taiyo Whales, 23
Tambi, Kaz, 205
Tampa, Fla., 15, 26
Tampa Bay Mutiny, 33
Tampa Bay Rowdies, 2, 28, 32, 33, 127, 128, 130, 133, 140, 187, 198, 206
Tarantini, Alberto, 142
Taylor Stadium (South Bethlehem), 62, 95
Taylor, William, 104
Team America, 202
Televisa, Grupo, 23
Time, Inc., 8, 21, 215
TimeWarner, 8, 21, 71, 215
Tintle, George, 10, 114, 116
Todd Field (Brooklyn), 151
Todd Shipyards FC (Brooklyn), 64, 91, 152, 154
Tokyo, Japan, 135, 192
Toronto Blizzard, 206, 208, 209

Index

Toronto Blue Jays, 21
Toronto Metros, 77, 124, 130
Toronto, Ontario, 77, 141, 188
Toye, Clive, 4, 12, 27, 28, 67, 76, 78, 79, 86,
 123-5, 127-9, 136, 142, 183-6, 216-9
 pre-NASL background, 68, 74
 executive in early NASL, 68-70
 start of Cosmos, 71, 74, 75
 pursuit of Pelé, 12, 75, 81-5
 departure from Cosmos, 13, 131, 132
 role in final days of NASL, 208, 209
Toyo Kogyo, 23
Trans-Atlantic Challenge Cup, 187, 190, 198,
 205
Trecker, Jim, 4
Trend, Harry, 57, 104
Trenton Caledonians, 58
Trenton FC, 167
Trenton, N.J., 171
Tribune Corporation, 20
Tueart, Dennis, 137, 140
Tulsa Roughnecks, 143, 145, 148, 186, 190,
 198, 202, 206, 207
Turner Broadcasting System, 21
Turner, Neil, 161
Turner, Ted, 120
21 Club, 86, 121

Udinese Calcio, 205
Ukrainian Nationals (Philadelphia), 2, 14,
 16, 161
Union Iron Works, 44, 113
United States Football Association, 7, 30, 51-
 4, 60, 64, 92, 93, 101, 107, 114, 115, 152,
 153, 160, 172, 173, 176, 180
United States national team, 11, 68, 76, 113,
 125, 166
United States Navy, 39, 40
United States Open Cup, 3, 4, 24, 33, 56, 65,
 69, 75, 92, 113, 172, 173 (see also National
 Challenge Cup)
United States Shipbuilding Co., 41, 42, 44
United States Soccer Federation, 17, 52, 54,
 185, 200, 210 (see also United States Foot-
 ball Association and United States Soccer
 Football Association)
United States Soccer Football Association,
 54, 67
United States Steel Corporation, 5, 41-4, 49,
 56, 61, 91
Urawa Red Diamonds, 23

Valentine, Carl, 145

Vancouver, British Columbia, 144, 209
Vancouver Whitecaps, 143-5, 198
Vandeweghe, Maurice, 65
Varsity Stadium (Toronto), 77
Vasco da Gama (Rio de Janiero), 18, 19
Veteran AA (Philadelphia), 105, 106
Veterans Stadium (Philadelphia), 32
VfB Stuttgart, 141
Viberg, Ernest, 114
Vickers, Albert, 40
Vickers' Sons & Maxim Ltd., 40, 41
Victor FC (Philadelphia), 60, 61
Victor Talking Machine FC (Camden), 60
Vila Belmiro Stadium (Santos), 83, 147
Villa Eden, 215
Vuckevic, Vojislav, 210
Vujovic, Dragan, 202

Walder, Jimmy, 10
Wall, Frederick J., 53
Walsh Chevrolet (Fall River), 173
Walt Disney Co., 20
Warner Brothers Pictures, 5, 71, 73
Warner Communications, 4-5, 7-8, 12, 14-5,
 18, 21, 25, 32, 33, 85, 121, 128, 132, 136,
 141, 189, 208, 211, 215, 217
 formation from Kinney, 70
 purchase of Cosmos, 73
 1982-83 Atari & legal troubles, 192-7,
 200
 1983-84 Murdoch-Siegel troubles,
 202-5
 post-Cosmos years, 213
Washington Darts, 70, 209
Washington, D.C., 122, 124, 126, 145, 146,
 202
Washington Diplomats, 11, 21, 122, 127, 133
Washington Park (Philadelphia), 51
Washington Redskins, 121
Waukesha, Wisc., 45
Wegerle, Steve, 187
Weiss, Solomon, 196, 197
Weisweiler, Hennes, 130, 146-8, 187-9, 218
Wembley Stadium (London), 81
West German national team, 131
West Hudson AA (Harrison), 45, 47, 48, 51,
 58, 64, 93, 95, 99, 103, 104, 107, 111, 113,
 152, 159
West Philadelphia FC, 56, 60
Westchester Premier Theatre, 195, 196
Wharton, Joseph, 39
White House, 122
White, Tec, 178

Whymark, Trevor, 144
Whyte, David, 96
Willey, Alan, 139, 201
William W. Wrigley Jr. Co., 16
Wilmington, Del., 44, 50, 88, 109
Wilson, Bruce, 13
Wilson, Giuseppe, 137
Wilson, James, 111, 114
Wilson, Woodrow, 88
Wissinoming FC (Philadelphia), 58
World all-star game (1982), 189
World Cup, 4, 30, 31, 67, 68, 72, 74, 78, 82, 83, 126, 131, 133, 137, 138, 142, 181, 195, 199, 200
World War I, 25, 39, 46, 64, 87-91, 108-10, 113, 162
World War II, 50, 213
Woosnam, Phil, 68-72, 74, 186, 189, 191, 208

Wrigley Field (Chicago), 184
Wrigley, Philip, 16, 17

Xisto, Jose Roberto Ribeiro, 86

Yakult Swallows, 23
Yankee Stadium (New York), 66, 70, 76, 77, 79, 86, 119, 124, 125, 128, 130, 132, 206
Yasin, Erol, 132, 142
Yawkey, Tom, 17
Yomiuri Giants, 23
Young, Roby, 78
Youngstown Sheet & Tube Co., 91, 176

Zenit St. Petersburg, 23
Zerega Oval (New York), 80, 81
Zito, 82
Zollner, Fred, 16, 17